GENDER, PATRIARCHY AND FASCISM

IN THE THIRD REICH

GENDER PATRIARCHY AND FASCISM IN THE THIRD REICH

THE RESPONSE OF WOMEN WRITERS

edited by ELAINE MARTIN

Wayne State University Press Detroit

Manufactured in the United States of America.
99 98 97 96 95 94 93 5 4 3 2 1

Library of Congress Cataloging-in-Publication Data

Gender, patriarchy, and fascism in the Third Reich: the response of women writers / edited by Elaine Martin.
p. cm.
Includes bibliographical references and index.
ISBN 0–8143–2420–7 (alk. paper).—ISBN 0–8143–2421–5 (pbk. : alk. paper)
1. German literature—20th century—History and criticism. 2. German literature—Women authors—History and criticism. 3. World War, 1939–1945—Literature and the war. 4. Fascism in literature. 5. National socialism in literature. 6. Patriarchy in literature. I. Martin, Elaine, 1949–
PT405.G45 1993
830.9'358—dc20 92–28667

Designer: S. R. Tenenbaum

For Jason Balgooyen

CONTENTS

ACKNOWLEDGMENTS

In recognition of the fact that all knowledge is interrelated and in many ways interdependent, we collectively thank those scholars who have preceded us and whose work has made our research and writing possible. Both feminist criticism and contemporary scholarship on literature of the Holocaust and the Third Reich have provided the groundwork upon which the essays in this volume build.

I personally wish also to thank the following individuals and institutions for their contributions—both large and small—in helping this volume become a reality: Ute Winston, Catherine Davies, William Doty, Matthew Winston, Thomas Kovach, Charlotte Armster, Ruth Getto, Richard Anderson, Mary Gray Porter, Robert Bell, Marti Balgooyen, the Fulbright Commission, the Deutscher Akademischer Austauschdienst, the National Endowment for the Humanities, and the Research Grants Committee of the University of Alabama.

EAM

ELAINE MARTIN

Women Right/(Re)Write the Nazi Past: An Introduction

> We will have no future until we have completely "seen" our past—whether we experienced it as perpetrator or as victim.
>
> Luise Rinser, *Gefängnistagebuch*[1]

Any literary text about a specific historical period is necessarily part story, part history, or perhaps it is the story *of* history. The meeting of history and literature in an individual text can be dynamic, even explosive, especially when the historical period in question is fraught with interpretive tensions, in the way that the Nazi era is. Certainly most critics would agree that all literature is ideological, and historical literature, such as the works discussed in this volume, is also political; that is, it offers interpretations of history that have political currency in the public negotiation of memory and legitimacy. As Geoff Eley writes in an article on the *Historikerstreit* (historians' argument), "taking a position on the origins of Nazism means simultaneously placing oneself in a present-related discourse about the bases of legitimacy in contemporary Germany" (172). Thus, what one writes, which events one reports, and how those events are interpreted matter very much indeed. For women writers, whose perspectives have traditionally been forced to the periphery of public discourse, being heard on the subject of the past means also having influence on the future. The conservative German historian Michael Stürmer seconds Eley's interpretation in his own summarizing statement: "In a land without history, whoever fills the memory, defines the concepts and interprets the past, wins the future" (cited in Craig 17).

In this volume both the authors under discussion and the scholars who write about them are interested in shaping the future by righting/writing the past; the former describe the effects of patriarchy, gender oppression, and fascist policies on women's lives and on their experiences under National Socialism, and the latter identify the interconnections of these factors and locate the individual life experiences within a larger literary/historical framework. In her book on postwar German novels about the Third Reich, Judith Ryan has noted:

> It should be established from the start that the actualities of history are, in a sense, peripheral to a study of this kind. More significant is the transmutation of history into opinion and ideology. We are faced, in effect, with a double displacement: first, of historical events into specific perceptions of history; second, of the perceptions into literary form (16).[2]

In writings by women, the "perceptions" of history in literary form undergo a third, gender-informed displacement: literature by women about the Nazi era integrates story and history from the unique perspective of *herstory.* The works discussed in this volume focus in varied ways on interconnections: on patriarchal fathers as individual tyrants, patriarchal family structures, and patriarchal social institutions; on fascisms in general and National Socialism in particular; on gender relations, women's lives, victimization, guilt, and responsibility; and on masculinity, aggression, and war. The individual elements form dizzying patterns of interlocked circles; the underlying subtext is violence, specifically the gradations of violence that range from the bittersweet power of paternal authority to the most overt form of organized violence, war. Because many works discussed in the essays focus on different combinations of linked factors, I briefly examine the factors themselves and begin with a look at these texts as "war literature," that is, as literary texts about (a) war.

The very appearance of war literature by women is of particular interest because in Western culture war has traditionally been viewed as a male phenomenon, that is, as something by, about, and curiously *for* men.[3] Sandra Gilbert, in her 1983 essay on World War I, notes the unique aspects of the Second World War in regard to the involvement of women; it was, she writes, "as much a war against women civilians as it was against male combatants, with a front indistinguishable from the home front" (449).[4] Traditionally, men left their homes as soldiers and went off to war; but this time the war came to their homes, and those who were "at home" were the women. German sociologist Annemarie Tröger supports Gilbert's interpretation of World War II as a new kind of war experience for women, one in which information passed down by mothers and grandmothers proved of little help. "The Second World War may be defined as a war against civilian populations," Tröger maintains. "Although in earlier wars," she continues, "civilian populations suffered—a cost deplored as the natural byproduct of warfare or justified as necessary to destroy the supply bases of the adversary—in World War II the war against the civilian population became a strategic goal in itself" (285).

Not only did women in World War II experience war differently than in previous conflicts, but they also have recorded and reflected upon those experiences in different ways. Writer Christa Wolf notes the "rows of book spines in the libraries" about the Nazi era which "are no longer measured in yards, but in miles," and cautions against a belief in sheer quantity as a mark of success in the process of *Vergangenheitsbewältigung* (coming to terms with the past). Quite the contrary. "The war is still unexplained," she maintains, "insufficiently discussed." For Wolf the root of the problem lies in an unspoken agreement among those who write about the period to avoid entire categories of topics and perspectives: "We have agreed to write about a certain aspect of the war, or to adopt a certain style when speaking of it, or to condemn it, but one feels a sort of omission in the writing, an avoidance of certain things which shake up the soul anew" (171). All the essays in this volume investigate these "certain things" that German writers have avoided, they probe the underlying psychological and sociopolitical reasons for the resulting omissions, and they reveal women's willingness to "shake up the soul." The war has been "insufficiently discussed," as Wolf claims, not only owing to personal omission or avoidance, but also because literature by women has been omitted and avoided by the canon-makers. As a review of the authors represented in this volume shows, although the majority of works appeared in the 1970s and 1980s, many writings about fascism and/or the war were published earlier, by such women authors as Irmgard Keun, Doris Dauber, and Virginia Woolf. As Margaret Higonnet et al. point out in the introduction to *Behind the Lines*, "Men's writing passed directly into the canon of twentieth-century literature, . . . women's wartime writings, on the other hand, passed into obscurity" (13). This has been true, until recently, not only of wartime writings but also of literature written since the war's end.

Historians like Claudia Koonz have identified another lacuna, namely that of factual information about women's involvement in and experiences during the Nazi period:

> After the publication of fifty thousand books and monographs about Hitler's Germany, it seems scarcely conceivable that any facet of those nightmare years remains unexplored, much less undiscovered. But in fact, half of the Germans who made dictatorship, war, and genocide possible have largely escaped observation. The women among Hitler's supporters have fallen through the historian's sieve, unclaimed by feminists and unnoticed by men (3).

Numerous works like Koonz's *Mothers in the Fatherland* and the anthology of essays *When Biology Became Destiny*, edited by Renate Bridenthal, Atina Grossmann, and Marion Kaplan, have in recent years significantly increased our knowledge of women's roles in Nazi Germany.[5] These new histories of women in the Third Reich make an inestimable contribution to overall scholarship on the era. Higonnet et al. view these new studies of women and National Socialism as the impetus for "a new historical perspective" and even "a rewriting of mainstream history" (4). But when Christa Wolf writes that "the war is still unexplained," she refers to a whole range of missing texts, primary and secondary, historical and literary. Those limitations inherent to historical study—shaped by events, documents, and testimony, and framed by interpretation—can be addressed by literary texts such as diaries, memoirs, autobiographies, essays, poetry, and fiction. In a recent *New York Times* review, Kit Reed wrote, for example, that "the biographical novelist has the liberty to reinvent the facts to get at the psychological truth" (33). Although not all the literary works discussed in this volume are (auto)biographical, one has a clear sense in reading about them that each author is indeed searching for a truth beyond the facts.

Those authors represented in this volume whose works have been written since the war, such as Zeller, Stern, Reichart,

Schwaiger, Rehmann, Wolf, Rinser, Bronnen, and Köhler, have been able to profit from the publication of both historical and literary texts about the Third Reich and the war. Eva Zeller addressed this topic in our 1986 interview when discussing the research she had conducted prior to the writing of her two autobiographical novels: "I read a lot of secondary literature, much of it by American authors because they had access to documents which we no longer have in Germany, or because we Germans have 'burned fingers,' and still do not have the necessary distance and objectivity. An American can deal with this historical material much more uninhibitedly than we Germans" (Interview 34).[6] Zeller's use of the term "burned fingers" calls to mind the paradox expressed in the title of Cordelia Edvardson's book, *Gebranntes Kind sucht das Feuer* (A burned child seeks the fire). The title, which is a word play on the German proverb "Gebranntes Kind scheut das Feuer," permits two different readings: the injured child seeks the source (reason, cause) of her suffering, or, although she has been burned, the child (here perhaps as metaphor for innocence and victimization), instead of running away from potential harm, is drawn or compelled toward it. This image of a fundamental duality, embodying as it does feelings of attraction/repulsion and innocence/guilt, explains in part the trauma for many writers discussed in this volume in deciding to write about the Nazi era.

In recent years journal articles and books have begun to appear that focus exclusively on women in the Third Reich. In addition to the works by Koonz and Bridenthal, Grossmann and Kaplan mentioned above, a number of published collections contribute specifically to the subject of *Frauenalltagsgeschichte* (history of women's quotidian lives) such as Gerda Szepansky's *"Blitzmädel" "Heldenmutter" "Kriegerwitwe": Frauenleben im Zweiten Weltkrieg* (Lightning Girls Hero-mothers War Widows: Women's Lives in World War II). This useful work consists of thirty-one interviews, which are largely retold in the words of the editor. Two further collections of this kind appeared in the late 1980s: *Behind the Lines: Gender and the Two World Wars* (1987) and *Arms and the Woman* (1989). The former focuses on twentieth-century wars, but not exclusively on literature; rather, it represents an interdisciplinary approach to the subject. The latter work does focus primarily on literary texts, but here the topic is war in general, rather than World War II in particular. In sum, as of this writing, I know of no single collection other than the present volume, which centers around women's literary treatments of the Third Reich. Even the excellent German work, *Opfer und Täterinnen* (Victims and perpetrators), edited by Angelika Ebbinghaus, approaches women's biographies from the perspectives of essay and document. Similarly, *Frauen gegen Hitler* (Women against Hitler), edited by Gerda Zorn and Gertrud Meyer, consists of reports by women who were in the resistance. The texts in this latter work have the advantage of having been written by eyewitnesses, but they are clearly oriented toward establishing what took place rather than interpreting or analyzing those events.

Thus, the present volume represents an introduction to and overview of a relatively unknown body of literature—one that centers on women's own descriptions and interpretations of their experiences formulated as literary texts. Nearly all the authors discussed in this volume, with the exception of Bielenberg, can be considered professional writers in that, at some point in their lives, they derived all or a portion of their income from their writings.

Most of women's writings about the Third Reich are autobiographical, either directly in autobiographies, diaries, and memoirs, or indirectly in autobiographical novels, short stories, and poetry.[7] This is also true for the majority of the authors discussed in the present volume. Despite the genre differences among the works, several common themes emerge that are not generally characteristic of men's works about the era.[8] Perhaps the most salient difference is the connection drawn—either overtly or implicitly—by many women writers between patriarchy and fascism, a theme that arises in all the essays in this volume, but is especially important to Gättens's discussion of language, gender, and fascism, to Figge's treatment of the literary reception of daughter-authored father books, and to Kecht's exploration of fascist family dynamics. Austrian writer Ingeborg Bachmann remarked in connection with her trilogy *Todesarten* that "the relationship between the sexes was a significant source for the development of fascism."[9] This is a theory argued also by Klaus Theweleit in his two-volume study *Männerphantasien* (*Male Fantasies*, 1987, 1989). Theweleit argues that the male identity of the *Freikorps* volunteers was shaped by the hatred and revulsion that characterized their relations with women, and that these feelings were, in turn, linked to the aggressive racism and anticommunism at the heart of the fascist movement. Another critic, Maria-Antonietta Macciocchi, has written on the connection not only of gender relations to fascism but also of sexuality to fascism. She argues, for example that "The body of fascist discourse is rigorously chaste, pure, virginal. Its central aim is the death of sexuality" (75). This provocative claim cannot be pursued at length here; suffice it to say that sexuality is a relatively unexplored but potentially important aspect of fascism and National Socialism. Overall, the interrelationship of racism, sexism, and fascism within the German patriarchal social structure is a complex topic and has engendered considerable discussion among scholars of the Nazi era, a discussion to which this volume seeks to contribute.

A second important perspective involves how the various authors discussed view the Nazi era in relation to a historical continuum that begins in the Weimar era or even earlier and continues through contemporary events.[10] This represents more than a new variation on the *Historikerstreit* (the argument on how National Socialism and its genocidal policies should be viewed: as aberration, represented in the *Sonderweg* (separate path) thesis, or as inevitability, as posited in the continuity thesis), because the context or framework within which the Third Reich is viewed in these works has international rather than national, that is, German, dimensions.[11] Christa Wolf, for example, draws numerous parallels between the Nazi era and both the Allende coup in Chile and the Vietnam War, events that were contemporaneous with her writing of *Kindheitsmuster* (*Patterns of Childhood*) in 1976. Both Irmgard Keun's life and writings, as illustrated in Horsley's essay, similarly embody not only the transitions between historical eras but also radical shifts in *Weltanschauung*—from the Weimar Republic and early Nazi years, including a temporary exile, to inner emigration and a precarious existence as a "submarine" in the underground.

Philippe Lacoue-Labarthe and Jean-Luc Nancy have made an important contribution to this discussion of history and ideology in their essay on the Nazi myth. Arguing that there is "a logic of fascism," they write: "There incontestably has been and there still is perhaps a German problem; Nazi ideology was a specifically political response to this problem; and there is no doubt whatsoever that the German tradition, and in particular the tradition of German thought, is not at all foreign to this ideology"

(295).[12] Going one step further, Lacoue-Labarthe and Nancy link the German tradition—via a discussion of the importance of classical Greece—with Western culture as a whole:

> This logic . . . belongs profoundly to the mood or character of the West in general, and more precisely, to the fundamental tendency of the *subject,* in the metaphysical sense of the word. Nazism does not sum up the West, nor represent its necessary finality. But neither is it possible to simply push it aside as an aberration, still less as a past aberration. A comfortable security in the certitudes of morality and of democracy not only guarantees nothing, but exposes one to the risk of not seeing the arrival, or the return, of that whose [*sic*] possibility is not due to any simple accident of history. An analysis of Nazism should never be conceived as a dossier of simple accusation, but rather as one element in a general deconstruction of the history in which our own provenance lies. (312)

This warning about the contemporaneity of fascist ideology would be seconded by women writers as diverse as Luise Rinser, Eva Zeller, Christa Wolf, and Carola Stern.

A third contribution of women's works is precisely this perspective of fascism as a contemporary phenomenon and the authors' insistence upon recognition of its continued threat. In our interview in 1979 Ingeborg Drewitz commented that "no one who was born later understands fascism, if she or he does not understand how it slipped into every life. Precisely for that reason it was dangerous, and wherever it exists in the world today, it is still dangerous."[13] On the same subject, Christa Wolf cites Kazimierz Brandys: "Fascism, as a concept, is larger than the Germans. But they became its classic example" (Wolf 36). One burning question for many of these women writers is why the Germans were so vulnerable to fascist ideas and ideals and thus became fascism's "classic example." Wolf links pre-Nazi vulnerability with postwar feelings of culpability and quotes a "famous Italian" as saying that, "twentieth-century men [*sic*] resent themselves and each other for having shown their capacity to live under dictatorship" (171).

Speculation on the appeal of fascist ideas and their potential audiences necessarily includes an investigation of the role played by traditional values, an investigation that reveals unmistakable

German proclivities and vulnerabilities. Christa Wolf minces no words on the subject of German moral or social priorities: "It seems easier to change a few hundred, or thousand, or million human beings into nonhumans or subhumans than to change our ideas about cleanliness and order and comfort" (199). Ruth Rehmann, as discussed in the essays of both Gättens and Figge, demonstrates in *Der Mann auf der Kanzel* (The man in the pulpit) how her pastor-father's unquestioning embrace of traditional German values led to his moral blindness, and Eva Zeller, as discussed in my essay on autobiography, concludes that the age-old Prussian values of "Gehorsamkeit, Treue, and Kamaraderie" (obedience, faithfulness, and comradeship) were skillfully altered and misused by the National Socialists within a populace that was politically too unsophisticated to recognize that transformation.[14]

The sanctity of the family, a concept that has a long history of willful misinterpretation and misapplication in women's struggles for equality and self-fulfillment, constitutes another "German" value that played a role in the radical policy reversals from the Weimar Republic to the National Socialist era.[15] Kecht explores one such intersection of public policy, social values, and the family in her essay on works by the Austrian writers Brigitte Schwaiger and Elisabeth Reichart. The threat to (patriarchal) social order posed by women emancipated under the Weimar constitution should not be underestimated. Melita Maschmann writes in *Fazit; Mein Weg in der Hitler-Jugend* (Sum total; My path in the Hitler youth): "It was considered good form back then to make fun of, even to attack, the women's movement, and especially feminists" (92).[16] Irmgard Keun's life provides a good example of how emancipated women were silenced, and Christabel Bielenberg, as a relatively independent Englishwoman, offers an outsider's view of the same phenomenon.

Neither can one discount the central importance of women to Nazi ideology and policy. Bridenthal et al. note that "gender was an extraordinarily salient category throughout the period" and that "its significance increased in the Nazi period because so much of Nazi rhetoric claimed that the government held population policy considerations paramount" (xiv). Not only were women at the center of Nazi policy, but they were also, according to historian Koonz, active players in the National Socialist phenomenon: "Far from remaining untouched by Nazi evil, women operated at its very center" (6). The question of women's involvement in the Nazi machinery can be seen from two sides: officially women were excluded from the party leadership, with the exception of Gertrud Scholtz-Klink who headed the bureau for women's affairs, but unofficially they helped both to bring the Nazis to power and to maintain them there. Gerda Szepansky writes, "Without women, the plans of the Hitler government would not have succeeded; without their industrious assistance, the war could not have been waged" (11).[17]

Women were just as guilty of being *Mitläufer* (collaborators) as were their male counterparts. Christa Wolf gives personal examples of this passive cooperation, saying of her protagonist Nelly, "She learned that it's a sin to be a bystander, and how sweet this sin can be. A lesson she never forgot, nor the temptation" (306). Eva Zeller records her first awakening to reality at eighteen when she is conscripted into the *Reichsarbeitsdienst* (national work corps) and loses all of her rights. Prior to this awakening she was, however, a total conformist who barely noticed missing neighbors, much less intervened to prevent their arrest; by her own admission she was more interested in love than in politics.

Zeller's apoliticism—even apathy—was typical of German women in general. Gerda Szepansky notes that "one would have to say that the majority of women was uninvolved politically; they adapted to the given situation, and were incapable of recognizing interconnections" (10).[18] Carola Stern has also admitted to passive compliance, saying of one particular incident, "this experience has played an important role throughout my life, primarily because one becomes so unsure of oneself" (Interview). Ingeborg Lauterstein, an Austro-American writer who grew up in Vienna during the war, also addresses this question of complicity and guilt; she records a painful scene in Vienna in which Nazis compel wealthy Jewish women to kneel in the street and scrub the paving stones while the uniformed men urinate on them. This event constitutes a moral turning point for the onlookers:

> Men danced around in circles, one by one, competing, goading. . . . Workingmen, the chimney sweep, looked on as though they were at the circus. They watched the Nazis make water on heads and hands and silk stockings. . . . [Then] the men were buttoning their trousers . . . The competition was over. Participants and onlookers, shamefaced, excited, frightened, or entertained—none of us would ever forget this scene. Memory of evil works like one of those clockwork automats in the amusement park, the Prater,

> where figures stand rigid until a coin sets them into motion, to move about and perform the same scene over and over again as long as the mechanism lasts. (151–152)

Lauterstein contrasts the bystanders' cruelty and insensitivity to the women ("The crowd liked to be entertained; they were ready to be amused at anyone's expense. They laughed as though they were at a show in the amusement park.") with their incongruous sympathy for the dog of one of the street-scrubbing women ("The crowd murmured, 'Poor dog . . .' Helpful hands urged the animal out of the circle."). At the end of the scene, a little boy's balloon escapes, and the bystanders assuage their guilt with exaggerated expressions of compassion for him: "Men and women turned to him in their great need to comfort. Catering to his futile grief helped them to feel they were kind, after all" (155).

Lauterstein records not only the confusion of emotions in an abnormal situation—excitement, shame, entertainment, fear—but also the ways in which people attempt to reassert feelings of normalcy. Rather than examine their inhumanity, they invest energy in diversionary activities (sympathy for a dog, compassion for a child). Carola Stern argues that "normalcy" could never be reestablished after such an incident because the very concept was in flux. For many people, any kind of *Gegenwelt* (alternative world) as Stern calls it, was lacking; as a result people had nothing against which to measure their acts and beliefs. Stern and numerous other writers depict in excruciating detail instances of personal *Versagen* (failure), that, when taken individually, seem perhaps insignificant, but when taken together, resulted in a moral bankruptcy of national proportions. Christa Wolf poses an important question as to which condition precedes the other: individual acts of cowardice and culpable behavior, or a prevailing permissive social attitude that makes such behavior acceptable. As she expresses it, "It's hard to determine which has to come first: the readiness of people to have their hearts prepared to sanction murder or the coffins that are being wheeled past them" (198).

Guilt is very much a topic in the women's works discussed in this volume, in particular because the authors are non-Jewish women and thus belong to the *Täterinnen,* to those who were perpetrators, rather than to the victims. Austro-American Ingeborg Day relates in *Ghost Waltz* that she heard the Holocaust scholar Elie Wiesel say one day on a television program, "I don't understand the victims, and I don't understand the killers. But the victims are my problem, and the killers are yours" (183–184).[19] One major task of women who write about Nazi Germany, and one they undertake unflinchingly, is to understand better "the killers." Wholesale murder requires collaboration at various levels—ranging from those who pull the trigger to nonintervening bystanders—and women were inevitably involved. Christabel Bielenberg, author of *The Past is Myself,* makes clear that "in a regime such as Hitler's, there could be no standing on the side-lines, but there were also no rules to the game; each to his [*sic*] own conscience" (98). Clearly, if women were involved, then the writers who experienced National Socialism are implicated themselves as well. "With my burned hand," Ingeborg Bachmann observed, "I write about the nature of fire."[20] Willard Gaylin writes in *The Rage Within:*

> True guilt is an excruciatingly painful emotion. Guilt sees us as both the one to be punished and the punisher. It is ourselves against ourselves. Or more exactly, ourselves against an image of ourselves the way we would like to be. It is the violation or failure of that image which produces the sense of guilt. Of course, the image must be there: we must first have developed a sense of ideal behavior. (67)

The problem in addressing the question of guilt, both for writers who lived through the Third Reich and those born after, is sorting out the competing sources of one's "sense of ideal behavior": pre-Nazi religious, familial, and social values versus the often conflicting, Nazi-informed models.

How do women writers deal individually with the question of guilt and personal responsibility? Many of them were children during the Nazi era; Eva Zeller, who was born in 1923, said in our interview, "I always have youth as my alibi." This would also be true of writers such as Ingeborg Drewitz (b. 1923), Ruth Rehmann (b. 1922), and Christa Wolf (b. 1929).[21] Others belong to the postwar generation, a number of whom are represented in this volume: Sarah Kirsch (Mabee's essay), Brigitte Schwaiger and Elisabeth Reichart (Kecht's essay), and Barbara Bronnen and Monika Köhler (Figge's essay). Still others began as Nazis but changed midstream, like Luise Rinser who ultimately was arrested and imprisoned for anti-Nazi activity. Diana Hinze's essay probes the difficulties of women like Rinser who have dual pasts, containing both Nazi and anti-Nazi phases, and also touches on the problems that these figures pose for researchers. Many other women went into exile; among those who did, Anna Seghers enjoys perhaps the greatest international recognition today. In this volume, Horsley's essay on Irmgard Keun and Rojer's essay on Doris Dauber describe in detail the trauma of the exile experience for women and make clear the long reach of the Nazi arm. And finally there were women who were truly enmeshed in National Socialism, who were party members and activists, were *entnazifiziert* (denazified) after the war, and subsequently used writing to explore and expiate their culpability, like Melita Maschmann in *Fazit* (for which the original subtitle was "Kein Rechtfertigungsversuch" [no attempt at self-justification]), Carola Stern, in her dual auto/biography of her own and her husband's lives, *In den Netzen der Erinnerung* (In the nets of memory), discussed in my essay, or Margarete Hannsmann in *Der helle Tag bricht an; Ein Kind wird Nazi* (The bright day dawns; a child becomes Nazi).

Women writers have approached the Nazi era and their own involvement with it—however far removed—in various ways: Sarah Kirsch changed her name, choosing the first name imposed on all Jewish women by the Nazis; Carola stern has tried to atone for her leadership role in the *Bund Deutscher Mädel* (Nazi youth group for girls) with years of work in Amnesty International;[22] Brigitte Schwaiger collaborated with Chawa Fränkel (Eva Deutsch), a Jewish woman from Galicia, to write the story of the latter's life during the Nazi years (*Die Galizianerin*);[23] and other professional writers like Christa Wolf and Eva Zeller have used the process of writing, "the laying bare of the innards" (Wolf 171), to expose new truths about what happened and to try and liberate themselves from the overwhelming burden of the past.

Although we have information about Jewish women's experiences of the Holocaust, both from scholars and from survivors, non-Jewish women's experiences have not been discussed as extensively.[24] Some women writers felt a sense of impropriety, as Luise Rinser explains in the foreword to the second edition (1973) of her prison diary (*Gefängnistagebuch*), originally published in 1946:

> The prison diary appeared as one of the first German books after the war. It quickly sold out. After the second printing I didn't want any more new ones. There were several reasons. First, I had heard so much in the meantime about the suffer-

> ings of those who had been in concentration camps, that my own experiences did not seem worth mentioning.[25]

Other women have said they needed time to gain emotional distance from the material, and some have indicated that they were unable to write because they were preoccupied with other responsibilities and duties. Because not much scholarship is available about literary treatments of non-Jewish women's experiences and reflections of the Nazi era, and because most primary works are relatively recent publications, the present essays open a new perspective on the Nazi era. Although that perspective is not monolithic, it does reveal a common pattern: what emerges from the women writers' accounts is a frightening sense of "normalcy," of apoliticism, and of indifference later sharpened by fear. Germans' self-perception as a civilized and cultured people prevented them from seeing and believing the injustices, crimes, and finally the atrocities being committed around them. Melita Maschmann summarizes at the end of her work: "The uncanny thing was that it was not gangsters and savages, but good-natured people endowed with intellect and a soul, who had allowed themselves to be seduced into approving of and serving absolute evil" (240).[26] The very ordinariness of the lives and the people described is a reminder of how fragile the boundary is between reason and irrationality, between normalcy and monstrosity, between legality and crime, and between legitimacy and usurpation.

Many literary works discussed in this volume offer, among other analyses, reasons for the special appeal of Nazism to girls and adult women. Writers who were children or adolescents during the Third Reich, such as Zeller, Rehmann, Wolf, and Stern, suggest the general vulnerability of young people to causes and their naive "belief that, one day, the world will be perfect" (Wolf 246), and they further describe the attractiveness to young girls of an escape from restrictive patriarchal family relationships—an escape that permitted them freedoms usually reserved for boys: physically strenuous outdoor activities, comradeship, leadership roles, creative outlets, and feelings of being both useful and taken seriously. Writers who were already adults during the Nazi era, such as Luise Rinser, Irmgard Keun, Christabel Bielenberg, and Doris Dauber, document the underestimated effects of mass psychology on a largely politically naive populace—a fact especially true of women because the emancipatory ideas of the Weimar Republic had touched relatively few women's lives. Writers from both these groups describe the willful confusion by numerous girls and women (as well as by boys and men) of religion, patriotism, and politics, whereby embracing National Socialism assumed the characteristics of a religious conversion. And finally, most writers in this volume show, either directly or indirectly, the attractiveness, to people with a weak self-concept and wavering sense of national identity, of rhetoric based upon (military) strength, nationalism, equality, sanctity of the family, and the promised dismantling of social privilege.

This volume had its origins in a conference session I chaired in 1987, "Women's Writings About the Nazi Era." Despite the somewhat prosaic session title, it became clear from the papers presented and the ensuing lively discussion, that the topic was anything but prosaic.[27] Because of the dearth of scholarly work on women's literary representations of the Nazi era, I resolved to bring together essays on the subject; three of the papers from that original session (Figge, Gättens, Hinze) were expanded into essays and became the backbone of this collection. All the essays were chosen because of their contribution to the basic thesis of the book: that patriarchy and fascism are interconnected concepts. My intent was, further, to introduce a broad range of women writers on this subject, in terms not only of their relative reputation (ranging from the well known to the unknown), but also in terms of a variety of other factors: their ages during (or after) the Nazi era; for the older writers, the variety of their experiences under National Socialism (both rural and urban—including life in Berlin—and life in exile and in the underground); differences in social class ranging from the aristocracy/upper middle class to the *Kleinbürgertum* (lower middle class) and working class; their political perspectives, especially their political orientation for/with/against Nazism; and finally, differences in nationality, including Austrian, German, and non-German (in this volume, British). I was also interested in genre differences—represented in this volume by biography, fiction, biographical fiction, and poetry.

The essays are ordered in this collection in a chronology roughly corresponding to the women writers' dates of birth. Exceptions to this order are the essays by Gättens and Figge, and my own, all of which discuss writers that belong to different age groups. Of course, there is no neat separation of "generations," and although writers may be of the same age group, they did not necessarily publish works on the Nazi era at the same time; for example, Christabel Bielenberg, born in 1909, first published her work in 1968. Despite these caveats, one can identify three main groups of writers. Those in the first group, born around the turn of the century such as Irmgard Keun, Luise Rinser, Doris Dauber, and Virginia Woolf, represent those women who were already adults in the Nazi era, and who wrote primarily before and during this period (with the notable exception of Rinser, who continued to publish for several decades after the war). Women in the next group of writers, born in the 1920s and 1930s, thus were children or adolescents during the Third Reich: Christa Wolf, Ruth Rehmann, Eva Zeller, Carola Stern, and Sarah Kirsch. Finally, a postwar generation is represented by the writers Barbara Bronnen, Monika Köhler, Brigitte Schwaiger, and Elisabeth Reichart. Because of these age differences, the authors' perspectives vary widely. With the earliest writers one has the strongest sense of eyewitness account, including even Virginia Woolf's "essay" which defies precise genre labels. The works by the middle group are already more layered with self-reflection and retrospective analysis—Christa Wolf's "rows of book spines in the libraries" clearly intervene between experience and narrative, between protagonist, narrator, and author. And finally, for the postwar generation, the intergenerational conflict, sometimes as a dialogue with, or search for, a deceased parent, takes a precedence that it does not have in the other works.

In these comments I have emphasized the diversity of the works discussed in this book, but they are also linked by common denominators. They represent women's unique experience of and response to National Socialism, and none of the writers discussed is Jewish (despite Sarah Kirsch's profound personal identification with victims of the Holocaust and her symbolic adoption of the name Sarah); thus they reflect essentially a non-Jewish, female perspective. Furthermore, what binds the essays in the volume together, and ultimately also the works they discuss, is the underlying feminist analysis of National Socialism that links patriarchal attitudes/institutions/familial structures with the rise of fascism. The essays in this volume are, as the word essay itself implies, an "attempt or endeavor." They reexamine previously accepted information about and interpretations of the Nazi era and put them to the test. The essays are not intended to provide a final word; rather, it is hoped that they will stimulate further study and revision, both for established scholars of the Nazi era and for students and scholars for whom the topic is relatively new.

NOTES

1. "Wir werden keine Zukunft haben, ehe wir unsere Vergangenheit—ob wir sie als Täter oder als Opfer erlebten—ganz und gar 'gesehen' haben." Luise Rinser's *Gefängnistagebuch* was one of the first West German postwar publications dealing with the topic of National Socialism and the war. This and further translations from Rinser's works are my own. Luise Rinser has become the subject of considerable controversy since the discovery of her early pro-Nazi writings. See Diana Hinze's essay in this volume for a complete discussion of the subject.

2. Judith Ryan's study includes only one woman, Christa Wolf, who, for a period in the 1970s and early 1980s became almost a token female in discussions of war literature. The other authors Ryan discusses are Thomas Mann, Günter Grass, Alfred Andersch, Heinrich Böll, Siegfried Lenz, and Johannes Bobrowski.

3. A brief review of World War II novels would support this perception that the war was a masculine event, both historically and literarily. The best-known writers who treat the subject are all men: Thomas Mann, Günter Grass, Heinrich Böll, Siegfried Lenz, Rolf Hochhut, Walter Kempowski, Jakov Lind, Martin Walser, Peter Handke, Uwe Johnson, Wolfgang Koeppen, Peter Härtling, and Christoph Meckel. Scholars, including women, reflect this male orientation. Like Judith Ryan, Donna Reid in *the Novel and the Nazi Past* discusses primarily male writers (Th. Mann, Grass, and Böll), and, in an epilogue on literature of the 1970s, investigates two more male writers (Handke, Johnson) and a single woman writer, Christa Wolf.

4. See Jane Marcus's "The Asylums of Antaeus; Women, War and Madness: Is There a Feminist Fetishism?" in *The Differences Within,* ed. Elizabeth Meese and Alice Parker (Philadelphia: John Benjamins, 1989) for a thorough critique of Sandra Gilbert's essay, especially pp. 53–58.

5. Other historians and scholars who have actively published their research on women in the Third Reich include Jill Stephenson, Leila Rupp, Dorothee Klinksiek, Gerda Szepansky, Rita Thalmann, Gisela Bock, Gerda Zorn, and Annemarie Tröger.

6. I interviewed Eva Zeller in Munich on 15 May 1986. This and all further references to this interview are my translation.

7. Works by women about the Nazi era are now numerous; the following are examples of the various genres: (1) diaries—Ruth Andreas-Friedrich's *Der Schattenmann* and *Schauplatz Berlin,* Luise Rinser's *Gefängnistagebuch,* Marie Vassiltchikov's *Berlin Diaries,* and Lore Wolf's *Ich habe das Leben Lieb; Tagebuchblätter aus dem Zuchthaus Ziegenhain;* (2) autobiographies—Luise Rinser's *Den Wolf Umarmen,* Christabel Bielenberg's *The Past is Myself,* Tatiana Metternich's *Bericht eines ungewöhnlichen Lebens,* and Carola Stern's *In den Netzen der Erinnerung;* (3) autobiographical fiction—Christa Wolf's *Kindheitsmuster,* Eva Zeller's *Solange ich denken kann* and its sequel *Nein und Amen,* Christa Reinig's *Die Himmlische und Irdische Geometrie,* and Ingeborg Drewitz's *Gestern war Heute;* and (4) fiction—Christine Brückner's three novels about the Quindt family, Erika Mitterer's *Alle unsere Spiele,* Ingeborg Lauterstein's *The Water Castle* and its sequel *Vienna Girl.*

8. Works that fit this category (in part because they are temporally comparable) would primarily be those published in the 1970s and 1980s, such as

Christoph Meckel's *Suchbild,* Peter Härtling's *Nachgetragene Liebe,* Peter Handke's *Wunschloses Unglück,* and Wolfgang Koeppen's *Tod in Rom.*

9. Quoted from an unpublished paper by Marie-Luise Gättens, presented at the American Association of Teachers of German (AATG) meeting, November 1987, Atlanta.

10. The essays in the volume *When Biology Became Destiny* thoroughly document the interconnectedness of the Weimar Republic and the Nazi era.

11. Another aspect to the debate is whether the "final solution" was a particularly German phenomenon, or whether such brutal and murderous policies are common to totalitarian regimes wherever and whenever they occur. The initial arguments of the *Historikerstreit* took the form of exchanges in newspaper and magazine articles in 1986 in publications such as *Die Zeit, Der Spiegel, Die Frankfurter Allgemeine Zeitung* (FAZ), *Der Frankfurter Rundschau,* and the *Rheinischer Merkur.* A summary of the debate was published in book form in 1987: *Historikerstreit: Die Dokumentation der Kontroverse um die Einzigartigkeit der nationalsozialistischen Judenvernichtung* (Munich: Piper, 1987). See also *Ist der Nationalsozialismus Geschichte?: Zu Historisierung und Historikerstreit,* ed. Dan Diner (Frankfurt/M: Fischer, 1988), and Geoff Eley, "Nazism, Politics and the Image of the Past: Thoughts on the West German *Historikerstreit,* 1986–1987," in *Past and Present* 121 (Nov. 1988): 171–208.

12. The discussion of the ideological roots of Nazism is not merely a recent phenomenon. For an early (1941) treatment of this subject, see Peter Viereck, *Metapolitics: The Roots of the Nazi Mind,* rev. ed. (New York: Capricorn, 1965).

13. "Niemand, der später geboren ist, versteht den Faschismus, wenn er nicht versteht, wie der sich eingeschlichen hat in jedes Leben. Genau deshalb war er gefährlich, und, wo immer in der Welt, ist noch immer gefährlich." From an unpublished interview I conducted with the author in her home, Berlin-Dahlem, 4 July 1979; my translation. A copy of the interview appears as an appendix in my dissertation, "Uncommon Women and the Common Experience: Fiction of Four Contemporary French and German Women Writers," Indiana University, 1982.

14. Renate Bridenthal and Claudia Koonz write in the opening essay of *When Biology Became Destiny:* "More than once since the Frankfurt School's famous study on authority and the family, it has been suggested that *the authoritarianism of the German family* contributed to the susceptibility of the population to the siren call of the leadership principle" (33, emphasis added).

15. For an excellent summary of the public debate about women's proper relationship to the family, see *Women, the Family, and Freedom,* vols. 1 and 2, eds. Susan Groag Bell and Karen M. Offen.

16. "Es gehörte damals zum guten Ton, über die Frauenbewegung, insbesondere über die Frauenrechtlerinnen, zu schimpfen und zu spotten." This and all further quotations from *Fazit* are my translations.

17. "Ohne die Frauen wären die Pläne der Hitler-Regierung nicht aufgegangen, ohne ihre tätige Mithilfe wäre auch der Krieg nicht führbar gewesen." This and all further quotations from *"Blitzmädel" "Heldenmutter" "Kriegerwitwe"* are my translations.

18. "Von der Mehrzahl der Frauen muss man wohl sagen, dass sie politisch desinteressiert waren, sich den Gegebenheiten anpassten, auch nicht in der Lage waren, Zusammenhänge zu durchschauen."

19. Continuing sentiments of anti-Semitism constitute a major issue in Day's autobiographical novel. About Yiddish she writes, for example, "Yiddish,

something hisses inside me, seething, ferocious, How I detest it, pidgin German, a sickening bastardization of my beautiful-beautiful-language-my-home-my-language-my-beautiful-beautiful—and [I] catch myself, terrified" (59). And, in similarly strong language she oddly blames the Jews for the Holocaust: "I felt: The legacy of the Holocaust has destroyed my father. I felt: The legacy of the Holocaust has irreparably damaged my mother's life. I felt: The legacy of the Holocaust has tarnished me beyond all methods of cleansing. I felt: I hate the guts of every Jew alive" (210).

20. Quoted in Wolf, p. 163.

21. Many women who were active in the BDM (Bund Deutscher Mädel) as girls—some even held leadership positions in the organization—could use the "tenderness of years" argument: Margarete Hannsmann (b. 1921), Melita Maschmann (b. 1918), Carola Stern (b. 1925), and Ingeborg Drewitz (b. 1923).

22. In our interview (10 June 1988, Cologne), Carola Stern said, "The healing process has been achieved less through the writing of the book, than through the long years of work in Amnesty International that I have done. I have the feeling that I worked off a double amount each year." ("Die Heilung war mir erfolgt weniger durch das Buch als dadurch, dass ich diese lange Amnestiearbeit gemacht habe. Ich habe das Gefühl, ich habe jedes Jahr doppelt abgearbeitet.") My translation.

23. For a critical evaluation of both *Die Galizianerin* and the Schwaiger/Deutsch relationship, see " 'Hoffentlich werde ich taugen.' Zu Situation und Kontext von Brigitte Schwaiger/Eva Deutsch *Die Galizianerin,*" by Dagmar C. G. Lorenz, *Women in German Yearbook* 6, ed. Jeanette Clausen and Helen Cafferty, 1991, 1–26.

24. See, for example, Marlene E. Heinemann, *Gender and Destiny: Women Writers and the Holocaust* (Westport, Conn.: Greenwood, 1986), especially the bibliography section: "Fiction, Memoirs, and Collected Testimonies," or Vera Laska, *Women in the Resistance and the Holocaust: The Voices of Eyewitnesses* (Westport, Conn.: Greenwood, 1983).

25. "Das 'Gefängnistagebuch' erschien als eines der ersten deutschen Bücher nach dem Kriege. Es war rasch vergriffen. Nach der zweiten Auflage wollte ich keine neue mehr. Es gab mehrere Gründe dafür. Der erste: ich hatte mittlerweile soviel gehört und gelesen von den Leiden derer, die in den Konzentrationslagern gewesen waren, dass mir daneben meine eigenen Erfahrungen nicht erwähnenswert erschienen" (5).

26. "Das Unheimliche lag eben darin, dass nicht Gangster und Rohlinge, sondern gutartige, mit Gaben des Geistes und der Seele ausgestattete Menschen sich verführen liessen, dem abgründig Bösen zuzustimmen und ihm zu dienen" (240).

27. The session on women's writings about the Nazi era was sponsored by the Coalition of Women in German at the 1987 American Association of Teachers of German (AATG) conference in Atlanta.

WORKS CITED

Bell, Susan Groag, and Karen M. Offen, eds. *Women, the Family, and Freedom: The Debate in Documents,* vol. 1, 1750–1880; vol. 2, 1880–1950. Stanford: Stanford University Press, 1983.

Bielenberg, Christabel. *The Past is Myself.* 1968; London: Corgi, 1984.

Bridenthal, Renate, Atina Grossmann, and Marion Kaplan. *When Biology Became Destiny: Women in Weimar and Nazi Germany.* New York: Monthly Review Press, 1984.

Craig, Gordon A. "The War of the German Historians," *New York Review of Books,* 15 January 1987.

Day, Ingeborg. *Ghost Waltz.* New York: Viking, 1980.

Drewitz, Ingeborg. *Gestern war Heute; Hundert Jahre Gegenwart.* Dusseldorf: Claassen, 1978.

———. Personal interview. 4 July 1979, Berlin-Dahlem. Printed as an appendix in Elaine Martin, "Uncommon Women and the Common Experience: Fiction of Four Contemporary French and German Women Writers." Ph.D. diss., Indiana University, 1982.

Ebbinghaus, Angelika, ed. *Opfer und Täterinnen; Frauenbiographien des Nationalsozialismus.* Schriften der Hamburger Stiftung für Sozialgeschichte des 20. Jahrhunderts. Hamburg: Delphi Politik, 1987.

Edvardson, Cordelia. *Gebranntes Kind sucht das Feuer.* Trans. from the Swedish by Anna-Liese Kornitzky. Munich: Hanser, 1986.

Eley, Geoff. "Nazism, Politics and the Image of the Past: Thoughts on the West German *Historikerstreit* 1986–1987." *Past and Present* 121 (Nov. 1988): 171–208.

Gaylin, Willard, M.D. *The Rage Within: Anger in Modern Life.* New York: Simon and Schuster, 1984.

Gilbert, Sandra. "Soldier's Heart: Literary Men, Literary Women, and the Great War." *Signs* 8, 3 (1983): 422–450.

Hannsmann, Margarete. *Der helle Tag bricht an; Ein Kind wird Nazi.* Munich: Deutscher Taschenbuch Verlag, 1984.

Higonnet, Margaret, Jane Jenson, Sonya Michel, and Margaret Weitz, eds. *Behind the Lines: Gender and the Two World Wars.* New Haven: Yale University Press, 1987.

Koonz, Claudia. *Mothers in the Fatherland: Women, the Family and Nazi Politics.* New York: St. Martin's, 1987.

Lacoue-Labarthe, Philippe, and Jean-Luc Nancy. "The Nazi Myth." Trans. by Brian Holmes. *Critical Inquiry* 16 (Winter 1990): 291–312.

Lauterstein, Ingeborg. *The Water Castle.* Boston: Houghton Mifflin, 1980.

Macciocchi, Maria-Antonietta. "Female Sexuality in Fascist Ideology." *Feminist Review* 1 (1979): 67–82.

Maschmann, Melita. *Fazit; Mein Weg in der Hitler-Jugend.* Munich: Deutscher Taschenbuch Verlag, 1979.

Reed, Kit. Review of *The Light Possessed* by Alan Cheuse, *The New York Times Book Review,* 7 October 1990, p. 33.

Rehmann, Ruth. *Der Mann auf der Kanzel; Fragen an einen Vater.* 1979. Reprint. Munich: Deutsche Verlags-Anstalt, 1981.

Reed, Donna. *The Novel and the Nazi Past.* New York: Peter Lang, 1985.

Rinser, Luise. *Gefängnistagebuch.* 1946. Reprint. Frankfurt/M.: Fischer, 1973.
Ryan, Judith. *The Uncompleted Past: Postwar German Novels and the Third Reich.* Detroit: Wayne State University Press, 1983.
Schwaiger, Brigitte, and Eva Deutsch. *Die Galizianerin.* Vienna: Paul Zsolnay, 1982.
Stern, Carola. *In den Netzen der Erinnerung; Lebensgeschichten zweier Menschen.* Reinbek bei Hamburg: Rowohlt, 1986.
———. Personal interview. 11 June 1988, Cologne, Germany.
Szepansky, Gerda. *"Blitzmädel" "Heldenmutter" "Kriegerwitwe"; Frauenleben im Zweiten Weltkrieg.* Frankfurt/M: Fischer, 1986.
Theweleit, Klaus. *Männerphantasien.* Vols. 1 and 2. Berlin: Verlag Roter Stern, 1977, 1978. [Published in English as *Male Fantasies.* Vols. 1 and 2. University of Minnesota Press, 1987, 1989].
Tröger, Annemarie. "German Women's Memories of World War II." In *Behind the Lines,* edited by Margaret Higonnet et al., 285–299. New Haven: Yale University Press, 1987.
Viereck, Peter. *Metapolitics: The Roots of the Nazi Mind.* Rev. ed. New York: Capricorn, 1965.
Wolf, Christa. *Patterns of Childhood* Trans. Ursule Molinaro and Hedwig Rappolt. New York: Farrar, Strauss, Giroux, 1984. Trans. of *Kindheitsmuster.* 1976. Reprint. Darmstadt: Luchterhand, 1979.
Zeller, Eva. *Solange ich denken kann.* Stuttgart: Deutsche Verlags-Anstalt, 1981.
———. Personal interview. 15 May 1986, Munich, Germany.

MARIE-LUISE GÄTTENS

Language, Gender, and Fascism: Reconstructing Histories in *Three Guineas*, *Der Mann auf der Kanzel* and *Kindheitsmuster*

I Virginia Woolf's analysis of fascism in *Three Guineas* focuses on the patriarchal relationship between men and women, and she argues that the unequal distribution of power between the genders is a key element for producing fascism. Contemplating the quote from a British newspaper of the 1930s, in which a man complains that working women take away men's jobs and thus make them unable to provide for a family, the speaker of *Three Guineas* offers this interpretation:

> There we have in embryo the creature, Dictator as we call him when he is Italian or German, who believes that he has the right, whether given by God, Nature, sex or race is immaterial, to dictate to other human beings how they shall live; what they shall do. Let us quote again: "Homes are the real places of the women who are now compelling men to be idle." (53)

The young man's complaint relates closely to the famous debate about the so called "double earners," that took place in Germany during the 1930s and fueled political passions, passions that ultimately served the National Socialists in gaining power. In this debate, married women who earned an income in addition to their husbands' were blamed for the vast unemployment during that time. The accusation was so far off the real economic impact of this small group of women that the significance of this issue in the political debates testifies to the power of traditional gender conceptions, which, when threatened, unleash a veritable flood of resentment. As the speaker of *Three Guineas* points out, the ability to provide for a family has been an essential component of what it means to be a man in this culture: "The desire to support wife and children—what motive could be more powerful, or deeply rooted? For it was connected with manhood itself" (138). The significance of women's employment in the political discourse of the thirties thus is not so much based on the economic impact of women's work but on its potential in altering the definition of what is male and what is female. Recently, feminist historians have stressed that the National Socialists' conservative gender policy was indeed a key element in gaining them widespread support and in consolidating their power (Bridenthal, 19).

Instead of turning the analyses of fascism to the countries Spain and Germany that experienced fascist rule in the thirties, *Three Guineas* focuses on democratic Britain; Woolf asserts that its gender relations could not only potentially produce fascism, but that men's power over women was itself a kind of fascist rule. The rejection Woolf's text experienced in the thirties within England was based on the fact, as Makiko Minow-Pinkney points out, that it violated the rules of (male) political discourse: "For the book deconstructs the conventional oppositions private/public, English liberalism/German and Italian fascism, on which the very identity of Woolf's social circle was constructed" (188). Indeed, *Three Guineas* argues that the reproduction of gendered subjects in the patriarchal family is the necessary ingredient for the development of fascism. For the fascist is a gendered subject: "It is the figure of a man; some say, others deny, that he is Man himself, the quintessence of virility, the perfect type of which all the others are imperfect adumbrations" (142).[1] Fascism thus depends on a male subject that constitutes itself through power and the control of others and on a female subject characterized by powerlessness and subjugation. *Three Guineas,* furthermore, exposes the complicity of the humanist tradition, "he is Man himself," in which men universalize their own experience while relegating women to "the other." Recently, Klaus Theweleit argued that the specific authoritarian patriarchal relationship between men and women in Wilhelminian Germany produced a life-destroying reality—fascism (Männerphantasien, I, 232).

Besides analyzing the importance of gender relations for the production of fascism, *Three Guineas* argues that it is of vital importance for women to know their own history in order to critically analyze their position in society. It offers a model of how women can read their history out of the male-dominated cultural text, and in doing so, it presents a historically specific female subject that, although subjected to patriarchy, is nevertheless an active producer of culture.

In the 1970s, a number of German women authors published texts that focused on their historical experience under National Socialism. These reconstructions of history are connected with the attempt to redefine women's position within the contemporary social order, an attempt that was influenced directly or indirectly by the women's movement. As in *Three Guineas* the concern for the past in these texts thus closely relates to present political concerns, which as the authors of the essay "Popular Memory" point out is always the case: "just as history-writing is necessarily a theoretical and political activity, so it is also a practice in and for the present. Theory, politics and contemporaneity are basic conditions of the practice, present even when denied" (240–241).

It is for its articulation of the three interrelated issues—gender relations and fascism, women's history, and the female subject—that I would like to analyze *Three Guineas* before turning to two German women's reconstructions of their history under National Socialism: Ruth Rehmann's *Der Mann auf der Kanzel* (1979, The man in the pulpit), and Christa Wolf's *Kindheitsmuster* (1976, *Patterns of Childhood*). While Woolf presents a more general theoretical reflection of the relationship between women's position within society and their position within the historical discourses, Rehmann and Wolf engage in specific readings of National Socialism from a female point of view. However, their readings also incorporate a critical examination of the historical discourses.

The notions of what is male and what is female are cultural conceptions into which all human beings are placed. These conceptions form a sex-gender system, which Teresa de Lauretis defines in the following way:

> The sex-gender system . . . is both a sociocultural construct and a semiotic apparatus, a system of representation which

> assigns meaning (identity, value, prestige, location in kinship, status in the social hierarchy, etc.) to individuals within the society. If gender representations are social positions which carry differential meanings, then for someone to be represented and to represent oneself as male or as female implies the assumption of the whole of those meaning effects. (Technology, 5)

The sex-gender system thus not only functions in the social structures that the texts analyze, for example British society of the 1930s in *Three Guineas* and German National Socialism in *Der Mann auf der Kanzel* (The man in the pulpit) and in *Kindheitsmuster*, (*Patterns of Childhood*), but also in the historical discourses that the three authors confront and in their own textual production. The authors themselves are implicated in the sex-gender system because the construction of gender occurs in all discourses and especially in feminist discourse, as de Lauretis points out. Although it is impossible to step outside gender, it is possible to undertake a critical analysis of the sex-gender system, to break open rigid conceptions on which this system is based, and thus to produce a shift in its significations.

Three Guineas focuses on the middle-class family as the institution that continuously produces gendered subjects and thus reproduces the existing cultural order. The essay is a passionate intervention against the sentimental discourse of the family, which presents the family as the peaceful heaven, in a world otherwise characterized by power and strife. Instead, according to Woolf, the regime of the family is characterized by "its cruelty, its poverty, its hypocrisy, its immorality, its inanity" (39). This at least is the perspective of the daughter, who until very recently was virtually locked up in the private house, with marriage as her only goal. The patriarchal fathers' conception of themselves as protectors and providers is rebuked as "infantile fixation." The deliberate misuse of the term designates the Victorian fathers' assertion of absolute power and control over their daughters, a totalitarianism *en miniature*. *Three Guineas* thus identifies the most significant moment in women's history when the door of the private house "was thrown open" and the daughters could leave to earn their own living. This moment is strikingly different from those that are considered the culminating points of patriarchal history, as there is no heroic subject involved and no empire built. Although a mere "sixpence," their earnings represent the most important step to independence for the daughters. Inside the family, financially dependent on men, obliged not to ruin their chances for marriage, the daughters can be nothing but the mirrors of men. For soothing and charming men are the only means of ensuring their livelihood. Through this, women contribute to producing a male subject who constitutes himself through power over others, which is also the vital ingredient of the fascist subject. Thus, although women's position in the family is characterized by powerlessness, it is not one of historical innocence. Indeed, *Three Guineas* stresses that women become complicit with the system of power upheld by middle-class men in their traditional familial role as supporters and soothers of men. Precisely because of this women have to break out of the regime of the family.

Woolf argues in *Three Guineas* that the middle-class family is based on economic inequality. Wives, who are supposedly entitled to half their husbands' income, in reality receive "board, lodging and a small annual allowance for pocket money and dress" (56). The assertion is proven by a painstaking analysis of annual expenditures as they are listed in Whitaker's Almanack. What seems to be the dry and inane listing of annual expenses from wine to cricket, through this brilliant analysis exposes the power relations between the genders. For who spends money on clubs (to which only men belong), on hunting, and cigars? The method at work here could be characterized as using the sex-gender system against what it is intended to conceal, the economic inequality of men and women. This strategy is characteristic of the critical method used throughout *Three Guineas.* The various discourses produced by men are "brush[ed] against the grain," to use Walter Benjamin's phrase, in order to expose the workings of the sex-gender system.

The complete economic dependence of middle-class wives and daughters determines their lack of social and political power: "Not only are we incomparably weaker than the men of our class; we are weaker than the women of the working class" (12), who can use their indispensible function in the production process as a weapon and strike. In contrast to this, middle-class women are completely dependent on the men of their class. Economic and intellectual dependence, furthermore, are connected. Economic independence thus means that middle-class women no longer need to support the causes of the men of their class. Ironically, the speaker of *Three Guineas* does indeed give the same significance to women's employment as the young man, quoted at the beginning, afforded it. She interprets women's work, however, quite differently: "For to help women to earn their livings in the professions is to help them to possess that weapon of independent opinion which is still their most powerful weapon. It is to help them to have a mind of their own and a will of their own with which to help you to prevent war" (58). Otherwise women are forced to support a sex-gender system based on a concept of maleness that depends as much on providing for a family as on maintaining male virility, which is closely linked to militarism. For the finest self-representation of this maleness, the speaker asserts, is the uniform of the soldier. Here again *Three Guineas* stresses the fundamental complicity of the educated man, who believes he is a democrat, with the fascist: "What connection is there between the sartorial splendours of the educated man and the photograph of ruined houses and dead bodies? Obviously the connection between dress and war is not far to seek; your finest clothes are those that you wear as soldiers" (21). *Der Mann auf der Kanzel* (The man in the pulpit) also uncovers the significance of the military for the formation of a male identity. In this text, the father, a Protestant pastor, carefully preserves his uniform from World War I. As an object of great reverence, it not only symbolizes the support of a nationalistic Protestant church for the military, but also points to the importance of the military for the construction of the male subject: the pastor insists that the military service made him into a man.

The speaker of *Three Guineas,* furthermore, humorously exposes the professions by ridiculing the pompousness of the professional robes middle-class men wear in Britain, as these form a veritable sign-system for upholding hierarchies, privileges, and power; for "it serves to advertise the social, professional, or intellectual standing of the wearer" (20). As self-representations of the male subject, the professional robes function importantly within the sex-gender system as de Lauretis defines it: "a symbolic system or system of meanings, that correlates sex to cultural contents according to social values and hierarchies" (Technology, 5). While the professional clothes of men "mean" power and curiously make them sexless, women's clothes function to emphasize their sexuality, or to be more precise, function to make them sexually attractive to men, which in this culture "means" social and political powerlessness; their sexuality disqualifies women within the professions. Contemplating the fact that women hold no well-paying positions in the government administration, despite the fact that a university education is open to them and despite reports that stress their professional efficiency, the speaker concludes:

> 'Miss' transmits sex; and sex may carry with it an aroma. 'Miss' may carry with it the swish of petticoats, the savour of scent or other odour perceptible to the nose on the further side of the partition and obnoxious to it. What charms and consoles in the private house may distract and exacerbate in the public office. (50)

For the professions are also ruled by the "fathers," who systematically exclude women, in order to retain their privileges. Thus the professions are characterized by "possessiveness," "jealousy," "pugnacity," and "greed" (74): characteristics which also foster war.

The choice between the private house and public institutions is thus bad. It is, nevertheless, essential for women, *Three Guineas* argues, to earn their living in the professions, as financial dependence on the father in the family is the most "odious form of slavery" (16). Yet, professional employment and financial independence of women do not guarantee the dissolution of the power structures that ultimately produce strife and war. On the contrary, women will tend to become implicated in these structures, as their gender possesses no transcendental virtue that protects them from seeking or upholding power. Now that women are about to be allowed to join "the procession" of professional men, they have to ask themselves if they indeed want to model themselves after men. For the demand for equality inevitably postulates men's position as the model, one that women are supposed to attain through a process of compensation and assimilation. *Three Guineas,* however, tries to precisely envision women in a position of equality (in the professions) without using men as the model. Instead of assimilation, it thus proposes that women use their history as a source of critique to provide them with the means for resistance within the public institutions. Woolf urges women to use the "four great teachers of the daughters of educated men—poverty, chastity, derision and freedom from unreal loyalties" (79). These four qualities, which were initially imposed upon women by patriarchal society, can be transformed into a political practice of nonassimilation. This practice aims to erode the power structures that uphold the social order: "By poverty is meant enough money to live upon" (80). The accumulation of wealth, which is based on the exploitation of others, however, must be avoided. Chastity, in this context, has for once not a sexual meaning, but "by chastity is meant that when you have made enough to live on by your profession you must refuse to sell your brain for the sake of money" (80). Derision signifies the refusal to participate in the system of professional and national honors: "Directly badges, orders, or degrees are offered you, fling them back in the giver's face" (80). Finally, "by freedom from unreal loyalties is meant you must rid yourself of pride of nationality in the first place; also of religious pride, college pride, school pride, family pride, sex pride and those unreal loyalties that spring from them" (80).

This "political program" is based on, to use Benjamin's phrase again, "brushing history against the grain," whereby the marks of oppression are transformed into tools of resistance. A resistance, nevertheless, which is not aimed at producing a counterpower but rather at eroding power by withdrawing consent. The past is thus used for political intervention in the present. This strategic reading of history, furthermore, indicates that a redefinition of women's position within the social order must always proceed from meanings initially imposed on women by the patriarchal order. There is no "true" character of woman beneath the patriarchal layers, for postulating such a character would precisely reconfirm a gender system based on "natural" gender differences. Instead *Three Guineas* argues that the culturally imposed difference of women can be used strategically to expose and erode the power structures of the social order. Reading history in *Three Guineas* thus does not mean that we gain access to the Truth about women, but rather functions importantly within the ongoing process of (re)-constructing ourselves as women within Western culture.

Three Guineas is written in the form of a fictitious letter of reply to a gentleman who has requested the speaker's support in the struggle against fascism. In its response to a man's summons to speech, *Three Guineas* articulates the power relations that underlie speech in our culture and exposes the political nature of address. The letter form articulates that speech is usually controlled by men and that women are usually not addressed to give advice in political matters: "since when before has an educated man asked a woman" (3). The gentleman's request—to help to prevent war by protecting culture and intellectual liberty—denies the narrator's specific identity as a woman by assuming a universal meaning of the terms fascism, war, culture, and liberty. It implicitly requires her to accept "his" definitions and thus to assume her prescribed position in his productions of meaning—silence or assimilated speech. The addressee is described as a middle-aged man, a prosperous lawyer who received his education in public schools and university and who now has wife, children, and a house. He thus belongs to those educational and professional institutions that practice the systematic exclusion of women; in other words, he is *the* representative of the various hegemonic discourses that keep the female speaker in the position of an outsider, as the speaker notes with exasperation: "Not a single educated man's daughter, Whitaker says, is thought capable of teaching the literature of her own language at either university. Nor is her opinion worth asking, Whitaker informs us, when it comes to buying a picture for the National Gallery, a portrait for the Portrait Gallery, or a mummy for the British Museum" (87). Speaking from a different position within the social order, women, the speaker insists, have their own historical and gender-determined perspective: "history is not without its effects upon the mind and body. Therefore her interpretation of the word 'patriotism' may well differ from his" (9). *Three Guineas* destroys the myth that men and women can engage in a dialogue that escapes the power that otherwise determines their relationship. Instead, it argues that power is always involved in the exchanges between men and women, especially when it is not acknowledged. The speaker's continuous mock reference with which she addresses the gentleman, while proceeding in her analysis that clearly goes against his intentions, exposes the usual authority structure between men and women and subverts this structure. The gentleman represents, what Benjamin has called the perspective of the victors from which history is usually told. The speaker, on the other hand, "brush[es] history against the grain" and assumes the perspective of those "who are lying prostrate" (256).

Three Guineas articulates the dilemma of all feminist interventions into the cultural order, which necessarily respond to patriarchal speech. Yet, a feminist analysis can not only expose the gendered nature of speech but also affect a shift in the significations of gender. The position of the outsider, which potentially means "the freedom from unreal loyalties," can be used as a critical perspective: "But our bird's-eye view of the outside of things is not altogether encouraging" (22). The speaker's perspective, furthermore, produces a gaze that defamiliarizes: "Your world, then, the world of the professional, of public life, seen from this angle undoubtedly looks queer" (18). "Queer" because that which is assumed to be natural, gender difference, is revealed as the historical and political effect of a specific sex-gender system.

The speaker of *Three Guineas* calls herself "the daughter of an educated man." She thus avoids the generalizing term "woman" which tends to obliterate social differences among women. "Daughter of an educated man," also roots the female subject in a specific history, namely that beginning with the Enlightenment, the project primarily shaped by educated men. The name continuously alludes to the fact that one key element of the Enlightenment—education—was withheld from women. "Daughter of an educated man, furthermore, points to the fact that there is no space beyond paternal domination in our culture which perpetually fixes women, as Sigrid Weigel contends, in the position of daughters (*Die Stimme,* 166). Instead of believing that speech in itself liberates the daughter from the father, *Three Guineas* reveals that the woman who writes is confronted with another, specific form of paternal domination, as she must confront the meanings imposed on her by patriarchal culture.

In *Alice Doesn't,* Teresa de Lauretis analyzes the process through which the "I" of Virginia Woolf's *A Room of One's Own* is defined as female or as she calls it "en-gendered." She proposes the term "experience," which she defines as

> a *process* by which, for all social beings, subjectivity is constructed. Through that process one places oneself or is placed in social reality, and so perceives and comprehends as subjective (referring to, even originating in, oneself) those relations—material, economic, and interpersonal—which are in fact social and, in a larger perspective, historical. (159)

Indeed, *Three Guineas* presents this process of experiencing oneself as female, precisely as social and as historical. Thus the speaker of *Three Guineas* is an avid and acute reader of her culture. The position from which she reads is one that defines her as female. She reads history books, biographies, common encyclopedias, and newspapers, in other words texts that are readily available to everyone who can read their own language. As a woman, born in the late nineteenth century, the speaker has no academic training, no access to special libraries or to the information one gains as an insider of institutions. Although an active participant in her culture, she thus reads from the position of partial outsider. The historical experience of her gender determines the perspective from which she interprets society: "your world as it appears to us who see it from the threshold of the private house; through the shadow of the veil that St. Paul still lays upon our eyes; from the bridge that connects the private house with the world of public life" (18). This position, which defines the speaker as female, is characterized by confinement, invisibility, and silence imposed on her by patriarchal authority, particularly the family and the church. At this moment, as the confinement and the silence have been partially broken, she is poised on the "threshold" between the private and the public world; in other words, her position with respect to the public discourses is that of a partial outsider. This position of the outsider generates her critique of the social order. In *Three Guineas,* constructing women's history is a critical enterprise, and although the "daughter" is free from "unreal loyalties," her approach to history is far from disinterested.

Woolf argues in *Three Guineas* that the occupation with history always means that the female historian has to work through the patriarchal structures that run through the historical discourses, and in Ruth Rehmann's *Der Mann auf der Kanzel* (The man in the pulpit) a daughter's search for her father's past leads her to do just that. In this text another "daughter of an educated man," turns to history in order to come to terms with paternal significance.[2] This time the daughter's task is further complicated by the fact that she deals with her *own* father. A tension thus runs throughout the text between the desire for fatherly affection, on the one hand, and historical accuracy, which requires critical scrutiny, on the other. This father is a Protestant pastor who silently accommodated his pastoral work to National Socialism. Having grown up in Wilhelminian Germany, he belongs to the group of conservative professionals who remained fundamentally antidemocratic throughout the Weimar Republic and who either openly supported or conformed to Nazi rule. The premise of the daughter's investigation into the father's past is that his deeply held Christian belief contrasted starkly with the Nazis' ideology, particularly their racial policy. The daughter's central question with respect to the father is, why did he not see what the Nazis were doing. Michael Schneider describes the pastor's complicity with the Nazis as "the amorality of nonperception, the consequences of which are no better than those of amorality which is based on opportunistic thinking, cowardice, or lack of scruples" (18).

Der Mann auf der Kanzel (The man in the pulpit) is concerned with perception, particularly political perception. Similar to *Kindheitsmuster,* (*Patterns of Childhood*), it reconstructs the formation of thought patterns as a kind of inner political texture. In both these texts, in contrast to the traditional bourgeois novel, the subject does not so much encounter history as is produced *by* history. Like *Three Guineas, Der Mann auf der Kanzel* (The man in the pulpit) unearths family structures that reproduce gendered subjects that in turn reproduce the existing cultural order. In both cases, we encounter a male subject whose identity is vitally linked to the nation/state. As in *Three Guineas,* the daughter's reconstruction of the father's past leads to a recognition of the paternal order.

As in many texts of the 1970s, in *Der Mann auf der Kanzel* (The man in the pulpit), the past suddenly breaks into the present. This eruption causes profound anxiety, as it signals that National Socialism, a period one has tacitly agreed to conceal, still has a profound impact on the present. As in many other texts, the daughter realizes her own avoidance of, what Margarete Mitscherlich and Alexander Mitscherlich have termed, *Trauerarbeit* (working through one's mourning). On a collective level this intrusion of the past reveals that the postwar period is based on evasion and avoidance. In *Der Mann auf der Kanzel* (The man in the pulpit) the involuntary encounter with the past causes the daughter to investigate her father's past, for she realizes that she has carefully separated her private recollection of her father from the context of the historical period—National Socialism. The following fond reminiscence of a member of the father's congregation makes the daughter realize that she has some important gaps in her memory:

> It was before her eyes, as if it were yesterday, how the dear pastor stood next to his Catholic colleague and the SA-mayor on the festive platform, decorated with flags full of swastikas and thanked in moving words the Lord of history for the happy turn—what an image of unity between a patriotic church and a Christian state! (13)

This mental photograph, for it has iconic qualities—whether rearranged by the woman's desire for a "perfect past" or accurately remembered does not matter—contains many issues that are at stake in the daughter's reconstruction of the past. The father's elevated position on the stage corresponds to his elevated social position that endows him with presence in the public theaters. The image points to a hierarchical system that arranges presences and absences, speech and silence, authority and nonauthority. His appearance together with the Catholic priest and the SA-mayor expresses accord between church and state. The pastor's words even suggest an active promotion of the National Socialist state. They employ God's authority to endow this state with legality and reveal a conception of a historical master-narrative whose supreme author is God. As a result, the human subject is relieved of the responsibility of intervening actively into the historical process.

Different levels of paternal authority constitute the pastor's consciousness. The text retraces the formation of this consciousness in his upbringing in a parsonage in Wilhelminian Germany. Again a mental photograph of the grandfather's house represents ideological structures through spatial structures. The grandfather's family is gathered around the dinner table. At the head of the table presides the father, surrounded in hierarchical order by his children. The youngest child, the pastor, sits at the bottom of the table, where he compensates for his low position with his storytelling skills through which he attracts the father's attention. Speaking, nevertheless, is firmly regulated by the father: "There is a kind of paternal clearing-of-the-throat, a-firm-look-into-the-eyes that suppresses daring talk immediately; they all knuckle under to him" (30). This image of the grandfather evokes the image of Martin Luther around his dinner table, where he delivered his famous informal lectures. The fact that he delivered these lectures at the family dinner table underlines the significance of the pater familias in Protestant dogma. Because he is responsible for the spiritual well-being of his dependents, he has the absolute authority over all discourses.

Paternal presence completely enfolds the pastor's childhood. Throughout his life he thus remains in the position of "the good son." For any rebellion against such a powerful father, who as a pastor more than any other father represents the authority of the word, would be too painful, lonely, and guilt-ridden. The pastor attempted to escape this overwhelming paternal presence once, with a trip to Italy after his graduation; afterward, he was reprimanded so effectively that no other attempt was undertaken. These words of paternal concern ensured the son's speedy return: "'you seek too many distractions, my dear son. I would like you to sit down quietly in your room and reflect upon your life and character. . . . More I don't want to say today, but I would like to express the hope, that my earnest word of love will awaken joyful obedience in your heart'" (34). This combination of love and authority, which in the case of a pastor is particularly closely linked to God's, effectively produces overwhelming feelings of guilt. For even though the father's scrutiny has its limits, God "can see one's heart." Max Weber argues in his famous essay, *The Protestant Ethic and the Spirit of Capitalism,* that in Protestantism, authority is not so much enforced through external means but firmly implanted into the subject's consciousness through a system of inner surveillance, which ensures the subject's own subjection under the paternal word. Michel Foucault's description of the implantation of the disciplines through a system of visibility and invisibility applies to this triangular relationship between God, father, and son: "Disciplinary power . . . is exercised through its invisibility; at the same time it imposes on those whom it subjects a principle of compulsory visibility. In discipline, it is the subjects who have to be seen. Their visibility assures the hold of the power that is exercised over them. It is the fact of being constantly seen, of being able always to be seen, that maintains the disciplined individual in his subjection" (187). The disciplined person finally internalizes this surveillance and thus provides his own correction. In his study, the pastor sits surrounded by the pictures of his fathers: Jesus, Martin Luther, the Kaiser, and his own father. At the end of the day, in his evening prayer, the pastor opens his heart to God, and God *surveys* his heart. God, thus, assumes the function of the supreme disciplinary power. The societal fathers receive their authority through their connection with the divine father. Thus the pastor's model for legitimate governance involves the rule, divine and worldly, of three fathers: God, the Kaiser, and the biological father. Herbert Marcuse has analyzed the patriarchal worldview inherent to Protestantism. Marcuse points to the fact that the abolishment of the Catholic hierarchy reinforced the authority of the pater familias. Authority, thus, becomes something "natural," as it is conceived as familial, having the father/son relationship as its model. The rule of the fathers always must be absolute and can be neither questioned nor terminated (76–77).

The pastor's conception of political power is modeled precisely on this father/son relationship. Throughout the Weimar Republic, his unfaltering loyalty belongs to the Kaiser, his *Landesvater* (father of the land). Every year he sends his Kaiser a birthday letter, and every year he is deeply disappointed about receiving a preprinted thank-you note, instead of a personal acknowledgment by his ruler. Permanence and loyalty are for the pastor the two essential ingredients for lawful rule. A critical analysis of the Kaiser's policy that led up to World War I represents an act of disobedience. The republic remains profoundly alien to him, as it is bound up with the multiplication of unlawful discourses, and he interprets its polyphony as "screaming" and "vulgarity." His terms for the republic express the breakdown of boundaries (social, physical, sexual) and are as denunciatory as those usually reserved for sexuality; *Affentheater* (monkey theater), *Quatschbude* (dwelling of babblers), *Klugschwätzer* (smart asses), *Schleimscheisser* (literally, those who shit slime), *Krämerseelen* (small-minded people, mercenary creatures), *Speichellecker* (literally, those who lick saliva), *Schlappschwänze* (literally, limp tails), *Profitgeier* (profiteers), *Verzichtler* (those who relinquished), *Verräter* (traitors). The main sins of the republic are threefold: it is based on profit; it generates too much talk; and it is the product of the defeat in World War I. The pastor is a proponent of the "stab in the back legend," according to which World War I was lost because of the collapse of the homefront caused by Jews, Communists, and Social-Democrats. Founded on betrayal, the republic's origin is thus illegitimate. The extremely aggressive nature of the pastor's language suggests that the collapse of the republic will not only cause no alarm but indeed will be welcome.

The pastor's terms for the speech of the republic, such as *Schleimscheisser,* all express lack of physical control. This is not the speech of the disembodied (male) subject. The republic's main violation consists in letting people speak whose speech lacks paternal authority (Jews, women, workers) and whose discourses are thus profoundly illegitimate. While the republic negotiates its relationship to the subjects through multiple and contradictory discourse, the *Kaiser* guarantees one supremely ordered social text whose configuration is represented best by the military with its strictly hierarchical order. As the military embodies the nation, the pastor believes that one can only completely become *his* subject in *his* army. The educational process thus culminates, even for future pastors, in military service. Lack of military service produces lack of proper subjects, another sin of the republic: "You could see at first sight that these young people had not served. They lack posture, polish, discipline, authority, and obedience. Things like that one simply cannot learn at the university, in party headquarters even less" (48).

For the pastor, who himself lacks soldierly qualities, the military represents primarily a supremely ordered social discourse in which speech and movement are strictly regulated and in which males are properly positioned. The military's ethical quality consists precisely in this ordering, through which it becomes, Foucault argues, the embodiment of "the perfect society": "Historians of ideas usually attribute the dream of a perfect society to the philosophers and jurists of the eighteenth century; but there was also a military dream of society; its fundamental reference was not to the state of nature, but to the meticulously subordinated cogs of a machine, not to the primal social contract, but to permanent coercions, not to fundamental rights, but to indefinitely progressive forms of training, not to the general will but to automatic docility" (169). In contrast to the supremely ordered mass of the soldiers, the "disorderly" mass of mostly working-class demonstrators represents not only social chaos but also the breakdown of the ethical order.

During World War I, the pastor immediately volunteered to offer his pastoral assistance to the war effort. The soldiers at the front seem to have been his most worthy congregation and he zealously consoled and assisted them in dying for the fatherland. In the postwar years, as he avoids confronting the slaughter of the war, the military retains its prestige for him. Gatherings with former officers are the pastor's favorite social events, the "cause" remains holy and his old uniform is carefully preserved and revered. There is an apparent continuity between the pastor's attitude towards the military and that of the Nazis, who after all regarded World War I as the birth of their movement.

As argued already in *Three Guineas,* the military, furthermore, functions importantly in the engendering process. The pastor insists that "only in the service of the young *Kaiser* did he really become a man, which women probably could not understand" (49). As women have been excluded from this experience for centuries, it is indeed difficult for them to understand, or as the speaker in *Three Guineas* puts it: "Complete understanding could only be achieved by blood transfusion and memory transfusion—a miracle still beyond the reach of science" (6–7). Women's lack of understanding of the military thus corresponds necessarily with a fundamental lack of understanding of the nation/state, an inability that also disqualifies women from being historians, as modern historiography is vitally rooted in the nation/state. In *Der Mann auf der Kanzel* (The man in the pulpit) the daughter's qualification as her father's historian indeed is questioned most dramatically by her oldest brother as she attempts to reconstruct the pastor's war experience.

The brother, who is now a pastor himself, regards the sister's project as an infringement, a form of presumption. He insists that no historical material will reveal the truth about the father and that as a nonbeliever she fundamentally lacks the insight to judge her father. The daughter realizes that her brother has erected parameters that categorically exclude her:

> "With all his love," he pushes me "aside," onto "the bench where the mockers are sitting," to the trespassers. . . . I deserve the following attributes from the family vocabulary "insolent," "annoying," "arrogant." I fundamentally lack "awe," "distance," "natural delicacy." I "snoop around," "meddle in things that are none of my business," . . . "presume the right to judge." (62)

All the attributes describe a breaking of boundaries that is connected to a lack of feminine modesty. The brother's defensive response is profoundly overdetermined. On the one hand, he reacts so defensively for political reasons. His sister's project centers around National Socialism, a period that has been tacitly removed out of the "family memory." On the other hand, the brother's response is based on "family politics," and his rejection of the sister's project is based on her gender. For him, as a representative of the paternal discourse, engaging in a critical evaluation of the father's relation to the dominant order, the sister trespasses upon an area she has no right to enter. For brother and father truth is not something produced out of certain materials within a certain context; instead, truth requires a specific endowment that guarantees access: one has to be a Christian, and one has to be male. For the brother, no matter how much of an effort the daughter undertakes, how many books she reads, how carefully she examines the issues, she will always produce nontruth.

No motherly influence seems to enter in any significant way into this paternal order that carefully structures presences: only middle-class and Christian fathers possess the full legitimacy to speak. The speech of all others (Jews, women, workers) is profoundly illegitimate. The expression of their political interests in the democratic system only produces nontruth: "The majority is dumb. What kind of people can that be who let themselves be put into power and then thrown out of it by majorities. Masses, mob, riffraff, pack, the 'street'" (99). The discourse of the street has to be firmly regulated, and, as the pastor's extremely aggressive language suggests, if necessary, it has to be done with force. The involvement of Jews is perceived as a particularly disgusting transgression of boundaries, as obtrusiveness; "The Jews have their sticky fingers in everything" (99). Women are allowed to use only a carefully assimilated speech; otherwise they cease to be women. The female curate who dares to disagree with the pastor in religious matters, forfeits her status as a woman by supposedly spitting while speaking: "He is convinced that zealous women inevitably spit, 'foaming mouth'" (149). Their speech thus lacks the proper disembodied quality that characterizes the speech of the fathers. Their speech, furthermore, produces the disruption of their bodies, which must be properly contained at all times.

In the parsonage, the mother is subordinated to the father's word. While the pastor's sphere is his study, a room that with its Bibles and compendia is loaded with meaning, the mother's sphere is the nursery, from which she upholds the small order, namely that of the household: "He does not perceive the order that serves first of all his work, his peace, his well-being" (92–93). Lacking direct access to the production of the discourses that enables the flow of desire in this world of carefully controlled bodies, the mother's position allows self-definition only in terms of sacrifice. As a result, her discourse is one of resentment, which she imposes, as a kind of revenge, upon her children:

> Only with reservation does she give the children the permission to go to a party. They are urged to be the first to depart, at the latest, "when the party really gets going," by no means should they be one of the last, when parties "deteriorate," "when barriers fall," in any case, they should "keep their distance," "practice reserve," "should not behave common." (96)

This profound fear of the breakdown of boundaries, shows the effort needed to contain all desire in order to be a good pastor's wife.

The pastor's deeply internalized concept of a hierarchical order produces his inability to perceive the criminal nature of the Nazi state. His profoundly antidemocratic attitude automatically censors all voices of dissent; thus, he is unable to hear any criticism or protest. This mechanism is also at work when he is directly confronted with the Nazis' persecutions of the Jews. Thus, he dismisses a Jewish friend's information about the deportation of the Jews as unregulated speech: "You must be mistaken. . . . There is much talk. You should not apply this to yourself!" (149). He simply labels as anti-German propaganda the assertion of a member of his congregation that dissenting Christians are deported to concentration camps: "KZ! . . . Are you also a victim of these toilet slogans, which were cooked up in the same witch's kitchen as the lies about the German atrocities during the invasion of Belgium" (129–130). As a liberal, critical press, with its dissenting voices only creates dissonance, the Nazis' abolishment of a free press is regarded as creating unity. Uncomfortable facts can thus automatically be dismissed as originating in illegitimate sources. This ordering of speech and silence, truth and falsehood, presence and absence structures perception in unison with an authoritarian, patriarchal order.

At the end, the daughter explains the pastor's nonperception with his own elevated position in this hierarchical order, which according to the daughter made it impossible for anybody to "really" talk with the pastor. His position up in the pulpit, on the "high horse," made communication with others impossible as speech within this order can only flow from the top down; again a spatial image describes the ideological structure of this hierarchical order. The daughter's psychological explanation, clearly a product of daughterly remorse, shows the difficulty in reconstructing history with one's own father as a participant. The connection between a beloved father and a murderous political order is hard to bear, for it disrupts the "idyllic" memory of one's childhood and retrospectively puts into question the relationship between "good" child and "good" parent. The daughter's brother makes it very clear that he considers her occupation with the father's past an overstepping of boundaries and "journalistic nosiness," as matters that are supposed to remain private are made public. The violation of the familial code is even greater when the daughter becomes her father's historian, as being his author involves retrospectively an almost complete reversal in the authority structure of their relationship. In *Der Mann auf der Kanzel* (The man in the pulpit), the daughter continuously struggles with her own sense that her project is a fundamental transgression, one connected with her sexuality. Thus she dreams that she lies naked in her bed and babbles incomprehensibly while her family stands around her bed and watches her. Throughout her project, she seeks out male advisers, her son and a teacher in particular, whose function is among other things to validate her as a historian.

Although writing about the father means a rebellion against a paternal order, which imposes silence on the daughter, she gains her legitimacy as the author of this history, as Sigrid Weigel points out, precisely from being *his* daughter and thus again through the father, which reproduces the father's central position within the cultural order (*Die Stimme,* 164). The daughter's relationship to the father in *Der Mann auf der Kanzel* (The man in the pulpit) thus remains profoundly contradictory; while her writing assumes critical distance and shows how the father was himself the product of an authoritarian order and "written" by the language of his time, the daughter's desire flows powerfully toward the father and seeks in him the source of all meaning. The text vacillates between presenting the father as a nonidentical subject, who is *not* in complete control, and presenting him as a unique, transcendental individual; or, to put it differently, he moves from being a subject *in* history to the subject *of* history. Yet the daughter's text, in contrast to the father's, which only allows one voice, incorporates many different voices, which are not seamlessly integrated. This draws attention to the fact that the past is reconstructed, a process that always involves a specific perspective. Thus, the source of this text is not some disinterested, disembodied author, but a daughter who is deeply entangled in her own text. As the figure of the father consists of multiple and contradictory parts so does the figure of the daughter-as-author. In contrast to the father's conception of history as God-directed, for the daughter history is humanly produced and thus requires the active participation of all historical subjects.

In contrast to *Der Mann auf der Kanzel* (The man in the pulpit), in *Kindheitsmuster* (*Patterns of Childhood*) the state assumes the traditional position of the powerful father.[3] Margarete Mitscherlich notes that while the petite bourgeoisie supported and participated in the reestablishment of a strictly patriarchal order under the Nazis, the personal father was experienced as weak and ineffectual (313). Bruno Jordan, the father in *Kindheitsmuster* (*Patterns of Childhood*), although successful with his grocery business, is a profoundly inarticulate man whose relationship to the public world is drastically circumscribed. Thus, he does not notice the Nazis' abolishment of democratic rights as he has never even been aware of these rights. His position as a grocer, furthermore, requires that he agree with the community on whose business he relies. It is thus a position fundamentally based on conformism, and Bruno Jordan is indeed a man who does not like to stand apart. His voting changes from the Social Democrats to the National Socialists, but he never becomes an actual sympathizer of the Nazis. He also welcomes the admission of his rowing club into the National Socialist sports' organization, for he profoundly longs to be in harmony with his environment. *Übereinstimmungsglück,* a happiness that is produced by being in agreement, is the greatest happiness for the Jordans. For the Jordans, happiness and conformity thus mutually depend upon each other. Otherwise Bruno Jordan practices primarily self-restriction and does not assume authority for shaping his daughter's view of the world. While Charlotte Jordan is outraged about her daughter's religious instruction, in which she learns that Jesus would today be a follower of Hitler, Bruno Jordan simply comments: "Just let him say what he wants. You can't stick your nose into everything!" (128).

In *Kindheitsmuster* (*Patterns of Childhood*), unlike *Der Mann auf der Kanzel* (The man in the pulpit), the mother/daughter relationship assumes central significance in the daughter's reconstruction of the past. Writing here is characterized by a powerful desire for the mother, whom the daughter simultaneously fears hurting with her writing. Thus, she dreams at the beginning of her investigation of the past: "Just then your mother comes in, even though she is dead, and sits down in the big room, something you had always secretly wanted. . . . Suddenly, a shock that penetrates even the roots of your hair: in the big room on the table lies the manuscript, with, on the first page, only one word, "Mother," in large letters. She'll read it, guess your purpose, and feel hurt" (10).

Kindheitsmuster (*Patterns of Childhood*) unearths the mostly silenced history of women under National Socialism, for as the authors of "Popular Memory" point out, even though all members of a society participate in the production of social memory, not all contribute equally. The history of women does not appear in the public discourses: "Usually this history is held to the level of private remembrance. It is not only unrecorded, but actually silenced. It is not offered the occasion to speak" (210). Because private memory is usually decontextualized from public memory, it tends to be dehistoricized as well. The Nazis' ideological appropriation of the figure of the mother makes it even more difficult, but at the same time more urgent, to write the history of mothers and daughters under National Socialism. *Kindheitsmuster* (*Patterns of Childhood*) represents precisely this attempt to historicize the mother/daughter relationship.

Structured around the mother/daughter relationship (Charlotte and Nelly Jordan under National Socialism and the narrator and her daughter Lenka in the present) the novel moves back and forth between past and present. The text constructs a female genealogy that encompasses four generations of women. This approach to family history is in opposition to the patriarchal genealogy, which culminated in the Nazis' notorious "family tree of Aryan descent." The text's focus on female figures and relationships shows, on the one hand, women's oppression and complicity, and on the other hand, their resistance and attempts at self-definition. The text presents the specific history of lower-middle-class, "German" women. While the text assumes in no way to speak for women of other social classes and ethnic backgrounds, it continuously reminds the reader of the fate of those who were persecuted and murdered by the Nazis. The history of the women described in *Kindheitsmuster* (*Patterns of Childhood*) is primarily one of conformism and complicity, but the text uses what was unrealized in the past, or as Ortrud Gutjahr calls it, that which could not yet be lived, as a potential for a future of nonassimilation and self-determination (54–55). As in *Three Guineas,* history is thus "brush[ed] against the grain" and used as a source of nonconformism. Thus Charlotte, the mother, is the only figure of the past who is described as having possessed the precondition of a moral conscience. This potential nevertheless exists rather submerged in Charlotte, who also practices primarily political self-restriction. Her powerful desire to be in good standing with the local authorities is exemplified in her thrashing of Nelly after she had a fight with a boy, to whose father, a police officer, Nelly complained about the boy's behavior: "Charlotte Jordan calls her daughter into the house and stands waiting for her behind the door, armed with the carpet beater, and beats her without listening to what she has to say, beside herself, screaming. . . . Who taught you to be a tattletale, who on earth, who? Then Charlotte drops onto a chair, bursting into tears, hands to her face, and says weeping: Do you have to get us on bad terms with that man, of all people?" (21). Yet in contrast to her husband Bruno, Charlotte engages in small acts of defiance against Nazi rule. Her association with Cassandra, furthermore, with whom she shares the gift of seeing, which in Charlotte's case is limited to ominous forebodings, connects Charlotte with a female tradition of resistance.

Although Charlotte's work exemplifies the domestication of women, her gaze at times betrays her nonassimilation to the social order: "Cassandra, behind the counter in her store; Cassandra aligning loaves of bread; Cassandra weighing potatoes, looking up every once in a while, with an expression in her eyes which her husband prefers not to see. Everything we do is an accident. An accident, this husband of hers. These two children about whom she has to worry so much. This house, and the poplar in front of it, completely alien" (165).

Like *Three Guineas* and *Der Mann auf der Kanzel* (The man in the pulpit), *Kindheitsmuster* (*Patterns of Childhood*) is concerned with the history of the family as the institution that produces gendered subjects and thus reproduces the existing cultural order. It focuses on the specific ways the female subject's engendering under Nazi rule implants her into the fascist order. Like *Three Guineas,* the text retraces the inscription of sexual difference through the various social and discursive practices. With Charlotte Jordan's rather harmless sounding, periodic exclamation to her children, "I really think you're not normal," the reconstruction of the inscription of sexual and racial difference that produces "the German girl" begins. For Nelly, Charlotte's questioning of her normality is extremely threatening. A retarded child in her neighborhood provides her with a terrible example of what it means *not* to be normal: "Not to be normal is the worst thing by far" (57). The significance of the term "normal" under National Socialism goes well beyond designating average mental and physical capacities. For once, it marks off socially acceptable from socially unacceptable behavior. Thus, Charlotte calls a girl who takes frequent evening walks with her boyfriend *triebhaft* (carnal). The girl is supposed to serve as a negative example for Nelly, for whom the meaning of the term carnal is nevertheless not explained. Charlotte's remark indicates that a woman's normality is primarily measured by her sexuality—a socially acceptable display of sexuality. To be considered too sexual for a woman means to be considered not normal. Normality can only be attained through *Beherrschung* (control): "Nelly will control herself. That's what every human being has to learn, or else he's no human being, says her mother. One really must learn to control oneself!" (58). While the standard for humanness is male, as Charlotte's language unintentionally reveals, for the construction of the German woman *beherrscht* (controlled) and *triebhaft* (carnal) form a key opposition.

Normality also requires strict orderliness through which the German family defines itself in opposition to other, clearly inferior families. Charlotte thus ceaselessly runs a campaign for cleanliness and orderliness: "Nelly was slovenly and untidy. Charlotte Jordan often was at her wits' end about how to teach her daughter to behave like a 'civilized Middle European'" (199). Normal and (Western) European form a mutually dependent unity, while non-normal and non-(or Eastern) European are the implied opposite terms.

Nelly, who is a "normal" German girl and thus within the Nazi view of the world belongs to an elite, is constantly summoned to keep herself *rein* (pure). The onset of her period causes Charlotte to implore her to keep herself even cleaner and to take good care of herself. In the League of German Girls, the girls proclaim: " 'We pledge to stay pure and to consecrate ourselves to Flag, Führer, and Fatherland!' " (135). While a woman traditionally was obliged to retain her purity for her future husband, whose possession she would become, purity is used strategically within the fascist order in terms of constructing a female fascist subject. The frequent parades within the Nazi youth movement, in which the participants collectively proclaimed their allegiance with sayings such as "we pledge to stay pure and to consecrate ourselves to Flag, Führer, and Fatherland!" produced through what Louis Althusser has called "hailing" the fascist subject. Althusser describes "hailing" as an act in which a cultural agent addresses an individual. The successful outcome of this address takes place when the person recognizes himself or herself in that speech. Through his or her response the individual becomes a subject, for as Althusser argues: "ideology 'acts' or 'functions' in such a way that it 'recruits' subjects among the individuals (it recruits them all), or 'transforms' the individuals into subjects (it transforms them all) by that very precise operation which I have called *interpellation* or hailing" (174). The collective proclamations under National Socialism are so significant precisely because they transform the individuals through these speech acts into fascist subjects. This is the reason why it seems almost impossible to forget the songs, which were sung during the parades. Despite her frequent lapses in memory, the speaker is able to remember the lyrics to almost all the songs of the Nazi youth movement.

Dr. Juliane Strauch, an ardent Nazi and Nelly's greatly admired teacher, has a favorite word: *Hingabe* (devotion), which literally means to give yourself completely. She obviously does not consciously refer to its sexual meaning, but instead uses it to designate complete devotion to the National Socialist state. Nevertheless, the subject's relationship to the fascist order is described in terminology that traditionally describes a woman's relationship to her husband. Nelly willingly emulates her teacher as her model in devotion. Yet reading about the *Lebensborn* (Well of Life), the Nazi institution in which SS-men impregnated German women solely for breeding purposes, she realizes that she is not willing to practice her devotion to such an extent. At this extreme point Nazi sexual policy clearly conflicts with middle-class notions of female chastity—Charlotte's admonition *not* to throw herself away. Nelly's response to the *Lebensborn* is representative for most middle-class girls' response at that time, for the Nazi sexual policy was only successful as long as it engaged middle-class morality.

The system of meaning that Nelly learns reveals that the engendering process forms a vital component within the construction of the fascist subject; or to put it another way, through the process of engendering, the female subject is implanted within the fascist order. Another set of associations connected to a second set of meanings of the word *rein* (pure) reveals even more clearly the intersection between sexuality and race under National Socialism. Nelly encounters an exhibitionist whose "sucking" gaze forces her to walk past him and to look at his exposed white "snake." Nelly is immediately aware of the fact that she cannot talk to anybody about this experience. The encounter produces in Nelly a profound loathing for spiders, toads, and lizards—animals commonly regarded as impure. In Nelly's imagination this experience is mysteriously associated with a story about a Jewish boy that Nelly overheard her parent's friend, Leo Siegmann, tell her parents. According to this story, Leo Siegmann's healthy racial instinct revealed itself already in the pre-Nazi era during his schooldays, when he had a Jewish classmate whom he felt like hitting every day. Nelly imagines this boy. She has never actually seen a Jewish boy. She fantasizes striking him; yet every time, exactly at the moment of hitting the boy, her mental film breaks. She thus cannot be completely sure whether she would be able to fulfill her "racial duty." In this chain of association the opposition between sight and blindness has become mixed up. Only blindness makes the appropriate production of hatred possible: " 'Blind hate,' yes, that would work, would be the only way. Seeing hate is simply too difficult" (134). Christel Zahlmann explains Nelly's inability to strike the Jewish boy with the fact that his image is not connected with sexual arousal and that he thus cannot become an object of hatred (177). Yet the association with *unrein* (impure) firmly connects sexual and racial components of meaning. Later during the day of the encounter with the exhibitionist, Nelly finds her aunt completely beside herself. Somebody has been spreading the rumor that she is half-Jewish. Charlotte's response is revealing, for she calls the rumor "pure blackmail." The same evening, seemingly out of context, Nelly proclaims in tears that she does not want to be Jewish. Charlotte's response—"How on earth does this child know what Jewish is?" (140)—displays self-imposed avoidance of the recognition that meanings are continuously constructed around the opposition Jewish/non-Jewish and pure/impure. The term that connects all the different components in Nelly's chain of associations is *unrein* (impure, unchaste):[4] "Nelly could no longer hear the word "unchaste" without having a simultaneous vision of vermin, the white snake, and the face of the Jew boy" (136). Nelly as a "German girl" is defined as pure, whereby racial and sexual purity depend upon each other. Thus only by retaining her chastity does Nelly retain her full status as a "German girl." The designation of impure, and consequently "subhuman" and "vermin," functioned as the linguistic preparation for the persecution and mass murder of Jews and other groups, for this language establishes a hierarchy between "valuable" and "valueless" life.

Certain key terms, *Glitzerworte* (glitter words), make the eyes of the adults glitter. These words arouse intense interest in Nelly, who knows that she can expect no detailed explanation of them, particularly from her mother. The simultaneity of speech and silence points to the fact that this is a field of signifiers of extraordinary significance for the fascist order. Charlotte's fateful *triebhaft* (carnal) belongs to this group as well as *artfremd* (alien to the species), a word that was probably not used in everyday conversations, but that could be found frequently in newspapers and other

Nazi publications, such as schoolbooks. Another term within this group, *Anlage* (predisposition) attains new significance within the context of the Nazis' eugenics. The Jordans explain this word in the following commonsensical way: Eugenics means that a healthy girl like Nelly should not be allowed to marry a retarded boy such as Heini. Which, as Charlotte points out, is quite obvious. The Jordan's explanation reveals their strategy of making this centerpiece of the Nazis' racial policy seem harmless while displaying a basic acceptance of the classification "valuable" and "valueless," on which the Nazis' eugenics policy is based. According to this policy people with venereal disease, consumption, and mental retardation are not supposed to marry. This classification led in subsequent years to the murder of 100,000 inmates of institutions within the context of the "euthanasia" project "T4" (Bock, 282).

Kindheitsmuster (*Patterns of Childhood*) exposes everyday language as permeated with racist terminology. It is a language that reveals widespread acceptance of the tenets of the Nazis' racial policy. This policy was based on a racist and biologist way of thinking that extends back into the nineteenth century and that vitally informs middle-class notions of sexuality. The Nazis' "race hygiene" imposed gender-specific norms on everybody, as the historian Gisela Bock argues:

> The use of eugenic sterilization was intended both to control procreation and, by defining and proscribing what was unacceptable, to impose a specific acceptable character on women and men: the hard-working male breadwinner, his hard-working but unpaid housewife, and children who were a financial burden to no one but their parents. This was the "valuable life": a gender-specific work and productivity, described in social, medical, and psychiatric terms. (274)

Normality is the key term within the sexual and racial terminology. As the goal of education and the standard for behavior, it prevails in all institutions in modern societies, as Foucault argues: "The judges of normality are present everywhere" (304). This is particularly true for Nazi society. Nelly's sense that "not to be normal is the worst thing by far" quite accurately reflects the ruthless imposition of norms on everyone in the Nazi state. Nelly's Aunt Dottie is not "normal" and lives in a mental institution. During one of Dottie's visits at her sister's house, Nelly meets this aunt. This scene shows how deeply norms for behavior are internalized by most people and how this leads to a rigid demarcation between normal and not-normal people. Dottie makes Nelly a sandwich with butter and lard. This sandwich arouses the outrage of the entire family because butter and lard on a sandwich is *not* normal. Immediately following this scene, it is mentioned, that Nelly was of course familiar with the term *lebensunwertes Leben* (life unworthy of life)—a concept taught at every school at that time. Nelly's Aunt Dottie dies between 1940 and 1941, the time of the Nazis' "euthanasia" project. Although Dottie's sister is completely crushed by her death, she remains silent about it. Nelly nevertheless senses something: "What Nelly did know, or sensed—for in times like these there are many gradations between knowing and not knowing—was that there was more to Aunt Dottie's death than met the eye" (197).

Within this language order, silences function just as importantly as speech, and subjects are integrated not only through regulated speech into the fascist order but also through regulated silences. Nelly's language learning process functions accordingly. From a very young age, Nelly knows "instinctively" when to speak and when to remain silent. The eight-year-old Nelly tells nobody that Elvira told her that all in her family are communists. The encounter with the exhibitionist also clearly falls under the verdict of silence, and so does Aunt Dottie's death. Nelly watches her great-aunt talk to an Eastern-European slave laborer—quite an unusual incident. When Nelly asks her aunt what they have talked about, she clearly is told a lie. Yet Nelly does not insist on knowing the truth as she senses a dangerous topic. Only many years later is she told that the woman was asking for diapers because a woman in the camp was about to give birth. The recollection of this scene suddenly unearths the repressed knowledge that they all silently knew about the camps. These silences always occur at the intersection of sexuality and race. *Schein-heiligkeit* (hypocrisy), the pretense of being innocent, of not knowing while knowing, characterizes the approach to both subjects.

While the adults operate with partial truths and impose silences, Nelly is called upon to tell the complete truth about herself and to keep nothing secret from her mother. Nelly is of course not able to follow her mother's demand: "Because, unknown to herself, this child's straight, truthful mind—to me, you're as transparent as a pane of glass, Charlotte used to say to her daughter—had designed secret hiding places to which she could retreat alone" (57). Her thoughts produce deep feelings of guilt in Nelly. Charlotte's relationship to her daughter is characterized by censorship, as she imposes strict silences in sexual matters and enforces a rigid normality in Nelly.

The narrative impetus—"to tell the complete truth about this child"—makes the author complicit with the disciplinary powers that enforce silence and speech. Thus the consistent use of the pronoun "you," in which the speaker addresses herself, gives her reflections the character of a self-interrogation. The relationship between speaker and child, furthermore, resembles that between police and perpetrator: "You'd have to stay on her trail, ruthlessly corner her" (120). Speech, enforced by torture, is the speaker's most horrible association about her own impulse "to make the child speak," to produce the truth. Similarly as in Foucault, this establishes a connection between the notion of the individual, who finds self-representation in the autobiography and the emergence of the individual through the examination in modern medicine, psychiatry, criminology, and education. *Kindheitsmuster* (*Patterns of Childhood*) brings to mind Foucault's observation: "We are entering the age of the infinite examination and of compulsory objectification" (189). Yet the speaker also expresses the hope that these power relations can be changed and that the author will not simply appropriate the figure of the past: "The child refuses to talk. Let's hope that whoever gets hold of her will not exploit her helplessness" (48).

The mother/daughter relationship is not only central for the reconstruction of the past, the speaker is also a mother and often reflects on the relationship to her daughter Lenka. It also serves as the model for the relationship between author and characters. For, despite its problematic history, it contains the potential of a nonhierarchical relationship based on nurturance. *Kindheitsmuster* (*Patterns of Childhood*) is characterized by a dialogic structure that works on many levels of the text: between the speaker and the female figure of the past, among the female figures of the past, between the speaker and her daughter, and between the speaker and the (female) reader.

Kindheitsmuster (*Patterns of Childhood*) places the subject within what Kaja Silverman calls, "historically circumscribed signifying operations" (129). This is true for the historical figure, Nelly, as well as for the speaker. The process of language learning places Nelly within the ideological framework of National Socialism, and the speaker's work on language uncovers the continuity of fascist structures in the present. Thus, the speaker decides that the word "normal" has lost once and for all its "innocent" meaning and can on longer be used to describe people:

> On the same day when you'd read material on concentration camps . . . ; when you'd seen psychiatric evaluations which characterized Adolf Eichmann—no doubt accurately—as "methodical, conscientious, animal-loving, and close to nature," as "sincere" and decidedly "moral," but above all as "normal" . . . ; on the same day when the repetition of the once respected word "normal" is creating in you a faint but penetrating nausea, as if the body's resistance to a kind of permanent poisoning had very suddenly weakened. (138–139)

The uncovering of continuing authoritarian and "normalizing" structures contradicts official German Democratic Republic interpretations, according to which East German society marked a clear break with National Socialism. Instead, *Kindheitsmuster* (*Patterns of Childhood*) points to the prevalence of behavior and attitudes learned under National Socialism: "How did we become what we are today?" (209).

The focus on present and past language use represents an important aspect in the approach to history in *Kindheitsmuster* (*Patterns of Childhood*), for as Linda Hutcheon puts it: "To reinsert the subject . . . into the context of its *parole,* its signifying activities (both conscious and unconscious) within a historical and social context, is to begin a redefinition not only of the subject but of history" (79). The subject in *Kindheitsmuster* (*Patterns of Childhood*) which is split into the one of the past, Nelly, and one of the present, the speaker, is defined by its historically determined use of language and other signifying practices. Engendered by patriarchal language, this subject is, nevertheless, as the subject in *Three Guineas,* also an active user and maker of culture. The breakdown of the GDR has confirmed the significance of this critical approach to history as a necessary break with authoritarian structures, but has also shown that it was never practiced by the historical apparatus of the GDR. Indeed, in retrospect it has become clear that the central axiom of GDR historiography, that the GDR was based on the principles of antifascism, functioned as a screen for the investigation of the past (and thus the present). As a result, the past complicity of the vast majority of GDR citizens with National Socialism and the continuation of authoritarian structures was never systematically examined by official GDR historiography.[5]

Three Guineas, Der Mann auf der Kanzel (The man in the pulpit), and *Kindheitsmuster* (*Patterns of Childhood*) expose the interrelationship between patriarchal and fascist structures. They show that fascism is fundamentally based on a specific notion of maleness and consequently of femaleness that grew out of the patriarchal gender system of the nineteenth century. As they focus on the significance of a gendered subject for the reproduction of an authoritarian order, they also attempt to break with the hierarchical structures that inform patriarchal history. All three texts use history as a political intervention against the imposed conformity of a rigid gender system. In Ruth Rehmann's *Der Mann auf der Kanzel* (The man in the pulpit) and in Christa Wolf's *Kindheitsmuster* (*Patterns of Childhood*) the speakers are also defined as mothers, which determines their perspective of the past. In these two texts being a mother and thus a transmitter of the past gives their projects a special urgency. For they realize that only by working through the past will they break its power over their lives. All three texts dislodge the myth that history can be written from a disembodied and disinterested perspective. Instead, the historical subject is not only a gendered one, but it is also entangled in a history that still powerfully affects her and, precisely because of this, requires her active intervention.

NOTES

1. Klaus Theweleit documents in *Männerphantasien* (*Male Fantasies*) the high social status of the military in German society from the turn of the century through National Socialism. The military, he argues, was regarded as the embodiment of German culture. The worship of the military had a significant impact on the development of German fascism.

2. All translations from *Der Mann auf der Kanzel* (The man in the pulpit) are mine. For further discussion of this novel, see Marie-Luise Gättens, "The Hard Work of Remembering: Two German Women Writers Re-examine Nationalsocialism," in *Taking Our Time: Feminist Perspectives on Temporality* and "Die Rekonstruktion der Geschichte: Der Nationalsozialismus in drei Romanen der siebziger Jahre," in *Frauen Fragen in der deutschsprachigen Literatur seit 1945.*

3. For further discussion of this novel, see Marie-Luise Gättens, "Mädchenerziehung im Faschismus: Die Rekonstruktion der eigenen Geschichte in Christa Wolfs *Kindheitsmuster,*" in *Der Widerspenstigen Zähmung,* "The Hard Work of Remembering," and "Die Rekonstruktion der Geschichte."

4. The English translation by Molinaro and Rappolt uses unchaste, which is, in my opinion, too narrowly sexual.

5. For a discussion of the historical development of the axiom of antifascism, see Antonia Grunenberg's article "Antifaschismus—ein deutscher Mythos."

WORKS CITED

Althusser, Louis. "Ideology and Ideological State Apparatuses." In *Lenin and Philosophy and Other Essays.* Trans. Ben Brewster. New York: Monthly Review Press, 1971.

Benjamin, Walter. "Über den Begriff der Geschichte." *Illuminationen.* 2d ed. Frankfurt: Suhrkamp, 1980.

———. "Theses on the Philosophy of History." In *Illuminations,* ed. Hannah Arendt. Trans. Harry Zohn. 5th ed. New York: Schocken Book, 1978.

Bock, Gisela. "Racism and Sexism in Nazi Germany: Motherhood, Compulsory Sterilization, and the State." In Bridenthal.

Bridenthal, Renate, Atina Grossmann, and Marion Kaplan. Eds. *When Biology Became Destiny: Women in Weimar and Nazi Germany.* New York: Monthly Review Press, 1984.

de Lauretis, Teresa. *Alice Doesn't: Feminism, Semiotics, Cinema.* Bloomington: Indiana University Press, 1984.

———. "The Technology of Gender." In *Technologies of Gender.* Bloomington: Indiana University Press, 1987.

Foucault, Michel. *Discipline and Punish. The Birth of the Prison.* Trans. Alan Sheridan. New York: Vintage Books, 1979.

Gättens, Marie-Luise. "Mädchenerziehung im Faschismus: die Rekonstruktion der eigenen Geschichte in Christa Wolfs *Kindheitsmuster.*" In *Der Widerspenstigen Zähmung. Studien zur bezwungenen Weiblichkeit in der Literatur vom Mittelalter bis zur Gegenwart,* eds. Sylvia Wallinger and Monika Jonas. Innsbruck: Innsbrucker Beiträge zur Kulturwissenschaft, 1986.

———. "The Hard Work of Remembering: Two German Women Writers Reexamine National Socialism." In *Taking Our Time: Feminist Perspectives on Temporality,* ed. Frieda Johles Forman with Caoran Sowton. Oxford: Pergamon Press, 1989.

———. "Die Rekonstruktion der Geschichte: Der Nationalsozialismus in drei Romanen der siebziger Jahre." In *Frauen Fragen in der deutschsprachigen Literatur seit 1945. Amsterdamer Beiträge zur Germanistik,* ed. Mona Knapp and Gerd Labroisse. Amsterdam: Rodopi, 1989.

Grunenberg, Antonia. "Antifaschismus—ein deutscher Mythos." *Die Zeit*, 3 May 1991.

Gutjahr, Ortrud. "'Erinnerte Zukunft' Gedächtnisrekonstruktion und Subjektkonstitution im Werk Christa Wolfs." In *Erinnerte Zukunft: 11 Studien zum Werk Christa Wolfs*, ed. Wolfram Mauscr. Würzburg: Königshausen & Neumann, 1985.

Hutcheon, Linda. "Subject In/Of/To History and His Story." *Diacritics* 16 (1986): 78–91.

Marcuse, Herbert. "Studie über Autorität und Familie." In *Ideen zu einer kritischen Theorie der Gesellschaft.* 3rd ed. Frankfurt: Suhrkamp, 1969.

Minnow-Pinkney, Makiko. *Virginia Woolf and the Problem of the Subject.* New Brunswick: Rutgers University Press, 1987.

Mitscherlich, Alexander, and Margarete Mitscherlich. *The Inability to Mourn.* Trans. Beverly R. Placzek. New York: Grove Press, 1975.

Mitscherlich, Margarete. "Die Frage der Selbstdarstellung. Überlegungen zu den Autobiographien von Helene Deutsch, Margaret Mead und Christa Wolf." *Neue Rundschau* 2/3 (1980): 291–316.

Popular Memory Group. "Popular Memory: Theory, Politics, Methods." In *Making Histories*, ed. Richard Johnson, et al. Minneapolis: University of Minnesota Press, 1982.

Rehmann, Ruth. *Der Mann auf der Kanzel: Fragen an einen Vater.* 3rd ed. Munich: Deutscher Taschenbuch Verlag, 1986.

Schneider, Michael. "Fathers and Sons, Retrospectively: The Damaged Relationship Between Two Generations." *New German Critique* 31 (1983): 3–51.

Silverman, Kaja. *The Subject of Semiotics.* New York: Oxford University Press, 1983.

Theweleit, Klaus. *Männerphantasien.* 2 vols. Reinbeck bei Hamburg: Rowohlt, 1983, 1984.

———. *Male Fantasies.* 2 vols. Trans. Erica Carter and Chris Turner in collaboration with Stephen Conway. Minneapolis: University of Minnesota Press, 1989.

Weber, Max. *The Protestant Ethic and the Spirit of Capitalism.* Trans. Talcott Parsons. New York: Charles Scribner's Sons, 1958.

Weigel, Sigrid. *Die Stimme der Medusa. Schreibweisen in der Gegenwartsliteratur von Frauen.* Dülmen-Hiddingsel: Tende, 1987.

Wolf, Christa. *Kindheitsmuster.* 8th ed. Darmstadt: Luchterhand, 1980.

———. *Patterns of Childhood.* Trans. Ursule Molinaro and Hedwig Rappolt. New York: Farrar, Straus and Giroux, 1984.

Woolf, Virginia. *Three Guineas.* New York: Harcourt Brace Jovanovich, 1966.

Zahlmann, Christel. *Christa Wolfs Reise 'ins Tertiär'.* Würzburg: Königshausen & Neumann, 1986.

RITTA JO HORSLEY

Witness, Critic, Victim: Irmgard Keun and the Years of National Socialism

One of the most fascinating and contradictory writers to experience life both under National Socialism and in exile is Irmgard Keun (1905–1982), who lived for three and a half years under Hitler, emigrated to spend four years in various European cities (and the USA) before being trapped in Amsterdam by the Nazi occupation in 1940. Forced to return secretly to Germany, she waited out the end of the war in perpetual danger of being identified and arrested as one who had written against the Nazi regime. After the war she began writing again, but failed to maintain her initial success and disappeared from public view until she was rediscovered in the mid-1970s. Keun's works, including seven novels, offer an ironic perspective of conditions and events in Germany from the close of World War I through the late Weimar Republic, the early years of the Third Reich and the experience of exile, to the postwar era. With one exception Keun did not construct her novels from the vantage point of distant recollection, but from recent observation, without the advantages and burdens of historical hindsight. Her first two novels, *Gilgi, eine von uns* (Gilgi, one of us, 1931), and *Das kunstseidene Mädchen* (The synthetic silk girl, 1932), touched a nerve of Weimar Germany with their witty, carefully observed portrayals of spirited young women and were sensationally successful: *Gilgi* was filmed, translated into seven languages, and serialized in the Socialist magazine *Vorwärts; Das kunstseidene Mädchen* was printed in the unheard-of first edition of 50,000 copies (Kreis 97).[1] Similarly, the novel of Nazi Germany *Nach Mitternacht* (*After Midnight,* 1937), published after Keun had emigrated, was based on her still fresh recollections of conditions inside the country and elicited the praise of Klaus Mann (also writing in exile), who found that the novel presented *deutsche Wirklichkeit* (German reality) as perhaps no other of its time (Mann 528). And *Kind aller Länder* (Child of all nations, 1938), based on Keun's life in exile and written virtually as she was experiencing it, evokes an urgent yet poignantly comic sense of chaos and despair. The proximity of these novels to the time they portray gives them a "documentary" immediacy that later works, colored by intervening events and the complexities of retrospection, may lack.

At the same time, Keun's novels are very much subjective constructs, "documentations" of her particular vision and artistic strategies. For example, all but her last novel center around and reflect the consciousness of a female protagonist, either a precocious girl or a seemingly naïve young woman from modest circumstances. From her position as a less privileged, less powerful outsider the narrator-protagonist presents an often sharp, often humorous perspective of society which unmasks middle-class hypocrisy and masculine or nationalist arrogance and authoritarianism. In reviewing Keun's œuvre as a whole, however, one is struck by an increasing loss in independence and spirit of these characters and by the gradual disappearance of a female voice. Compared to the struggling but rebellious "New Women" of her first two novels, the adult protagonists of the later novels appear ever more passive and victimized, and secondary women figures are often drawn with a harshly negative, even misogynist, brush. And while Gilgi and Doris articulate the primary perspective of their accounts, in Keun's last two novels, narrated by a child and by a man respectively, the woman's voice is virtually silent.

Thus one question a study of Keun's literary treatment of the years of National Socialism must address is how her own experiences during this period may have figured in such a shift in her construction of reality. The intermingling of autobiography and fiction in Keun's novels has long been assumed, although much about her life remained in the shadows, a fact that has been attributed in part to society's lack of interest in women's cultural achievements.[2] The chaos of the period in which she lived and wrote, her reluctance to speak about the most painful parts of her life, and the difficulty of sorting out fact from fiction in Keun's own statements and letters have also worked against a definitive biographical account. The publication in 1988 of letters written between 1933 and 1947 to a previously unknown lover and a study of Keun by Gabriele Kreis (1991) fill many gaps in her biography and reveal that the correspondence between her life and her fiction is even greater than previously thought.[3] At the same time, both the letters and Kreis's perceptive biography underscore the fictive quality of Keun's recollections and assertions and warn that more than the usual caution is required in assessing the "documentary" significance of her texts, both fictional and autobiographical. Many details that had been accepted about Keun's life, such as stories of her persecution by the Gestapo, must now be revised, whereas many elements of the novels previously thought fictional can now be recognized as drawn from real life.

Keun's tendency to fictionalize her life, to invent in her recollections and letters a reality that she preferred, may also provide a key to understanding her representation of women. Gabriele Kreis chose for the title of her Keun-biography the quotation from a letter of 1933: "*Was man glaubt, gibt es*" (What you believe, exists) and suggests that Keun's fabrications often corresponded to her life-long need to be "*etwas Besonderes*" (something special, Kreis 49). In her career as a writer, in particular a woman writer, Keun experienced both fulfillment and frustration of such a need, as her success in the relatively liberal Weimar Republic gave way to the repression of National Socialist Germany and the deprivations of exile, illegal hiding inside Germany and the struggle for survival after the war. One might expect that the conflicts traditionally endured by women artists, such as that between the patriarchally defined feminine role and the goals of a self-identified artist, would be exacerbated in the historical context in which Irmgard Keun lived out her ambitions, as conservative and misogynist attitudes toward women replaced more progressive ones in the culture at large. That Keun was reinforced in such a double-identity is illustrated in the well-known praise from the beginning of her career by Kurt Tucholsky: "Sie hat Humor wie ein dicker Mann, Grazie wie eine Frau" (she has the sense of humor of a fat man, the grace of a woman) a brand of commentary that continued throughout her career (as in Krechel 113). Indeed, the intense desire to find acclaim in the (male) world of literature both "as a woman" and as an author propelled Keun throughout her life and was surely an important factor in her successes as well as in her eventual decline under the tragic sway of alcohol. The ever greater strain required to maintain this contradictory identity would have left its traces in her writings: her increasingly hopeless portrayals of women as passive victims or malevolent shrews and her need to exaggerate her accomplishments and importance may reflect two complementary sides of an internalized message of female inferiority. At the same time, Irmgard Keun was able to penetrate the mists of self-delusion and hypocrisy with a wit and trenchancy matched by few other novelists; perhaps this too was the result of a contradictory sense of herself as outsider looking in at many realms, not least formidable—and vulnerable—of which was the domain of masculine cultural privilege.

Keun was born in Berlin, the first, "difficult" child of middle-class, liberal-minded parents and the sister of a more easily managed brother, four years younger, of whom she was at first intensely jealous (Kreis 17). When Irmgard was barely eight the family moved to Cologne, where her father became the director of an oil refinery. Here she felt herself an outsider, in part because of her accent, in part because she attended a more advanced school than the other children her age: "I didn't fit anywhere, and it was awful."[4] This early sense of being different, of not belonging, would become a recurrent theme in Keun's novels, and anticipated her literal exile by some years. Irmgard Keun early developed a sympathy for those outside the mainstream of the middle class and found in their situation and perspective the critical point of departure for her often satirical views of respectable society ("Gespräch" 72). At the same time, a teacher recalls, as a girl Irmgard resisted order and discipline and learned only what interested her; her later defiance of authority was already prefigured in her habit of playing hooky from school, and her need to gain recognition took the form of misbehaving or acting the clown (Kreis 49–50). In contrast to her brother Gerd, a "good student" who went on to the college preparatory *Gymnasium* and then the university (Kreis 49, 63), Irmgard attended the less academic girls' *Lyzeum* and was then taken into her father's office to work two years as a clerk, before she could persuade her parents to send her to acting school in Cologne in 1923. She played minor roles in Hamburg and then Greifswald, and when her contract there was not renewed in 1929, she returned to office work in Cologne. Keun's experience in these typical female occupations formed the basis of her first two novels, which are important as both background and contrast to the works written under the impact of National Socialism and exile.

Gilgi (1931) presents the struggle of an emancipated young office worker to maintain her independence and make something of her life despite the obstacles of an obsessive first love affair, an unwanted pregnancy, and the unemployment and general despair of late Weimar society. Doris of *Das kunstseidene Mädchen* (1932), already less optimistic about the chances for advancement than Gilgi, abandons clerical work altogether when she is fired after resisting her boss's advances and is drawn to the mecca of Berlin, where she hopes to become famous and make her fortune as a *Glanz* (glittering star), reminiscent of the secretary-turned-actress in such popular Weimar films as *Dolly macht Karriere* (Dolly's Career, 1930). Her adventures in the bewildering metropolis do not bring such a fairy-tale solution, however; after a series of erotic encounters and exposure to the poverty and the anonymity as well as the excitement of Berlin, Doris instead reaches a kind of disillusionment about the myths of glamour and luxury that governed the dreams of many young women of her society. Keun's Weimar novels combine lively wit with a sharp gift for social and psychological observation and satire, in particular of bourgeois hypocrisy and patriotic pieties. The novels counterpose a forthright defense of women's right to independence and sexual pleasure against narrow moralizing and the double standard as well as male insensitivity and arrogance. Keun mocks conservative or fascist platitudes, as when Gilgi listens in vain for *die Stimme des Bluts* (the voice of her blood 40) to confirm that the woman she has just met is indeed her biological mother, or when Doris defends her own and her mother's sexually free and self-determined way of life against the official ideal of woman as *eine deutsche Mutter von Kindern* (a German mother of children 85).

As Heide Soltau has pointed out, Keun, like her contemporary Marieluise Fleisser, goes beyond most women's novels of the 1920s in that she shows problematic as well as positive aspects of the image of the New Woman, including women's own internalization of patriarchal values (Soltau 229–232). While Gilgi takes it for granted that she can have both an independent career and sexual freedom—she simply moves out when her conventional bourgeois parents object to her social life—her relationship with the older, more educated Martin is problematized to show its costs to her in self-determination and independence, and she finally leaves him. Love itself is viewed with ambivalence: although Keun argues in these two books that women have a right to erotic experience outside marriage, she also shows sex as leading to disaster—

not only through the inevitable pregnancies that cause financial ruin to Gilgi's friends Hans and Hertha but also through Martin's erotic demands, which prevent her from bringing them money in time to stave off their suicides. Similarly, in *Das kunstseidene Mädchen* the prostitute Hulla commits suicide because her friend Doris is distracted by a seductive male and fails to intervene.

The protagonists, although they identify with the down-and-out and are vaguely sympathetic with socialist ideas, find the prevailing political discourse basically too complicated and abstract. Typically they turn to more highly educated or activist males for political enlightenment, only to be treated as sex objects or emotional sounding boards by the men, whose long-winded, oblivious arrogance provides one of the comic pleasures of Keun's texts. As the author Elfriede Jelinek observed, Keun unmasked such masculine linguistic privilege as perhaps no other woman had (Jelinek 223). Conversely, and perhaps as a response to masculine domination of the economic and cultural realms, the female characters take on a naïveté of speech and perspective that is at least equally a source of comic enjoyment and a trademark of Keun's fiction. Although such artfully naïve perspective and diction are effective vehicles for Keun's criticism of bourgeois narrowness and patriarchal attitudes, her protagonists nonetheless suffer for their lack of linguistic and intellectual sophistication. Gilgi is tormented by her inability to articulate her thoughts to herself or her partner, while Doris grasps at every linguistic straw to appear as elegant and sophisticated as the world she yearns to join.[5] To a certain extent we might see in Gilgi's and Doris's insecurities a projection of their author's sense of educational disadvantage and inadequacy. To be sure, Keun was famed for her ability to speak virtually *druckreif* (in a manner fit to print), but compared to the more serious male writers she associated with she was herself educationally disadvantaged. As she commented in an interview from her last years: "I didn't consider myself to be intellectual at that time. . . . I was told often enough that I was unusually intelligent. I didn't think so myself, I thought I was quite stupid."[6]

Like their author, Gilgi and especially Doris are outsiders, feeling themselves excluded from a class or family community and viewing their society from its margins. Both leave home to seek greater independence; both eventually lose their jobs as office workers; both leave their "middle-sized city" for the more impersonal freedom and opportunity of the metropolis; finally, both leave men they love to face the world alone. As Doris says, "That's just it—I don't have anyone of my own kind. I don't belong anywhere at all" (215).[7] They illustrate the ambivalent status of self-chosen exile: freedom coupled with isolation and alienation, a condition their author too often experienced. Keun's rejection of the conventional fairy-tale "happy end" of romance or success—the final scene of both novels is a railroad station, the protagonist's fate uncertain—points to an open question in late Weimar society concerning the future development of women's roles. It was a question for which Irmgard Keun, writing from her own sense of feminine possibilities, had no clear answer.

These two novels made Keun famous overnight; she had suddenly become *ein Glanz* herself, a newly discovered young prodigy. (On the advice of her future husband, Johannes Tralow, Keun had adjusted her birthdate, claiming to be five years younger than she was in reality.) Reaping popular and critical acclaim, she was highly praised for her humor by no less an author than Kurt Tucholsky. Only voices from both political extremes were less friendly; the leftist Bernhard Brentano scolded Gilgi's inadequate solidarity and political engagement, but right-wing accusations of Doris's supposed immorality and defamation of German womanhood pointed in a more ominous direction (Kreis 80–82, 97 Ball, Brentano). Keun's liberal treatment of sexual mores and her irreverence toward traditional values caused her to be an early target of the Nazi policy of cultural *Säuberung* (purification), an author of *schädlichen und unerwünschten Schrifttums* (harmful and undesirable literature), of "asphalt-literature of anti-German tendency," or literature of "cultural nihilism" and "free-floating intellectualism" (Kreis 133). In the spring of 1933 her name was placed on the precursors of the official blacklists for the "purification" of bookstores and for the "orientation" of publishing houses, and soon thereafter her books were confiscated and destroyed (Roloff 51–54; Kreis 133–135). On 15 December 1933, Keun wrote to her secret lover Arnold Strauss that various newspapers where she had sought to publish some short pieces had told her they were no longer allowed to print any of her works (*Briefe* 46). The Reich Culture Chamber Law, passed on 22 September 1933, required that anyone having anything to do with the production of culture must belong to one of the seven departments of the *Reichskulturkammer* (Reich Chamber of Culture, *RKK*), for literature the *Reichsschrifttumskammer* (Reich Chamber of Literature, *RSK*) (Ritchie 71). The letters to Arnold Strauss show Irmgard Keun struggling constantly to complete work she hoped would be acceptable and to find some way to publish it during the years she remained in Germany after 1933. Although opposed to the Nazis, she was desperate enough to seek membership in the *RSK*, but was refused admission in late 1934 and in subsequent attempts (e.g., *Briefe* 148; Kreis 136). On 29 October 1935 and again in early 1936, Keun was so foolhardy as to file suit against the government for the income she had lost through the regime's confiscation of her books. This act failed to win her any of her lost money, but according to the available documentation, it also had no negative consequences, in contradiction of Keun's own postwar accounts that she had subsequently been arrested and tortured by the Gestapo, freed only on payment of a huge ransom by her father, and consequently forced to flee the country (e.g., Kreis 157).[8] In petitions she later formulated in order to receive support from cultural and governmental agencies as one politically persecuted by the Nazis, Keun also claimed to have refused offers to join the *RSK* (Kreis 216, 278). But even if Keun did make up the dramatic story of being interrogated at Gestapo headquarters (a version of which would appear in her novel *Nach Mitternacht*), she nonetheless was forced to emigrate in order to continue her career as a writer, hardly begun but spectacularly successful. She could no longer publish or sell anything in Germany.

And even without active persecution by the Nazis, Irmgard Keun's life in Germany prior to her emigration was filled with stress and anxiety. She was under pressure from her publisher, experiencing difficulty writing her next book, and suffering ambivalent feelings about having suddenly become a famous person subject to harsh as well as positive criticism (Kreis 98–108, 117). In 1932 she married Johannes Tralow, a novelist, dramatist, and theater and film director twenty-seven years her senior. Tralow encouraged his wife as a writer and provided as much financial support as he was able in response to her often extravagant demands. Although she needed and used him, Keun chose for much of the time to live apart. In the summer of 1933 she became the lover of the young physician Arnold Strauss and then his fiancée; she told Tralow nothing of this affair, nor, until the last minute, of her long-held plans to emigrate (Kreis 158). To account for her supposedly sudden departure for Holland in 1936 she told him—a story later published—that she had to flee for having boldly slapped a Nazi who had insulted a Jewish friend of hers; the story was later refuted in print by the friend (Kreis 156–159).

Irmgard Keun's gift for invention was put to even greater use in the 271 (surviving) letters she wrote to her lover, who emigrated first to Holland (1933), then to Italy (1934) and finally to Montgomery, Virginia (1935). Nevertheless they are also our primary source of information about the author's character and experiences during the years 1933–1940, and they reveal much of her sense of herself as an author and the stresses of the Nazi and exile years. Arnold Strauss, the only son of a solid, middle-class Jewish family, firmly intended to make Keun his bride, over the objections of his parents, for whom she was "trop bohème," in the words of cousin Fritz Strauss (*Briefe* 93). Against Arnold's wishes Keun insisted on concealing the relationship, especially from Tralow, who was still potentially worried that her relationship with a Jewish man would make it still more difficult for her to publish in Germany if it were known. A major theme that emerges from the letters to Arnold Strauss before her own emigration is Keun's absolute commitment to her work, her determination to persist and be successful in spite of the personal and mounting political obstacles: "On top of everything else there were the daily battles with my publisher and always new complications. I can't explain that to you now. Heaven only knows how I'll get out of this mess. . . . I love my work more than anything in the world. But working *now* and *here?* . . . If it depends on performance, ability, work, I have no fear. . . . But to have to deal only with senseless, arbitrary highhandedness? And how am I supposed to work when they won't let me?" (*Briefe* 19).[9] Less than two weeks before this letter of 18 August 1933, *Das kunstseidene Mädchen* had been confiscated in Prussia (August 7) and Bavaria (August 8) and was destroyed a few months later on October 13 (Kreis 133).

From the beginning of the correspondence in the summer of 1933 Keun was clearly considering the possibility of emigration, in order to be able to write and publish, but did not want to burn her bridges in Germany until she was certain of the situation "outside" (*Briefe* 23). She wrote to Arnold that she was working feverishly on her novel manuscript "Der hungrige Ernährer" (The Hungry Provider) and that she had falsely told her publisher it was already completed, in hopes of receiving further advance royalties (*Briefe* 24). Meanwhile she worked on a collection of *Kindergeschichten* (children's stories) which she hoped—in vain—she might still be able to publish in Germany. At the end of February 1936, she learned that friends' continuing efforts to get her into the *RSK* had been unsuccessful, and that "is perhaps a good thing" (*Briefe* 157).[10] For now she had a firm offer from the "most highly respected publishing house" in Holland, Allert de Lange (*Briefe* 157), and accompanied by her mother, she finally left Germany to arrive in Ostende, on the Belgian seacost, on 4 May 1936 (Kreis in *Briefe* 163). In one of her first letters from Ostende, she expressed her relief: "I have time and peace and quiet—finally after a long, long time peace and quiet again (knock on wood!!!) . . . I can still hardly believe that I'm not in Nazi-land any longer and can really write, speak and breathe freely" (*Briefe* 165).[11]

Keun's ambivalence about committing herself to Arnold Strauss infuses the letters and is always tied to her ambitions as a writer. Over and over she responds to his urging that she join him in exile with the protest that she must first establish herself as a writer in Germany, then Europe (e.g., letter of 19 April 1935, *Briefe* 113); always there is one more book that must be completed and published before she dare think of leaving. The traditional feminine conflict portrayed in *Gilgi* between autonomy and work and the demands of a relationship was one Keun felt very sharply: "sometimes my work is something that makes itself independent and personifies itself—and then I love it like my most beloved man, because it's the only thing that helps me out of everything. . . . Why didn't you take me with you? Maybe now I'll never come" (*Briefe* 17–18).[12] Keun viewed the "respectable" feminine roles as incompatible with her calling as a writer: "If one wants to write well and naturally, one can't live like a polite society lady—you must never want that" (*Briefe* 133).[13] Even worse would be the routine boredom of a housewife's role, as she insisted to Arnold Strauss, who was then setting up his household in Montgomery: "And then I'll also need cigarettes and decent alcohol and I have to go to a pub every day too in order to write. I can't just sit around the whole day at home—I always need a change of atmosphere and I have to be able to see and observe things. If I really had to lead the life of a housewife I'd soon get dull and miserable. Is that clear?" (*Briefe* 134).[14] From Ostende Keun made herself even clearer: "I'm fond of you, but I don't give a damn about marrying you. . . . I'd rather let myself be beaten to death in a German concentration camp than to live out my existence in gratitude and humility at your side" (*Briefe* 177).[15]

In these letters Irmgard Keun revealed herself to be, even accused herself of being, egocentric and demanding; she wrote much about herself, her successes, her trials, whatever caught her attention, often without much thought to her partner: "when I have a pencil in my hand I simply *can't* write anything but whatever is important to me in the moment of writing—Then I totally forget that I'm writing to you" (*Briefe* 17).[16] Increasingly, the letters are devoted to reproachful pleas or demands for money, as Keun manipulated the fiction of or belief in their engagement to milk her distant lover for sums to tide her over for many emergencies large and small; she admitted herself that she was careless about money (e.g., *Briefe* 293) and exaggerated her financial plight to coax still more from him. With very few exceptions, Arnold complied; even his skeptical parents eventually sent her a regular allowance at their son's request, although they believed that her interest in him was insincere, and shortly before their own deaths by suicide, wrote urging him to free himself from "this Circe" (*Briefe* 300).

Keun was disingenuous in her correspondence with Arnold Strauss, just as she had been toward her husband Tralow and her publisher, and it is often difficult to assess the truth value of her assertions and accounts. Certainly Keun deceived Arnold when she wrote that her year-and-a-half long relationship with the Austrian novelist Joseph Roth, whom she met in Ostende, was merely a friendship. Yet she could also be direct and very honest in warning Arnold about her real needs and the risks involved in a relationship with her; many letters express longing and, toward the end of the correspondence, desperate need for his emotional support. The long-distance, "literary" relationship with the devoted and reliable Arnold Strauss was important for Keun as writer and human being; her biographer Kreis observes that Arnold played an important role as Keun's last reader during the years before her emigration. In her letters Keun found a way to maintain her identity as a writer, to invent her reality and know it was being read and admired (Kreis 153, *Briefe* 304–305). Arnold provided her with a form of stable if remote contact and continuing security during the uncertain, tumultuous years before and during her emigration. In the early stage of the relationship they wrote each other almost daily, and Keun's letters are often up to ten pages long. Her letters were also a way to retain human emotions in a dehumanizing time, as a letter from Amsterdam of 17 April 1939 suggests: "My little one, I've suffered a lot in the last year and had gotten so dull and numb. Now I'm beginning to melt a little again, and I always want to write you everything so that I don't freeze shut" (*Briefe* 268).[17]

Keun's experiences in exile were not entirely negative, however, particularly at the beginning. She soon became part of a company of German writers who gathered in the summer of 1936 in

Ostende. In her *Bilder aus der Emigration* (Images from Exile, first published in 1947), Keun characterized and recalled anecdotes about Egon Erwin Kisch, Ernst Toller, Stefan Zweig, Hermann Kesten, and Joseph Roth, as they read each other their manuscripts, talked about politics, and visited each other's "offices," each at a regular table in a different café.[18] Keun, working on her novel about Nazi Germany (*Nach Mitternacht*), was encouraged by her colleagues and her publisher; her letters show it was a stimulating environment for her as an author. Moreover, she was inspired by their political élan and sympathized with the Communist party members Kisch, Willi Münzenberg, and others. Arthur Koestler recalled: "Keun was on our side and took part in our discussions about the events in Spain, where the civil war had just broken out" (Bronsen 472). Writing to Arnold, she criticized the bourgeois capitalism of the United States and complained about its class differences: "It won't be long before I'm politically quite on top of things. You have your duty as a doctor, and now I have mine in the struggle against fascism" (*Briefe* 178, 180).[19] Keun later recalled the political as well as personal demoralization caused by the news that one after another of the exiled authors had committed suicide: "It hit so especially hard when one of the political authors committed suicide. That is, during emigration and simply by virtue of the fact of emigration every writer was actually political, and every suicide meant giving up the fight and discouragement in our own ranks, and triumph and affirmation for the enemy" (*Wenn . . .* 150).[20]

Keun soon became the companion of Joseph Roth, a prolific writer who spurred her on to write even when she wanted to stay in bed with the "serious depressions" she often suffered with her menstrual period: "You are a writer, you are not to be a woman, but a soldier" (*Briefe* 181).[21] Keun wrote Arnold that Roth was a wonderful friend from whom she was learning a tremendous amount, but did not report that they were soon sharing a hotel room (Bronsen 475). Roth was a long-time and fierce opponent of the Nazis, but at this period in his life he had given up his earlier socialist leanings for more conservative sympathies with the former Austrian monarchy. Presumably any potential movement of Keun's toward the left would not have flourished in his company. Roth may possibly have been a good influence on Keun's self-discipline—she told about the "writing-Olympics" they engaged in: "Usually he has more pages than I do by evening" (*Briefe* 182).[22] But his influence as a heavy drinker was less benign. Kisch wrote to a cousin in Vienna encouraging him to get to know his two friends Roth and Keun while they were there but warned him against getting drunk in the process: "the two of them drink like holes" (Bronsen 654, n. 73a).[23] Keun accompanied Roth on his travels to Brussels, Amsterdam, Wilna, Lemberg, Vienna, Salzburg, and Paris. The constant financial and political difficulties that had filled Keun's frantic letters and telegrams across the Atlantic are described with more detachment in her recollections:

> Roth and I . . . were soon used to depending on something or other that we couldn't count on at all. And again and again money did come from somewhere—from the publisher, from a newspaper or through foreign translations. We never suffered real need, and never were hungry, at least not at that point.
>
> We constantly had financially embarrassing moments. For example our visa would have run out and we had to go to another country, if possible in an expensive Pullman train, because that was the easiest way to avoid the passport control. The hotel bill had to be paid. No money could be expected from the publisher until enough manuscript pages had been sent in. But one didn't have enough manuscript pages. By working at a boiling pace one would be that far in fourteen days at best. One needed the money, however, in three days at the latest. (*Wenn . . .* 143–144)[24]

In spite of the increasingly chaotic conditions of her life, Keun published four books between 1936 and 1938. The first was *Das Mädchen, mit dem die Kinder nicht verkehren durften* (The girl with whom the children were not allowed to associate), mostly written before her emigration and published in 1936 in Amsterdam by Allert de Lange. The series of episodes from petit bourgeois Cologne at the close of World War I, again following many of her own experiences, features Keun's typical naïve-clever narrator-protagonist, in this case a high-spirited preadolescent girl who speaks the truth as she sees it. Her lively narrative punctures conventions of respectability and patriotism and satirizes adult authoritarianism and hypocrisy. Keun was pleased by the enthusiasm this book generated among the critics in Holland, in particular by a reviewer who compared her to Dickens (*Briefe* 184), but she considered her novel-in-progress, based on her recent first-hand observations of life inside the Third Reich, to be much more important (*Briefe* 171).

Keun finished *Nach Mitternacht* in early 1937 in the Café Roma in Lemberg, Poland, and it was published by the second major Dutch publisher of German émigré(e) literature, Querido, in the same year. Her original publishing house Allert de Lange had found the book too provocative politically and feared losing its German advertisers if it were to publish it (Kreis 196–197). The novel, which provides an ironic and perspicacious account of conditions and attitudes in the first years of Hitler's Germany, was translated into six languages by 1939, was praised by critics such as Klaus Mann and Fritz Erpenbach, and is generally considered her best and most important book (Steinbach 2). About writing *Nach Mitternacht* Keun later said: "I was very committed politically, and that last period in Frankfurt and in Germany in general became very alive for me. And so I could get rid of everything that had burdened me" ("Gespräch" 72).[25] Because of its outspoken mockery and condemnation of Nazis, from Hitler down to the most small-time of opportunists, the book made Keun even more notorious inside Germany. When her divorce was finalized on 26 May 1937, the German decree listed among the grounds that she, the defendant, "had displayed through her publications and other expressions of opinion a kind of behavior which represents for any German a contrariness to duty which can hardly be surpassed" (as quoted in Roloff 57).[26]

Once again the key to Keun's satire is the artfully naïve perspective of her narrator, another simple young woman of modest background but clear-sighted powers of observation and common sense. Susanne or "Sanna" Moder is also a cousin to Gilgi and Doris in that she has left her petit bourgeois home and family to seek a wider horizon in the city, where she—again—feels herself an outsider socially and intellectually. The theme of a young woman's quest for self-identity important in the first two novels is relatively muted in this novel, however; Sanna remains largely in the observer role until she finally reaches, like Keun herself, the difficult decision to leave Germany. As she moves from her Mosel village of Lappesheim first to Cologne and then to the more metropolitan Frankfurt, Sanna tries to make sense of a world that appears absurd to her innocent eyes. Through her protagonist's precise observations of the day-to-day behavior of "Kleinbürger" (the petit bourgeois) and the literary intelligentsia under Nazism, Keun reveals mechanisms of fascist domination and their psychosocial roots. The novel, which begins in a Frankfurt pub and ends a little over twenty-four hours later with the escape of Sanna and her lover Franz across the border, shows how completely the private lives of the characters are intertwined with underlying political forces. Using a technique of flashbacks and cutting somewhat reminiscent of film, Keun both suggests how the present has roots in the past and builds the tension and suspense of her story.[27] As often in her novels, the satirical, comic impulse, which dominates at the beginning, gradually gives way to a sense of increasing desperation.

Sanna's double-edged, naïve yet knowing perspective, and Keun's masterful use of metaphor are particularly effective in the depiction of the Führer's visit to Frankfurt, an exposé of the Nazis' obsession with image politics, as well as of the worshipful fascination of their German public. Sanna describes the preparations for Hitler's appearance: "In front of the Opera House was a turmoil of people and swastika flags and garlands of fir branches and SS people. It was a commotion of excited preparations, like Christmas time in a well-to-do family with several children" (25).[28] This comparison of the Nazi demonstration with a family celebration makes the connection between political events and traditional middle-class German values and suggests how the Nazis were drawing on long-standing cultural traditions. At the same time the comparison deflates, by domesticating it, the image of high seriousness and importance the Nazi leaders wished to project. A similar double-edged ironic light is shed on both Hitler and his followers, by the comparison to a carnival (mardi gras) procession: "And slowly an automobile drove past; in it stood the Führer like Prince Carnival in the carnival parade. But he wasn't as funny and happy as Prince Carnival and he didn't throw any candies or little bouquets, but only raised an empty hand" (31–32).[29] Hitler may have been in large part show, but his was not a warming or cheering appearance.

The metaphor of theater, of a grand spectacle, is further developed as Sanna describes how she and her friend Gerti wait on the balcony of a restaurant across from the Opera House (itself a significant location) where Hitler and the other dignitaries are to appear. All the building's balconies are already packed with eager spectators. "Behind us were sitting elegant gentlemen and ladies, who were behaving quietly and with high-class attentiveness, the way they do in the loge of a theater" (30).[30] Like "accomplished movie actors" the leading Nazis can never rest but must "surely always be thinking in order to be able to constantly present a nation with novelties" (33).[31] Hitler himself is presented as a martyr to the cause of show: "The Führer alone lays down practically his whole life to be photographed for his people. Just imagine such a tremendous performance: letting yourself be photographed without interruption with children and favorite dogs, outside and in rooms—over and over" (33).[32] The scene ends on a prophetically ominous note, a dance of death that combines the satire with a symbolic foreshadowing of the inhuman terror to come:

> There stood these rulers now personally on the balcony of the Opera House. They were still illuminated, otherwise night fell. The lights of the square were put out so that the *Reichswehr* (army) could be properly appreciated. For they had shining steel helmets on and flaming torches in their hands; holding them they danced a kind of ballet to the sounds of military music. . . .
>
> The world was large and dark blue, the dancing men were black and uniform—without faces and mute, in black motion. (34)[33]

The image of the Nazi theater spectacle gains cultic dimensions in the response of Sanna's Aunt Adelheid to Hitler's oratory; this woman, portrayed as the epitome of opportunism and brutality, has the same worshipful-erotic response to Hitler as to her favorite actor and hangs pictures of both in her bedroom (76). Keun's satire also discloses how National Socialist manipulation of public consciousness functioned through the terror it induced. For example, Sanna describes her fear of listening to Göring's radio speeches; after building up the listeners' pride at belonging to the glorious German *Volk* that can overcome anything, he lets loose "a wild ranting . . . : that everyone who offends against the Will to Build will be smashed" (74). Sanna, terrified by such tirades because she is never sure whether or not she falls into the latter category, is constantly afraid that she will reveal that she does not understand the "National Socialist *Weltanschauung*" (world view), cause enough to be hauled in before the Gestapo (82). The Nazi mystification of its demagogic ideology into a vague "world view" that is always invoked but can seldom be explained by its practitioners (36–37) is revealed as a powerful mechanism of control in this novel. The uncertainty of exactly who or what is to be condemned, together with the apparatus of arbitrary punishment, result in an atmosphere of terror in which everyone is afraid of everyone else.

Keun shows a world in which the ruling ideology has effectively saturated both public and private spheres, so that even the women's restroom is no longer truly "private." "Earlier it was always so cozy when two girls would go to the restroom together. You powdered your nose and quickly had an important conversation about men and love. . . . Now politics has even penetrated this air. Gerti says: "nowadays you even have to be grateful if there's no attendant sitting there to whom you have to say 'Heil Hitler' and then leave a tip for the privilege" (39–40).[34] It is potentially dangerous to join friends at the *Stammtisch* because a careless word could lead to denunciation by a jealous neighbor. One woman tells Sanna that she keeps her husband at home to protect him; when he objects that it's like a concentration camp she points out, "'dat janze Volk sitzt als im Konzentrationslager, nur die Regierung läuft frei erum'" (The whole nation is sitting in a concentration camp, only the government can run around loose, 86). The ever-present radio, broadcasting speeches and patriotic anthems (the *Deutschlandlied* and the Horst Wessel Song) reaches into every home, as well as the pubs and cafés. Sanna is denounced by her own aunt, after what she has thought are innocent remarks about Göring's and Hitler's speeches.

The National Socialist attack on literary culture is satirized in the figure of Sanna's half-brother Algin, before Hitler a successful novelist who, like Keun herself, had written social-critical novels portraying modern urban life. Now, however, he is reduced to writing the only kind of literature acceptable, that which idealizes simple life of the *Volk* and nature: "The reason for clods of earth is that the poets must praise them, so they don't get foolish ideas and start thinking about what's happening in the cities and with the people." (11)[35] Algin represents a type of writer-intellectual whose career is cut short by the Nazi regime, yet who halfheartedly tries to accommodate himself to the new situation, much as Keun saw in the figure of Johannes Tralow. His opposite is Heini, the liberal journalist who has tried to warn and enlighten through his writing, but who now hardly writes any more, for "political reasons" (89). In his thorny charm, his relentless opposition to the Nazis, his impecunious situation, and his ability to drink quantities of alcohol and stay clear-headed, Heini may have been modeled partly on Joseph Roth—or on one side of Keun herself; his name also suggests an affinity to the ironic and critical exiled poet Heine. Heini's clear-sightedness leads him to despair, however; he describes himself as "a mouse trying to hold back an avalanche by its squeaking," and, predicting a long and hopeless period of bloody violence for Germany, he shoots himself in the climactic final party scene of the novel, just before midnight (164).[36]

Besides unmasking the ways Nazi cultural politics manipulated and controlled public consciousness, *Nach Mitternacht* takes aim at the readiness of many Germans to profit from the new order. Members of the SS, the SA, and common citizens are shown to be motivated by feelings of inferiority and narcissism, by the desire for power and material success usually at their neighbor's cost, in their apparent enthusiasm for the National Socialist world view. From something as harmless as the excitement of secret *Klopfzeichen* (knock-signals) to gain entrance to a bar late at night (53) to the constantly retold and embellished stories of Hitler's visits to his family and of his attendance at the Nürnberg Party Convention (36), SS-man Kulmbach reveals his dependence on membership in the movement to prop up his self-image (52). The petit bourgeois families Silias and Breitwehr vie with each other for the distinction of having their daughter be the one to present Hitler with a bouquet on his visit to Frankfurt; both act on the same class-based desire to appear more important than one's neighbors that had motivated Frau Breitwehr in her scheme to acquire an expensive fur coat.

Sanna's Aunt Adelheid illustrates more sharply than any other character Keun's point that National Socialism offered a vehicle to express, in everyday life, the underlying brutality and self-serving hypocrisy already present in the authoritarian personality structure of many Germans. Adelheid's destructive selfish qualities have their primary locus in the family itself, where she has browbeaten her son Franz until he has become a silent, humble creature, unable to defend himself against her. When Hitler came to power, Adelheid "became political" and joined the Nazi women's organization as a way to associate with "better ladies" as a "German woman and mother" (13). She now seizes upon the chance to denounce Sanna to the Gestapo as a way of getting revenge because Sanna has made Franz happy and less subservient to his mother. Sanna's description of the Gestapo headquarters presents this betrayal, based on opportunistic, petty motives, as typical; the room is full of citizens wishing to file accusations against personal enemies: "And ever more people stream past; the Gestapo room seems to be an absolute place of pilgrimage. Mothers are denouncing their daughters-in-law, daughters their fathers-in-law, brothers their sisters, sisters their brothers, friends their friends, drinking buddies their drinking buddies, neighbors their neighbors" (80).[37]

The Nazi permeation of the private sphere is also illustrated in the various romantic relationships of the novel. The most striking example is the love between Sanna's friend Gerti and Dieter Aaron, the son of a wealthy Jewish merchant and a dominating "aryan" mother. (On 15 September 1935 the Nuremberg Laws had been proclaimed, stripping Jews of political and civil rights and forbidding marriage or extramarital relationships between them and non-Jews.) Gerti, similar to Keun herself in her compulsive pleasures in provoking pompous Nazis through her wit, also defies authority in her choice of a lover, just as we now know Keun did. Sanna observes: "It's hard enough to know all the regulations of the authorities for business life . . . and now one also has to know all the regulations for love, that certainly won't be easy" (40).[38] In the marriage of Sanna's brother Algin, Keun shows more subtly the effects of political and social conditions. Algin had married Liska because it fit with his new status as a successful author to have an expensive apartment, elegant furniture, and a beautiful indolent wife who looked up to him as to a "creating god." His marriage was part of the "magnificent theatrical production" he created through his surroundings (19). The theater metaphor indicates that this prototype of a bourgeois marriage is also an aspect of the show and self-delusion that characterized the apolitical middle class. But now Liska's role as a pampered ornament, her pleasure at taking long baths, and being adored by her husband are at an end; her husband's career has been so damaged by the political situation that he no longer indulges her whims but is preoccupied himself with how to survive. When the meddling Betty Raff, another of the unrelievedly negative female figures in this novel, easily plants in Liska's mind a completely unrequited passion for Heini, the superficiality of the marriage is made even clearer.

In the culminating party scene of the novel the unreality and irrelevance that characterize the activities of the apolitical Liska and her social class are symbolized. As though to emphasize the artificial, self-deluded quality of the lives and relationships of those present, Keun has Liska decorate the apartment as an imaginary restaurant in her desperate attempt to force Heini to notice and respond to her. Here Keun's criticism of the educated middle class aims at its denial of the evil of National Socialism; with the exception of Frau Aaron, descended from an old Prussian family, these characters are not shown as ardent supporters of the Nazis as are many from the lower middle class, but they have reached varying degrees of accommodation with the regime. The wealthy Jewish merchant Aaron favors the Nazis over the Communists out of misguided self-interest, and both he and the Jewish Doctor Breslauer have refused to acknowledge the deadly implications of Nazi rule (145). In this final scene of desperate festivity Keun compresses political, personal, and social crises into one long prefiguration of *Weltuntergang* (the end of the world). Although the surrealist, dreamlike hours of tension and waiting evoke in Sanna and the reader a sense of paralysis, as midnight approaches reality can be denied no longer: Gerti and Dieter are discovered making love and are separated permanently by Frau Aaron; Heini commits suicide; Liska recognizes the illusoriness of her infatuation and the end of her marriage; Betty Raff finally gains her objective, power over the now completely unresisting Algin. For Sanna too the turning point comes "after midnight," this symbolic end point of dark reckoning. Her sudden vivid recollection of the brutal Nazi murders of Communists in a Cologne prison, a concrete episode of actual history set into the trancelike party scene, helps Sanna to see clearly herself: to remain in Germany will mean death for her lover Franz, who has killed a Nazi. With this insight and her love for Franz, she is able to muster the courage, strength, and wit to organize their successful escape over the German border.

In the figures of Aunt Adelheid, Betty Raff, Frau Aaron, and others Keun has created strikingly negative images of women—grasping, power-hungry, cruel or cold, sexually unfulfilled, and unattractive. The author appears to trade here on traditional stereotypes; she expects that her readers will join her in laughing at and condemning these women, who, as in the case of Adelheid in particular, are also among the most repugnant Nazis. Some clearly misogynist lines are also given to Heini, a character who generally seems to speak for Keun (102–104). Moreover, it is the male Heini who is given the authoritative antifascist voice: through his biting comments Keun casts her arrows much more directly than through Sanna's naïve descriptions. Such images and attitudes contradict the generally positive portrayals of women in the Weimar novels, where feminine independence was presented as a desirable quality. In *Nach Mitternacht* the women's options appear to have narrowed along the traditional spectrum of "femininity": the positively presented women conform to traditional feminine virtues of sex-appeal, nurturance, political and intellectual naïveté, and deference to male authority. The outspoken Gerti does exhibit a dangerous, spirited independence against the Nazis, primarily, however, in her love for a Jewish man.

Because the negatively portrayed women are also most often identified with National Socialist mentality, one might be tempted to interpret the creation of such exceptionally unpleasant characters as Keun's way of symbolizing the Nazi deformation of women's character and roles. In figures like the resentful, ambitious Aunt Adelheid or the mother of Bertchen Silias, Keun illustrates the particular vulnerability of relatively powerless, modestly educated, and conventionally narrow-minded women of the German middle class to seduction by Nazi ideology. Moreover, the relative absence of independent New Women of Gilgi's or Doris's stripe reflects the changed social reality of the Third Reich and its call for women to return to more traditional roles. At the same time, however, in its apparently unquestioning presentation of such negative feminine stereotypes, the novel comes close to reflecting misogynist perspectives common to National Socialism itself.

While Keun was writing this novel in 1936, moreover, she was in largely male society; during the first months at Ostende she was the only female author in a group of men, and although this was a rare period of stimulation and solidarity with literary colleagues, she experienced here too the double identity of woman and artist. In her desire for recognition in both roles she may well have assumed typical "male" perspectives herself. In his recollection of the first meeting with her, Hermann Kesten emphasized the contradiction that Keun both cultivated and suffered: "In the hall of the Hotel Métropole I found a pretty young girl, blond and blue-eyed, in a white blouse, who smiled sweetly and looked like a young lady one would like to go dancing with right away." But as soon as she began to speak about conditions in Germany she was "naive and brilliant, . . . no longer a young lady with whom one wanted to go dancing, but . . . a prophet who accuses, . . . a political person" (Kesten 426–427).[39] Keun would perhaps most intensely experience this double role in her relationship with Joseph Roth, whose lover-companion she was during the composition of *Nach Mitternacht*. Keun said that Roth was "the only man who ever fascinated" her so that his words often "took root in [her] soul!" (Bronsen 476).[40] A letter to Arnold Strauss refers to Roth's attitudes: "He doesn't like women and it is terribly depressing when he proves to one the inadequacies of the female sex. And he has a way of speaking such that I take every one of his words as gospel" (23.8.36; *Briefe* 189).[41] According to Keun's recollections, Roth imposed his strongly traditional notions of how a woman should behave within their relationship: "He wanted to make something out of me that I wasn't. Often he would say to me: 'A woman doesn't behave that way.' 'A lady doesn't do such a thing.' For decency's sake I couldn't speak with the taxi driver. I wasn't allowed to carry a package. He wanted to make a humble maid out of me, to train me to 'delicacy.' He forced me into the role of a pitied creature, until I believed it myself; he would wear me down so much that I had to cry" (Bronsen 502).[42] With the increasing effects of his alcoholism Roth became ever more controlling and so obsessively jealous that Keun felt herself "more and more driven into a corner," and when she finally left him in Paris in early 1938, it was with the "feeling of having escaped an unbearable strain" (Bronsen 502).[43] It seems very possible, given the intensity of Joseph Roth's influence in her life, that Keun's female characters in *Nach Mitternacht* and the following novels would bear the mark of such attitudes. Even Sanna, the modest protagonist of *Nach Mitternacht,* feels at the end of the novel that she must suppress herself for the sake of her lover: "I must make myself appear weaker than I am, so that he can feel strong and love me" (172).[44]

After completing *Nach Mitternacht* Keun faced the dilemma of the emigrée author of social criticism, no longer in direct contact with life in her own country, yet limited in what she could say about her experiences in exile. She recalled in 1947: "What I had to write about National Socialist Germany as I knew it I had written. I couldn't write another novel about it. From now on I didn't know it any longer from my own experience" (*Wenn . . .* 153).[45] Yet to write about the reality of exile was also difficult, because it would involve criticism of conditions in countries where one was at best a barely tolerated guest; one did not wish to appear ungrateful or to reveal information that might endanger oneself or other emigré(e)s, whose existence was already precarious enough. Moreover, even if an emigrant did write an good book, there was the problem of who would read and review it—the Nazis had extended their domination over most of German-speaking Europe, and translation was not always a very likely option (154–156).[46]

"All these considerations became so oppressive that I was afraid I would never be able to write another book in my life" (156).[47] Nevertheless, in spite of these problems and the chaotic conditions of her life, Irmgard Keun was able to draw on her experiences in exile to produce and see printed (she was more fortunate than others in having a publisher) two more novels before she was forced by the advance of the Nazis to go underground and flee back into Germany in 1940.

Of *D-Zug dritter Klasse* (Express train, third class, published in 1938 by Querido) Keun wrote to Arnold Strauss: "My new book is better and more beautiful than all the rest, you'll really love it. The only thing is, it's a little crazy" (*Briefe* 232; Christmas, 1937).[48] As though illustrating Keun's later complaint about the problems of writers in exile, this novel has much less explicit social or political reference to conditions inside Germany than *Nach Mitternacht* and received little popular or critical attention at the time—nor has it since. The one reviewer who correctly identified the underlying theme of "the oppression of women" complained that this subject so overwhelmed the book that it left no room for "larger matters" (Blum 119).[49] A book particularly close to Keun's heart (Kreis 198), *D-Zug* offers penetrating psychological portraits, a suspenseful plot, and desperate humor. The novel's brilliant analysis of the abusive relationship of Lenchen and Karl (modeled on Keun and Roth) in particular may be read as disclosing relations between men and women, which, as Ingeborg Bachmann asserted, lie at the roots of fascist domination (Bachmann 144). Writing *D-Zug* in the wake of her months as Joseph Roth's companion, Keun presents an uncommented but ironically tinged and acutely perceptive portrait of a timid young woman who has let herself become engaged—to three men simultaneously—out of fear of hurting someone's feelings or out of sheer passivity and the need to be in a relationship, however damaging or unfulfilling. Keun most likely termed her book "somewhat crazy" not only because of the grotesque, daft figure of Aunt Camilla and the other somewhat eccentric travelers, but also because of the bizarre predicament of the main character. Of course, this situation corresponded fairly closely to her own life because as we now know, she herself had been married to Johannes Tralow, was engaged to Arnold Strauss, and traveling with Joseph Roth at the same time.

The theme of deception of self and others, significant in *Nach Mitternacht* is also developed in the gradually unfolding stories of the seven characters who occupy a third-class compartment in a train traveling from Berlin to Paris. The narrative perspective, a "point of view" or interior monologue that shifts from character to character or group of characters, undermines any notion of a single, unified version of reality and forces the reader to adopt simultaneously a sympathetic identification with the characters and an ironic, critical view of them. As in *Nach Mitternacht,* filmic techniques of flashback and cutting characterize the novel's structure: the time frame consists of a relatively condensed period for the present action itself—the time of the trip from Berlin to Paris, lasting approximately two days and a night—which is interrupted and expanded by the past recollections and life stories of the characters. Again, the setting of the train (or of a train station) is significant—these characters too are in search of "a new life" (*D-Zug* 81), and they hope to exchange a disappointing, entrapping, or terrifying existence for something better. But also typically, the goal of the journey is indistinct; Keun's characters, particularly Lenchen (like Doris, Gilgi, and Sanna), have the "double gaze" that characterizes the perspective of many critical women writers—the structures of the past and present are perceived as "no longer" liveable, yet an alternative is "not yet" in view.[50] "New life meant above all not having the old life anymore" (81).[51]

In the figure of Lenchen Keun, like Marieluise Fleisser and much later Ingeborg Bachmann, presents a woman as she has been "damaged" by patriarchy. Introduced as the passive victim of circumstances with her three unintended fiancés, Lenchen is a tragicomical variation of woman psychologically trained by her society to powerlessness. Reviewer Blum saw in her an exposé of the ideal woman of reactionaries everywhere, in particular of Nazis—"die holde Magd, die weibliche Frau" (the lovely maid, the feminine woman, Blum 120). As a girl Lenchen's imagination has been shaped by romantic images from popular German culture which lead her to fantasize an unreal life filled with dreams of ethereal sentimentality:

> Everything that had to do with flowing gowns was beautiful, mysterious, good and noble. In fairy tales these gowns were worn by elves and good fairies, kings' daughters wore them and lovely brides. . . . Germanic maidens charged into battle in white flowing gowns, and slender ladies of castles stood

> clothed in flowing white at night on balconies to let their golden tresses blow in the wind and to be carried off by bold knights on white steeds. (18–19)[52]

In the real world—Lenchen chooses a career in the theater, where she hopes to live out her fantasies—her lack of a strong self-concept leaves her vulnerable to overwhelming anxiety. "Her life continued to consist of anxiousness. She was afraid of the strange city, afraid of her landlady, afraid of waiters in a restaurant, afraid of her director, afraid of the audience" (25).[53] With no ambition for herself, only the fear of disappointing others, particularly her parents (31), Lenchen has been socialized to please; appearance is more important than the reality of her own desires. She becomes involved with each of her lovers in turn out of weakness, because, as she says of the first, "together with him she wasn't afraid anymore, and was hardly homesick" (26).[54] From Berlin she writes to one man in South America and another in Stuttgart, constantly postponing the marriage dates and half-believing the comforting lies she writes. Not so easily put off is the drinker and bully Karl, who dictates her behavior and thoughts and torments her with mistrust and jealousy. Lenchen dreams of freeing herself from Karl, but again and again reverses herself or is simply unable to act. Her sense of self is not strong enough to oppose Karl's definitions of reality—he berates her for being inferior and immoral—and instead she escapes into sentimental fantasy. Particularly telling is Lenchen's recurrent daydream of a mysterious, comforting stranger and her admission that "she had never been in love with a real man" (103).[55] This fantasy of a strong male protector is the corollary of her narcissistic self-image as a delicate, vulnerable angel in white. And it is part of what chains her to the dominating, abusive Karl. To avoid confrontation or acting on her own feelings, Lenchen constructs an ever more hopelessly entangled web of lies by telling Karl whatever will placate him, and she deceives herself in the process. She becomes so caught up in her imagined stories that she can often no longer sort out truth from fiction, reality from fantasy in her own thoughts. In this, Lenchen shows a striking affinity to the author herself.

The timid Lenchen is a far cry from Keun's earlier spunky protagonists, and the other significant, though virtually silent female figure of the novel, Aunt Camilla, is presented as a grotesque eccentric, an older, caricatured version of the once independent woman of the 1920s. Unmarried, an original inventor and thinker, she is considered to be either crazy (as her family has always believed) or as "at most old-maidish, as very talented, and otherwise as fully normal," by some in the family who are worried by the Nazi theories of inheritance of insanity (70).[56] Her "technical abilities" are presented as absurdly useless: she works feverishly, destroying one thing to create something less valuable. She also writes, plays the piano, draws, and speaks foreign languages, as it were representing all the amateur talents such a modern "bluestocking" might have developed. There seems to be no possibility for her to earn an income; rather she is dependent on her siblings for her livelihood. Camilla does not follow the normal rules of social behavior and polite conversation, dresses in her own fashion and is stubborn. Lenchen does not find her any less "normal" than the rest of the family, simply more honest and direct. But in the Third Reich such a woman, who is "different," whether actually crazy or not, presents a danger to the family as evidence of possible genetic "abnormality" and might be denounced by a hostile neighbor (74). Indeed, she has become increasingly withdrawn and suspicious of others, so that the family decides she must be removed from Germany to a sister in Paris. This figure and Lenchen's relationship to her can be viewed through more than one lens. On the one hand, Camilla's behavior is genuinely bizarre and is presented with a kind of black humor that seduces the reader into finding her comical. On the other hand, she symbolizes victimization by a society that has no place for those who deviate from its narrowly circumscribed norms, here for example those of marriage, submissiveness, and domesticity. In her lack of a husband or even the hint of interest in men, Camilla breaks the patriarchal "rules" of conventional society, particularly in the time of the Third Reich. In this she is, ironically, related to Lenchen, the only relative she can tolerate, for Lenchen, with her three men, has also broken the rules. In spite of herself and precisely through her extreme manifestation of patriarchal socialization, Lenchen has also turned the system of male domination on its head: each of her three fiancés sends money and letters, works and plans in order to make her his "own," and believes in fact she is his own. Lenchen herself, however, lives most truly in the world of her fantasies, and is, with Camilla, both victim and unwitting rebel in her sexist and fascist society.

Like *Nach Mitternacht, D-Zug dritter Klasse* also contains sketches of minor women characters whose stereotypical attributes of meddlesomeness and bossiness cause undeserved suffering to men and to the more acceptable, "feminine" women. In addition to such negative stereotyping, which the narrator appears to exploit as a source of comic effect, there are numerous examples of brutality against women. Here, where a more serious, critical perspective is present, the overall picture is of a society characterized by male violence and female victimization. A young man tells how his mother, along with her children, is tyrannized by his penny-pinching father so that she is forced to lie to cover up small rebellions such as buying a pound of pears for her children: "Thin and small, my mother stood before my tall, dark father. 'Why are you lying?' he asked. 'Because I'm afraid,' said my mother" (107).[57] (Again, the theme of a woman's lying is introduced; here even more clearly than in the case of Lenchen, it is a response of survival by the relatively powerless woman over against the dominant male.) Another character, a fruit-dealer, recalls how he was virtually coerced, while intoxicated, into going to the room of a Berlin prostitute, where he was pressured for ever more money until, in desperation, he threw the woman out the window, as he now believes (91). In this case the narrator steps back from the fruit dealer's rather harsh recollection of the prostitute to comment: "One felt sorry for the fruit dealer, one thought with empathy of his wife and their children, . . . no one thought of the girl who had been thrown out of the window. If the fruit dealer had broken up a sink in the men's room or burned a carpet of his relatives—one would perhaps also have managed a bit of regret for what had been destroyed" (94).[58] The episode is relevant to Lenchen's life; she recalls how Karl had just three days ago thrown a heavy flower jar at her, barely missing her head (101), and fears that she too will be thrown from a window in Paris (95). The fruit dealer carries with him a pack of pornographic pictures, which he proudly displays; Lenchen, who tries to avoid looking at them (as she avoids seeing the reality of her life), cannot help but see one of the pictures: "A naked man was hitting a naked woman, who smiled in a polite and uninvolved way like a sales clerk who was wrapping up some soap for a customer, or a waitress serving a piece of cake" (122).[59]

Thus, in spite of its generally ironic and humorous tone and treatment of the plot, *D-Zug dritter Klasse* shows a world in which ominous undertones of violence, misogyny, and the pornographic image of women are part of everyday reality. It is a world in which the important female characters are stylized as either timid and dependent—"feminine"—or as desexed and eccentric, either caught in a spiral of deception and fantasy, or virtually silenced. Drawn from her personal experiences of a tormented relationship with Joseph Roth and the accompanying strains of her life in exile, this novel captures Keun's pessimistic vision of a woman's existence in Europe under growing Nazi domination.

After completing *D-Zug dritter Klasse,* Irmgard Keun finally visited Arnold Strauss in the United States. Sailing to New York, where she wanted to talk with the American publisher of *Nach Mitternacht,* Blanche Knopf, Keun also saw the authors Ernst Toller and Anton Kuh, and applied for and received a small stipend from the American Guild for Cultural Freedom, an organization which assisted artists in need (Kreis 211, 216). In Virginia Beach, near Norfolk, Virginia, where Arnold had rented a small cottage for her, Keun stayed from mid-May to early August 1938, working on her next book, *Kind aller Länder* (Child of all countries), which was largely based on her life in exile. According to her landlady Keun was thought to be a German spy "because she kept to herself and typed late at night" (Kreis 218). In the exile novel the passages that refer to the America-visit suggest to her biographer that Keun and Arnold Strauss had little left in common (Kreis 219–220), although in her letters to him following her departure she still wrote as the fiancée who planned to return.

Back in Amsterdam, Keun was overwhelmed by the war anxiety now permeating Holland; it seemed clear the Nazis would soon invade the rest of Europe. The ominous political developments further undermined Keun's ability to cope with an increasingly precarious reality. "My little one," she wrote Arnold, "I need you so much. With you I'll quickly get normal and well, as far as that's possible for me. I'll probably never be completely normal" (*Briefe* 249).[60] Recovering from a serious siege of bronchitis, she vowed to give up drinking: "I'm quite clear in this moment and I'm not deceiving either you or myself. I know that with a little outward calm and order there will also be calm and order inside me. Since we've known each other, Arnold, my life has been one giant chaos. And you must believe me: I experience and feel much that has happened and is happening in the world more bitterly and painfully than many other people" (*Briefe* 250).[61] Keun now began serious efforts to return to America. But in a bitterly ironic twist, her desire to rejoin Arnold Strauss now seemed to be hindered by *his* hesitations or faulty judgment; instead of supporting her wish to return quickly on a tourist visa, Arnold instructed her to obtain an immigration visa, a lengthy and uncertain process of waiting for one's number to be included in the quota of immigrants to be admitted by the United States. Because of this strategy, neither Irmgard Keun nor Arnold Strauss's parents, who were now also living in the Netherlands and hoping to emigrate, would leave Europe. In early September 1940, after the Nazis had occupied the Netherlands, Lucy and Arthur Strauss took their own lives, while Keun went underground and returned secretly to her family in Cologne.

Before those events, however, and while she was still making desperate efforts to obtain a visa, Keun managed to finish *Kind aller Länder,* published by Querido in 1938. *D-Zug* was not selling well: "precisely from me people want more 'optimistic' things" (*Briefe* 248).[62] Keun had early been labeled a humorist, and in spite of *D-Zug's* witty analysis of characters and relationships, the underlying hopelessness of the novel apparently did not correspond to her audience's expectations. But her publisher had high hopes that *Kind aller Länder* would be more widely appealing, with its wistful, comical observations of life in exile by the ten-year-old Kully. In fact, this, her sixth novel, was almost as successful as *Nach Mitternacht* had been, and Keun was congratulated by the critic Fritz Erpenbeck not only as an "extraordinary narrative talent," but also as a "master of original composition" (as in Kreis 227).[63]

Reflecting the uprooted situation of the emigré family, Kully's account is more a kaleidoscopic series of recollections and impressions than a development of plot or character, and is convincingly structured according to the associative logic of a child's mind and feelings. The novel evokes a sense of absurd, endless movement without a goal, every arrival soon superseded by a new departure. The narrative largely follows the course of Keun's own travels with Roth, expanded by her journeys, after the break with him, to Nice, Bordighera, and the United States. Kully's father, a writer, has had to leave Germany with his wife Annchen and their daughter because of his criticism of the regime, and now, as Keun and Roth had, he struggles to find the money to keep afloat. His major strategy in this endeavor captures the tragicomical absurdity of his efforts: he has discovered the "pawn value of wife and child" (*Wenn . . .* 144),[64] and repeatedly leaves Kully and her mother virtually hostage in hotels while he criss-crosses Europe concocting futile fantastical schemes to get rich and redeem his family. Kully's father is a kinder, gentler patriarch than the alcoholic Karl of *D-Zug*, but a patriarch nonetheless. He acts with total lack of consideration for his wife's needs or wishes; he is a philanderer who spends his nonexistent money on other women; his speeches and letters are pauseless monologues that reveal no sensitivity to or interest in a partner's possible responses. The father's lengthy monologues also reveal him to be blind about himself and deluded about his feverish schemes for raising money; this man's "optimism," his constant, restless dashing off to new cities, new contacts, new hare-brained ideas from which he predicts success and salvation, seem to be reflex reactions denying the bleakness of his real circumstances. In this he is another manifestation of Keun's theme of self-deception.

The child Kully, like Gilgi, Doris, and Sanna before her, tries to make sense of the world around her, and her puzzled observations from a child's perspective lay bare the paradoxes of adult behavior and arrangements, particularly incomprehensible during this era of disruption and alienation. Such phenomena as laws and regulations, money, borders and visas, and experiences of loss and abandonment, death and decay are the subjects of Kully's earnest musings. In this book the naïve perspective, while preserving the unmasking function of the outsider to adult society, is less critical and rebellious than the narrator-protagonist of *Das Mädchen, mit dem die Kinder nicht verkehren durften,* and Keun suggests rather the dependence of the child in a world of unreliable adults and unpredictable forces. An underlying despair permeates this novel in spite of the witty, ironic satirizing of the author-father and the frequent humor of Kully's naïve point of view. The muted, hopeless sadness of Kully's mother, who longs for a settled home life and the child's repeated experiences of loss give the book a haunting quality. Kully can no longer see or write her Jewish friend in Germany or visit her favorite uncle in Vienna, and even the animals she plays with in lieu of other children confront her with mortality. Kully comes to think that it might be better to be dead and "be happy," as she has been told by adults (42); and when her family has learned of another suicide, she wishes "that people would not even be born at all any more" (126).[65]

While the perspective in this novel is that of a young girl, the voice of the adult woman in *Kind aller Länder* is barely heard. Kully's mother Annchen—the diminutive"-chen" underlines (here as for Lenchen in *D-Zug*) her infantilization—is another passive female, lumped together with her daughter in total dependence on her husband: "My mother and I are a burden to my father, but since he's got us, he wants to keep us" (*Kind* 8).[66] Annchen, separated from her own parents because of her husband's politics, longs for a life in which she might make a home, cook, and care for her family. But her rather bohemian husband cannot tolerate such a settled existence and insists on a life of superfluous luxury, choosing none but the best hotels and restaurants in spite of his lack of money and growing debts. He rebuffs Annchen's occasional efforts to influence his ways, and she falls into a position of silent suffering. Although she and Kully are together much of the time, we seldom hear her speaking, in contrast to the long letters and speeches of the often absent father. In a unique gesture of silent, almost unconscious rebellion, Annchen, unhappy with her husband's decision to take the family to America, manages to become ill and miss the ship on which he and Kully sail. But this reminiscence of the earlier protagonists Gilgi and Doris, who also separate from their men, only underlines the gap between them; while the Weimar women choose, despite an uncertain future, to leave men who have set limits to their individual identities, Annchen simply fails to accompany her husband, in part through his own blundering, and disappears from sight.

In portraying the exile experience, Keun has given primary weight to the perspective of the lonely, thoughtful, and often baffled child; the charming but impossibly unrealistic, irresponsible writer-father takes second place in terms of a realized character and voice. The absence of a strong adult feminine psyche capable of dealing with the difficult circumstances of exile existence or even of struggling to change her life as Lenchen did, seems to represent a further regression in Keun's vision of women's potential in the late 1930s. At the same time the grouping of characters into infantile and dependent females on the one side and the deluded and impractical writer-father on the other may correspond to the divided self of Keun the woman-writer, as projections both of her restlessly nomadic and flamboyant life as a well-known author and of her inner need to be taken care of.

In the months following the completion of *Kind aller Länder* it must have become increasingly difficult for Keun to maintain a reasonable context for writing, although her letters to Arnold Strauss mention a new novel in progress (e.g., 22 July 1939), a manuscript that was apparently never completed or published.

From this period a small number of poems do survive, which are published as *"Gedichte aus der Emigration"* (Poems from exile) in *Wenn wir alle gut wären* (158–165, 263) and in *Briefe* (266–267). These poems testify to the extremity of her situation; in *"Wahnsinn"* (Madness) she writes of approaching insanity: "Softly and wildly it spoke to me. / Defenseless and desiring I pray: let it happen" (*Wenn* . . . 164).[67] Another poem, *"Der Hofnarr"* (The court jester), conveys a sense of growing despair and inability to continue writing in her expected humorous style. The jester has become boring and is dismissed by the king:

> Mitten im strengsten Dienst verlor ein Hofnarr sein Lachen.
> Da gefroren die Tränen in seinen Augen zu Eis vor Schreck,
> Und er konnte nicht mehr schlafen aus Angst zu erwachen. (164)
>
> In the middle of the most demanding service a jester lost his laugh.
> At that the tears in his eyes froze in terror,
> And he could no longer sleep for fear of awakening.

The letters to Arnold Strauss of this last year in exile describe the panic of exiles and other residents of Amsterdam in anticipation of war and a Nazi invasion of Holland; Keun felt herself in constant danger of being turned over to the Germans (*Briefe* 280, 286) and became unbearably anxious: "I am so terribly nervous and irritable that I can hardly bear to be together with other people, simply out of the fear that I'll suddenly begin to scream or go raving mad over some remark" (*Briefe* 287).[68] Unable any longer to cope with the "constant fear for her own and others' lives," Keun now also endured real hunger and insomnia (289–290). She felt her isolation particularly acutely, but precisely in these months Arnold Strauss wrote less often, apparently finally doubting the sincerity of her love. Keun's desperation can be heard through her attempt to reassure him: "I feel nothing but love and longing, and I implore you: Don't leave me alone, please don't leave me alone now, because I won't be able to survive. . . . If I don't hear from you right away or if I can't leave here, I'll die" (early January 1940; *Briefe* 291).[69] In the same period she also wrote her former husband Tralow letters filled with similarly desperate sentiments: "I think constantly of you and have a terrible longing for you! . . . And I'm suffering immeasurably. I don't know how to help myself and others can't help me either" (Kreis 231).[70]

During these last months in exile Irmgard Keun made contact with Arnold's parents, Lucy and Arthur Strauss; their letters to Arnold alternate between delighted accounts of good times together, praise for Irmgard's charming and witty personality, and complaints that she was unreliable and deceptive, an alcoholic chain smoker given to "pathological fibbing" and stealing (*Briefe* 296–299). They report that she had been seen "drunk several times (5x) in the presence of quite ordinary male company" (*Briefe* 299).[71] Arnold's parents, who repeatedly urged him to give up the dream of marrying Irmgard Keun, may well have been motivated partly out of self-interest because they too were dependent on him for their survival; hence their comments must be taken with some caution. Their description of her behavior is probably generally accurate, however, because it corresponds to reports from others who knew her (e.g., Kreis 235). His parents' warnings do seem eventually to have influenced Arnold Strauss, however, who had also met Marjory Ware Spindle, his future bride, in the summer of 1939 (*Briefe* 307). In her last letter to Arnold from Amsterdam, dated 3 March 1940, Keun defended herself against the reproaches, prompted by his parents, that she had fabricated the seriousness of her financial situation and reiterated her desire to be with him. Her loyalty to Europe and its suffering is unchanged, however: "But in my feelings and my imagination and my longing, you're always living here with me" (*Briefe* 293).[72] Stronger than her fear and desperation are her determination to witness, share, and survive the agonies of her culture, "with the last human and animal desire to survive everything, to keep on existing" (*Briefe* 294).[73]

Her strong, elemental survival instinct and love of Europe, together with the desire to return to her mother (as one gathers from her own and Lucy Strauss's letters)—as well as the absence of other options—led Keun to escape from Nazi-occupied Holland by returning to Germany. In a letter to Hermann Kesten written after the war (10 October 1946), Keun describes how she fled from Amsterdam to the Hague, without papers and with almost no belongings: "I had more or less resigned myself to the idea of not staying alive, and was relatively calm. Earlier—when I was still waiting for the catastrophe—I had almost lost my mind with anxiety" (*Wenn . . .* 168).[74] Here she made the acquaintance of a German military police officer whom she claimed to have charmed into helping her obtain papers in the name "Charlotte Tralow" with which she reentered Germany (*Wenn* . . . 168–169, Kreis 231). False reports in the international press that Keun had committed suicide in Amsterdam contributed to the success of this daring act, as well as to her survival underground until the end of the war (Kreis 235).

Keun later recalled the first two years of her "inner emigration" as the most difficult because at that time few Germans doubted an ultimate Nazi victory: "Everything was so disgusting to me that I wasn't even careful any more. I flitted all through Germany" (letter to Hermann Kesten, 10 October 1946; *Wenn* . . . 169).[75] Aided by old friends and supported by her parents, Keun spent time in Bad Godesberg, where she was friends with anti-Nazi doctors, and in Starnberg and Berlin ("Gespräch" 69). Still boldly outspoken, she made no secret of her opposition to the Nazi cause, but apparently did no writing during this time (Kreis 238). In 1943 she and her parents received the news that her only brother Gerd had been killed in Russia, and they themselves later experienced repeated bombing and artillery raids, which finally destroyed the Keuns' two houses in Cologne. "Only in the last year I became afraid of the air raids, and my fear intensified more and more . . . I took Phanodorm constantly in order to be somewhat sleepy and calm" (*Wenn* . . . 170).[76]

Keun had almost euphoric recollections of the first months following the arrival of the American troops, in spite of the hardships: "The first period was magnificent. Somewhat dreadful too" (*Wenn* . . . 171).[77] The American soldiers were friendly and helpful; it seemed like a new beginning: "I liked it. I found even . . . somehow . . . the landscape quite romantic . . . was happy about everyone who was still alive" ("Gespräch" 70).[78] But soon the deprivations of the postwar period, as well as the political climate, caused Keun to complain to her fellow writer Kesten in New York: "I feel so strange and lost here—like back then when I left Germany. Or even worse. I hate being here, and I have only one wish, to be able to get away again" (letter, 10 October 1946, *Wenn* . . . 168).[79] The material conditions of life were miserable: "Nothing to eat. No furniture, no clothes, no sheets or towels. Everything, absolutely everything totally lost. . . . No place to live. My parents so helpless" (*Wenn* . . . 171).[80]

Keun was particularly depressed that writers who had compromised enough to remain in Germany under the Nazis were now resurfacing as the acknowledged literary voices: "I very consciously intend to keep my distance from the literature here" (*Wenn* . . . 175)[81] Her letters to Kesten show a continuing determination to leave Germany in spite of her wish to be near her parents; but bureaucratic regulations of the occupation forces seem to have complicated her efforts (16 April 1947, 23 August 1947, *Wenn* . . . 182, 184). By the spring of 1948 her desire to leave for the United States has a more resigned tone: "I do wish I could come there once" (*Wenn* . . . 191).[82] But her sharp criticism of German society, in particular its intellectuals, persists. In her first letter from October 1946 she had written: "The people in Germany are just as they always were. They're not wearing swastikas on their suits anymore, but otherwise nothing has changed with them" (*Wenn* . . . 173).[83] Scornful of how easily former Nazis now streamed into churches, forgetting or denying their past involvement (16 April 1947, *Wenn* . . . 180), by 1948 Keun sounds even more discouraged: "The others want to forget and fit themselves in again, I will not and cannot forget as long as I live, and I won't fit myself in anywhere here either. . . . I don't want to educate the populace either. If bombs, danger of death, and hunger haven't made them any smarter, then I certainly can't teach them anything" (189).[84]

Nevertheless, in spite of the material deprivations, the discouragement, and alienation, Keun did begin writing again, contributing short satirical pieces to newspapers and to the radio and enjoying initial popular success (e.g., *Wenn* . . . 182). Her topics include such conditions and themes of postwar Germany as the black market, the "shortage of men," and the behavior of former Nazis. In 1947 she published *Bilder und Gedichte aus der Emigration* (Images and poems from exile), the account of her first months in exile with colleagues Roth, Kisch, Kesten, Stefan Zweig, Tucholsky, and poems written during 1929–1940. This volume, expanded by satirical pieces and anecdotes, was reprinted in 1954 as *Wenn wir alle gut wären.* In 1950 Keun published one of the first novels portraying and criticizing postwar society, *Ferdinand, der Mann mit dem freundlichen Herzen* (Ferdinand, the man with the friendly heart), based on episodes she had written for radio broadcast. Here for the first time Keun chose a male narrator-protagonist for a novel, and the explicitly feminine perspective is completely absent. Like his female predecessors in his role as a naïve but perceptive outsider, however, the returning soldier Ferdinand describes a society of black market operators, militarists, profiteers, and superficially "denazified" fascists. The eccentricity of many of the characters and episodes suggests the disjunctures and provisional quality of postwar life up to and immediately following the currency reform of 1948. But the truly trenchant passages of social observation and criticism are too often outweighed by superficial caricature, aimed mostly at women who have "failed" in patriarchal terms and are stereotyped as grasping, domineering, or foolish man-chasers. Although highly praised in Hermann Kesten's foreword, the novel did not bring the critical or popular success of earlier books (Kreis 269).

In the first years of the postwar period, Keun nevertheless had found an enthusiastic audience, insofar as publication possibilities existed. All of her earlier novels were reprinted in Germany, beginning in 1946 (*D-Zug dritter Klasse*), followed by *Gilgi* (1948), *Das Mädchen, mit dem die Kinder nicht verkehren durften* (1949), *Kind aller Länder* (1950), and *Das kunstseidene Mädchen* (1951). It is perhaps typical of the political and cultural climate that Keun's antifascist novel, *Nach Mitternacht,* was republished first in the German Democratic Republic (GDR, 1956), and did not appear in the Federal Republic until 1961, printed by a small progressive press (Fackelträger, Hannover). By contrast, her greatest popular success came with her book of "children's stories," *Das Mädchen, mit dem die Kinder nicht verkehren durften,* which first appeared inside Germany in installments in the *Rheinische Zeitung* of Cologne during the autumn of 1948, after having been read over the former Nordwestdeutscher Rundfunk (NWDR, Northwest German Radio) to tremendous listener response (Roloff 60, n. 61). While this novel is also critical of German social attitudes and institutions, it portrays a more remote period, the end of the First World War, and is more gentle in its social criticism than *Nach Mitternacht* or Keun's other novels. And of course, a book written from the perspective of a child would have been received as particularly appropriate for a woman author.

Although Keun's books were initially reprinted and she began to take up her career again, she did not succeed in making or maintaining connection with contemporary literary developments. The increasing silence of women in her novels was extended to real life: Irmgard Keun published no larger works after *Ferdinand* and nothing new after 1962, the year that *Blühende Neurosen. Flimmerkisten-Blüten* (Blooming neuroses. Cinemablossoms), satires from the world of film, appeared. Eventually Irmgard Keun disappeared from the literary scene; she stopped answering letters, and her whereabouts were unknown to the public and many of her former friends (Krechel 123–124). Not until the mid-1970s was she rediscovered, living in poverty and ill health in an attic room in Bonn. In 1977 Gert Roloff lamented in his excellent early introduction to Keun's life and work that all her books were out of print and without likelihood of republication (Roloff 67).

To some degree Keun no doubt suffered the fate of many authors exiled by the Third Reich: with the hardening of the lines in the cold war in the late 1940s, initial West German interest in exile literature—especially that with a critical perspective—quickly dissipated, and indeed many former emigré(e) writers encountered resentment and bias (Walter 9–15). Thus the bulk of the œuvre Keun produced while in exile was not seriously received or reviewed in Germany until more than thirty years after the end of the war. The discouragement of no longer being part of the higher literary mainstream, the isolation and alienation of living in a repressive political and cultural climate, the early need for money and resulting pressures to meet frequent deadlines all contributed to Keun's diminishing literary productivity. Yet Gabriele Kreis's recent book unveils more fully the personal factors that were also involved in Irmgard Keun's decline as an author some thirty years before her actual death. Chief among them was her heavy use of alcohol over decades, although this cannot be separated from other lifelong problems and conflicting characteristics: recurrent anxieties and depressions on the one hand, bravura and flamboyance on the other; the desire for recognition and a sometimes exaggerated sense of her achievement versus self-doubt and insecurity; a need for freedom yet a strong impulse of dependence on others; the inability to manage money or the practical demands of daily life; finally, the thoroughgoing intermingling of truth and invention that had become second nature to her.

Keun had settled in the bombed out house of her parents in Cologne and lived there for years in a shambles until she finally decided to have it rebuilt in 1962. Her mentor at NWDR (Northwest German Radio) and friend from 1946 to 1949, Lutz Kuessner, recalled how she required alcohol as a stimulus for her writing; how much trouble she had with deadlines; how in spite of her fondness for elegant clothing she had lost all sense of her real appearance and would not notice that her stockings were ripped or her feet unwashed when she went out (Kreis 253, 262, 267). In 1951 Keun filed for financial compensation as one who had been "politically persecuted" under the Nazis; her application, enhanced through what now appear to have been prevarications and exaggerations (e.g., her claims to have been arrested by the Gestapo, and to have refused to join the *Reichsschrifttumskammer*), brought her a one-time settlement of 82,300 Marks. Keun was also highly successful at marketing works she had already sold and earned significant royalties, though she produced little that was new after the early 1950s. For some time she was financially much better off than many, although as always, money slipped through her fingers. In 1951 Keun had given birth to a daughter, Martina; she was a loving mother but erratic in her ability to care for the child, who was often watched by friends, among them Annemarie Böll, wife of author Heinrich Böll. In spite of efforts by friends such as the Bölls to give her a new start, Keun was not able after the early 1950s to produce writing of quality. By the late 1950s her money had dwindled, and she had alienated many former friends and supporters by her difficult, often outrageous behavior under the influence of alcohol (Kreis 269, 283). In 1962 she was committed to the state hospital in Düren for four and a half months, where she was prevented from drinking but otherwise had no special treatment program because alcoholism was not recognized as a disease at the time (Kreis 288). After her release she was determined not to drink any more; but as her money ran out and her debts grew, this wish became one more self-delusion. Finally in 1966 Keun was committed to the state hospital in Bonn, with the diagnosis "Geistesstörung infolge Sucht" (mental derangement because of addiction, Kreis 289). After one year of treatment, she was kept another five years, sharing a room with two schizophrenic patients because there seemed to be no other place for her to go. During this time she did concentration exercises, still hoping to write again, and she was allowed to leave and return to the hospital at will. Released in 1972, Keun lived for one year with a friend in Cologne, then, again thanks to a friend's support, in her own tiny flat in Bonn.

In the final few years of her life, with the more progressive atmosphere of the 1970s and a growing interest in exile literature, Irmgard Keun experienced one more time a brief period of fame. She accepted invitations to read from her works, gave interviews, and saw her books republished, beginning in 1979, by Claassen. *Nach Mitternacht* was made into a film, and in 1981 Keun was named the first recipient of the Marieluise Fleisser Prize of the city of Ingolstadt. But this belated recognition came much too late for Irmgard Keun the writer. Invited to write her autobiography, she chose the title "Kein Anschluss unter dieser Nummer" (This number is no longer in service, literally: no connection under this number), and talked of writing a fictionalized autobiography, or "life novel." Although she claimed to have written pages of manuscript, nothing was ever found (Unger, "Nachwort," *Wenn . . .* 256–257). The title, an image of failed communication, suggests Keun's alienation, her own "inner exile" in the years following the war, and underlines her distance from her own early protagonists, who in spite of their outsider-consciousness were intended to be "One of Us," as her first novel proclaimed. The years of anxiety and excess, suffering and loss, neglect and privation had taken their toll. Irmgard Keun died on 5 May 1982 of a lung tumor, having characteristically defied her doctors' advice that she could lengthen her life by limiting her use of tobacco and alcohol.

A summarizing attempt to assess the overall impact of the Nazi years on the life, career, and reputation of Irmgard Keun must recognize both continuities and disruptions, achievements and losses. Viewed in their entirety, Irmgard Keun's works make up a remarkable chronicle, bearing critical, ironic, and clear-sighted witness to conditions and attitudes of Germany for more than thirty years of its most fateful history. Common to all Keun's writing is her unerring ability to penetrate the façade of propriety and self-righteousness and reveal the underlying motivations of selfish, hypocritical, or self-deluded men and women. Arnold Strauss had written of her in 1934: "Everyone is terribly afraid of this young, deeply insecure and shy creature, because she basically listens to the thoughts, not the words of people and it's very uncanny to get answers to your thoughts instead of your words, especially from a humorist" (*Briefe* 51–52).[85] Keun's unmasking of pretense and delusion often takes the form of demonstrating how sociocultural values shape individual consciousness through the channels of mass media and entertainment. Fragments of popular love songs permeate the pages of *Gilgi.* Doris is inspired by the movie culture of the early 1930s to her dreams of glamor and stardom, and at one point imagines herself on stage; as she acts out this fantasy she becomes totally identified with the image: "I . . . am a stage" (*Das kunstseidene Mädchen* 125).[86] In *Nach Mitternacht* the Nazis as well as the bourgeois intelligentsia are satirized through the metaphor of theater, which lays bare the importance that both placed on appearance. Lenchen's career as a half-hearted actress in *D-Zug dritter Klasse* symbolizes her lack of an authentic self-identity, and she resorts to self-deluding fantasies and lies in a futile effort to compensate for this lack and the vulnerability to psychological domination that results from it.

There was surely a correlation between Keun the acute observer and analyst and Keun the practitioner of this discrepancy between appearance and reality, between imagined fiction and factual truth. As we now see from her letters to Arnold Strauss and from the information uncovered by Gabriele Kreis, Keun herself was a master at exaggerating and fabricating events, and such first-hand experience may have sharpened her ability to recognize and analyze such (self-)deception in others. How aware she was of her own practice of creating preferable alternatives to the "facts" is less clear, particularly at the end of her life. Given to challenging authority and "official" versions of behavior and events from an early age, Keun had always had the spirit and audacity to substitute her own story when it suited her. Often such inventions served a very practical purpose: to make possible her simultaneous relationships with men she wanted or needed, to obtain money from Arnold Strauss, Tralow, her publishers, or government agencies, to survive difficult circumstances. And often, as Kreis's sensitive study suggests, they reflected a more deeply rooted drive to win recognition. Keun was motivated by this need both as woman and as (woman) writer. She persisted in her belief that she was irresistibly attractive to men to the end of her life; if only she had an elegant enough coat, she could "catch any man" (e.g., Kreis 289), and she frequently remarked to Kreis that all the men immediately wanted to marry her (Kreis 112). This often repeated credo of success in the realm of sexual attractiveness found its counterpart in Keun's self-presentation as an author, as when she would inflate her publication data (e.g., Kreis 260) or stage ostentatiously regal appearances as a celebrity, for example during her visits to the GDR (Kreis 285).

But such assertions of success and importance may also be viewed as the paradoxical manifestation of a hidden insecurity, of a never ending struggle against obstacles within and without. Even in her early letters Keun apparently tried to present herself in what she must have believed a more positive light, to counteract real or imagined criticisms. We hear her, for example, reassuring Arnold Strauss how well and successfully she is working and cautioning him not to worry or nag her: "You know, the more people worry about my work, the less well I can work" (9 March 1934; *Briefe* 52–53).[87] Under the pressure of expectations and need, she not only claimed to have written manuscript pages that did not exist but also fabricated reasons why she had not answered a letter sooner (one even suspects this in some of the letters to Kesten, e.g., 11 February 1947, 16 April 1947, *Wenn . . .* 174, 180). Such excuses and exaggerations echo the negative self-image of the "Porträt einer Frau mit schlechten Eigenschaften" (Portrait of a Woman with Bad Qualities), an ironic self-portrait from the early 1950s that suggests both criticism of traits she attributed to herself and a coquettish defense against such criticism. "Sometimes I can't stand myself. . . . Then it's hard to think of a single good thing about me" (*Wenn . . .* 124).[88] In accusing herself of such faults as laziness, cowardice, self-indulgence, enjoyment of pleasures, and insufficient self-discipline, Keun is of course partly making light of the traditional German virtues of hard work, thrift, and self-sacrifice. Yet her self-portrait also acknowledges that she does not live up to such values, including those that might be expected of a writer: "I'm not noble. I don't write books to improve humanity, but to earn money. I can't judge whether I would also write if I did have enough money, since I've never yet had enough money" (124).[89] One is tempted to speculate that Keun had an image of what she should be like, as though still trying to be a "good daughter" or a "good author," an image that she felt she often failed to measure up to and at times may have pressed her to fabricate more "acceptable" versions of her life.

Early in her career Keun had known the split consciousness of a woman attempting to achieve in a male world, a problem exacerbated by her experience under National Socialism and in exile. The early letters to Arnold Strauss indicate her determination to establish herself as a writer in spite of the obstacles presented by the political situation and her own self-doubts. Her judgment of herself could be harsh and reflects the dilemma of the creative female who knows that as a woman she is expected to be modest and limited in her ambitions: "Some faults, which are only human and which I can easily tolerate in others, I hate in myself like the plague. For example vanity and primitive craving for recognition. And self-delusion. . . . I sometimes feel such rage at myself that I could strangle myself" (23 January 1934, *Briefe* 49–50).[90] She chides herself for being "arrogant" in demanding more from herself than from others, and yet has *irrenhausreif Depressionen* (depressions fit for an insane asylum) when she has not accomplished as much work as she expected of herself (*Briefe* 49–50).

Keun's critics and censors may have contributed to such a sense of a divided self. Although she was particularly proud of Kurt Tucholsky's praise of her first novels, it represents the kind of well-meaning but patronizing and limiting labeling a woman author had to expect: "A woman writer with humor, well look at that! . . . If she keeps working, travels, has a major love affair behind her and an average love at her side—: something can come of this woman someday" (Tucholsky 180).[91] It is impossible to imagine a male writer being "praised" in such a way. Such commentary tells an author what is expected of her and sets parameters that define and limit her. Similar messages were conveyed by the censorship Keun encountered under Hitler; not only were her two first novels declared immoral and blacklisted, the more serious short stories and sharper satires she wrote and tried to place before her emigration were not considered "appropriate at the moment" for publication: "Any old ludicrous shit is easier to sell. . . . At most I am allowed to have the humor of a ninety-year-old canoness" (13 June 1934, *Briefe* 73).[92] During her exile Keun did not suffer such direct censorship, but the conservative shift in her female characters suggests that she may nevertheless have been influenced by the misogyny and ideology of traditional roles for women propagated by the Nazis, under whom she had lived for three years. Moreover, her contacts during this period would also have encouraged her to adopt an increasingly "male-identified" perspective. As she later said of the colleagues and artists with whom she associated: "They accepted me as their equal. They were practically only men, you know" ("Gespräch" 62).[93] As a token woman Keun would have been subjected to pressure, consciously or unconsciously, to conform to the attitudes and values of her male colleagues, in particular the views of her lover-companion Joseph Roth.

Deprived of the possibility of continuing her career during the five years between her return to Germany and the end of the war, Keun had to begin over again, amidst discouraging and difficult conditions. During this time the effects of Keun's long and heavy use of alcohol became an increasingly destructive factor, gradually eroding her ability to write. Her anxieties and depressions, the ever-present deadlines for frequent radio broadcasts, the general chaos and material deprivations of the first postwar years—all must have further fueled her impulse to drink, a habit that had plagued Keun at least from the early 1930s when the first meeting with physician Arnold Strauss had been arranged by a mutual friend in the hope that he might help with this problem (*Briefe* 12). In a number of respects Keun's dependence on alcohol can be interpreted as part of her struggle to be both woman and author. As a young woman of the 1920s and 1930s, she would have viewed liberal indulgence in alcohol and cigarettes as a part of her rebellion against conventional middle-class standards, especially for women, and as a sign of equal membership in the predominantly male society of actors, writers and other artists she associated with ("Gespräch" 62). Moreover, both her husband Tralow and her later companion Roth were drinkers (Kreis 113). Keun apparently also needed the stimulus of alcohol to write even early in her career, as her early letters to Arnold indicate; one wonders whether she used it to overcome anxieties or insecurities she may have felt as a relatively naïve, inexperienced author intruding upon traditionally male terrain. Gabriele Kreis suspects Keun may have drunk in order to ward off fear of failure (*Briefe* 12) and later fear of the very success she craved (Kreis 253). The extreme uncertainties and disruptions of her life and career through the Nazi and exile years, largely experienced by Keun as a woman on her own, were further cause for reliance on the transitory relief brought by intoxication. Like her fanciful revisions of uncomfortable, inconvenient or truly painful facts, alcohol could blot out the anguish of an often overwhelming reality.

Like their author, Irmgard Keun's female characters reflect the contradictions experienced by women in patriarchal society. Even Gilgi and Doris, the most emancipated, combine ambition and self-doubt, the desire for independence and the turn to male authority. Their struggles to articulate and communicate their thoughts and feelings, to be taken seriously by the men in their lives, make up a central theme of the novels; in the relatively more open atmosphere of the Weimar Republic women's desire for self-determination and respect could be represented. But even here such ambitions appear unrealizable; Gilgi and Doris must choose between being autonomous human beings and being "women," and both leave their lovers when the impossibility of being both becomes clear. The lack of a recognized place for such women in their society is reflected in the open-endedness with which both protagonists conclude their stories. The young women's original dreams and desires are unmasked as illusory; what remain are rejection of the existing options and uncertainty about the future. The absence of a concrete positive political or personal ideal is seen even more dramatically in the later novels, written under the sway of the Third Reich and its traditionalist prescriptions of women's role. In the novels of Nazi Germany and exile Keun's women defer to men in virtually all respects, and their desires and dreams are increasingly "negative," symbolized by departure from an undesirable context. Sanna actively leaves an oppressive political system behind for the life of an emigrant. Lenchen hopes for a vaguely romantic and liberated "new life" without her previous lover, but she is barely able to act on her constantly retracted decision. Annchen, finally, is not even given the voice to tell us what she wants but disappears from the narrative, too passive either to fight or to leave. Although they give insight into the sexism of the particular contexts they portray, these characters also exemplify, more starkly than in the Weimar novels, the limitedness of prefeminist vision.

The gestures of departure, escape, self-exile—from family, job, lovers, hometown, and country—that recur throughout Keun's novels as a response to oppressive conditions and conflicts permeated her life as well. When asked why she had given up writing and withdrawn from contact with the outside world in the period after the late 1950s, Keun answered that she had been tormented by an obsession to flee: "I always felt as though I were a fugitive. I wanted to get somewhere and I didn't know where I was supposed to go" ("Gespräch" 71).[94] This obsession continued to the end of her life: *"Ich habe immer Fluchtgefühle, immer"* (I always feel the need to escape. Always.). But it was a feeling she had known throughout her life: the desire to "get away" after a certain time. In this compulsion she also claimed to be trying to escape from herself ("Gespräch" 73). Keun's critical view of women, which we might today characterize as "male-identified," thus included a measure of self-hatred. In her "Portrait of a Woman with Bad Qualities" she had written: "with few exceptions I prefer men to women. My reasons for this are many. I myself would not like to be a man; the thought that I would then have to marry a woman terrifies me" (*Wenn . . .* 125).[95] While Keun knew early and clearly that she wanted a career and success as a writer, political and social conditions presented many obstacles to her realization of this goal, particularly as a woman. In the conservative, misogynist atmosphere of the years following the Weimar Republic, the absence of a supportive feminist context and perspective further fostered a divided self-image and lack of clear positive models. The only visible path to self-preservation may have lain in simply breaking out, rejecting the given. "Let me go somewhere else! Nothing holds me down!" ("Gespräch" 73).[96]

NOTES

For helpful information and assistance I wish to thank Dr. Gabriele Kreis, Hamburg; Dr. Uta Biedermann, Stadtbücherei Köln; Historisches Stadtarchiv Köln (Wilhelm Unger Nachlass). For criticism and support I am indebted to Kay Goodman, Renny Harrigan, Barbara Hyams, Peter Ott, Luise F. Pusch, Robert Spaethling, Margaret Ward, Christiane Zehl-Romero. I also wish to thank the Fulbright Commission and the American Council of Learned Societies for their support of this project.

1. All translations from the German are my own, unless otherwise noted. For references to extant English translations of Keun's novels, see list of Works Cited.

2. Krechel 122 notes that we would know nothing of Keun's life during much of her exile were it not for the information gathered for the biography of Austrian author Joseph Roth, her companion for one and one-half years.

3. Irmgard Keun, *Ich lebe in einem wilden Wirbel: Briefe an Arnold Strauss 1933–1947,* selected and edited by Gabriele Kreis and Marjory S. Strauss (Düsseldorf: Claassen, 1988), cited hereafter as *Briefe; "Was man glaubt, gibt es." Das Leben der Irmgard Keun* (Zürich: Arche, 1991), cited hereafter as Kreis.

4. "Ich passte nirgends hin, und es war scheusslich" ("Gespräch mit Klaus Antes" 64, cited hereafter as "Gespräch").

5. For a fuller discussion of the problematics of language in these two novels, see my article " 'Warum habe ich keine Worte?' "

6. "Für intellektuell hielt ich mich damals nicht. . . . [Es] wurde mir oft genug gesagt, . . . dass ich ungewöhnlich intelligent sei. Das fand ich selbst nicht, ich fand mich ganz doof." Undated recorded interview with Wilhelm Unger. Wilhelm Unger Nachlass, Historisches Archiv Köln.

7. "Aber das ist es ja eben, ich habe keine Meinesgleichen, ich gehöre überhaupt nirgends hin." Similarly Gilgi says: "I don't belong anywhere" (Ich . . . gehöre nirgends hin" 124).

8. Indeed, the correspondence among the various offices, including the Gestapo and the RSK, appears to demonstrate rather an effort to be correct in rejecting Keun's claim, which she apparently submitted to courts in several jurisdictions, before assuming that the case was closed (cf. Kreis 155–156).

9. "Zu allem ergaben sich auch noch tägliche Kämpfe mit dem Verlag und immer neue Komplikationen. Ich kann Dir das jetzt nicht erklären. Der Himmel

mag wissen, wie ich aus diesem Schlamassel herauskomme. Ich . . . liebe meine Arbeit mehr als alles auf der Welt. Aber *jetzt* und *hier* arbeiten? . . . Wenn's auf Leistung, Können, Arbeit ankommt, habe ich keine Angst. . . . Aber nur noch mit sinnloser Willkür zu tun haben? Und wie soll ich arbeiten, wenn man mich nicht lässt?"

10. "Ist vielleicht gut so."

11. "Ich habe Zeit und Ruhe—seit langem, langem endlich mal wieder Ruhe (unberufen!!!) . . . Ich kann's ja noch gar nicht glauben, dass ich nun nicht mehr im Nazi-Land bin und wirklich frei schreiben, sprechen, atmen kann."

12. "Manchmal ist meine Arbeit etwas, was sich unabhängig von mir macht und personifiziert—und dann liebe ich sie wie meinen am meisten geliebten Mann, weil sie das einzigste ist, was mir immer raushilft aus allem. . . . Warum hast Du mich nicht mitgenommen? Jetzt komme ich vielleicht nie mehr mit."

13. "Wenn man gut und natürlich schreiben will, kann man nicht leben wie eine artige Gesellschaftsdame—das musst Du nie wollen."

14. "Und dann brauche ich auch Zigaretten und anständigen Alkohol und muss jeden Tag mal in ein Lokal, um zu schreiben. Ich kann nun mal nicht den ganzen Tag zu Haus sitzen—ich brauche immer wieder mal eine veränderte Atmosphäre und so nebenbei was sehen und beobachten können. Wenn ich so ganz und gar das Leben einer Hausfrau führen müsste, würde ich bald matt und kläglich werden. Ist das klar?"

15. "Ich hab' Dich lieb, aber mir liegt ein Dreck dran, Dich zu heiraten. . . . Ich würde mich lieber in einem deutschen Konzentrationslager totprügeln lassen, als mein Dasein dankbar und demütig an Deiner Seite zu Ende zu leben."

16. "Wenn ich einen Bleistift in der Hand habe, *kann* ich einfach nur das schreiben, was mich in der Sekunde des Schreibens angeht.—Ich vergess' dann ganz, dass ich an Dich schreibe."

17. "Mein Kleines, ich habe viel gelitten in dem letzten Jahr und war so dumpf und starr geworden. Jetzt fange ich an, wieder etwas aufzutauen, und ich will Dir immer alles schreiben, damit ich nicht zufriere."

18. "Bilder aus der Emigration," as reprinted in Irmgard Keun, *Wenn wir alle gut wären*, 140, cited hereafter as *Wenn . . .*

19. "Es wird nicht lange dauern, dass ich politisch ziemlich exponiert bin. Du hast Deine Aufgaben als Arzt, ich habe jetzt meine Aufgaben im Kampf gegen den Faschismus."

20. "Es traf so besonders hart, wenn einer von den politischen Schriftstellern Selbstmord beging. Das heisst, in der Emigration und allein schon durch die Tatsache der Emigration war eigentlich jeder Schriftsteller politisch, und jeder Selbstmord bedeutete Kampfaufgabe und Entmutigung in den eigenen Reihen und Triumph und Bestätigung für den Feind."

21. "'Sie sind ein Schriftsteller, Sie haben keine Frau zu sein, sondern ein Soldat.'"

22. "Meistens hat er abends mehr Seiten als ich."

23. "Wenn Du sie kennenlernst, werde ich mich sehr freuen, aber besauf Dich nicht dabei, die beiden trinken wie die Löcher."

24. "Roth und ich . . . waren bald daran gewöhnt, uns immer auf irgend etwas zu verlassen, womit wir gar nicht rechnen konnten. Es kam dann auch immer wieder von irgendwoher Geld—vom Verlag, von einer Zeitung oder durch Auslandsübersetzungen. Richtige Not haben wir nicht gelitten und auch nicht gehungert, damals jedenfalls noch nicht.

Peinliche Momente der Geldverlegenheit gab es dauernd. Da war zum Beispiel das Visum abgelaufen, man musste in ein anderes Land reisen, möglichst im teuren Pullmanzug, weil man da noch am ehesten der Passkontrolle entgehen konnte. Die Hotelrechnung musste bezahlt werden. Geld vom Verlag war erst wieder zu erwarten, wenn man genügend Manuskriptseiten eingeschickt hatte. Man hatte aber nicht genügend Manuskriptseiten. Bein einer Arbeit mit Siedehitze konnte man allenfalls in vierzehn Tagen soweit sein. Das Geld aber brauchte man in spätestens drei Tagen."

25. "Da war ich nun stark engagiert, und da wurde die letzte Zeit in Frankfurt und in Deutschland überhaupt sehr lebendig für mich. Und da konnt' ich alles loswerden, was mich belastet hatte."

26. "Hat die Beklagte . . . bei ihren Veröffentlichungen und sonstigen Meinungsäusserungen ein Verhalten an den Tag gelegt, das für jeden Deutschen eine kaum zu überbietende Pflichtwidrigkeit darstellt."

27. Sautermeister 50. Sautermeister offers a detailed analysis of stylistic and thematic elements of this novel.

28. "Am Opernplatz war ein Getummle von Menschen und Hakenkreuzfahnen und Tannengirlanden und SS-Leuten. Es herrschte ein Durcheinander von aufgeregten Vorbereitungen wie bei einer Weihnachtsbescherung wohlhabender Eltern mit mehreren Kindern."

29. "Und langsam fuhr ein Auto vorbei, darin stand der Führer wie der Prinz Karneval im Karnevalszug. Aber er war nicht so lustig und fröhlich wie der Prinz Karneval und warf auch keine Bonbons und Sträusschen, sondern hob nur eine leere Hand."

30. "Hinter uns sassen elegante Herren und Damen, die benahmen sich still und mit vornehmer Aufmerksamkeit wie in der Loge von einem Theater."

31. "Muss sicher dauernd nachdenken, um einem Volk immer Neuigkeiten vorführen zu können."

32. "Der Führer gibt doch schon allein fast sein ganzes Leben hin, für sein Volk fotografiert zu werden. Man stelle sich nur so eine ungeheure Leistung vor: ununterbrochen sich fotografieren zu lassen mit Kindern und Lieblingshunden, im Freien und in Zimmern—immerzu."

33. "Da standen diese Herrschenden nun persönlich auf dem Balkon des Opernhauses. Sie blieben erleuchtet, sonst wurde Nacht. Die Lichter des Platzes wurden ausgelöscht, damit die Reichswehr zu richtiger Geltung Kommen konnte. Denn die hatte blinkende Stahlhelme auf und brennende Fackeln in den Händen, damit tanzte sie zu militärischen Musikklängen eine Art Ballet. . . .

Die Welt war gross und dunkelblau, die tanzenden Männer waren schwarz und gleichmässig—ohne Gesichter und stumm, in schwarzer Bewegung."

34. "Früher war es immer so gemütlich, wenn zwei Mädchen mal gemeinsam auf die Toilette gingen. Man puderte sich und sprach schnell Wichtiges über Männer und Liebe. . . . Jetzt ist die Politik auch in diese Luft eingedrungen. Gerti sagt: es sei schon viel wert, wenn auf so'ner Toilette keine Toilettenfrau sitze, der man Heil Hitler sagen müsse und dafür noch zehn Pfennig geben."

35. "Der Sinn der Erdschollen besteht darin, dass die Dichter sie besingen müssen, um nicht auf dumme Gedanken zu kommen und nachzudenken, was in den Städten los ist und mit den Menschen."

36. "Eine Maus, die durch Piepsen eine Lawine aufhalten will."

37. "Und immer mehr Menschen strömen herbei, das Gestapo-Zimmer scheint die reinste Wallfahrtstätte. Mütter zeigen ihre Schwiegertöchter an,

Töchter ihre Schwiegerväter, Brüder ihre Schwestern, Schwestern ihre Brüder, Freunde ihre Freunde, Stammtischgenossen ihre Stammtischgenossen, Nachbarn ihre Nachbarn."

38. "Es ist ja schon schwer, immer die Massnahmen einer Behörde für das Geschäftsleben zu kennen . . . und nun muss man auch noch alle Bestimmungen für die Liebe kennen, das ist bestimmt nicht leicht."

39. "In der Halle des Hotels Métropole fand ich ein hübsches, junges Mädchen, blond und blauäugig, in einer weissen Bluse, das lieb lächelte und wie ein Fräulein aussah, mit dem man gleich tanzen gehen möchte." . . . "Naiv und brilliant, . . . und kein Fräulein mehr, mit dem man tanzen gehen wollte, sondern . . . eine Prophetin, die anklagt, . . . ein politischer Mensch."

40. "Der einzige Mann, der mich je gefesselt hat, so dass manches Wort von ihm in meiner Seele Wurzeln schlug."

41. "Frauen mag er nicht und es ist schrecklich deprimierend, wenn er einem die Unzulänglichkeit des weiblichen Geschlechts beweist. Und er hat eine Art zu sprechen, dass ich jedes seiner Worte wie ein Evangelium hinnehme."

42. "Aus mir wollte er etwas machen, was ich nicht war. Oft sagte er mir: 'Eine Frau benimmt sich nicht so.' 'Eine Dame tut sowas nicht.' Mit dem Taxichauffeur durfte ich anstandshalber nicht sprechen. Ein Paket zu tragen, war mir nicht erlaubt. Er wollte aus mir eine ergebene Magd machen, mich zur 'Zartheit' erziehen. Er drängte mich in die Rolle eines bemitleideten Wesens hinein, bis ich selber daran glaubte, er zermürbte mich so, dass ich weinen musste."

43. "Immer mehr in die Enge getrieben." . . . "Gefühl, einer unerträglichen Belastung entronnen zu sein."

44. "Ich muss mich schwächer zeigen, als ich bin, damit er sich stark fühlen und mich lieben kann."

45. "Was ich über das nationalsozialistische Deutschland, so wie ich es kannte, zu schreiben hatte, hatte ich geschrieben. Noch einen Roman konnte ich nicht darüber schreiben. Von nun an kannte ich es ja auch nicht mehr aus eigenem Erleben."

46. See also Sylvia M. Patsch 304–306.

47. "Alle diese Erwägungen wurden so beklemmend, dass ich fürchtete, nie in meinem Leben mehr ein Buch schreiben zu können."

48. "Mein neues Buch ist besser und schöner als alle anderen, Du wirst es sehr lieben. Es ist nur etwas verrückt."

49. "Die Unterdrückung der Frau," . . . "grössere Dinge."

50. Sigrid Weigel first developed these concepts in her essay "Der schielende Blick" 105, and Monika Shafi has applied them to Keun's *Das kunstseidene Mädchen* 324.

51. "Neues Leben hiess vor allem, kein altes Leben mehr haben."

52. "Alles, was mit wallenden Gerwändern zu tun hatte, war schön, geheimnisvoll, gut und edel. In Märchen wurden diese Gewänder von Elfen und gütigen Feen getragen, Königstöchter trugen sie und liebliche Bräute. . . . Germanenjungfrauen zogen mit weissen, wallenden Gewändern in die Schlacht, und schlanke Burgfräulein standen weisswallend gekleidet nächtlich auf Altanen, um goldene Locken im Winde wehen zu lassen und von kühnen Rittern auf weissen Zeltern entführt zu werden."

53. "Ihr Leben bestand auch weiterhin aus Angst. Sie hatte Angst vor der fremden Stadt, Angst vor der Zimmerwirtin, Angst vor Kellnern im Restaurant, Angst vor dem Regisseur, Angst vor dem Publikum."

54. "Mit ihm zusammen hatte sie keine Angst mehr und kaum noch Heimweh."

55. "In einen wirklichen Mann war sie nie verliebt gewesen."

56. "Allenfalls . . . etwas altjüngferlich . . . sehr begabt und im übrigen . . . vollkommen normal."

57. "Dünn und klein stand meine Mutter vor meinem grossen, schwarzen Vater. 'Warum lügst du?' fragte er. 'Weil ich Angst habe,' sagte meine Mutter."

58. "Man fühlte Mitleid mit dem Früchtehändler, man gedachte mit Teilnahme der Frau und ihrer Kinder, . . . an das aus dem Fenster geworfene Mädchen dachte niemand. Hätte der Früchtehändler auf einer Herrentoilette ein Waschbecken zertrümmert oder bei seinen Verwandten einen Teppich verbrannt—man hätte vielleicht auch ein wenig Bedauern für das Zerstörte aufgebracht."

59. "Ein nackter Mann schlug eine nackte Frau, die dazu höflich und unbeteiligt lächelte wie eine Verkäuferin, die einem Kunden Seife einpackt oder wie ein Servierfräulein, das einem Gast Kuchen hinstellt."

60. "Mein Kleines, ich brauche Dich so sehr. Bei Dir werde ich schnell normal und gesund sein, soweit das bei mir möglich ist. So vollkommen normal werde ich wohl nie werden."

66. "Ich bin ganz klar in diesem Augenblick und lüge weder Dir noch mir selbst etwas vor. Ich weiss, dass bei ein wenig äusserer Ruhe und Ordnung auch in mir selbst Ruhe und Ordnung sein wird. Seit wir uns kennen, Arnold, war doch mein Leben eine einzige grosse Wirrnis. Und Du musst mir glauben: Vieles, was auf der Welt geschah und geschieht, erlebe und fühle ich bitterer und schmerzhafter als viele andere Menschen."

62. "Gerade von mir wollen die Leute 'optimistischere' Sachen."

63. "Aussergewöhnliches Erzählertalent . . . Meister origineller Komposition."

64. "Des Versatzwertes von Frau und Kind."

65. "Dass Menschen gar nicht mehr erst geboren werden."

66. "Meine Mutter und ich sind meinem Vater eine Last, aber da er uns nun mal hat, will er uns auch behalten."

67. "Sanft und wild hat er zu mir gesprochen. / Wehrlos und begehrlich bete ich: es sei."

68. "Ich bin überhaupt so wahnsinnig nervös und gereizt, dass ich ein Zusammensein mit Menschen kaum noch ertrage, einfach aus Angst, dass ich plötzlich anfange zu schreien oder über irgendeine Bemerkung tobsüchtig werde."

69. "Ich fühle nichts als Liebe und Sehnsucht, und ich flehe Dich an: Lass mich nicht allein, lass mich jetzt bitte nicht allein, weil ich es sonst nicht mehr aushalte. . . . Wenn ich nicht sofort von Dir höre oder vorher fortkann, sterbe ich."

70. "Ich denke dauernd an Dich und habe schreckliche Sehnsucht nach Dir! . . . und ich leide masslos. Ich weiss mir nicht mehr zu helfen, und andere können mir auch nicht helfen."

71. "Mehrmals (5x) betrunken in ganz gewöhnlicher Männergesellschaft."

72. "Aber mit meinem Gefühl und in meiner Phantasie und in meiner Sehnsucht lebst Du immer hier mit mir."

73. "Mit der letzten menschlichen und tierischen Lust, alles zu überleben, bestehen zu bleiben."

74. "Ich hatte mich so ziemlich damit abgefunden, nicht am Leben bleiben zu können, und war verhältnismässig ruhig. Vorher—als ich noch auf die Katastrophe wartete—war ich vor Angst fast verrückt geworden."

75. "Mir war alles dermassen ekelhaft, dass ich schon gar nicht mehr vorsichtig war. Ich sauste kreuz und quer durch Deutschland."

76. "Erst im letzten Jahr hatte ich Angst vor den Fliegerangriffen, und die Angst steigerte sich immer mehr. . . . Ich habe ununterbrochen Phanodorm gegessen, um etwas schläfrig und ruhig zu sein."

77. "Die erste Zeit war herrlich. Etwas grauenhaft auch."

78. "Mir hat's gefallen. Ich fand sogar . . . irgendwie . . . die Landschaft recht romantisch . . . freute mich über jeden, der noch lebte."

79. "Hier fühle ich mich so fremd und verloren—so wie damals, als ich aus Deutschland ging. Oder noch schlimmer. Ich hasse es, hier zu sein, und ich habe nur den einen Wunsch, wieder fort zu können."

80. "Nichts zu essen. Keine Möbel, keine Kleider, keine Wäsche. Alles aber auch alles restlos verloren. . . . Keine Wohnung. Die Eltern so hilflos."

81. "Von der Literatur hier will ich ganz bewusst abgesondert bleiben."

82. "Ich wünschte doch, ich könnte einmal nach dort kommen."

83. "Die Menschen in Deutschland sind genau wie sie immer waren. Sie tragen keine Hakenkreuze mehr am Anzug, aber sonst hat sich nichts mit ihnen geändert."

84. "Die andern wollen vergessen und sich wieder einordnen. Ich will und kann nicht vergessen solange ich lebe, und ich will mich hier auch nirgends einordnen. . . . Ich will auch das Volk nicht erziehen. Wen Bomben, Todesnot und Hunger nicht klüger gemacht haben, dem kann auch ich nichts beibringen."

85. "Alle haben eine schreckliche Angst vor diesem jungen, im Tiefsten unsicheren und scheuen Geschöpf, weil sie im Grunde nicht den Worten, sondern den Gedanken der Menschen lauscht und es sehr unheimlich ist, auf seine Gedanken statt auf seine Worte Antworten zu bekommen, zumal von einer Humoristin."

86. "Ich bin eine Bühne."

87. "Weisst Du, je mehr man sich um meine Arbeit kümmert, um so weniger kann ich arbeiten."

88. "Zuweilen kann ich mich nicht leiden. . . . Es fällt mir dann schwer, noch irgendein gutes Haar an mir zu finden."

89. "Ich bin nicht edel. Bücher schreib'ich nicht, um die Menschen zu verbessern, sondern um Geld zu verdienen. Ob ich auch dann schreiben würde, wenn ich genug Gelde hätte, kann ich nicht beurteilen, da ich noch nie genug Geld gehabt habe."

90. "Manche Fehler, die allgemein menschlich sind und die ich an anderen gern toleriere, hasse ich an mir wie die Pest. So zum Beispiel Eitelkeit und primitive Geltungssucht. Und Selbstbelügen. . . . Ich habe manchmal eine solche Wut auf mich, dass ich mir selber den Hals zuwürgen könnte."

91. "Eine schreibende Frau mit Humor, sieh mal an! . . . Wenn die noch arbeitet, reist, eine grosse Liebe hinter sich und eine mittlere bei sich hat—: aus dieser Frau kann einmal etwas werden."

92. "Momentan . . . nicht genehm. Irgendeine neckische Schleisse ist leichter loszuwerden. . . . Allenfalls ist mir der Humor einer 90jährigen Stiftsdame gestattet."

93. "Die nahmen mich ja auf als ihresgleichen. Es waren ja fast nur Männer."

94. "Ich fühlte mich immer wie auf der Flucht. Ich wollte irgendwohin und wusste nicht, wohin ich sollte."

95. "Hab' ich, von wenigen Ausnahmen abgesehen, Männer lieber als Frauen. Meine Gründe dafür sind mannigfaltig. Ich selbst möchte kein Mann sein; der Gedanke, dann eine Frau heiraten zu müssen, schreckt mich."

96. "Woanders hin! Mich hält nichts fest!"

WORKS CITED

Bachmann, Ingeborg. *Wir müssen wahre Sätze finden. Gespräche und Interviews.* Ed. Christine Koschel and Inge von Weidenbaum. Munich and Zurich: Piper, 1983.

Ball, Kurt Herwarth. (Review of *Das kunstseidene Mädchen.*) *Der Hammer* 31 (1932):251.

Berglund, Gisela. *Deutsche Opposition gegen Hitler in Presse und Roman des Exils. Eine Darstellung und Vergleich mit der historischen Wirklichkeit.* Stockholm: Almqvist & Wiksell, 1972. (Stockholmer germanistische Forschungen 11). 215–221.

Blum, Klara. "Irmgard Keun." *Internationale Literatur. Deutsche Blätter.* 9. Jg., Heft 6 (1939). (Reviews of *Nach Mitternacht, D-Zug dritter Klasse, Kind aller Länder.*)

Brentano, Bernhard. "Keine von uns. Ein Wort an die Leser des *Vorwärts.*" *Die Linkskurve* 4/10 (1932): 27–28. (Review of *Gilgi.*)

Brinker-Gabler, Gisela, ed. *Deutsche Literatur von Frauen.* Vol. 2. Munich: Beck, 1988.

Bronsen, David. *Joseph Roth. Eine Biographie.* Cologne: Kiepenhauer & Witsch, 1974. Reprint. Munich: Deutscher Taschenbuch Verlag, 1981 (dtv 1630).

Erpenbeck, Fritz. "Eine Frau tritt in die Front. Zu Irmgard Keuns Roman: *Nach Mitternacht.*" *Internationale Literatur. Deutsche Blätter.* 7. Jg. Heft 6(1937): 139–142. (Review of *Nach Mitternacht.*)

———. "Manchmal habe ich Heimweh." *Das Wort.* 4. Jg., Heft 3 (1939). (Review of *Kind aller Länder.*)

Horsley, Ritta Jo. "Irmgard Keun." *Dictionary of Literary Biography.* In Vol. 69: *Contemporary German Prose Fiction: 1945 to the Present,* ed. Wolfgang D. Elfe and James Hardin. Detroit: Gale Research, 1988. 182–188.

———. "'Warum habe ich keine Worte? . . . Kein Wort trifft zutiefst hinein.' The Problematics of Language in the Early Novels of Irmgard Keun." *Colloquia Germanica* 23, 3–4 (1990): 297–313.

Jelinek, Elfriede. "'Weil sie heimlich weinen muss, lacht sie über Zeitgenossen.' Über Irmgard Keun." *die horen* 25 (Winter 1980): 221–225.

Kesten, Hermann. "Irmgard Keun." In his *Meine Freunde, die Poeten.* Munich: Desch, 1959. 423–434.

Keun, Irmgard. *Gilgi, eine von uns.* Berlin: Universitas, 1931. Reprint. Bergisch Gladbach: Lübbe, 1981 (Bastei-Lübbe Taschenbuch).

———. *Das kunstseidene Mädchen.* Berlin: Universitas, 1932. Reprint. Bergisch Gladbach: Lübbe, 1980 (Bastei-Lübbe Taschenbuch). Trans. by Basil Creighton as *The Artificial Silk Girl.* London: Chatto, 1933.

———. *Das Mädchen, mit dem die Kinder nicht verkehren durften.* Amsterdam: de Lange, 1936. Reprint. Bergisch Gladbach: Lübbe, 1981 (Bastei-Lübbe Taschenbuch). Trans. by Leila Berg and Ruth Baer as *The Bad Example.* New York: Harcourt, 1955.

———. *Nach Mitternacht.* Amsterdam: Querido. 1937. Reprint. Bergisch Gladbach: Lübbe, 1981 (Bastei-Lübbe Taschenbuch). Trans. as *After Midnight.* Trans. Anthea Bell. London: Gollancz, 1985. Trans. James Cleugh. New York: Knopf, 1938.

———. *D-Zug dritter Klasse.* Amsterdam: Querido, 1938. Reprint. Bergisch Gladbach: Lübbe, 1984 (Bastei-Lübbe Taschenbuch).

———. *Kind aller Länder.* Amsterdam: Querido, 1938. Reprint. Bergisch Gladbach: Lübbe, 1983 (Bastei-Lübbe Taschenbuch).

———. *Ferdinand, der Mann mit dem freundlichen Herzen.* Düsseldorf: Droste, 1950. Reprint. Bergisch Gladbach: Lübbe, 1982 (Bastei-Lübbe Taschenbuch).

———. *Wenn wir alle gut wären: Kleine Begebenheiten, Erinnerungen und Geschichten.* Düsseldorf: Fladung, 1954. Revised and enlarged edition. Ed. and with a "Nachwort" by Wilhelm Unger. Cologne: Kiepenhauer & Witsch, 1983.

———. "Woanders hin! Mich hält nichts fest': Irmgard Keun im Gesprächt mit Klaus Antes." *die horen* 27 (Spring 1982): 61–75. Cited in text as "Gespräch."

———. *Ich lebe in einem wilden Wirbel: Briefe an Arnold Strauss 1933–1947.* Selected and edited by Gabriele Kreis and Marjory S. Strauss. Düssseldorf: Claassen, 1988. Cited in text as *Briefe.*

Krechel, Ursula. "Irmgard Keun: die Zerstörung der kalten Ordnung. Auch ein Versuch über das Vergessen weiblicher Kulturleistungen." *Literaturmagazin* 10 (1979): 103–128.

Kreis, Gabriele. *"Was man glaubt, gibt es." Das Leben der Irmgard Keun.* Zurich: Arche, 1991.

Mann, Klaus. "Deutsche Wirklichkeit." *Die Neue Weltbühne.* 17 (1937): 526–528. (Review of *Nach Mitternacht.*)

Patsch, Sylvia M. "'Und alles ist hier fremd.' Schreiben im Exil." In *Deutsche Literatur von Frauen.* Vol. 2, ed. Gisela Brinker-Gabler. Munich: Beck, 1988, 304–317.

Ritchie, J. M. *German Literature under National Socialism.* London & Canberra: Croom Helm; Totowa, N.J.: Barnes & Noble, 1983.

Roloff, Gerd. "Irmgard Keun—Vorläufiges zu Leben und Werk." *Amsterdamer Beiträge zur neueren Germanistik* 6 (1977): 45–68.

Sautermeister, Gert. "Irmgard Keuns Exilroman *Nach Mitternacht." die horen* 27 (Spring 1982): 48–60.

Serke, Jürgen. "Irmgard Keun." *Die verbrannten Dichter.* Weinheim: Beltz and Gelberg, 1977. 162–175.

Shafi, Monika. "'Aber das ist es ja eben, ich habe ja keine Meinesgleichen.' Identitätsprozess und Zeitgeschichte in dem Roman *Das kunstseidene Mädchen* von Irmgard Keun." *Colloquia Germanica* 21 (1988): 314–325.

Soltau, Heide. "Die Anstrengungen des Aufbruchs. Romanautorinnen und ihre

Heldinnen in der Weimarer Zeit." In *Deutsche Literatur von Frauen,* ed. Gisela Brinker-Gabler. Vol. 2. Munich: Beck, 1988. 220–235.

Steinbach, Dietrich. "Irmgard Keun." *Kritisches Lexikon zur deutschsprachigen Gegenwartsliteratur.* (Munich: edition text und kritik, 1985). 19. Nachlieferung (19th Supplement).

Stephan, Alexander. *Die deutsche Exilliteratur 1933–1945. Eine Einführung.* Munich: Beck, 1979.

Tucholsky, Kurt ("Peter Panter"). "Auf dem Nachttisch." *Die Weltbühne* 28, 5 (1932): 180. (Review of *Gilgi.*)

Walter, Hans-Albert. *Bedrohung und Verfolgung bis 1933. Deutsche Exilliteratur 1933–1950.* Vol. 1. Darmstadt und Neuwied: Luchterhand, 1972. (Sammlung Luchterhand 76).

Weigel, Sigrid. "Der schielende Blick: Thesen zur Geschichte weiblicher Schreibpraxis." In *Die verborgene Frau,* ed. Inge Stephan and Sigrid Weigel. Berlin: Argument, 1983, 83–137.

OLGA ELAINE ROJER

From German Journalist to Argentine Exile: Doris Dauber and the Nazi Years

Of the estimated 500,000 exiles who fled Germany, Austria, and Czechoslovakia between 1933 and 1941, well over 100,000 settled on the Latin American continent.[1] The Republic of Argentina received the largest number of German-speaking exiles, an estimated 45,000 to 50,000, among whom were several dozen exiled authors, journalists, and publishers.[2] These literary exiles emigrated with hopes of political and artistic freedom, but in Argentina they found not only circumscribed freedoms but also the realities of poverty, discrimination, and alienation. For most writers in exile, their new lives in Argentina were marked by artistic stagnation, a limited audience, and little financial reward. In 1940, however, the fate of the German exile writer improved with the founding of a German-language publishing house in the Argentine capital of Buenos Aires, where most had settled. From 1940 to 1945, the Editorial Cosmopolita published some twenty works by German-speaking authors living in Argentine exile. Noteworthy among Cosmopolita's publications is an autobiography written by the German journalist and socialist Doris Dauber who fled to Argentina from Nazi Germany in 1933.[3] Unlike many other autobiographical writings by exiles, Dauber's personal narrative provides not only a woman's perspective of events but also a reflection of the economic and political peripeteia of a socialist's life.

Women's autobiographies have often been dismissed as unimportant and nonliterary,[4] and indeed Dauber's *Eine Nacht-Ein Leben* (One night-one life, 1945) was initially turned down by the director of the publishing house who feared that few people would want to read the life story of an unknown woman. It is fortunate that the work was ultimately published at the insistence of a prominent local German exile, who argued in favor of Dauber's story. Fellow socialist August Siemsen stressed the fact that human experience is gendered and that the personal narrative of a female exile, even if unknown, is essential and should not be ignored.[5]

Eine Nacht-Ein Leben remains one of the few surviving documents to describe the experiences of an independent, educated, politically active, single woman in Nazi Germany and Argentine exile. The publication also documents Nazi government policies regarding women's rights, or rather, lack thereof, in the Third Reich. When Hitler came to power in 1933 and implemented his one-party state, the *Weltanschauung* toward the role of women became one of "childbearers of a nation" (Stephenson 6). In the Nazi view, as Jill Stephenson describes in *Women in Nazi Society*, the main difference between men and women was that "man was essentially productive, and woman fundamentally reproductive" (8). In the same view, "man was creative, while woman was imitative" (8). According to Nazi philosophy, a woman should exhibit her "natural" qualities of sympathy and self-sacrifice and should shed the "unnatural" ones of independence, intelligence, or competitiveness (9). As an educated, single, independent woman, with left-wing political leanings, Dauber was anathema to the Nazis. As a committed socialist and ardent defender of women's rights in Nazi Germany, she became an enemy and threat to the state. Actions by the Nazis toward members of the radical left, communists, and socialists (the so-called "political criminals") were fierce and included incarceration, at times even the death penalty (Röder xxix). When an official warrant was issued for Dauber's arrest in 1933, she fled Germany. Dauber's remarkable odyssey as recounted in her personal narrative is the focus of this essay.

Doris Dauber arrived in Buenos Aires in 1935 after a hazardous flight through France, England, and Ireland. If Dauber, a progressive journalist and ardent socialist, had hoped to continue her long-established fight against the Nazis from this country of refuge, she was disappointed. Argentina's Prussian-trained military government, increasingly fascist after 1930, did not welcome the exiles. In fact, the government's unmistakable pro-Nazi stance prompted Hitler to select this country as the center of his South American foreign policy. Early on Argentina became the main artery for Nazi political activity throughout the continent (Kannapin 81). For all arriving exiles, Argentina presented a supreme challenge, but Germany's political exiles in particular faced tremendous hardships, provoked largely by local Nazi sympathizers and pro-Nazi native elements.

"Life is difficult for the Argentine woman," writes Dauber in a postexile publication *Als ich drei Berufe hatte. Argentinien wie es wirklich ist. Eine Reportage* (When I had three jobs. Argentina as it truly is. A Report, 1950).[6] She continues: "But it is even more difficult for the female immigrant, especially the political immigrant, who finds herself in a constant battle with authorities" (106).[7] A confrontation with local authorities almost led to her deportation. She recalls: "Because of a clash with the Argentine political police in the year 1936 I was unwelcome in Argentina. I was considered an annoying foreigner. Back then, my deportation by Argentine authorities was postponed although not totally ruled out." She adds with subtle irony: "I was aware of my importance after seeing thick official files on the subject. There was no doubt about it, they did not want me in Argentina" (112).[8] Dauber's statement was no exaggeration. Argentina's political history from 1930 to 1945 was one of chaos and confusion. A military coup d'état, staged by factions of the Argentine military on 6 September 1930, not only had resulted in a government that discarded the Argentine tradition of military abstention from politics but also had left the army to rule supreme. Any semblance of democracy was lost in subsequent years. The ensuing political climate prompted a German political exile to caution fellow refugees: "As an immigrant, the best thing to do is to be silent" (Olden 78).[9]

As an experienced journalist, Dauber obtained a position as an editor at the *Argentinisches Tageblatt,* the only established democratic German-language newspaper in Buenos Aires. The job did not, however, last. Although the reasons for Dauber's departure are not clear, she alludes to them in *Als ich drei Berufe hatte:* "My professional life began with a stroke of luck. I found a position as editor at the anti-fascist German-language newspaper. But after a year I no longer pleased the editor-in-chief, he did not please me either, and I had to leave" (106).[10]

From its inception, the *Argentinisches Tageblatt*, founded in 1889 by the Swiss Alemann family, enjoyed widespread popularity in Argentina and on the entire Latin American continent. During the 1930s in particular, this daily newspaper became a pillar of moral support for exiles and anti-Nazis.[11] Despite its solid reputation, the paper's political stance at times triggered criticism from political exiles. Socialist circles, in particular, criticized the paper's conservative stance and its business orientation. As one socialist exile complained:

> Although this newspaper was consistently antifascist, in it one could find little socialism. . . . Socialists had a difficult time with Alemann. . . . His main interest was in the business aspect of the newspaper. For him the newspaper existed mainly for business reasons. Had business gone well, only then could one talk politics with him. (Mittenzwei 71)[12]

Shared political convictions undoubtedly facilitated cooperation with Alemann, a fact that may have contributed to the departure of the ardent and outspoken socialist Dauber.

The loss of her job at the *Argentinisches Tageblatt* brought Dauber many difficulties. Although financially dependent upon her writing, she found it almost impossible to get published in her native language. The local political climate impeded not only political activity by left-wing foreign nationals but literary output as well. By the late 1930s a number of laws in Buenos Aires severely restricted writing activities. Censorship activities increased even more dramatically at the onset of World War II, when the Argentine government, in an effort to secure a continued appearance of neutrality, sharpened its control. Dauber's poignant articles, political and strongly critical in tone, often faced censorship. She recalls: "My articles were popular and published often. But if I dared to express my opinion about fascist actions by the Germans, the Argentine government immediately issued a ban on my writing" (*Als ich drei Berufe hatte*, 109).[13]

Increased censorship was not the only problem facing the literary exile. Prospects for German-speaking writers, regardless of their political conviction, were dim. Publishing possibilities in the exile's native language were few. The half dozen German-language exile journals that appeared in Buenos Aires during the late 1930s were mainly oriented toward politics, not literature, and they struggled under severe financial difficulties. They offered only limited opportunity for contributions; fees were minimal. Publishing in the local Spanish-language press required a thorough knowledge of Spanish, which few exiles possessed. Only the *Argentinisches Tageblatt* offered the exiles a true outlet for their writings, so Dauber's sudden departure from the paper eliminated this possibility for her.

Faced with increasing difficulties earning a living as an independent writer, Dauber was forced to seek other income. In *Als ich drei Berufe hatte,* she describes how she would rush between part-time jobs, ranging from translator to nightwatchwoman in a mental institution, to make ends meet. No easy feat as she recalls: "With the earnings of these . . . jobs . . . I could not live luxuriously. I barely earned enough to pay for an inferior, second-class half-board" (109).[14]

As a committed socialist, aware of the worker's rights in the workplace, Dauber often clashed with Argentine employers on the issue of employee benefits. Indignant after being fired because of her insistence on obtaining health benefits, Dauber angrily criticizes the Argentine workplace:

> When working in a factory, you experience for yourself, what it means, that there is no legislation concerning health and labor. . . . If you should have the misfortune of getting sick or being in poor health, then you are lost . . . not a penny is obtained by the ailing person. Health insurance, which would pay for physician and pharmacy bills, health benefits, with which one could survive, there is no such thing in Argentina. . . . I took a job as librarian in a chemical-pharmaceutical factory. . . . I lost this job, because I wanted paid sick leave. (*Als ich drei Berufe hatte.* 72, 75, 106)[15]

Dauber's ardent fight in the 1930s for health and employee benefits was well ahead of its time, for these issues would not receive major attention until the presidency (1946–1955) of Juan Domingo Perón.

Despite increased frustration with her plight in exile and growing mental and physical exhaustion, Dauber nonetheless succeeded in writing an autobiography. *Eine Nacht-Ein Leben* was published in 1945 by the Editorial Cosmopolita, and it stands out among the works published by Cosmopolita between 1940 and 1945.[16] The reasons for its unique status are discussed at length later in the essay.

The Freie Deutsche Buchverlag or Editorial Cosmopolita, as it was soon renamed, was founded in Buenos Aires in 1940. Under the directorship of James I. Friedmann, a Jewish refugee and former bookseller and publisher from Berlin, Cosmopolita published some twenty works by authors living in Argentine exile.[17] Cosmopolita's production was comprehensive; it encompassed anti-fascist novels, a poetry collection, a political treatise, and works written for entertainment. A total absence of any German publications in a dried-up Argentine market necessitated, according to Friedmann, this diversity of material. "The publishing activities during this period, should therefore not be judged solely from a literary standpoint," (Muttersprache 233)[18] Friedmann hastens to caution the reader (Friedmann was referring here to the fact that, with the outbreak of the war on the European continent in the late 1930s, local book supplies were depleted.)

Prose in general, and novels in particular, were Cosmopolita's most popular literary genre. Although written in exile, few of the published works could be classified as novels *of* exile—that is, novels in which the authors turn to the exile experience for their creative material. Few authors treated the condition of exile in their fictional works. Many preferred to reserve the rather personal account of life in exile for what were then considered the bona fide literary genres, such as the autobiography and memoir. Others worried about the element of appeal: novels dealing with the problems and hardships of life in exile stood little chance of being sold. Still others found it difficult to deal with their present situation and host environment in their works. Instead, there was a preoccupation with the immediate past. Authors attempted to come to terms with the complex events that had led to exile. Evidently it was only after arriving at an understanding of these events, that the author could begin to examine her/his present host environment. A characteristic feature therefore of Cosmopolita's novels is their concentration on the events that led to exile. Authors restricted themselves to scenes set in Nazi Germany or Austria, where Jewish destinies were portrayed and Nazi and Austrian politics studied (Kamla 1–6).

The novels published by the Editorial Cosmopolita differed little from one another in style, theme, or political viewpoint and were, with one or two exceptions, of minimal literary quality. Being rather self-conscious collections of episodes, the novels often lacked internal cohesion. In many, the action was melodramatic. In others, simple stories were augmented with components reminiscent of trivial literature, such as episodes of pursuit and long-winded, unessential discussions about individualism and politics. In still others the author's personal experiences got in the way and reduced objectivity (Strelka 26). "Objectivity is a luxury you cannot afford when you are starving; when you cannot find a function, cannot find a Raison d'être in a country," lamented a German exile author (Müssener 50).[19] Willful subjectivity was unmistakable in most of Cosmopolita's publications. In sum, the exile authors connected with the publishing house generally failed as novelists. Because it exceeds the scope of this essay to expound on the many reasons why the authors failed at writing quality literature in exile, suffice it to say that numerous factors, including unsettled and unsettling working conditions combined with emotional, psychological, financial, even linguistic difficulties, were largely to blame. To blame also was Cosmopolita's primary aim as a commercial venture striving for sales success. Commercially oriented publication choices did not necessarily promote quality literature; neither did the fact that almost all the authors published by Cosmopolita were literary beginners (Rojer 197). With this in mind, it is all the more remarkable that among the twenty works published by Cosmopolita, the only two deserving of mention are written by women: Doris Dauber's *Eine Nacht-Ein Leben* and Livia Neumann's *Puerto Nuevo-Neuer Hafen* (New Harbor 1943).[20]

The exile authors Dauber and Neumann, of German and Austro-Hungarian descent respectively, shared remarkably similar backgrounds. Both received a university education, which, as mentioned earlier, in itself was unusual: Dauber had a Ph.D. in literature, philosophy, and history, and Neumann had training in psychology. Both were former journalists as well. Dauber had worked for, among other papers, the *Frankfurter Zeitung* and Neumann for several Viennese dailies among them the *Neuer Wiener Journal,* where she wrote a column entitled "Seelenklinik." In Argentine exile, Neumann also became an editor for the *Argentinisches Tageblatt,* a post she held for years. (It is not clear if the two women worked for the daily at the same time and if they knew one another.) The two authors also portrayed in their works their experiences as women in Nazi-occupied Germany and Austria and in Argentine exile.

Of the two publications, Dauber's autobiography is probably more interesting to today's reader because it chronicles the life story of a woman who consciously defied the rules and was therefore forced to negotiate her way through two patriarchal societies.[21] The context of the narrative, the temporal and geographical locus in which the life story is embedded, is equally unique for it offers the reader an insight into the political and social structures of 1930s Europe and Latin America. In contrast, the adventures of Neumann's married heroine in the fictional novel *Puerto Nuevo-Neuer Hafen* are less authentic. In the 431-page novel, the author turns to the exile scene for her subject matter (the only novel *of* exile published by the Editorial Cosmopolita). Neumann portrays, against an action-packed background, a young couple's struggle—he a Jew, she an "Aryan" of noble birth—against the ideologies of the time and the difficulties of life in exile. Their marriage is strained by not only immigrant life in Argentina (the difficulties of everyday life are realistically sketched) but also the persistent amorous advances of a local Nazi who hopes to conquer the young wife. The simple story is augmented with elements reminiscent of trivial literature which significantly lessen its literary integrity. Among the German exile population on the Latin American continent, however, Neumann's novel was well received: "The first great novel of free German literature which masterly portrays the destiny of all those in South America," read the review in *Aufbau* in New York.[22]

Dauber's autobiography *Eine Nacht-Ein Leben* initially stood little chance of being published by the Editorial Cosmopolita, which favored the more popular genre of novel. Cosmopolita's editors argued against publication, but at the insistence of Dr. August Siemsen, a former socialist member of the Reichstag and leader of the local political exile organization Das Andere Deutschland, the work was nonetheless published. Siemsen had a persuasive counterargument: "What independent women write about themselves, even if they are unknown, is often more interesting than the memoirs of the most well-known diplomat" (7).[23] In the work's preface Siemsen argues:

> In this book we are not dealing with a typical, but rather with a unique, case. It is unique, because the life of the author has been determined by illness. Yet the life and struggle of this woman are an integral part of our present capitalist world with its exploitation, wars, fascism and immigrant destinies. And so the book, above and beyond its human value, is also interesting because it portrays an independent woman, a sick woman, in the center of this world (8).[24]

Cosmopolita, it should be noted, incorrectly classified the autobiography as a novel, probably to enhance salability of the work.

Dauber's autobiography is a skillful chronicling of events in a swift forward motion and at times displays appealing self-irony. It can be divided into three distinct time periods: the author's youth and early adulthood in turn-of-the-century Germany and the early Weimar Republic, her student days in a disintegrating Weimar Republic and early Nazi era, and her adult years in exile in Argentina. Within this framework, the autobiography interprets political, social, and family relations. The dynamics of gender expectations and norms emerge clearly from Dauber's personal narrative. It reveals how the author—although she would not have called herself a feminist—challenged and defied such norms, both in Nazi Germany and in exile. Her difficulty in conforming to various societal dictates is a recurring theme in the work.

To interpret Dauber's autobiography, the term narrative form, which describes the framework used to narrate the life story, should be mentioned.[25] Dauber apparently is conscious of the genre, and the narrative form of the 199-page autobiography is rather traditional. A large part of the autobiography, approximately the first third of it, deals with family relations and childhood memories. The narrative first becomes interesting for today's reader during the author's student days when she becomes a conscious social and political actor. Fifty pages detail Dauber's activities as an ardent socialist and anti-Nazi. Upon completion of her doctoral program in the early 1930s, Dauber ardently embraces the fight for women's rights in Nazi Germany as an abortion rights activist. This part of the autobiography, in which Nazi government actions against women's rights are described, is both riveting and historically accurate. The final pages of the autobiography describe Dauber's ordeal as an exile on the European continent and in Argentina. The effect of continuous personal upheaval is a major theme of the autobiography, and this may account for Dauber's search for self-identity throughout the work.

From a literary point of view the autobiography has some minor flaws. Repeated indulgences in excessive self-glorification detract from its literariness. One example is Dauber's description of the Nazis: they are portrayed as caricatures, whereas the author is always portrayed as a hero. The countless political and economic disputes the author engages in with people from all walks on the theories of Marxism and the shortcomings of capitalism reflect a self-righteousness that strikes today's reader as somewhat naive. The work, however, should not be judged solely in literary terms. What makes the autobiography so interesting and valuable is not so much its literary quality as its historical value. *Eine Nacht-Ein Leben* remains one of the few surviving documents to chronicle the daily hardships of an unmarried woman in both Nazi Germany and in Latin American exile. The lack of literary excellence is offset by the work's value as a first-person documentation of a critical time in modern history seen from a woman's perspective.

Initially insecure about writing her autobiography, Dauber soon realized that chronicling her life's experiences could become an act of survival "because I had to conquer my life, had to free myself from my personal experience . . . from this life which had been a continuous struggle" (10).[26] The feverish recollections of the seriously ill and at-times delirious author, who is suffering from a general inflammation of the nerves, constitute the opening phrases of the autobiography:

> I am screaming so loudly that they can hear me in the neighboring house. I don't want to cry, but the tears are flowing. Now again. But why? Death must be very beautiful, with its immense, eternal peace. If only dying were not so painful! (16)[27]

She continues:

> I would like to live, experience much more. I cannot die now, right in the middle of this world tragedy of war. I must see how things will change for the better after the war. . . . What was there really in my life to make it so worthwhile? Or was it in vain? I would like to relive my life—at least for now in my thoughts. Perhaps the thoughts will help drown the pain (16).[28]

An interpretation of family relations during her youth and young adulthood follows, in which Dauber analyzes inward struggles and emotional experiences. The sudden mental illness and early death of her father, a physician, clouds her youth and future. Dauber was very fond of her father, whom she describes as an intelligent and enlightened man. This contrasts sharply with the negative description of Dauber's mother, a middle-class conservative, who did not approve of the independent life-style and political and social activities of her daughter. Dauber's early rejection of traditional religion—she became an atheist soon after the death of her father—may have further alienated her mother who was a devout Christian. Dauber explains that she rejects the concept of a God but that she does believe in a moral code of behavior, akin to Kant's categorical imperative:

> There does not exist a God for me. We only have natural and human laws. The human being has the obligation toward him/herself and all of humankind to be as good as possible in all he/she says and does. That is the only immortality there is: good deeds and acts are immortal. (46)[29]

Dauber's relationship with her sister Ilse, older by two years, and a married schoolteacher, is cordial. Ilse is apolitical and remains in Germany during the Nazi years. The painful experience of the early death of Dauber's father leaves her with deep psychological complexes and a lifelong battle with numerous physical maladies. Dauber writes that the physical illnesses began after the death of her father, and they therefore may well have been psychosomatic. The illnesses continued into her adult life and could therefore also have been physical outlets for or manifestations of the difficulties she experienced because of her nontraditional life-style. She writes:

> True, some was bad luck, like the early death of my father. But, regarding these numerous illnesses, which far exceed the figure of a hundred, . . . these uncountable accidents, these money losses. About these you can only laugh, although only then, when they are behind you. I, however, have not yet experienced a true, liberating laugh. Otherwise, this book would not be necessary. (10–11)[30]

As the daughter of a pure "Aryan" family of ministers and physicians, Dauber's future in Nazi Germany seemed secure. But as a student, Dauber consciously jeopardized this security by being politically active. Dauber contends that she became socially and politically aware during World War I, as an eighteen-year old, when she realized that war was an act of madness. "I could not define national honor. . . . I only know: the war is madness!" (48).[31] She became a critic of Wilhelminian Germany, a supporter of the industrial proletariat, and a confirmed pacifist. She ardently read the early dramas of naturalist playwright Gerhart Hauptmann and the critical turn-of-the-century novels of Heinrich Mann. However, not until Dauber was a graduate student in the mid-1920s did she become a confirmed Marxist. She writes that she wanted to join the great fight of the masses against exploitation and suppression. "Only in this manner, by fighting for justice in the world, can I overcome myself, can I avoid being controlled by physical pain, can I be a winner in the fight against my destiny" (119).[32] In 1929, Dauber joined numerous political groups and social organizations.

After completing graduate studies in German philosophy, history, and literature at the universities of Leipzig, Cologne, and Kiel, Dauber received her Ph.D. from the University of Leipzig; she does not specify in what year she receives her doctoral degree. She settled in Frankfurt am Main where she became a correspondent for the *Frankfurter Zeitung.* Dauber's continued political activity prompted reactions from local Nazi groups. She recounts:

> Every morning, when I return loaded with material from the newspaper, I am forced off my bike at any number of street corners, in order to engage in street discussions with the Nazis. This does not make me very popular among them. One day as a way of showing their opinion of me, I am thrown into a shop window. I don't get hurt however. . . . During these politically exciting years from 1929 to 1933, we find ourselves [Dauber and like-minded political activists] every evening in a meeting or gathering (119).[33]

Her intensely held political beliefs, bravery, and independence—so strongly exhibited in her twenties—continued to shape her later exile experience.

After her stint as a journalist, Dauber became the secretary and active supporter of Dr. Else Kienle, physician and director of the "Stuttgarter Beratungsstelle des Reichverbandes für Sexualhygiene und Geburtenreglung" (The Stuttgart Counseling Center of the National Association for Birth Control and Sexual Hygiene), a nonprofit organization that promoted sex education and contraceptive advice. Dr. Kienle, together with the communist physician and author Friedrich Wolf, was one of a handful of physicians to militantly oppose the anti-abortion statutes in the Third Reich (Kiessling 420–421).

Germany's Communist party had a tradition of campaigning for legalized abortion and contraceptive advice, based on proabortion legislation in the Soviet Union (Stephenson 57). In Nazi Germany, where the increase of the Aryan race was a high priority, the subject of abortion and contraception was controversial. Paragraph 218 of the Criminal Code stated that anyone discovered performing an abortion for payment would be severely punished. A law enacted by the Nazi government on 28 February 1933 enabled police authorities to close most birth control organizations throughout the country. A handful survived, but they conducted activities in secrecy. Additional laws were instated in May 1933, which called for imprisonment or implementation of stiff fines on anyone offering abortion facilities. In 1943 yet another law was introduced, which authorized the death penalty for anyone found to have performed an abortion (Stephenson 58–69).

Dauber's public support for the work of Dr. Kienle and her insistence on the abolition of paragraph 218 prompted an official warrant for her arrest in 1932. She recalls: "I have committed . . . serious sins against the authority of the state. . . . There is the matter of the abortion statute. By working as secretary for Frau Dr. E. K. . . . I am guilty of a crime." She adds: "In addition, and this could cause the most difficulties, I have been working on the preparation of a referendum to change the notorious statute 218. In numerous mass meetings, I have been the principal speaker against this statute" (123–124).[34] A four-hour hearing conducted by a public prosecutor followed Dauber's arrest, and it resulted in an unexpected release. When Dauber courageously held yet another speech against the notorious statute, she faced renewed arrest. "At a large and well-attended rally, I am once again holding a speech on the subject of women's rights and social issues, causes I am fighting for. The attending police officer, who together with four of his cronies has to make sure that nothing is said that could violate the emergency decree, becomes restless and reaches for his notebook" (125).[35] Faced with renewed arrest and possible imprisonment, Dauber was forced into exile; she fled to Paris in 1933.

The time in Paris, where she worked as a maid, was uneventful. She recalls: "In my position as maid, I am slowly becoming a megalomaniac. In my thoughts I often dabble with mathematical problems, for you have to occupy yourself mentally with something when you scrub floors and do dishes. Thinking solely of your destiny leads to melancholy, and that is of no use to me" (152).[36]

After thirteen months in Paris, Dauber learned of her impending extradition to Germany and fled once again, this time to England. "At the human rights league [in France], I receive the pleasant news that the German authorities have demanded my extradition. Charge: death to two hundred and thirty-two unborn children. That is absurd," Dauber writes with her characteristic mixture of irony and directness. "They are simply shifting the charge against Frau Dr. E. K. onto me, since she is in a country which does not allow for extradition on the basis of an offense against statute 218. France, however, does have a special extradition treaty with the Reich for this offense" (163).[37] Once in England, Dauber was warned by a journalist for the *Sunday Express* of her recent *Ausbürgerung* (loss of citizenship) and her death sentence by the Nazis. Fearing an extradition procedure, the British government asked her to leave. Quakers initially procured a job for her in Ireland, and after several months there, they provided her with a first-class ticket on a freighter to Argentina. The year was 1935.

The last part of the autobiography portrays daily struggles, especially financial ones, in an alien and hostile environment. The gloomy picture presented is no exaggeration. Argentina of the 1930s and 1940s was far from an immigrant's paradise. The cities suffered from unemployment and overt exploitation of the working classes; inflation had reached an all-time high, and wages were low. Housing was chronically short and rents inflated. *Villas miserias* (slums) and *conventillos* (run-down tenement houses) were scattered throughout the city. As a primarily agricultural country, Argentina could not accommodate the largely professional skills of the German refugees. According to a local Jewish aid committee, the only positions open to refugees were as housekeepers (generally for females only), technically trained specialists, manual workers, butchers, and laborers.[38] With few possessions, often destitute, the German refugees would accept almost any job. Dauber explained: "From the very beginning, almost all . . . German immigrants have been forced to hold two to three jobs simultaneously" (*Als ich drei Berufe hatte* 110).[39]

Dauber's average income of 50 pesos a month did not last very long. The author's detailed account of how each of the 50 pesos was spent reveals both the desperation of her circumstances and the mental energies consumed by quotidian cares: "A small attic room costs twenty five pesos. I need five pesos for transportation . . . , three pesos a month are spent on cigarettes. . . . I smoke the cheapest ones I can possibly buy, and to totally quit smoking, that I simply cannot do" (*Eine Nacht* 182).[40] She continues:

> At the beginning of the month I put 5 pesos aside for shoe repairs, a haircut, soap and such things. Twelve pesos are left. Twelve pesos for thirty breakfasts, thirty lunches and thirty dinners. Forty centavos a day to survive with. I convince myself, that with bread, butter, milk and bananas, for ten centavos each, I am adequately nourished. But this is apparently not so. I keep losing weight, till my face, forty-two kilos with a height of one meter seventy-seven, frightens even me. (183)[41]

Working several jobs, sometimes two a day, while combating numerous illnesses, Dauber still does not capitulate. With irony and humor she enumerates the menial jobs she was forced to accept in Argentina in an effort to make ends meet:

> Maid, nightwatchman in a lunatic asylum, box wrapper in a mail order firm, not exactly positions of high social standing. But one can descend the stairs even further. And I do so, to its lowest steps, yet without ever "losing a bead out of my crown." On the contrary, as with all the previous jobs, my horizon is broadened. I become a lavatory attendant in a night club, the only opportunity I encounter to earn some money. In this job, I amuse myself tremendously. (*Eine Nacht* 190)[42]

She continues with increased irony:

> The opening and closing of the doors are switch-on signals for me. The door opens . . . I am a lavatory attendant, nothing else. Diligently, I wipe the toilet bowl, hand a comb, offer a towel, take out the clothes brush and say "thank you" in one of four languages, depending on the nationality of my customers. The perfect lavatory attendant. The door closes. I am alone. Quickly I reach for a book. . . . My other self begins its secret life with figures of literature. (191)[43]

The final pages of Dauber's narrative end in personal triumph. The recollections slowly subside as her fever goes down, and the crippling nerve inflammation is conquered. "Dead? No! A person can die only when her life has been fulfilled. Mine is still unfulfilled. I still have much to do. . . . I suddenly know that for a fact.

I want to sit. . . . And I am sitting. I have conquered the paralysis" (199).[44] The review in the April 1945 issue of *Das Andere Deutschland,* a local German-language exile magazine, perhaps best summarized the work: "*Eine Nacht-Ein Leben,* cannot be classified as 'schöne Literatur,' rather it is a book written by life itself."[45]

The fifty-year old Dauber had spent a total of twelve years in Argentine exile by 1947. Although she was a member of the local political organizations Das Andere Deutschland and Verein Vorwärts,[46] and occasionally wrote articles in the newsletter of the latter organization, her political activity in Argentina remains virtually unrecorded. That Dauber at times was politically active in her country of refuge is confirmed by a few lines appearing in the June 1947 issue of *Das Andere Deutschland.* In the article, members of the organization express both their gratitude for Dauber's participation in numerous activities and reveal that Dauber was granted permission by military officials to return to postwar Germany to accept an editorial position in Leipzig.[47] Her autobiography, however, mentions little if any political activity in Argentina and reflects little social interaction between herself and this patriarchical society. Rather, Dauber gives the impression of feeling isolated and of suffering from this isolation. This sense of isolation may well have contributed to her writing an autobiography, brought on by the need, more acutely felt in exile, to establish a self-identity.

The autobiography *Eine Nacht-Ein Leben* integrates personal narrative with an exposé of history and society. The author chronicles, from a woman's perspective, how social and political conditions in Nazi Germany influenced and shaped the course of a life. The dynamics of gender inform the entire autobiography. One example is the controversy over women's education in the Third Reich. The autobiography details how the author's advanced degree was yet another strike against her. According to the Nazis, higher education had "defeminized" German women. In *Nazi Germany: It's Women and Family Life,* Clifford Kirkpatrick describes how women leaders were blamed for the absence of millions of babies in the Third Reich and university women for Germany's biological crisis and the decline of the population both in quantity and quality (234). (Hitler needed a young and strong population to realize his *Lebensraum* ambition). Kirkpatrick recounts how the Nazis claimed that the academic generation of 1890 to 1900 had an average of 2.4 children, whereas the recent generation (of the 1920s) had produced only 0.3. Laws were enacted to limit the enrollment of women in universities, and in the winter of 1932–1933 only 15.8 percent of the 122,847 students in the German universities and technical schools were women (236).[48] One of these women was Dauber.

Dauber's political status in Nazi Germany could be defined as marginal. She was continually harassed by the Nazis because of her independent views and unmarried status. Her later status as an immigrant woman in Argentine exile enforced this marginality. Before writing her autobiography Dauber viewed herself as marginal and believed her life's story to be unessential. The preface to the autobiography begins with an apology to the reader: "I am writing this book even though I believe that there truly is no justification for it" (12).[49] Dauber displays false modesty here, for her life story not only evidences historically important activity but also presents a representative account of what happened to feminists in the Nazi era and a reflection of the physical and emotional price they paid for their sociopolitical beliefs. Although initially insecure, Dauber's effort pays off. The concretization of her personal narrative, the act of giving shape, form, and meaning to her life, becomes a liberating act and convinces the author of the significance of both her life and its story.

After Dauber's return to Leipzig in 1947, she worked for the local publishing house Volk und Wissen for six years. During these years Dauber published a report on the social conditions and the position of women in Perón's Argentina. Dauber's feminist interests are more clearly focused in this critique of women's position in Argentina. The 141-page publication, *Als ich drei Berufe hatte. Argentinien wie es wirklich ist. Eine Reportage* (1950), consists of short accounts that run between one and four pages. Under such headings as: "Die Wohnungsfrage" (the problem of housing), "Heimarbeiterinnen" (women home laborers), "Ausbeutung" (exploitation), "Frauen" (women), "Die Klassenfrage" (the class problem), Dauber discusses the realities of a socially structured gendered hierarchy, the gender division of labor, and the power relations between men and women. In the section on "Frauen," she criticizes gender expectations and norms. She writes:

> Until recently the woman who earned her own living was held in contempt. This was expressed by the fact that all

> women who did so were addressed with the informal [tú] by men. Only *'maestras'*, [schoolteachers], were exempt from this informal address. Female office workers . . . are officially paid ten percent less than their male counterparts. In reality the payment is forty percent below those of the men. (98).[50]

At first, Dauber applauds Perón for the many social reforms he introduces in Argentina. Soon however, she is disappointed and criticizes Argentina's president for not granting women a seat in parliament. "Perón promised women much, and one promise he kept: he gave them voting rights. He could risk doing that. He thereby eliminated future opponents. . . . However, that they would not decide their own fates, that women did not realize. . . . This step [voting] added nothing to the liberation of the [Argentine] woman" (103).[51] Under the heading "Wohnungsfrage," the author criticizes living conditions in the run-down tenement houses of Buenos Aires where the poor lived. "Here you are happy when yet another day has passed in which endless conflicts have not led to murder" (15).[52] These short and critical accounts reveal a literary style that became a Dauber trademark: sparse, realistic prose with an ever-present dose of irony.

Dauber died prematurely—probably as the result of her accumulated physical and mental hardships—in Leipzig in 1953 at the age of fifty-five. But in the few years in Leipzig after the war, Dauber found her long-sought happiness. In the afterword to *Als ich drei Berufe hatte,* she writes:

> In Autumn of 1947, I returned to the Soviet occupied zone in Germany. I have not regretted it for one moment and will not regret it, for here my greatest wish has been fulfilled: cooperating meaningfully, contributing to the building of a better future in which no war will senselessly destroy that which has just been built. With continued world peace, through the building of a socialist economy, all people will be able to live as people. It is in the fight for this goal, that life becomes worthwhile. (unpaginated)[53]

The autobiography *Eine Nacht-Ein Leben* is an eyewitness account of one woman's destiny intertwined with the tragedies of history. With most German exile works written in Argentina during the 1930s and early 1940s irretrievably lost, today's reader will not find a truer witness.

NOTES

1. Herbert A. Strauss, "Jews in German History: Persecution, Emigration, Acculturation," In *International Biographical Dictionary of Central European Emigrés 1933–1945,* ed. Herbert A. Strauss and Werner Röder (München: K. G. Sauer, 1983), vol. 2, part 1, a–k, xi, xii.

2. Only a few well-known authors, for example Balder Olden, Werner Bock, and Paul Zech, fled to Argentina after 1933. None of their exile works, however, were published by Cosmopolita.

3. Doris Dauber was born 4 September 1897 in Wurzburg. She spent her youth in New York, where her father practiced medicine. Because of her father's mental illness, the family returned to Germany. The autobiography does not describe the time spent in New York. Dauber died 4 February 1953 in Leipzig. There is little information available on Dauber. Only a few lines appear on the cover page of her autobiography, and she is mentioned in two short articles that appear in the journal *Das Andere Deutschland* in Argentina. Wolfgang Kiessling devotes several pages to her in his publication *Exil in Lateinamerika* (Frankfurt am Main: Röderberg Verlag, 1981), 416–423.

4. Katherine Morris, "Women Remembering: Autobiography as a Source of German-Jewish Cultural History in Brazil," unpublished essay. Morris writes: "Traditional approaches to the assessment and analysis of women's autobiographies have denigrated the feminine *Weltanschauung* as trivial and have often overlooked the possibility that women may have developed their own tradition of self-awareness as well as their own genres of writing" (2).

5. A very progressive statement by the socialist August Siemsen. Siemsen a German journalist, teacher, and former Reichstagsmember fled into exile in 1933. After three years in Switzerland he continued on to Argentina. In July 1937, the fifty-three-year-old Siemsen founded the political exile organization Das Andere Deutschland (DAD) in Buenos Aires. As Argentine authorities no longer permitted the founding of German political organizations in the late 1930s, DAD had to take the form of a journal to pursue its political objectives. Objectives were initially to aid arriving exiles with financial, legal, and moral support, but soon activities expanded to include the formation of an anti-Nazi front. DAD aided Argentine authorities investigating fifth column activities on Argentine soil. Siemsen, who was chief editor of *Das Andere Deutschland,* most probably knew Dauber quite well since she both contributed articles to the journal and participated in organized events. Winfried Seelisch, "Das Andere Deutschland. Eine politische Vereinigung deutscher Emigranten in Südamerika," Diplomarbeit (Berlin: Otto Suhr Institut, 1969).

6. "Die argentinische Frau hat es schwer." All translations are by the author of this essay.

7. "Noch schwerer hat es die Emigrantin—vor allem die politische Emigrantin—die in dauerndem Kampf mit den Behörden steht."

8. "Wegen eines Zusammenstosses mit der politischen Polizei im Jahre 1936 war ich in Argentinien unbeliebt. Ich galt als lästige Ausländerin. Eine Ausweisung meiner äusserst wichtigen Person—von meiner Wichtigkeit wurde ich durch dicke Aktenbündel überzeugt—war damals aufgeschoben, aber nicht aufgehoben worden. Also war ganz klar, man wollte mich nicht in Argentinien haben."

9. Balder Olden, *Paradiese des Teufels, Biographisches und Autobiogra-*

phisches. Schriften und Briefe aus dem Exil (Berlin: Rütten und Loening, 1977). "Man . . . kann als Immigrant nichts Besseres tun, als still sein."

10. "Mit Glück fing mein berufliches Leben an. Ich fand eine Stellung als Redakteurin an der deutschsprachigen antifaschistischen Zeitung. Aber nach einem Jahr gefiel ich dem Chefredakteur nicht mehr—mir gefiel er auch nicht—und ich musste gehen."

11. Peter Bussemeyer, *50 Jahre Argentinisches Tageblatt. Werden und Aufstieg einer auslandsdeutschen Zeitung* (Buenos Aires, 1939).

12. Werner Mittenzwei. *Carl Meffert, Clément Moreau. Ein Leben auf der Suche nach der Brüderlichkeit des Menschen* (Berlin: Henschel Verlag, 1977). "Diese Zeitung gab sich zwar konsequent antifaschistisch, aber in ihr konnte man nichts Sozialistisches finden. . . . Sozialisten hatten es mit Alemann schwer. . . . Ihn interessierte in erster Linie das Geschäftliche. Die Zeitung . . . existierte . . . für ihn hauptsächlich aus geschäftlichen Erwägungen. Klappte jedoch das Geschäft, so liess auch politisch mit sich reden."

13. "Meine Artikel wurden gern gedruckt. Aber als ich wagte, kritisch zu deutschen faschistischen Methoden Stellung zu nehmen, erliess die argentinische faschistische Regierung schleunigst für mich ein Schreibverbot."

14. "Mit dem Verdienst aus diesen . . . Berufen . . . konnte ich nun nicht etwa luxuriös leben. Ich verdiente nur so viel, dass ich eine schlechte Halbpension bezahlen konnte."

15. "Wenn man in einer Fabrik arbeitet, spürt man es sehr deutlich am eigenen Leib, was es bedeutet, dass es keine Arbeiterschutzgesetze gibt. . . . Wenn man . . . das Pech hat, krank zu werden oder öfter zu kränkeln, dann ist man überhaupt verraten und verkauft. . . . Keinen Pfennig erhält der Kranke. Krankenversicherung, die Arzt und Apotheke bezahlt, Krankengeld, von dem man sein Leben fristen kann, das gibt es in Argentinien nicht. . . . Ich nahm eine Stellung als Bibliothekarin in einer chemischpharmazeutischen Fabrik an. . . . Diese Stellung verlor ich, weil ich Krankheitstage bezahlt haben wollte."

16. The following works were published by the Editorial Cosmopolita between 1940 and 1945:

Günther Ballin, *Zwischen Gestern und Morgen*, Roman, 1945
Adolf Borstendörfer, *Die letzten Tagen von Wien*, Roman, 1944
———, *Graf Ciano*, Roman, 1944
José Hernandez, *Martin Fierro*, translated into German by Adolf Borstendörfer, Poetry, 1945
Doris Dauber, *Eine Nacht-Ein Leben*, Roman, 1945
Fred Heller, *Das Leben beginnt noch einmal. Schicksale der Emigration.*
Paul Walter Jacob, *Zeitklänge, Dirigenten-Profile und Komponisten-Porträts*, 1945
Hans Jahn, *Babs und die Sieben. Eine lustige Geschichte für Kinder von 12 bis 80 Jahren*, 1944
Hans Jahn und Karl Kost, *Herz an der Rampe, Ausgewählte Chansons, Songs und Dichtungen ähnlicher Art*, 1944
Karl Kost, *Menschen essen Stickstoff*, Roman, 1945
Johan Luzian, *Der ungläubige Thomas*, Roman, 1945
Livia Neumann, *Puerto Nuevo-Neuer Hafen*, Roman, 1943
———, *Hab Mut zum Glück! Betrachtungen über alle Seelenprobleme*, 1942
———, *Der Meisterspion. Das Geheimdossier des Falles Redl*, Roman, 1945 (written under pseudonym S. E. Kelly)

August Siemsen, *Die Tragödie Deutschlands und die Zukunft der Welt. Aufsätze und Reden,* 1945

17. The thirty-eight-year old James Illy Friedmann arrived in Argentina in 1938. One of the few German exiles in Latin America to do so, Friedmann recorded his experiences in Argentine exile in a detailed unpublished memoir, "Muttersprache-das Vaterland der Heimatlosen. Erinnerungen und Dokumentation eines deutschen Verlegers in der Emigration mit anschliessender Anthologie aus vergriffenen Büchern, Zeitschriften und Zeitungen, Argentinien 1938–1946," 3 vols. Unpublished manuscript located at the Deutsche Bibliothek in Frankfurt am Main.

18. "Die verlegerische Tätigkeit damals, darf mithin nicht nur rein literarisch beurteilt werden."

19. Helmut Müssener, "Schweden ist gut-für die Schweden. Aspekte geglückter und missglückter Integration in Schweden nach 1933," *Leben im Exil. Probleme der Integration deutscher Flüchtlinge im Ausland,* Wolfgang Frühwald and Wolfgang Scheider, eds. (Hamburg: Hoffmann und Campe Verlag, 1981). "Objektivität ist ein Luxus, den man sich nicht leisten kann, wenn man verhungert; wenn man in einem Land . . . keine Funktion, keine Raison d'être fand."

20. Livia Neumann-Szekely was born on 10 April 1912 in Budapest and grew up in Vienna. She contributed articles to several Viennese dailies. She left for Argentina in 1938. In Argentina she contributed to the local newspapers *Argentinisches Tageblatt* and *Jüdische Wochenschau.* Wilhelm Sternfeld and Eva Tiedemann, *Deutsche Exil Literatur 1933–1945* (Heidelberg: Verlag Lambert Schneider, 1970), 368.

21. The Personal Narratives Group, ed., *Interpreting Women's Lives* (Bloomington: Indiana University Press, 1989). This important publication on feminist theory and personal narratives, provided the theoretical framework for the interpretation of Dauber's life story.

22. Excerpt of a review of *Aufbau,* New York, reprinted in the book announcement pages following Livia Neumann's novel *Der Meisterspion.* "Der erste grosse Roman der freien deutschen Literatur, der das Schicksal aller nach Südamerika Verschlagenen meisterhaft gestaltet."

23. "Was auf sich gestellte Frauen von ihrem Leben zu erzählen haben, das ist, auch wenn sie 'namenlos' sind, oft interessanter als die Memoiren eines noch so bekannten Diplomaten."

24. "In diesem Buch haben wir es allerdings nicht nur mit einem typischen, vielmehr mit einem singulären Fall zu tun. Singulär ist er deshalb, weil das Leben der Verfasserin weitgehend durch Krankheit bestimmt wird. Aber das Leben und der Kampf dieser Frau spielen in unserer heutigen Welt des Kapitalismus und der Ausbeutung, der Kriege, des Faschismus und der Emigrantenschicksale ab. Und so ist das Buch über das Persönliche hinaus auch deshalb interessant, weil es eine auf sich selbst gestellte Frau, eine kranke Frau, inmitten dieser Welt . . . zeigt."

25. *Interpreting Women's Lives,* 12–13.

26. "Weil ich mein Leben überwinden muss, vom bisher Erlebten loskommen muss. Von diesem Leben, das ein ständiger Kampf war."

27. "Ich schreie, dass man mich im Nachbarhaus hört. Ich will nicht heulen, aber die Tränen fliessen. Jetzt auch wieder. Warum eigentlich? Der Tod ist doch sicher sehr schön, die grosse, die unendliche Ruhe. Wenn nur das Sterben nicht so schwer wäre!"

28. "Ich möchte leben, noch vieles erleben. Ich kann jetzt nicht sterben, mitten in diesem Weltunglück des Krieges. Ich muss sehen, wie alles nach dem

Kriege sich zum Besseren wendet. . . . Was war eigentlich in meinem Leben, das es mir so lebenswert machte? Oder war es wirklich vergeblich? Ich will mein Leben noch einmal leben—wenigstens jetzt in Gedanken. Vielleicht übertönen die Gedanken die Schmerzen."

29. "Es gibt für mich keinen Gott. Es gibt nur Naturgesetze und Menschengesetze. Und der Mensch hat die Verpflichtung, vor sich selbst und vor der Menschheit, so gut wie möglich zu sein, in allem, was er sagt, in allem, was er tut. Das ist die einzige Unsterblichkeit: die guten Taten und Worte gehen nicht verloren; sie wirken fort ins Unendliche."

30. "Gewiss, manches war Unglück, wie der frühe Tod meines Vaters. Aber über diese vielen Krankheiten, die die Zahl hundert weit übersteigen, . . . über ungezählte Unglücksfälle, über Geldverlust, da kann man nur lachen—allerdings meist erst, wenn es vorbei ist. Aber zum richtigen, befreienden Lachen bin ich doch noch nicht gekommen. Sonst wäre dies Buch nicht nötig."

31. "Ich kann mir unter "nationaler Ehre" nichts vorstellen, ich weiss nur: der Krieg ist Wahnsinn!"

32. "Nur so, wenn ich für stärkere Gerechtigkeit in der Welt kämpfe, kann ich mich selbst überwinden, kann ich verhindern, dass das körperliche Leiden mich beherrscht, kann ich Sieger im Kampf gegen mein Schicksal werden."

33. "Jeden Vormittag, wenn ich mit Material beladen von der Zeitung zurückkomme, werde ich an irgend einer Ecke vom Rad geholt, um in eine Strassendiskussion mit Nazis einzugreifen. Das macht mich bei diesen nicht gerade beliebt. Und als Zeichen ihrer Meinung über mich fliege ich eines Tages in ein Schaufenster. Aber ich tue mir nichts dabei. . . . Jeden Abend dieser politisch erregten Jahre 1929 bis 33 sind wir in einer Versammlung oder Sitzung."

34. "Ich habe . . . schwere Sünden gegen die Staatsgewalt auf dem Kerbholz. . . . [Es gibt] die Angelegenheit mit dem Abtreibungsparagraphen. Gegen den habe ich als Sekretärin von Frau Dr. E. K. gesündigt. Ausserdem, was erschwerend ins Gewicht fallen kann, bin ich mit der Vorbereitung eines Volksentscheids für Abänderung dieses berüchtigten Paragraph 218 beschäftigt. Ich habe in vielen Massenversammlungen das Hauptreferat gegen diese Gesetzesbestimmung gehalten."

35. "Ich spreche in einer stark besuchten, sehr grossen Versammlung einmal wieder über die frauenrechtliche, soziale Frage, für deren Lösung ich mich einsetze. Der Polizeioffizier, der mit seinen vier Mann aufzupassen hat, dass nichts gesagt wird, das gegen die Notverordnungen verstösst, wird etwas unruhig und zückt sein Notizbuch."

36. "In meinen Dienstmädchenstellungen werde ich langsam grössenwahnsinnig. Ich gebe mich in Gedanken viel mit mathematischen Problemen ab, denn mit etwas muss man sich doch geistig beschäftingen, wenn man Böden schrubbt und Teller wäscht. Nur über sein Schicksal nachzudenken, führt zu Trübsinn, und den kann ich nicht gebrauchen."

37. "Auf der Liga für Menschrenrechte [in Frankreich] bekomme ich die angenehme Nachricht, dass die deutschen Behörden meine Auslieferung verlangt haben. Anklage zweihundertzweiunddreissigfacher Mord an ungeborenen Kindern. Das ist einfach toll. Man wälzt einfach die Anklage gegen Frau Dr. E. K. auf mich ab, weil sie in einem Lande ist, das keine Auslieferung wegen des Paragraphen 218 kennt, während mit Frankreich ein besonderer Auslieferungsvetrag bei diesem Vergehen besteht."

38. Asociación Filantrópica Israelita, ed. *Zehn Jahre Aufbauarbeit in Süd-*

amerika, 1933–1943 (Buenos Aires: Hilfsverein Deutschsprechender Juden, 1943), 32–33. "Frauen und Mädchen im Haushalt, technisch geschulte Spezialisten, Handwerker, Schlächter und Schwerarbeiter."

39. "Fast alle anderen deutschen Emigranten sind schon seit langem gezwungen, zwei bis drei Berufe nebeneinander zu haben."

40. "Fünfundzwanzig Pesos kostet ein kleines Dachzimmer, fünf Pesos brauche ich für Fahrgeld . . . drei Pesos gebe ich im Monat für Zigaretten aus. Ich rauche die billigsten, die man überhaupt zu kaufen bekommt, und ganz darauf verzichten kann ich nicht."

41. "Fünf Pesos lege ich mir Anfang des Monats beiseite für Schuhreparaturen, Haarschneiden, Seife und solche Dinge. Zwölf Pesos bleiben übrig. Zwölf Pesos für dreissig Frühstücke, dreissig Mittagessen und dreissig Abendbrote. Vierzig Centavos pro Tag zum Leben. Ich bilde mir ein, mit Brot, Butter, Milch und Bananen für je zehn Centavos ernähre ich mich ausreichend. Aber es ist anscheinend nicht so. Ich nehme dauernd ab, bis mich mein Gesicht—zweiundvierzig Kilo bei ein Meter dreiundsiebzig Grösse—selbst erschreckt."

42. "Dienstmädchen, Nachtwächterin im Irrenhous, Paketpackerin in einem Versandgeschäft sind nicht gerade sozial hochstehende Berufe. Aber man kann die Treppe noch tiefer hinabsteigen. Und ich steige sie hinab bis zur untersten Stufe, ohne dass mir eine Perle aus der Krone fällt. Im Gegenteil: wie bei allen früheren Berufen erweitert sich mein Horizont. Ich werde in einem Nachtlokal Klosettfrau, die einzige Verdienstmöglichkeit, die sich mir bietet. Meistens amüsiere ich mich köstlich dabei."

43. "Öffnen und Schliessen der Türe sind für mich Schaltsignale. Die Tür öffnet sich . . . ich bin Klosettfrau, nichts weiter. Eifrig wische ich über den Klosettdeckel, reiche den Kamm, halte das Handtuch hin, zücke die Kleiderbürste und sage 'danke' in einer der vier Sprachen, je nach der Nationalität meiner Kunden. Ganz perfekte Klosettfrau. Die Tür schliesst sich. Ich bin allein. Ein rascher Griff zum Buch . . . mein zweites Ich beginnt sein geheimes Leben mit den Gestalten der Literatur."

44. "Tod? Nein! Der Mensch kann erst sterben, wenn sich sein Leben erfüllt hat. Meines ist noch unvollendet. Vieles steht mir noch bevor . . . ich weiss es plötzlich ganz genau. Ich will mich setzen. . . . Und ich sitze. Ich habe die Lähmung überwunden."

45. L.H., "Doris Dauber, 'Eine Nacht-Ein Leben'," *Das Andere Deutschland* Jg. 7. Nr. 93. April 1945: 30. "Eine Nacht-Ein Leben ist kein Werk der schönen Literatur, es ist ein Buch, das das Leben selbst schrieb."

46. The Verein Vorwärts was a German political organization, founded in Buenos Aires in 1882 by thirteen socialists who fled Bismarck's Germany. From its inception, the organization's main objective was to spread socialist principles in Argentina. Members of the organization helped form the Argentine Socialist party in 1896.

47. "Doris Dauber," *Das Andere Deutschland*, Nr. 143. 1 June 1947: 2.

48. Kirkpatrick writes: "A limitation was placed by the National Socialists on higher education for women. . . . Barriers to higher education for women effectively eliminate feminine competition. Lack of professional opportunities deprives professional education of value. In 1934 the German woman who approached the end of an arduous professional training looked out on a world in which vocational prospects in the various fields of endeavour were none too bright." See also Gertrud Baumgart, *Frauenbewegung Gestern und Heute* (Heidelberg: Winter, 1933), and

Irmgard Reichenau, *Deutsch Frauen an Adolf Hitler* (Leipzig: Adolf Kelin Verlag, 1933).

49. "Und so schreibe ich es [die Autobiographie], trotzdem ich glaube, dass es eigentlich keine Berechtigung hat."

50. "Bis vor kurzem wurde die Frau, die sich ihren Lebensunterhalt selbst verdiente, verachtet. Das drückte sich schon darin aus, dass die Frauen, die dies tun, von allen Männern . . . geduzt werden. Von dieser Duzerei waren nur die Maestras, die Lehrerinnen, ausgenommen. . . . Die Büroangestellten . . . werden offiziell zehn Prozent schlechter bezahlt als ihre männlichen Kollegen. In Wahrheit liegt die Entlohnung meist vierzig Prozent unter der Männer."

51. "Perón hat den Frauen viel versprochen, und etwas hat er gehalten: Er hat ihnen das Stimmrecht gegeben. Er konnte es wagen. Er hat sich dadurch keine Gegnerinnen geschaffen. . . . Allerdings, dass sie doch nicht ihre Geschicke selbst in die Hand nehmen durften, das haben die Frauen nicht gesehen. . . . Diese Massnahme ist auch kein Schritt zur Befreiung der Frau."

52. "Hier ist man froh, wenn wieder ein Tag vergangen ist, an dem der tägliche unaufhörliche Streit nicht zu einem Mord geführt hat."

53. "Im Herbst 1947 bin ich in die damalige sowjetische Besatzungszone Deutschlands zurückgekehrt. Ich habe es keinen Augenblick bereut und werde es nicht bereuen, denn hier ging meine grosse Sehnsucht in Erfüllung: sinnvoll mitzuarbeiten, beizutragen zum Aufbau einer besseren Zukunft, in der kein Krieg sinnlos das eben Errungene zerstört. Im dauernden Völkerfrieden, durch den Aufbau einer sozialistischen Wirtschaft, werden alle Menschen Menschen sein. Und im Kampf dafür lohnt es sich, zu leben (Leipzig, im Oktober 1950)."

WORKS CITED

Asociación Filantrópica Israelita, ed. *Zehn Jahre Aufbauarbeit in Südamerika 1933–1943*. Buenos Aires: Hilfsverein Deutschsprechender Juden, 1943.

Bussemeyer, Peter. *50 Jahre Argentinisches Tageblatt. Werden und Aufstieg einer auslandsdeutschen Zeitung*. Buenos Aires, 1939.

Dauber, Doris. *Als ich drei Berufe hatte. Argentinien wie es wirklich ist. Eine Reportage*. Rudolstadt: Greifenverlag, 1950.

———. *Eine Nacht-Ein Leben*. Buenos Aires: Editorial Cosmopolita, 1945.

Friedmann, James I. "Muttersprache-das Vaterland der Heimatlosen. Erinnerungen und Dokumentation eines deutschen Verlegers in der Emigration mit anschliessender Anthologie aus vergriffenen Büchern, Zeitschriften und Zeitungen, Argentinien 1938–1946." Ms. Deutsche Bibliothek, Frankfurt am Main, 1968. 3 vol.

Kamla, Thomas Anthony. "The Theme of Exile in the Novel of the German Emigration." Ph.D. diss., University of Wisconsin, 1973.

Kannapin, Klaus. "Zur Politik der Nazis in Argentinien von 1933 bis 1943." In *Der deutsche Faschismus in Latein-Amerika,* ed. Heinz Sanke. Berlin: Humboldt Universität, 1966.

Mittenzwei, Werner. *Carl Meffert, Clément Moreau. Ein Leben auf der Suche nach der Brüderlichkeit des Menschen.* Berlin: Henschel Verlag, 1977.

Morris, Katherine. "Women Remembering: Autobiography as a Source of German-Jewish Cultural History in Brazil." Unpublished essay.

Müssener, Helmut. "Meine Heimat fand ich hoch im Norden—Schweden ist gut—für die Schweden. Aspekte geglückter und mißglückter Integration in Schweden nach 1933." In *Leben im Exil. Probleme der Integration deutscher Flüchtlinge im Ausland 1933–1945,* ed. Wolfgang Frühwald and Wolfgang Schieder. Hamburg: Hoffmann und Campe Verlag, 1981.

Neumann, Livia. *Puerto Nuevo-Neuer Hafen.* Buenos Aires: Editorial Cosmopolita, 1945.

Olden, Balder. *Paradiese des Teufels. Biographisches und Autobiographisches. Schriften und Briefe aus dem Exil.* Berlin: Rütten und Loening, 1977.

Röder, Werner. "The Political Exiles: Their Policies and Their Contribution to Post-War Reconstruction." In *International Biographical Dictionary of Central European Emigrés 1933–1945,* ed. Herbert A. Strauss and Werner Röder. München: K. G. Sauer, 1983. Part 2, xxvii.

Rojer, Olga Elaine. *Exile in Argentina 1933–1945. A Historical and Literary Introduction.* New York: Peter Lang, 1989.

Seelisch, Winfried. "Das Andere Deutschland. Eine politische Vereinigung deutscher Emigranten in Südamerika." Diplomarbeit. Berlin: Otto Suhr Institut, 1969.

Stephenson, Jill. *Women in Nazi Society.* New York: Barnes and Noble, 1975.

Sternfeld, Wilhelm, and Eva Tiedemann. *Deutsche Exil Literatur 1933–1945.* Heidelberg: Verlag Lambert Schneider, 1970.

Strauss, Herbert. "Jews in German History: Persecution, Emigration, Acculturation." In *International Biographical Dictionary of Central European Emigrés 1933–1945,* ed. Herbert A. Strauss and Werner Röder. München: K. G. Sauer, 1983. 2 vols. Part 1, a–k.

Strelka, Joseph P. "The Novel in Exile: Types and Patterns." In *The Writers' Experience,* ed. John M. Spalek and Robert F. Bell. Chapel Hill: University of North Carolina Press, 1982.

The Personal Narratives Group, eds. *Interpreting Women's Lives.* Bloomington: Indiana University Press, 1989.

DIANA ORENDI HINZE

The Case of Luise Rinser: A Past That Will Not Die

In August 1987, four years after the death of Paul De Man, one of the giants of deconstructive literary theory, a Belgian graduate student found in the archives of *Le Soir* approximately one hundred articles published in that Belgian paper by De Man between 1940 and 1941.[1] Written during the time of German occupation, most of these book reviews, literary essays, and cultural contemplations proved innocuous. One, however, was unabashedly antisemitic. The storm that immediately arose and threatened to topple one of the gods of literary criticism—posthumously no less—has not abated in the last five years. The basic questions De Man's foes and friends seek to answer are, of course, ethical: Were the propagandistic utterances against Jewish writers contained in his *Le Soir* article merely dictated by fear of political repercussions? Were they thus a sign of moral weakness submitting to convenience? Or were they the honest expression of political-philosophical convictions? Whatever the verdict of this debate, hotly discussed at specially convened conferences, De Man's image would be tarnished: he would either surface as a rather weak-kneed opportunist and collaborator with the German occupying forces; or much worse, the alternative conclusion would enforce a radical revaluation of all De Man's ensuing utterances. Was he ever a true fascist and, if so, for how long and to what degree?

Statements made by the critic himself about this period of his life as well as what sketchy facts are known about it abound in such contradictions that an approximation of truth may lie in only one source: the text. Appropriating the critic's own tools to lay bare what may be hidden, De Man's theses of language's fundamental undecidability and tenuousness lead in the right direction. In his critical writings developed during the 1960s and after, De Man claimed that an author's intentions remain unclear and thus open to any interpretation by the reader and critic and that intentions remain secret to the author as well. This blindness to her/his own intentions removes the text to a location where there is neither absolute truth nor any degree of lasting certainty of meaning. According to De Man, the author's unconscious desire for privacy and escape forces him/her to withdraw behind a protective wall that critics can never dismantle more than partially.

In De Man's unconventional interpretation of Rousseau's line "I confess that I refuse to confess," critics have detected his own refusal to come to terms with youthful misdemeanors and ensuing feelings of guilt. The degree of guilt and the atonement befitting it remain, however, elusive as long as the perpetration hovers in the realm of allegation. The ultimate irony of the De Man case may well arise out of the critic's own theses: while the ultimate truth about the nature of his crimes lies beyond our grasp, the text constructed from both his evasive actions and his theories serves to indict him, possibly in such a measure that the punishment exceeds the crime.

As a tragic figure toppled not so much by the magnitude of his misdeeds but by the flaw of dishonesty, De Man's case could serve as a paradigm for one malaise of twentieth-century intellectuals: an initial fascination with fascist ideas that is later disavowed when the full extent of fascism's crimes against humanity are revealed. Rather than be implicated, many European artists and intellectuals denied their own past and hid behind lies and dissimulation.

There are striking parallels between the case of the Belgian-turned-American De Man and that of the German writer Luise Rinser who was born in 1911. Rinser, who has lived in Italy for the last thirty years, is an equally prominent, if less esoteric, highly prolific writer of fiction and diaries. The stations of the life and literary development of this writer—just recently touted Germany's most widely read woman novelist (*Bild der Frau*)—are well known because her involvement in an array of social causes has also made her a highly visible public figure. Trained as an elementary school teacher, she left this profession in 1938; her first novel, *Die Gläsernen Ringe* (Glass rings) appeared to favorable reviews in 1940; in 1944 she was incarcerated on grounds of *Wehrkraftzersetzung* (acts of sabotage against the government) for half a year but was freed before the end of the war. The book that made her famous, *Mitte des Lebens* (Life's center) and its sequel *Abenteuer der Tugend* (Adventure of virtue)—until now considered largely autobiographical—appeared in 1950 and 1957. Nina, heroine and alter ego of her creator, is presented as an avid resistance fighter from the very beginnings of the Third Reich, a fiercely independent woman who risks her life for political and racial victims of the regime. She is jailed for treason, yet has the largesse upon being freed by the occupying forces to save the life of an SS man who is dying of blood poisoning. It was only logical that from such beginnings, which made her into a symbolic figure of antifascism and the resistance, Luise Rinser would turn to postwar political and social causes; she has accordingly been a vociferous spokeswoman for the feminist movement, the antinuclear debate, the ecological battle, the advancements of rights of prison inmates, and the fight for rights of gypsies. It will come as a severe shock to the large group of Rinser devotees that parts of their heroic and steadfast figurehead's past have now been revealed to contain previously undisclosed secrets as compromising as anything in Paul De Man's past.

During a stay in the literary archives of Marbach, West Germany, in the summer of 1987, I discovered a series of mostly prose texts—two of which were openly profascist—written by Rinser; they had appeared between 1934 and 1936 in *Herdfeuer,* a Nazi magazine.[2] Only one of these, a poem "Junge Generation" (Young generation) had been made known to the general public by the editors of the neo-Nazi *Deutsche Nationalzeitung* with whom Rinser has been embroiled since the late 1960s in a nasty court battle about the alleged authorship of this "Hymn to Adolf Hitler" (1935). She has now lost two rounds of the battle against editor Kurt Ziesel, an unreformed Nazi who maintained the right to call her a "Nazi poet" in his publication. In a long-winded and ambiguously phrased renunciation of her initial denial, Rinser finally had to concede defeat in this matter in 1981. Yet her private disclaimers of any involvement in fascist thoughts or deeds continue unabated, as does her immense popularity.

She uttered such protests of innocence again with great fury and vigor during a two-day interview that she generously granted me in her home outside Rome in 1987.[3] So adamant in her denial of early infatuation with NS ideas was she that it became abundantly clear that if the truth were to be appropriated at all, it would have to be found beyond the realm of conscious self-analysis. Since the publication of Goethe's *Truth and Fiction,* there has, of course, been no need to question the fact that both the soul searching in which authors engage during interviews and the production of autobiographies are made up of equal amounts of fiction and coquettery. These self-reflections thus become part of the oeuvre, as much a figment of fantasy as any work so labeled, rather than sources of objective information.

If read against the grain of what is conventionally known about her past, Rinser's texts reveal to the critical reader visions of a mind driven maniacally from early on to perform feats of achievement. This passionate drive to excel, to stand out, to be admired for her uniqueness explains the immense force with which she has always hurled herself into righteous causes as well as endeavors that proved fatally flawed. "It is my will that you shall be great," the fifteen-year old addresses herself in her diary; indiscriminate in her desire for fame—and no doubt infatuated with Nietzschean ideas—she envisions herself in the "role of a leader (Führer) or a prophet, obsessed by a blind and unlimited will to achieve something grand, it [did] not matter what, it just [had] to be grand."[4] In her autobiography of 1981, *Den Wolf Umarmen* (Embrace the wolf), Rinser portrays herself as a precocious child who at once rebelled against and was shaped by her strictly Catholic middle-class environment in rural upper Bavaria. The strongly competitive system left her with an overarching worldly ambition, while the religious element of her upbringing forced her into exercises of asceticism and self-denial. From these basic contradictions spring many of the conflicting forces making up the writer's personality. A fascinating feature of *Den Wolf Umarmen* is the fashion in which the Rinser of 1981 invests her persona of 1918 not only with extraordinary intellectual capacities but also with strange and mystical powers of hypnotism and extrasensory perception, granting her in various situations the power over life and death for others and herself. Unmindful of how smoothly she erases the borders between reality and fiction, she paints an image of the youthful Rinser spared time and again thanks to what she calls an "undisturbed relationship with death."

"Gods are mortal, and we must let them die, when their time has come," proclaims the aged writer musing about herself forty years earlier, looking back at her life in 1939. "I never drove my gods into catastrophes, I let them fade away, those divine images of earlier stages of development" (139). But the gods she maintains she permitted to fade away have refused until today to die; they keep coming back to haunt her. It has proved a fundamental misperception that she would be able to go from one metamorphosis to the other unscathed.

The gods Rinser had thought to transcend in 1936 were the dogma and the trappings of the then new National Socialist regime. Looking at her beginnings, she sees herself raised apolitically to be a mere "Yes-sayer," and she accuses her parents' generation of "letting us run blindly into the danger" (196) of the Nazi ideology. The elders' fear of socialism, handed down to the young, drive them into the arms of the greater scourge. At this point in the book a fascinating pattern begins; it consists of alternating gestures of denial for her own involvement and gestures of defense for those who did submit to the Nazi lure. While Rinser presents herself as sensing intuitively the evil of the new regime, she does admit that "it would have been possible that we fell victim to fascism which promised to eradicate all that was old and decayed" (197). The twenty-two-year-old student at the University of Munich finishing her degree in elementary education and psychology, like so many of her generation, must have been enthralled by the new regime's promises for regeneration and national grandeur. Furthermore, her upbringing in rural Bavaria had instilled in her a preference for the simple life, so that the fascist nostalgia for a preindustrialized Germany and its anti-intellectualism held great appeal for the young woman waiting for her first teaching position in a Bavarian village."It was hard to detect the border between what we longed for and that which actually was in preparation . . . the pied pipers were clever," (255) Rinser—as so many would later ruefully admit—reflects about this period. Although she claims to have felt instinctive revulsion at the pomp of the parades, she goes so far as to concede (supposed quote from diary of those days): "I understand the seduction of the NS-celebrations; something takes effect there which leads to a mindless participation, a state of intoxication and daze. In me personally this experience creates the need for a renewed commitment to the mind" (287). The theme of the intellect opposing and negating the aura of mindless fascination emanating from the Nazi demon was to become the major leitmotif in Rinser's reconstruction of her—more or less subconscious—battle with NS ideas. But this is a retroactively infused element; it is nowhere to be detected in her writings of this period which contradict clearly her pretense of having remained an objective observer and outsider. She had agreed to set up and lead a *Bund Deutscher Mädel* (BDM) Camp in upper Bavaria where leaders for this women's organization were to be trained.[5] "We desperately need leaders," she writes in a report about this venture appearing in *Herdfeuer* of March/April 1934. "All those who are joyfully and forcefully dedicated to the new youth organizations (HJ, BDM) have to observe with disquiet and a nagging worry how here and there that strong initial enthusiasm threatens to ebb and return to the old bourgeois ways. . . . And why? Because we lack leaders. Or rather because those who lead today . . . frequently do not know what leadership means, how deeply leadership obligates and what its requirements in terms of human qualities and technical know-how are" (127).

That was certainly not a defect from which the teacher-trainee suffered who had early-on mentally prepared for just such a position. For that reason she felt it incumbent upon herself to take matters in hand; initiative for the leadership training camp had to come from the "Volk": "I placed one day before the Obergau-administration a plan which had been worked out to the smallest detail." Sensing that "time was precious," she pressed on to get her project approved and to utilize that initial burst of energy lifting the nation's spirit. In the report there follows an in-depth description of the daily regimen consisting of the well-known mix of strict discipline and inculcated enjoyment. Rounds of communal tasks such as cleaning, cooking, arts and crafts, skiing, and singing of hymns fill the day with robust if spartan pleasures. "If you are spoiled, you don't belong to us. There are only straw-filled mattresses and covers." The three goals on which camp training focused were: emphasis on discipline; the experience of the group, of comradery; and finally, because it was a girls' camp, the development of the "type of the new German woman." Rinser sees two types of girls represented in her camp: the feminine, quiet one on the one hand, the courageous, "SA-type" on the other. While the former loved singing, dancing, and crafts, the other preferred discussing politics and athletic activities. (Dare we interject the question here of which category Rinser fell into?) The consensus on where the happy medium would be found reads in Rinser's formulation like a classic prescription taken from a BDM brochure: "We want 'women' again, but women who are also 'pals': healthy, energetic, athletically trained, courageous, open, free, natural in all movements of their body, their hearts and their minds, free of all over-refinement and decadence. . . . Above all, we want woman, motherly woman. We do not want a fighter in the public sphere. . . . Our highest priority: the breeding of healthy human beings" (130f). The report ends with a renewed oath of eternal loyalty to the Führer "under the sign of the *Hakenkreuz* which obligates us." In the wake of this exhilarating experience, the young teacher expresses confidence in braving attacks by cowardly citizens who want to see fast success without being willing to sacrifice of themselves. She comes away with contempt for them but hope for her generation: "Idealism is not the same as optimism. We coined this motto in our camp: 'idealism is to see and feel the dirt—and yet to go on working'" (131).

What is there to say? We have to be willing today to take these embarrassing utterings as a document of misguided youthful fanaticism. Idealistic fervor characterized the Hitler Youth movement to whose dreams of reform Rinser subjected herself blindly and unquestioningly. Yet, regardless of the fact that she did undergo a change of heart later on, the truth about her initial philosophical-political faltering stands. Her beginnings in the fold of the Nazi camp are not to be denied, and, if the author does so today, all of her ensuing work in the literary and the public sphere needs to be reconsidered in the light of this obvious dishonesty. What remains believable of Rinser's valiant postwar involvement in social causes, her fight for freedom from all forms of oppression, and—most embarrassing of all—her vehemently voiced moral outrage over former and reborn Nazis in the German political and cultural scene? How much of this righteous posturing still rings true, or is her credibility and reputation tainted beyond repair by the unearthing of a past she thought to have left behind? I certainly will not attempt a definitive answer, finding it painful myself to reconcile the image of the former once respected Rinser with the newly discovered one. Yet, even at this late date, an admission of culpability might have been her response to the open confrontation with the media that followed on the heels of the discovery. This would at least have partially exonerated a writer to whom so many, especially among the young, have looked up with admiration. But Rinser does not consent to this solution that, albeit the most obvious, is also the most difficult requiring a great measure of largess and humility. "I will not do what so many politicians try: claim a black-out, amnesia," Rinser wrote in a rebuttal to an article by Juergen M. Moeller who outlined her Nazi past and analyzed the *Herdfeuer* texts. However, she then proceeds to do just that; pointing out that she never even joined the BDM, although she fleetingly "toyed with the idea of making a career out of work in the youth movement"; she concedes to having written the report: "It seems logical, although I don't remember doing it . . . and I can't explain the enthusiastic journalistic tone, unless I was forced to it [the tone]. . . . Whatever, that was the end of my work for the BDM" (*Tageszeitung*). It was not the end of her publishing in *Herdfeuer*, however. At least four more pieces appeared there until 1936 even if the writer claims ignorance today as to how they got into the "obscure magazine": "Harmless poems and stories . . . written before 1933 that had nothing, but absolutely nothing to do with the NS—I was 18 to 20 years old."

That this disclaimer borders on the meaningless if not ridiculous must have occurred to Rinser herself. She no doubt knows that one of her earliest literary mentors, Ernst Jünger, whom she read and emulated avidly in those days has been called "a proven opponent of the NS while being as undoubtedly instrumental in bringing it about" (Grimm). Handed to her by a young SA-man to whom she almost became engaged, Rinser had read Jünger's *In Stahlgewittern* (Storms of steel) of 1920 and *Der Kampf als Inneres Erlebnis* (Battle as inner experience) of 1922. Not surprisingly, numerous excerpts from these two works appear in Ernst Loewy's *Literatur unterm Hakenkreuz* (Literature under the sign of the Swastika), one of the most comprehensive documentations of Nazi literary texts. As Rinser writes in her autobiography, she was fascinated by Jünger's meticulously styled prose and set herself the task of appropriating his finesse in the art of close description. The story of a defoliation of a lily, later appearing as a chapter of *Die Gläsernen Ringe* in 1941, testifies to this intent. Jünger's central themes "death, total war, and the depersonalization of modern man" (Stern) initially intrigued the young Rinser; but she confesses that his cold and intellectualized aestheticism and elitist isolationism soon caused her disenchantment, even horror. "He may be a good stylist, but he is a coiner of counterfeit," she evaluates the other writer retrospectively, "you learn from him, but then you forget him" (*Den Wolf Umarmen* 17). What she today calls Jünger's "necrophilia," his pathological attraction to death, allegedly revolted her; but it did not keep her from seeking his personal acquaintance in 1940, an episode described in the most ambiguous of terms in *Den Wolf Umarmen,* about which she today reminisces full of unmistakable regret: "Fate did not permit him to include me in his life . . . nothing came of this relationship" (26). Jünger books, sent to her by their author, magically survived all bombing raids, "as though protected by a demon" (16). Nor had she abandoned her adulation of Jünger at the time of their meeting in 1940, when she had just completed the manuscript of her first book; in her correspondence with the older writer who at that time was observing the war from a rather exclusive vantage point in Paris, she informs him that he had unwittingly served as godfather to *Die Gläsernen Ringe.* When this memoir of her childhood appeared a year later, the novel's concluding sentence, "I realized that . . . the sharp and clear law of the mind would guide my life," was clearly modeled upon a phrase contained in Jünger's *Auf den Marmorklippen* (On the marble cliffs) of two years before, in which he proclaimed his intent to "resist solely through the power of the mind." But we have moved ahead here skipping several beats in the stages of Rinser's literary development. Back in 1934, disenchantment with the new political movement had not set in, and she would have been far from ready to follow anyone, even Jünger, into the withdrawn realm of "inner emigration" as she did in 1940. Now, her ambition and her enthusiasm drove her to make a literary debut of sorts.

Let us return for the moment to Rinser's characterization of her juvenalia as "harmless and innocent" of any Nazi contamination. Although it may be debatable what clearly constitutes Nazi literature, some guidelines have been established. As evidenced in critical analyses and documentations of this period, typical Nazi literature falls into three main categories: there are writings concerned with the idea of the "Volk," often termed the literature of "blood and soil"; there are works celebrating the idea of the heroic nature of war and the nation's need to prepare for it; and finally there are hymnal works adulating the sacred figure of the "Führer." Something for each of these headings is to be found in the treasure chest of Rinser's youthful literary production: most readers are familiar with the Hitler hymn reprinted ad nauseam by the *Deutsche Nationalzeitung.* Although this would not be readily apparent, judging from the radically different function of the two pieces, there are clear parallels between the hymn "Young Generation" and the BDM camp report considered earlier. In both pieces the universe is ruled by the same dichotomy between the sphere of the "satiated bourgeois" and that of the young, "marked by their oath to the great 'Führer.'" The lines "unsheltered, we keep an icy watch on towers and summits during sharp morning storms," are unmistakable echoes of the wind-tossed experiences collected in the paramilitary world of the women's ski camp. "Cool, hard and knowing is this conscious generation," in whose name the author swears to be loyal until death, "a sworn guardian of the sacred soil / the great "Führer's silent ambassadors," who will "watch, conquer, or die / because we are faithful."[6] Anthologies full of similar banalities written as devotional pieces to Hitler appeared with regularity in those years, and most authors in the fascist camp openly contributed to what Loewy calls "the death sentence of German literature" (275). But an author did not have to grovel quite as abjectly to be in the sacred cove, that is, to find a publisher for products that would have been refused as unqualifiedly poor writing a few years earlier. Now, any writing celebrating the "salt of the earth," the life of the farmer, and realistically describing his battle against the forces of decadent civilization and the close relationship of race and homeland was eagerly accepted by publications propagating "literature as a life force" (Langenbucher). Antiprogressive and anti-intellectual, this literature was designed to bring about a national rejuvenation through a return to the romanticized and idealized ways of an earlier period. Two of the remaining four Rinser short stories could be categorized as "blood-and-soil" writing; they capitalize on the nation's new taste for pieces utilizing regional dialects and depicting the hard yet heroic life of the rural population. These were elements the fledgling writer not only knew from close observation but must have intentionally used as tools in the reform battle she saw herself and her generation waging. "Die Traud. A Legend on All Souls Day from the Ammergau," (1934) published in the November/December issue of *Herdfeuer,* is written in the form of an oral narration. Appropriating Bavarian dialect as far as it lends itself to printing, the legend uses the standard repertoire of folk tale motifs; there is the charming fiddle player who first promises love to Traud, the only daughter of a wealthy farmer, but then he is seduced by a black-haired servant girl. When this steamy affair predictably ends with a child on the way and everyone's lives in ruins, overly proud Traud makes a pact with death not to embrace any other than him. After a number of prophecies and curses required by the formulaic structure of this genre, each major player has either been drowned, sucked empty of blood, or has danced himself/herself to death. Had this piece been meant as a farce or parody, it could not have been more full of cliches and prefabricated segments. Unfortunately, we cannot even grant Rinser the benefit of this doubt because there were more such products for which the rubric "harmless" would be entirely too benign. "Agnes," a much longer story was printed in the May/June 1936 issue of *Herdfeuer:* "Farmer Michael Weigant is lord and master on the Wildhartsberg. . . . The best in his manor: his blond, strong and hard-working wife and the three boys. And between the two oldest boys the girl, Agnes, as slim and fine as a young hazelnut branch: blond, light-eyed and tall like her father, mother and brothers." This southern Germanic idyll is disturbed by the arrival of Piet, a farmer's son from northern Germany who falls in love with Agnes: "Proudly sings his blood. Hot and forceful. 'You, I like you.' She puts her arms around his head and laughs at him. He puts her down on the floor. He thinks: 'How soft she is! Like a young animal. A deer; oh, my hands are so hard and full of calluses. I don't want to hurt her.' The coocoo screams. Seven times. Twelve times." Ignorant and innocent, Agnes is afraid of being pregnant; she drowns herself. Piet, the intruder from the North, harbinger of love and death, takes up his wandering again, having assured the father of his innocence. The hearty handshake with which the two men console each other, makes it amply clear: in this realm of undisputed patriarchy, the death of a foolish young thing, innocent and beautiful though she was, can be overcome as long as the male hegemony and its rigid work ethic survive intact. Rinser, who is, of course, known for her feminist stance today, conforms here completely with the fascist expectations of woman as serving male needs for the nation's glory: "shy, quiet and soft . . . her dominant function is subservience and fertility" (Loewy 124). Gazing after Piet who walks into the sunset, farmer Weigant muses while surveying his land: "Good bye, boy; but now horses, giddy-up. The land has to be broken. Let's start plowing." As J. M. Moeller quips in his critical evaluation of Rinser's *Herdfeuer* texts mentioned earlier, "prose like this may not have to be broken, but certainly forgotten as quickly as possible."

In the summer of 1935 "I tried for the first and last time to be blind and deaf and mute. I took the right for myself to be for once apolitical and live a very private life. I was in love, no I loved" *(Den Wolf Umarmen* 320), Rinser writes in her autobiography about the following period that signaled major changes in her life. Yet, the puzzled reader of her self-reflections asks, why does Rinser find it necessary to make excuses for leading the happily oblivious life of a young woman in love? Does she still feel herself under the charge that she had early-on imposed upon herself, the task of finding fame and grandeur tied somehow to the notion of assuming the role of a public figure? Her appeals to the reader's forgiveness do not make any sense unless a radical shift of allegiances was about to take place. Of course, having denied it in the first place, she would never admit here that the intoxicating effect of the Nazi ideology had slowly come to an end to be replaced by merely private concerns. Her true guilt feelings focus on the fact that she had left the public sphere without having metamorphosed into a full fledged opponent of the regime, a solution appearing so much more convenient and attractive in retrospect.

In 1936, Rinser came under the tutelage of composer Heinrich Kaminski by way of her fiance, Kaminski's master student, Horst Günther Schnell. In his review of *Den Wolf Umarmen,* Winfried Martini claimed in 1981 that it was Kaminski, then fairly well known, who now effected a political conversion in Rinser, getting her to read for the first time the great philosophical and literary texts of India and China and eventually leading her to the acquaintance with her next role model, Hermann Hesse. In the environs of Kaminski's highly cultured and refined household, Rinser, the tomboy elementary school teacher whose main pastimes had been mountain climbing and skiing, was now also introduced to the finer points of music and the arts. In turn, her romanticized swooning for the present political regime was exposed as the foolish and short-sighted misconception it was. She underwent the change of mind required of so many of her contemporaries at this time when the evil nature of the NS system revealed itself. Her autobiography's reader would expect, of course, not so much details of searching discussions but at least a portrayal reflecting some measure of gratitude and appreciation: had she not, after all, been saved from the gates of hell by the enlightened circle around Kaminski and Schnell? Yet the scenes in the composer's country home are described with so much rancor and barely hidden animosity that Martini calls them the "fatal climax" of her already flawed autobiography. Again she lashes out at others instead of directing insightful criticism where it belongs: the fundamental hypocrisy needed to depict this period in her life must have chafed painfully. Her benefactor thus becomes the butt of her ridicule. As a secondary figure, he assumes the role of stepping stone; her eyes were now lifted to the image of a new divinity.

> Thus we, brothers who are mistaken
> Can still feel love in all this conflict
> And not judgment and hatred
> But patient love
> Loving tolerance leads
> Us closer to the sacred goal.[7]

This last stanza of the Hesse poem "Besinnung" (Contemplation) copied by Rinser in a notebook of 1936, causes her the following reflections: "Later generations, the young of today cannot know that this poem had a significant political effect. During the Hitler regime, when there was only 'blood-and-soil literature', crude and silly farmers' novels written by intellectuals who had no idea what a farmer was, and war novels celebrating the battle and death, and Hitler youth poems—to read in a time like this such an acknowledgement of the power of the intellect, that was comfort and gave us hope, that encouraged us to join the resistance" (*Den Wolf Umarmen* 329). In the light of what we considered in Rinser's own publication record, this statement has to be taken as only one of many painful revelations contained in her autobiography. Undeniably honest, however, must have been Rinser's disillusionment with Nazi ideas and her desire in this period to turn away from the old idols, surrounded as she was by intellectuals and artists who had never fallen prey to Hitler's ideology. Thus it was Hesse, his work and his personal advice transmitted through a series of letters, who now became the young teacher's "refuge from National Socialism . . . a kind of guru." His eternally young wisdom appealed to her and Schnell as it would to the postwar generation in Germany and abroad. Rinser eagerly took up the task central to Hesse's message: a call for individuation, a search for the path to the inner self to be achieved through a rebellion against civilization's limiting constraints. A pacifist since his participation in World War I, Hesse, though unsympathetic to the new regime in Germany, was very cautious during these early years in his exhortations to Germans about open political opposition. In the voluminous correspondence with Germans requesting advice from the sage living in Switzerland, Hesse admonished above all the restraint, patience, and tolerance reiterated in the verses of the poem "Contemplation." Only after the war was he to proclaim his outrage against timid half-heartedness and caution his correspondents in Germany that he could take seriously only those Hitler opponents who had been in a concentration camp "with both feet" (*Betrachtungen und Briefe* 448).

Consequently, the search for self Luise Rinser embarked on at this time did not entail an active participation in the political underground, a connotation erroneously to be deduced from the above quoted passage from *Den Wolf Umarmen.* Rather, the withdrawal from the public into the private sphere found expression in the writing Rinser was about to begin, her first larger novella, *Die Gläsernen Ringe.* With this memoir of her early years up to the age of sixteen, Rinser chose a genre popular with many other German writers who, although opposed or at least indifferent to the regime, had chosen to stay in the country and wanted to continue to be published. Like Rinser, they had abdicated the political arena and retired to an inner realm, had chosen not exile but "inner emigration." As H. D. Schäfer has pointed out in an excellent and exhaustive treatment of this group of writers, Günter Eich, Karl Krolow, Peter Huchel, Wolfgang Koeppen, Ernst Schnabel, Friedo Lampe, Rudolf Krämer-Badoni, and Marie-Luise Kaschnitz produced a body of "qualitatively significant literature" between 1933 and 1945. Although after the war many denied their popularity and even their start during the Third Reich or exaggerated difficulties with censorship, even well-known publishing houses such as Suhrkamp (where *Die Gläsernen Ringe* appeared in 1941) during the early years of the regime were permitted to specialize in the publication of nonfascist literature.

The "inner emigrants"—opposed politically as much to socialism as to National Socialism—were by nature antiprogressive, nonidealistic, and individualistic. Because survival was their only agenda, calls for an active overthrow of the government could not be the focus of their works; their criticism thus limited itself to veiled invectives against the anti-intellectualism of the regime. Their attitude was typically apolitical, reaffirming in a vague sense the spirit of European humanism. This aura of largely aloof noninvolvement was confirmed by the literary forms chosen by this group: the diary, sermon, legend, travel sketch, feuilleton. The preferred tone was that of private confession, of melancholy recollection. To facilitate the escape from immediate concerns, writers sojourned into the *heile Welt* (intact world) of their childhood past or faraway fantasy places. As Reinhold Grimm has pointed out, it is the image of the untouched epicenter, "the center of the cyclone" (referring to Benn) that best expresses the focal experience of "inner emigration." Not surprisingly, these writings abound with visions of island romances, asylums in quiet corners, and garden idylls. This "regression to remote realms," as Walter Benjamin has called it, characterizes perfectly the writing Rinser remembers as an act of desperation in 1939; looking back at the young woman expecting her first child, living in simple circumstances far away from the beloved Chiemsee village in the south, she writes in *Den Wolf Umarmen:* "she has to save herself, the rabid dog is after her, it is panting and it has Hitler's eyes and Hitler's voice, and it has declared war on Poland, on the world and on life. She has to save herself, because of the child, and there is only one path towards salvation: she has to write" (11).

Looking for models in the works of both her literary mentors, Ernst Jünger—who had by then joined the "inner emigrants" with his *Auf den Marmorklippen*—and Hermann Hesse, Rinser dived deeply into her earliest memories. Consequently, *Die Gläsernen Ringe* shows a curious combination of both authors' imprints. Stylistically, Rinser was still enamored of Jünger's closely honed descriptive detail. But while she strove to imitate the language of the writer who, as we recall, served as godfather to this her first major work, the universe she created was suffused with Hesse's spirit and peopled with Hesse-inspired characters. Hesse's *Narziss und Goldmund* of 1930 probably was the single most dominant influence on *Die Gläsernen Ringe,* starting with the locale in a monastery and extending to the artist-protagonist's split into the sensual-erotic and the ascetic-intellectual. The typically Hessian homoerotic constellation of two males finds its equivalent in Rinser's portrayal of a latently lesbian relationship between the female protagonist and an adored teacher. Hesse's nature child, Lise, the gypsy girl who first introduces Goldmund to the pleasures of sexual love, has a parallel in the "wild boy" befriending Rinser's prepubescent persona whose magical attraction she flees. The book's final scene echoes the by now familiar leitmotiv of the mind's indomitable power, a sentiment with which she was sure to recap both Hesse's and Jünger's central message: the sixteen-year old Rinser-persona is brought to realize the destructive and evil forces lurking all around her as well as in her subconscious; playing once more the magical game of the "glass rings," rings in a pool of quiet water caused by her throwing of small stones, she recognizes the "wonderfully strict pattern" that will govern her life: "not the confused and dark suffering of the physical, but the sharp and clear law of the logos, the intellect" (160). Hesse, predictably, was delighted and wrote the young author: "I read with true enjoyment the pure and noble German you write and was also delighted about the conclusion of the book and its affirmation of the spiritual" (*Den Wolf Umarmen* 12). The small book was received very favorably by both the reading public and the official critics; Rinser recalls, "I never again had such uniformly positive, even enthusiastic reviews." But this, she muses, should not surprise anyone, considering the competition: "Hitler-ordered blood-and-soil literature, war books, and boring farmers' novels." In a review in the *Neue Schweizer Rundschau* of December 1941, Rinser is applauded for her "descent into the dream-like remote realm of youth," done in descriptive passages of a "timeless, visually satiated" language. Its very classicality erected a protective wall against the onslaught of the political chaos surrounding the book's genesis. Although it follows that *Die Gläsernen Ringe* is anything but an antifascist document, Rinser has at times called it thus (Konzag) and points to the fact that she was forbidden to publish further in 1943. As far as this can be ascertained, ten editions of *Die Gläsernen Ringe* were printed until 1943, at which point Suhrkamp Verlag was not issued any further supply of paper for books not high on the list of desirable writings. The fate of being silenced by this war emergency befell many "inner emigrants," but it should not be construed as a sign of persecution by the regime or a restrictive measure leveled for the antifascist content of the publication.[8] Rinser is still listed in *Kürschner's Literaturkalender* of 1943 under the double name she was then using, Luise Rinser Schnell.

But the period of exile in an interior realm of quietude had now come to an end: in 1942, shortly after the birth of their second son, Horst Günther Schnell was drafted—Rinser today thinks he was placed into a *Strafbataillon* for his openly antifascist remarks, a claim impossible to verify—and fell on the Russian front in 1943. With two infants, Rinser took refuge in a ramshackle little house near Salzburg. She was solely responsible for her family; she had left the teaching profession; and she had not produced any further fiction. The novel *Hochebene* was written a little later and not published until 1948; nor is it likely that it would have been published in those days. A venture offered to her by a high-ranking Nazi to write the film script for a propaganda film fell through when she could not come to a compromise on the script with the film's director; more "harmless Kitsch" she calls it today, but it did leave her with a 2,000-Mark advance. Once more she had apparently tested how far her ambition would let her charge into the world before her conscience would call her back. She had no doubt arrived at a dead end, both privately and professionally. The full ire of her always passionate nature logically now turned upon the source of all her present misfortune: the Nazis had become her arch enemies. With this turn, her development into an outspoken opponent of the regime had finally come full circle. Full of the missionary zeal so characteristic of her, yet incautious and impetuous to a fault, she was soon in deep trouble with the authorities. The sabotage activities she engaged in were typical of all Germans who fell within the categories of the *Mitläufer,* those Germans who quietly assented to the regime's activities, and the active resistance fighters. Like others termed officially *Heimtückefälle* (cases of sabotage), Rinser had tried in small ways to subvert the now-hated government: she listened to foreign radio stations, communicated with Polish and Russian prisoners of war working in the area, refused to join the party or even contribute to Nazi charitable causes, corresponded with "enemies of the nation" (Hesse), and finally married a communist who was also a homosexual. This last item—bizarre by any account—had more than any other action, attracted the curiosity of the authorities, and the couple had been spied upon for two years before Rinser was finally arrested. Her arrest came immediately upon the heels of a denunciation by a former good friend of the writer's who had appealed to her for help; Rinser advised this friend to caution her husband to leave the troops because the war was practically lost and just about over. Consequently, Rinser was charged with defeatist activities and detained in the Traunstein women's prison from October 1944 to February 1945 while awaiting trial. This period is described in her *Gefängnistagebuch* (*A Woman's Prison Journal*),[9] published in 1946, it documents the dehumanizing effect of imprisonment but also attests to Rinser's indomitable energy and vitality. She was held in *Untersuchungshaft* (detention while awaiting trial) and released upon intervention by Karl Ritter, the highly positioned NS official who had offered her the failed propaganda film venture a few years earlier. Whether she was charged with "high treason" and whether a death sentence was actually pending are two more Rinser claims impossible to verify today.

There can be no doubt that the brutalizing effect of imprisonment had a lasting impact on the writer's development and that

Rinser then was at her farthest remove from the early infatuation with NS ideas. But she had at this point already begun to disavow categorically any such previous involvement; the process of conscious amnesia had set in and was dictating to her a reconstituted self-image modeled on those requirements that were now politically correct and necessary. The past had become a burden and a liability that was easy to toss off in the general chaos of the "zero hour;" these efforts were even more plausible and convincing in light of her recent incarceration. Rinser had taken up her correspondence with Hesse again, and although her letter of 1946 reporting on recent experiences is not extant, Hesse's response is telling enough; this reply, (*Betrachtungen und Briefe* 445–453), first published in a daily newspaper, was also to be a significant factor in establishing the image of Rinser as valiant antifascist in the public eye that later became prevalent. Hesse begins by categorizing the various letters he has been getting from Germany since the collapse of the Third Reich. Complaining about the generally larmoyant tenor of most of these letters and the total and incomprehensible absence of any admission of culpability in the recent debacle, Hesse's reaction is bitterness and disgust. He is the first to raise an issue here on which prominent social psychologists were to focus only twenty years later: Hesse charges the Germans as a nation with the infamous *Unfähigkeit zu trauern* (inability to mourn), a failure to come to terms with the aftereffects of atrocities committed in the nation's name. But Rinser's letter he praises as of a totally different nature: not a cliche word, not a complaint nor a charge. Deeply moved by her personal fate, so threatened and so close to death, he assures her that he was not really surprised by what happened to her: "for I had never imagined you with one foot in prison or camp and with the other in the party but never doubted that you stood on the right side, as courageous and conscious as befits your bright eyes and your intelligence. And that naturally meant grave danger" (450).

Thus, imprisonment had earned Rinser the "red badge of courage" needed to become the representative of that small group of politically astute and daring Germans to whom Hesse and the world were looking for rebuilding Germany at this time. To the seventy-year-old Hesse, Rinser's letter and her very existence constituted one of the few hopeful signals "for the continuation of a truly spiritual Germany," which he was confident to find only in such "wonderfully joy-giving credos of tenacity and courage, of hope and readiness unblinded by illusion. I thank you for this. Protect the seed, remain faithful to the light and to the spirit, there are only few of you, but perhaps you are the salt of the earth." Rinser was fully prepared to fulfill the task implied in Hesse's praise, and the publication of the *Gefängnistagebuch,* coming immediately after his letter, proves this point. In her foreword to the slim volume, she argues against the intent of many of her compatriots to forget as quickly and as completely as possible: "those who say it is dangerous to conjure the abyss of evil, should consider that it is much more dangerous to kill truth by *totschweigen* (silence) and to escape into a world of the "pure intellect" into which the memories of evil's crimes are not admitted. Everything that is banned forcefully from humanity's memory, will surface one day and powerfully demand its right" (*Gefängnistagebuch* Foreword).

The moral outrage expressed here so forcefully has been the center of the Rinser credo in the last forty years. Linked with it is an undeniable undertone of self-righteousness, a privilege supposedly due her on grounds of exclusion from complicity. If things were as they seem, the voluminous oeuvre the author has produced in the time since then should be a testament to at least one isolated German writer's "ability to mourn." However, the signals her texts emit sadly do not warrant granting her such exceptional status. To perform the tasks of grieving and remembering adequately, the mourner, as Alexander Mitscherlich and Margarete Mitscherlich pointed out in their groundbreaking book *The Inability to Mourn* of 1967, "has to recognize wrong convictions as such, has to be capable and willing to make changes, and must be able to confront all that was wrong." Rinser was, in fact, now asked to help others overcome shame and enter into the process of reform, repentance, and reentry into a normal life. In 1946, she was hired by the new government to give lectures to an assembly of four hundred German prisoners of war, former SS men undergoing de-Nazification. She chose the title: "Hitler in uns selbst. Versuch einer Analyse des Nachkriegsdeutschen," (Hitler in ourselves. An attempt at an analysis of the postwar German, *Den Wolf Umarmen* 398). Many of these men left the room in protest after listening to some of her invectives. "I understood them. They did not give in and grovel; their manliness did not permit that and their oath of loyalty. I was almost impressed by them" (398). There is a basic ambivalence here, a stance that was to dictate essentially the ways in which Rinser would deal with the dark and unresolved problem of the past—the nation's and her own.

"Today it is less a question of what [a writer] was or did then [during the fascist period] but rather what he/she is and does today; more precisely we need to look at the ways in which . . . the past is dealt with," proclaimed Ernst Loewy (353), citing the example of writers such as Gottfried Benn who had remained unenlightened about the true nature of the fascist state long after its debacle. Discussing Benn's case, the critic continues: "That he lost his way in 1933, . . . may be excusable. In 1950 . . . it is shameful. It is a total declaration of the mind's bankruptcy before a power which held him captive even long after its demise." With this in mind, let us return here to issues brought up in our initial discussion of the De Man story; trying to approximate the truth in the Rinser controversy will entail performing a similar exercise of deconstruction on her texts; we might then be able to dismantle the protective wall erected by the writer's will to erase traces, to smooth over tell-tale signs. "One of the themes of deconstruction is that the position you try to separate yourself from tends to reappear as a repressed motif in your own texts," (Wiener) Gerald Graff said in pondering the De Man case, and this observation finds strange applicability in the case of the writer here under scrutiny. Much of Rinser's work revolves around the general question of culpability; several books and short stories focus directly upon the issue of involvement with fascism. But the scenarios Rinser chooses are sublimations, exhibiting the desire to construct post facto a reality that might have been. Frequently at the center of her plots are Germans who help those pursued by the regime, Jews or political refugees. This is, of course, most central in *Mitte des Lebens* (Life's Center), whose heroine Rinser's readers have always identified closely with their creator. "She is not really me, but she has some of my characteristics," *Den Wolf Umarmen* 410) the writer says today of Nina, the courageous protagonist who not only is active in the resistance starting with smuggling those in danger over the border as early as 1933 but also procures poison for a political prisoner to help him commit suicide, saves a Jewish child during the Crystal Night, and discusses with rage and disgust the question of euthanasia with fellow students at the University of Munich. Even if her writing was not a conscious attempt to fit herself with a past more redeeming than the truth—and no one can be quite sure about this—the effect of such a construct bears considering: if there were, indeed, as many Germans as noble and selfless as Rinser leads us to believe, the fascist disaster would shrink proportionately to their number in the eyes of the world. There is thus a grave danger in presenting figures like Nina or plot constellations such as we find in Rinser's "Jan Lobel aus Warschau" and "Hinkela" (1956), short stories written in the first years after the war. Both stories present escaped Jews who find refuge and succor in the homes of Germans. The Jew is seen as an alien, the other, who forces his entry into the sphere of the central female figures. Rinser here utilizes one of the constellations developed during the time of her apprenticeship as a writer. In the *Herdfeuer* story "Agnes," Piet from the northern realms who enters Agnes's world with such tragic consequences, already served the same purpose. The "other" has now acquired a new identity, but his function in the plot development still stands: the outcast and refugee who is taken in as a guest, sets into motion a cycle of joy and love as well as jealousy, suffering and finally death; these men come to liberate women's spiritual and sexual needs, acting as life-giving forces in the static existence typical of female roles. Both Jan (in "Jan Lobel from Warsaw") and the Jewish child in "Hinkela" are redeemer figures who free all of those with whom they come into contact in their new environment from their isolation and catatonic withdrawal. Both are shot to death when they resume their escape, but they leave behind "death in life," a void that cannot ever be filled as in Jan Lobel's case; or they mediate even more directly between life and death by dragging along their beloved victims, as in the case of the unnamed Jewish child in "Hinkela" who takes his protector into the hail of German bullets when they try to escape thirty miles outside Auschwitz. Thus, these Jewish figures are assigned the status of reverse Christ figures: they are initially permitted to grant happiness, peace, and love, but after their act of redemption they lead their loving captives straight into the apocalypse. The miserable and undignified death they themselves die then appears as nothing but a logical consequence of their intrusion, not a senseless crime perpetrated against the innocent. This can be done because there is no clear assignation of guilt anywhere in the Rinser universe; having the Nazi system act as some vague and anonymous evil in the background does not allow specific charges or single out individual responsibilities. And yet it is only when we "consciously come to terms with feelings of guilt and shame and their causes that we can overcome and integrate them into our conscience," Margarete Mitscherlich has pointed out. But Rinser denies this by insisting on a fundamental ambivalence in the design of her characters and her world in general. Nothing, she claims, should be painted in black and white or in one-dimensional terms. A statement of crucial significance surfaces in *Mitte des Lebens,* when Nina agonizes over how to write about the episode in which she saved the two SS men:

> Let's face it, we are no heroes, we just act like it, we are all a little cowardly and a little calculating and selfish and far from greatness. And that . . . I would like to show: that we are both bad and good at the same time, heroic and afraid, small and generous, everything close together, and that it is impossible to know what prompted us to a certain act, a good or a bad one. I don't like people who want to make everything so simple, when everything is so terribly confusing. (106)

And in a sudden and unexpected fit of rage that betrays more than she could have intended, Rinser turns upon her reader and accuses him/her of being one who "demands such stories where everything dissolves smoothly," stories full of heroism, self-denial, and political immaculateness; "there are no even equations in life," she warns, and thus literature that works on evoking cheap effects and grand gestures remains to her nothing but "posed photos." In a world as complex as she draws it, everyone is equally deserving of compassion, everyone has a claim upon suffering, everyone, in other words, has the potential to be considered a victim. This must necessarily result in a dangerous erasing of all borders, and consequently questions about individual responsibility and complicity become invalid. Rinser's strategy by which clearly defined fronts are eroded is best demonstrated by using the "Jan Lobel" story: at the end of the war, the patriarch of the household in which Jan, the escaped Jew, has found refuge returns. Max Olensky is painted as the archetypal German soldier, a man who by losing the war has also lost his manhood and who returns to a country and a home where everything has been devastated and where he has been displaced. But he can feel no hatred against the wife who cheated on him: "How is a woman like that to be blamed?" he asks. Likewise, he forgives his daughter, his son and his mother who have all fallen under the fascination of Jan's charm. The intent here is to demonstrate that suffering is not the exclusive claim of one particular group. Because everyone is equally caught in the web of aberration, every human being deserves the grace of forgiveness. This, however, demeans the specific situation of the Jews in Germany during the Third Reich: in Rinser's view—which, of course, many Germans share—the crimes of dehumanization and deprivation committed against this group differ in no way from those committed upon all Germans in their war-ravaged country. Subtle mechanisms of apologetics are at work here plying the reader into accepting life as a generally diseased situation. Rinser's oeuvre may express empathy for the suffering of humanity, but by not extending her sympathies specifically to the Nazi victims, she fails in the task of mourning their horrible fate. By not clearly placing blame where it belongs, she fails in reminding her readers of the guilt they need to remember collectively.

In her latest book, *Silberschuld* (Silver's guilt, 1987) Rinser has addressed the question of collective guilt head-on. Utilizing the metaphor of the descent into the mines of the past, into the depth of memory, she does not unearth the half expected, half hoped for admission of past failings. Instead her protagonist surfaces from the subterranean caves with the triumphant revelation that all of humankind's basic misdeeds are linked to material greed. Humanity needs to be liberated from this scourge and the aged writer's persona—reminiscent of the adolescent Rinser's drive for martyrdom and leadership—has taken up the challenge. She descends to effect a redemption from the collective crimes of her forefathers, and in the final fireworks in which all jewels and amassed riches are exploded she grants herself and humankind a sweeping amnesty for the deeds of the past. Even though Rinser's delving into remembrance deviates from the adamant gestures of evasion characteristic for her previous work, she still fails to arrive at the essential recognition: there is no indication that she wishes to acknowledge the memories of collaborationist impulses. As long as her denials remain steadfast, however, her personality and her work will be under the dark cloud of suspicion. Like Paul De Man she has become, permit me to quote myself here, "a tragic figure toppled not so much by the magnitude of her misdeeds but by the flaw of dishonesty."

NOTES

1. A selection of critical essays on this topic: Jacques Derrida, "Like the Sound of the Sea Deep within the Shell," *Literary Inquiry* (Spring 1988); Hans-Thies Lehmann, "Paul De Mans Dekonstruktionen," *Merkur*, Nr.472 (Juni 1988); Delmore Schwartz, "The Case of Paul De Man," *New York Times Magazine*, 28 August 1988; Jon Wiener, "Deconstructing Paul De Man," *The Nation*, 9 January 1988.

2. The *Herdfeuer* texts were pointed out to me by Mr. Pfeifel, the able librarian of the Schiller Nationalmuseum's literary archives. The material found in the 1936 issues were secured with the gracious help of staff members in the Library of Congress, Washington, D.C.

3. I was a guest for two and a half days at Rinser's mountain villa in Rocco di Papa outside Rome in August 1987. The writer at first graciously consented to lengthy taped interviews during which she freely offered her interpretations and opinions on her own and other modern writers' works. She flew into a rage, however, whenever the slightest mention was made of her own possibly collaborationist past. Judging from Rinser's reaction, this matter is a source of torment to her. It became obvious that direct confrontation was not going to elicit the truth. Suffice it to say that I left less than satisfied; in fact, I was quite bewildered and embarrassed to have witnessed this show of dissimulation.

4. All quotations from this book are my own translations.

5. Bund Deutscher Mädel, Association of German girls and women during Third Reich.

6. "Junge Generation," Rinser.

Von den Grenzen des Landes hören wir nächtens
Fieberndes Wühlen dumpf und böse in der Erde.
In den Fabriken schlagen die Hämmer, schmieden
Eisen hart und kalt zu nackter Todeswaffe.

Gefährlich riecht es um Mitternacht aus Feindland
Geheim brauen giftig schwelende gelbe Mordgase.
Um die Ecken der Städte schleicht grinsend der Tod
Unter uns schüttert der Boden vom Bohren schlafloser Wühler.

In den weichen Dunstnestern des Tales aber liegen,
Eng sich wärmend und satt, die guten Bürger
Und träumen schnarchend vom ewigen Frieden,
den ihnen ein sanfter verbindlicher Bürgergott schenkt.

Wir aber, angerufen von ewig eisernem Wort,
Wir, des grossen Führers gezeichnet Verschworene,
Ungeborgen in scharfen Morgenstürmen,
Halten auf Türmen und Gipfeln klirrende Wacht.

Kühl, hart und wissend ist dies wache Geschlecht,
Nüchtern und heiliger Trunkenheit voll,
Tod oder Leben, ein Rausch, gilt uns gleich—
Wir sind Deutschlands brennendes Blut.

Todtreu verschworene Wächter heiliger Erde,
des grossen Führers verschwiegene Gesandte,

Mit seinem flammenden Zeichen auf unserer Stirn,
Wir jungen Deutschen, wir wachen, siegen oder sterben,
denn wir sind treu!

7. "Besinnung," Hermann Hesse
Besinnung
Darum ist uns irrenden Brüdern
Liebe möglich in aller Entzweiung
Und nicht Richten und Hass
Sondern geduldige Liebe
Liebendes Dulden führt
Uns dem heiligen Ziele näher.

8. This point is made by H. D. Schäfer in his essay on "inner emigration," quoted above.

9. Published in a translation by Michael Hulse in the United States in 1988.

WORKS CITED

"Deutsche Jugend in der Dichtung." *Neue Schweizer Rundschau.* NF, vol. 9. December 1941.

Grimm, Reinhold. "Im Dickicht der Inneren Emigration." In *Die Deutsche Literatur im Dritten Reich,* ed. Horst Denkler. Stuttgart: Reclam, 1976.

Hesse, Hermann. "Ein Brief nach Deutschland. 1946." *Betrachtungen und Briefe.* Berlin: Suhrkamp, 1958.

———. *Narziss und Goldmund.* Berlin: Fischer Verlag, 1930.

Jünger, Ernst. *Auf den Marmorklippen.* Stuttgart: Klett, 1967.

———. *In Stahlgewittern.* Berlin: Mittler, 1920.

———. *Der Kampf als Inneres Erlebnis.* Werke, vol. 5. 1922. Reprint. Stuttgart: Klett, 1960.

Konzag, Marianne. "Gespräch mit Luise Rinser." *Sinn und Form* 36 (July/August 1984).

Langenbucher, Hellmuth. "Die Aufgabe der Dichtung in unserer Zeit." In *Rufe in das Volk.* München: Deutscher Volksverlag, 1942.

Loewy, Ernst. *Literatur unterm Hakenkreuz.* Frankfurt: Europäische Verlagsanstalt, 1966.

"Luise Rinser steht zu ihren Fehlern." *Bild der Frau* (Februar 1988).

Martini, Winfried. "Flammenzeichen auf der Stirn." *Rheinischer Merkur* 19 (8 May 1981).

Mitscherlich, Alexander, and Margarete Mitscherlich. *Die Unfähigkeit zu trauern.* München: Piper, 1967.

Moeller, Jürgen M. "Deutschlands brennendes Blut." *Tageszeitung* (TAZ) (10 February 1988).

Rinser, Luise. "Aus einem Oberbayrischen BDM-Führerlager." *Herdfeuer* (March/April 1934).

———. "Die Traud. Eine Allerseelenlegende aus dem Ammergau." *Herdfeuer* (November/December 1934).

———. "Junge Generation." *Herdfeuer* (January/February 1935).

———. "Agnes." *Herdfeuer* (May/June 1936).

———. *Die Gläsernen Ringe.* Berlin: Suhrkamp, 1941.

———. *Gefängnistagebuch.* München: Desch, 1946.

———. *Hochebene.* Kassel: Schleber, 1948.

———. *Mitte des Lebens.* Frankfurt: Fischer, 1950.

———. *Abenteuer der Tugend.* Frankfurt: Fischer, 1957.

———. "Jan Lobel aus Warschau." In *Ein Bündel weisser Narzissen.* Frankfurt: Fischer, 1956.

———. *Den Wolf Umarmen.* Frankfurt: Fischer, 1981.

———. "Hinkela." In *Geschichten aus der Löwengrube.* Frankfurt: Fischer, 1986.

———. *Silberschuld.* Frankfurt: Fischer, 1987.

———. *A Woman's Prison Journal.* Trans. by Michael Hulse. New York: Schocken, 1988.

———. "An meine Freunde und Feinde." *Die Tageszeitung* (TAZ) (February 1988).

Schäfer, Hans Dieter. "Die nichtfaschistische Literatur der jungen Generation im NS Deutschland." In *Die Deutsche Literatur im Dritten Reich,* ed. Horst Denkler. Stuttgart: Reclam, 1976.

Stern, J. P. *Ernst Jünger. A Writer of Our Time.* Cambridge: Bowes & Bowes, 1953.

Wiener, Jon. "Deconstructing Paul De Man." *The Nation,* 9 January 1988.

ELAINE MARTIN

Autobiography, Gender, and the Third Reich: Eva Zeller, Carola Stern, and Christabel Bielenberg

Autobiographical works on the Nazi era proliferated in the 1970s and 1980s to a point where scholars (and readers) in the 1990s have a rich selection available for consideration. One of the first works published in this wave of literature was Christa Wolf's *Kindheitsmuster* (*Patterns of Childhood*), which, since its initial appearance (East Germany 1976, West Germany 1979, U.S. 1980), has become a classic example of the genre. I have chosen to focus in this essay on three lesser-known works, which are, in a sense "literary children" of *Kindheitsmuster;* each of the three represents a different autobiographical treatment of the Nazi era.[1] I chose widely varied works as an illustration of the range of autobiographical writing on the subject; also the several points of intersection—and what they say about the universality of women's experiences under Nazism—are thus reinforced. After providing background information on the three works and exploring some of their textual differences, as well as differences of authorial perspective, I focus my attention in the remainder of the essay on the interplay between recent theory on women's autobiography and these three texts, which are restricted by time and place to descriptions of a very specific as well as singular historical experience. Of particular interest to me in this essay are the following problems: genre definition, including the relative balance of the three components of aute/bios/graphia; literary self-constitution as it is influenced by the interwoven elements of patriarchy, fascism, gender, religion, and sexuality; and concepts of victimization. I conclude with a discussion of the image of the mirror and its unique function in these autobiographical works.

The three authors Eva Zeller, Carola Stern, and Christabel Bielenberg have been chosen from among numerous others because of the diversity of life experiences they represent and the very different types of works they have written about the shared experience of National Socialist Germany. Eva Zeller is a professional writer, whose two novels, *Solange ich denken kann* (As far as I can recall, 1981), and its sequel *Nein und Amen* (No and Amen, 1985), are examples of autobiographical fiction. Her two novels, which she considers a single work, show distinct parallels with Christa Wolf's *Kindheitsmuster,* although Zeller told me in our 1986 interview that she read Wolf's novel only after completing her own. Carola Stern was a journalist for years and had written several biographies before attempting her autobiography, *In den Netzen der Erinnerung* (In the nets of memory, 1986). Stern's work is of special interest because she simultaneously writes her own autobiography and the biography of her husband in the same book; she contrasts their very different lives, hers as a Nazi, his as a Communist. By contrast, Christabel Bielenberg had no writing experience when she composed *The Past is Myself* in the late 1960s, a project that took her two years. Bielenberg's case is also unique because her book has had a complicated publishing history. It went undiscovered for almost fifteen years, when suddenly in the early 1980s it became a sort of bestseller. Her experience is similar to that of Austrian writer Erika Mitterer who told me that she sought a publisher for thirteen years before finally finding one in the late 1970s. Mitterer's novel, *Alle unsere Spiele,* was translated into English only in 1989, more than twenty years after it had been written. As for Bielenberg, not only did her book enjoy a marketing success, but the BBC also made a television movie of the work. It was shown on PBS in the United States in March 1989 with the title *Christabel,* and the book is marketed in the United States under that name.

These works differ in several important ways. The authors experienced dissimilar aspects of the National Socialist era based on differences of class, nationality, and political orientation. Bielenberg not only belonged to the upper class but also, as an Englishwoman ("I am British to my Irish core"), she had a totally different, and in some respects privileged, perspective on events. By contrast Zeller came from a middle-class family; her father was a well-known scholar, and her mother a pianist. Stern's family was lower middle class and lived in a rural area in Pommern. On the political spectrum, Bielenberg's (English) family, her husband's (German) family, and their friends were all liberals and anti-Nazi; Peter Bielenberg was even peripherally involved in the July 20th assassination plot against Hitler. Quite at the other end is Carola Stern, whose family embraced National Socialism and who enthusiastically joined the NSDAP (National Socialist party) at the age of eighteen. In the middle of these two political extremes is Zeller, who grew up between her bitterly divorced parents, between a politically naive mother who supported the regime and a politically sophisticated, cautiously anti-Nazi father.

The approach to the autobiographical project also differs in these works, partly as a result of the authors' differing purposes and areas of expertise. Zeller, a professional writer with numerous novels and volumes of poetry and a degree in *Germanistik* to her credit, has produced a lyrical, self-reflective work that, like Wolf's *Kindheitsmuster*, repeatedly calls its own project into question. Zeller not only holds up a mirror to her past, but she also finds herself in a veritable hall of mirrors that reflects multiple, layered images, some of them uncomfortably, even frighteningly distorted.

By contrast, Stern's journalistic orientation is evident in her documentary-style auto/biography. She has produced a largely unreflective, event-oriented text that derives its greatest merit and interest from the textual juxtaposition and interweaving of the two life stories. Rather than hold up a mirror, like Zeller, Stern uses the perspective of a movie camera with which she records unfolding images. Her role in *In den Netzen der Erinnerung* is that of photojournalist, who records the past in one long pan shot.

Bielenberg, the literary novice, regarded *The Past is Myself* (1968) initially as a project to set the record straight about a friend, Adam von Trott zu Solz, who was executed in the wake of the failed July 20th plot. A singer by training, Bielenberg said in our interview that she composed sentences in terms of their rhythm and melody, but she viewed the autobiography primarily as a recounting of events, a perspective that is reflected in the anecdotal structure of her work. Rather than the reflected images of a mirror or a movie camera perspective, Bielenberg offers the reader a trip through the family photograph album, static vignettes that she fixes page by page.

Despite these important structural differences, the three works are also interrelated in ways that increasingly lend themselves to illumination through feminist autobiography theory. This field of scholarly inquiry has grown rapidly in the past decade and has much to offer specialized studies such as this, which focus on very specific subsets of autobiographical literature by women. Numerous scholarly works published in the 1980s on women and autobiography help fill in "that ghostly absence" of autobiographical works by women in the canon, by which one "would be forced to conclude that women had written virtually no autobiographies" (6), as Domna Stanton noted in 1984. These new theoretical works have also contributed to the continuing debate on the nature of autobiography, its relation to history and literature, and the whole question of the self and the very existence of a subjective "I."[2]

Most critics of autobiography address the question of definition, both reviewing the evolution of various traditional definitions of autobiography and offering new possibilities. Sidonie Smith begins broadly: "Since all gesture and rhetoric is revealing of the subject, autobiography can be defined as any written or verbal communication" (19). This position parallels that of James Olney, whom Smith cites earlier in her essay: "Autobiography is not so much a mode of literature as literature is a mode of autobiography" (cited in Smith 3). But Smith does qualify her initial statement with the following:

> More narrowly it can be defined as written or verbal communication that takes the speaking "I" as the subject of the narrative, rendering the "I" both subject and object. From that operational vantage point, autobiography includes letters, journals, diaries, and oral histories as well as formal autobiography. (19)

Smith restricts her own discussion to works of formal autobiography that she defines as works "written to be published and thus addressed to that arbiter of all cultural ideologies, the public reader" (19).

Like Smith, I have chosen to discuss works that are "formal autobiographies," ones that were consciously and self-consciously produced for publication. Domna Stanton's contribution is also useful in further identifying the three works under discussion in this essay. Stanton reflects in her definition the historical tradition by which women's autobiographical writings were devalued: men claimed that "women could not transcend, but only record, the concerns of the private self." Stanton suggests, that contrary to this claim, an understanding of women's autobiography might rest precisely on their engagement "in self-transcending political and philosophical questions" (7). Given the moral and ethical tensions associated not only with the Nazi era as historical event but especially with later interpretations of it, we rightfully expect, as readers, any autobiographical writing on this subject to be deeply engaged with political and philosophical issues—the only question remaining is the extent to which this writing is self-transcendent and is perceived as such by the writer herself.

Although they are individually very different, Zeller, Stern, and Bielenberg have all written what Smith terms formal autobiographies. The authors themselves have different perceptions of the genre to which their works belong, and they would probably disagree with Smith's definition. One could take the distinction of formal autobiography a step further with Zeller's two novels, clearly examples of *literary* autobiography. The other two writers, although they say their works are autobiographies rather than autobiographical literature, use various techniques of fiction, a practice that "widens the sphere of relevance of autobiographical material which might otherwise be seen as restricted by time, individual, and geography," as Barbara Saunders claims. "The fictional elements create an *imaginative* context (not strictly factual)," Saunders continues, "where the focus of attention is no longer fixed on the accuracy of the biographical detail presented, but on the broader relevance of one man's [*sic*] life to the experience of others" (3). All three authors have used literary techniques "to explore those aspects of human experience which are hidden by purely factual biography" (Saunders 3): Bielenberg uses motifs and metaphors, litotes, direct address, parable-type stories, and special punctuation; Zeller uses motifs, dialect, repetition, song texts, dreams, and a self-conscious, intruding narrator; Stern frames her story, alternates past and present perspectives, interweaves two simultaneous life stories, and uses dialect, rhetorical questions, an interview style, and, at one point, a different narrative voice (her husband's).

Although the question of how much fiction exists in a given autobiography—and what this does to the text's authenticity—

provides a useful framework for analyzing an autobiographical text, Sidonie Smith offers another fruitful approach by deconstructing the concept of autobiography into its component parts, *aute* (sense of identity), *bios* (experience), and *graphia* (textuality) (16). Earlier Domna Stanton had removed the *bios* entirely, but Bella Brodzki and Celeste Schenck reinstated it with the argument: "We strongly believe that the duplicitous and complicitous relationship of 'life' and 'art' in autobiographical modes is precisely the point" (13). At the risk of oversimplifying, one could separate the three authors' works according to the aspect of autobiography they emphasize: Stern focuses on the *aute* (her quest for guilt-free adulthood), Bielenberg on the *bios* (an emphasis on historical scenes), and Zeller on the *graphia* (problems of the literary transformation of history). This distinction sketches only the *grandes lignes,* however, and in reality, all the authors do interweave, in varying proportions, the three aspects of autobiography in their works.

A review of the three authors not only demonstrates this multiple interest they share but also highlights those areas in which they differ. Eva Zeller, for example, who is an accomplished poet as well as a novelist, is especially concerned with form, and she is the only one of the three to claim that her works are autobiographical novels, not autobiographies. It remains unclear, though, just how important this distinction is. James Olney says it is "immensely important" (250), but Philippe Lejeune states there is "no difference between an autobiography and an autobiographical novel." Similarly, Burton Pike concludes that, "all autobiography is fiction."[3] Theory aside, Zeller's two novels do differ from Stern's and Bielenberg's works in that her narrator is both self-conscious and self-reflective, and she calls the autobiographical project itself into question by offering various interpretations of events, doubting the reliability of the memory, and questioning the accuracy of her own account. But it would be a misrepresentation to restrict Zeller to an interest in *graphia.* Particularly in her first volume, *Solange ich denken kann,* she is very much in quest of her self-identity (*aute*) when she examines the troubled relationship she had with her father throughout childhood and adolescence and painfully probes its influence on her development at different stages. The second volume, *Nein und Amen,* by contrast, alternates interest between her continued adolescent search for self and the events of the war that increasingly encroached on her life (*bios*).

Carola Stern's work is similarly complex. First, she structures it around the parallel events in both her and her husband's lives (*bios*). She also conducted considerable research before writing: she read old newspapers, interviewed family members, former classmates, and inhabitants of her village, and read secondary literature. She explained in our 1988 interview: "My weakness is reflection. I prefer to relate something rather than reflect on it."[4] Stern said she tried to compensate for this inability to reflect by evolving a multiplicity of forms (*graphia*). But she also argued in our interview that *aute* is a necessary ingredient in any autobiography: "One does not write an autobiography if one is not extremely interested in oneself. . . . I am interested in people, and among all people, I am most interested in myself" (41). Christabel Bielenberg's book would, however, challenge Stern's insistence on the essential nature of *aute*.

Of the three authors, Bielenberg is the only one who does not seem to be directly in quest of her identity. Of course her position as a foreigner—although she had adopted German citizenship—has meant that she has not had to deal with her involvement with National Socialism in the same way as native-born Germans such as Zeller and Stern. However, as she herself points out, "In a regime such as Hitler's, there could be no standing on the sidelines" (98); furthermore, she did live in Germany throughout the Nazi years, and her husband was German. Although her preoccupation with *aute* is in no way overt, I shall argue later that it poses an important subtext in *The Past is Myself.* Clearly biographically related events of wartime Germany are the center of Bielenberg's anecdotally structured text, highly polished beads on an autobiographical string. In our interview, Bielenberg agreed that "each chapter could be a short story in itself," and she connected her string-of-stories structure to photographic visualizations: "I have to see a clear photograph in front of my mind, and around that photograph I build my story."[5] Although an anecdotal structure does correspond to one of the several traditional forms of autobiography, contemporary versions of this structure often promise much more than mere *bios*.

James Olney in his essay on "The Ontology of Autobiography," interprets Yeats's autobiography as anecdotal also, but Olney argues that "these anecdotes are something other and more than simply historical or factual. In them Yeats seeks to capture character at its most typical, thus catching a glimpse of the essence that lies behind (or . . . above) the accident" (261). I would make a case for a similar interpretation of Bielenberg's anecdotes. One of her means of transcending the purely biographical is to provide dramatic concluding statements (almost punchlines) to many of her anecdotes, conclusions that invite a broader interpretation. Describing a Christmas scene in 1941, for example, she details how Peter, her husband, had brought home three goslings, months earlier, which had become family pets. Finally he brings himself to dispatch one, and it is prepared for Christmas dinner. But their young son "was not to be deceived. He had controlled himself until it reached his plate and then, flinging down his knife and fork, he had burst into tears and rushed from the room crying: 'You just can't eat friends'" (202). Given the historical moment, the kinds of moral and ethical choices the adults faced daily, and the fact that both Peter and his friend Adam von Trott zu Solz—also present at the dinner with his family—worked in the German Foreign Office and were involved with the July 20th plot, it is clear that Bielenberg intends the child's objection to have larger sociocultural ramifications.

In writing her book, Carola Stern also consciously searched for punchline-style sentences that she referred to in our interview as *Klapssätze* (literally striking, hitting sentences). Stern uses these sentences to expand the meaning of passages that are otherwise basically focused on events (*bios*); often they reflect her interest in the textual aspects of her work. She gives as one example the concluding sentence to a chapter where she describes herself as a bored teenager in a provincial village who naively and ignorantly longs for action, for some sign of the war, and who wishes to be in the middle of things. When, to the girl's horror, the neighboring town (Peenemünde) is totally destroyed in a bombing raid, Stern closes with the set-off comment: "Well, now she has her war" (174).[6] Two chapters later, she employs the same device. Her naive mother, politically blind and believing to the end, claims in the last weeks of the war, "Now the *Wunderwaffen* (miracle weapons) are coming." Carola Stern, as author, ironically corrects her mother forty years later: "But the Russians came" (206).

To conclude the discussion of *aute, bios,* and *graphia* in relation to these three writers, I must comment on Bielenberg's relationship to the textual or *graphia* element at greater length. In our interview she denied paying conscious attention to certain stylistic elements such as motifs: "I never write anything consciously; it just arrives. I am living it, and it arrives." I asked again, "So you did not seek symbols to represent experiences?" She replied, "No, I do not think I did; I do not think I would" (19). When I later asked if she felt an intermediary, reflective stage, (i.e., asking oneself "What would be an effective construction at this point?"), Bielenberg responded, "No, I have never had that at all; it's just writing. It is only when I see a sentence that is musically all wrong for me, that I start working on it" (20). Bielenberg's musical ear stands her in good stead throughout the work. In the interview she cited a passage of which she is particularly proud, a passage she spent two days writing. The well-crafted concluding sentence to this passage is: "This longed-for moment, and I could not rejoice, but just stood there silently, watching the bonfires as they dimmed, glowed red, and went out, one by one, up and down the valley" (284). According to Bielenberg, the addition of "one by one" finally balanced this sentence for her. Although Bielenberg is not a professional writer in the sense of Eva Zeller or Carola Stern, neither could one say that she is either disinterested in or unskilled at the textual aspect (*graphia*) of her work.

One characteristic of traditional male autobiography has been the underlying belief that the autobiographer's life has in some way been exceptional and therefore worth writing and reading about. Bella Brodzki and Celeste Schenck have compared male and female autobiographies in their work *Life/Lines*, which they consider an extension of the theoretical work begun by Domna Stanton. They begin their introductory essay by investigating a number of characteristics of traditional male autobiography and suggest that these may not apply to the female autobiographical tradition. One of these characteristics centers on the concept of the autobiographer-as-paragon; it is important to the autobiographies by Stern, Zeller, and Bielenberg. "The very authority of masculine autobiography," Brodzki and Schenck write, "derives from the assumption by both author and reader that the life being written/read is an exemplary one" (2–3). But these women authors see themselves and their experiences in the Nazi era not as especially exemplary, rather as representative of a broad spectrum of "ordinary" people. This is particularly true of Zeller and Stern who recounted in my interviews with them that they have received letters from numerous readers, who claim that their experiences have been accurately reflected as well. Stern said in our interview, for example, that her book was "representative for northern Germany, for the northern German provinces. . . . It is also typical for all those who had no alternative world[view]" (40).

Bielenberg's situation is somewhat different from the two Germans. In our interview, she did not compare her experience with that of other foreigners in Germany, but she did refer numerous times in our interview to her "liberal upbringing" that she felt predetermined many of her thoughts and responses; to this extent her experience would be applicable to others who shared liberal upbringings. In *The Past is Myself,* she emphasizes that she was not uncommonly brave: "Writing this down, back in the protection of my white hills, I would not want to convey, that because I was not afraid, I would consider myself essentially a brave person. I am not. No one knows how they are going to behave in real danger until they are faced with it" (232).

The reverse of this sense of one's life as typical and representative is the conflicting "need to differentiate the self from others," as Domna Stanton remarks in her essay (16). Seemingly irreconcilable impulses, the perceptions of one's life as both representative and unique are linked by Stanton, Brodzki, Schenck, and Mary Mason through a "relatedness to others." According to Brodzki and Schenck, "This 'delineation of identity by alterity,' as Mary G. Mason defines it . . . , this self-definition in relation to significant others, is the most pervasive characteristic of the female autobiography" (8). Stanton gives as examples of "others" (in the case of the Duchess of Newcastle) father and husband, but "others" must certainly be more inclusive in different works. For Stern and Zeller, the separation begins with the narrative voice, which Stanton refers to as "the split subject" (16). Like Christa Wolf, who is known for her self-division in *Kindheitsmuster* into "she," (Nelly, the child), "you" (German: *du*), and "I", Eva Zeller alternately refers to her subject protagonist as "Eva" (her identity in the mother's village), "E-M" (her identity when with the father in Berlin, further split into the preexisting Eve/Mary dichotomy), and "I" (increasingly used as she matures and begins to assume responsibility for her actions). Stern refers to herself with the third-person "Eka" throughout the text, but this name represents real-life splits. Stern's real name is Erika Assmus (abbreviation Eka); Carola Stern is a professional name she adopted as a journalist. Her identity splits further owing first to the assumed name Stern, which many people thought was Jewish, and second, having married late in life, she is also legally Frau Zöger. She recounted in our interview that she continues to use the three names/identities interchangeably according to circumstances.[7] *In den Netzen der Erinnerung* itself reflects this willful confusion of identities: it is an *auto*biography authored by Carola Stern, but both the protagonist and the narrator are Eka Assmus.

Bielenberg's work reflects to a lesser extent these "problematics of subjecthood" (Stanton 16) in a formal narrative way, but her identities were also radically split during the Nazi era. Although she spent the war years in Germany and had assumed German citizenship upon marriage in September 1934, Bielenberg said in our interview, "I never felt German. . . . I felt very sympathetically close to Germans, but never, never German" (7). She characterized her psychic split as "straddling a fence" and made clear her personal dilemma: "I think after a bit I was so involved with the German side of the story because we only had friends who were anti-Hitler . . . [but] naturally I was homesick for England. I had two brothers fighting on the other side; I did not know whether they had been killed or not" (7). Bielenberg felt set apart from Germans further by the way she was raised: "There were certain peculiarities about me, due to my liberal upbringing, which did not conform to the image of a young wife as viewed by worthy Hamburg burghers" (17). As an independent woman, she was definitely unlike German women of her age and social status about whom she writes: "Independence, financial or otherwise, was not a state of affairs to be encouraged in a German woman; it might arouse and set in motion quite a number of disturbing phenomena which had up to date slumbered very peacefully in the German social scene" (17). Bielenberg's narrative remains first-person throughout, with the exception of one chapter told in her husband's voice. She did not feel the need to distance herself from the text with a third-person voice, in the same way as either Zeller or Stern, because she was already distanced by being multiply an outsider (English, upperclass, liberal, financially independent, anti-Nazi). "Being written by an Englishwoman . . . makes a difference," she pointed out in our discussion. "So many of the German books are sort of *plaidoyers,* and they still have a guilty conscience. I have no guilty conscience; it was not my people that was going around the bend" (8). All three authors thus experience in some way the split subject in terms of identity, although not always formally through narrative designation(s) of the self.

One can also make a strong argument that all three writers define themselves in relation to "others" outside themselves, as Schenck, Stanton et al. suggested above. For Carola Stern, the primary other is her husband Heinz Zöger whose life story she tells parallel to her own. She felt it imperative to include his life as a Communist as a *Masstab* (yardstick) against which to measure her own youthful involvement with National Socialism. She said that Heinz would not have been able—either emotionally or in terms of literary ability—to write his own story, and her greatest fear throughout the project was that her husband would say, "I cannot continue; I am no longer willing to talk about it" (Interview 15). Stern mentioned that her husband suffered an emotional collapse while viewing a film on the Spanish Civil War and she emphasized the residual emotional pain of the victims (based on suffering) compared to that of perpetrators such as herself (based on guilt and shame). In the book, Stern resorts to the method of an interviewer to elicit information in Heinz's own voice, but when she presses him unbearably on painful topics, he attacks her: "Just think about it! Just think about it! You question [me] like the Gestapo! . . . Just think about it, they said! It will all come back to you! Let's stop for today. Tomorrow we will continue with the interrogation" (181).

Christabel Bielenberg found herself in a situation similar to Stern's vis-à-vis her husband, Peter, who was clearly a "significant other" for her throughout the war and has remained so since. She felt that "his story was the German story and must be told" (Interview 17), but she judged that he could not tell it himself. She jokingly commented, "I know he cannot write. He wrote himself dry when we were engaged; he wrote a letter every day" (Interview 16). But on a more serious note, Bielenberg felt that her husband was emotionally unable to write about his life during the Nazi era. Like Heinz Zöger whose emotions lay just beneath the surface, Peter Bielenberg suffered both spiritually and physically from being forced to remember. "Peter, when it becomes something to do with his friends or to do with that period of time loses his voice completely and has to go out of the room," his wife commented (Interview).

For Zeller's narrator, the male significant other is divided between two persons: in the first volume, her father plays a determining role, and in the second volume her life is redefined in terms of her young fiancé, Dirk. Her father is a physical and intellectual colossus who constantly finds fault with her as a child when she is obliged to visit him during vacations. Zeller represents him through the motif of a large, strutting, puffed-up tom turkey who pecks at her whenever she gets too close. She initially rejects both him and his political beliefs, but his efforts to wean her away from her support of National Socialism finally come to fruition when she is a young adult. The child and father stand in an earth-sun relation to one another. The sun-father is a strong and vital force, but he is also self-consuming in his intensity and dangerous to those who venture, Icarus-like, too close. The earth-child clearly revolves around this source and is aware of its dual life-giving and destructive potential. Important, too, both the narrative focal point and narrative voice belong to the earth-child. The emotional dynamics underlying this relationship are ultimately Ptolemaic, not Copernican.

The second volume, *Nein und Amen,* could be read as a memorial to Zeller's first husband, who was her first love—today she says her only love—and who was killed on the Russian front in the final months of the war. The eighteen-year-old Eva focuses her existence entirely on Dirk, commenting: "From now on I want to orient myself only toward Dirk . . . there are only places where Dirk is and those where he is not" (*Nein* 130). Zeller describes their love in bittersweet terms, combining the perspectives of the original passionate and totally interdependent relationship with her retrospective knowledge of the doomed nature of their love. She notes that their infatuation is not to be counteracted by later events "because there will not be a 'later' for us, no after-the-war" (*Nein* 158–159). She does experience a postwar relationship with her father, but she is apparently unrelenting in her rejection of him. In sum, whereas her father negatively circumscribed her identity in *Solange ich denken kann,* Dirk represents a positive force of identification, a healthy "other" in *Nein und Amen.*[8]

For both Eva Zeller and Carola Stern, the mother is also a significant other. She is less so for Christabel Bielenberg because of their geographical separation during the years treated in her narrative and because Bielenberg (b. 1909) was already an adult during the Nazi era, unlike Zeller (b. 1923) and Stern (b. 1925) who were children and adolescents. Not only do their mothers play an important role, but Zeller also relies on a strong grandmother and a panoply of maternal aunts, and Stern counts an entire ancestry of *starke frauen* (strong women), the *Heesters* or fisherwomen, of the northern German seacoast where she was born and raised. Stern commented in our discussion: "After I became an adult, I quickly realized that I had grown up in an absolute matriarchy" (33). A woman already known for her strength, Eka's mother, Ella Assmus, became even stronger after her husband's premature death. But in political decisions, her strength alone proves inadequate. Because men in their community always took care of politics, she lacks what the narrator terms "political yardsticks and experience. Accustomed to advising others, now she cannot even advise herself. . . . Ida Schwandt [the maternal grandmother] had left her daughter the legacy of good common sense, with which, under normal circumstances, she would have gotten through life quite well. But the circumstances were not normal" (63). Thus Ella the mother becomes a Nazi, and Eka the daughter follows in her footsteps, the former as *Ortsfrauenschaftsleiterin* (leader of the local Nazi women's group) and the latter as *Jungmädelführerin* (leader of Nazi girls' group). Mother and daughter remain believers and supporters until the bitter end, when fleeing westward before the advancing Russians, they finally abandon their uniforms and insignia. Stern attributes this blindness in part to the lack of an alternative viewpoint: "The Assmus family had practically nothing to hold up against fascism. No alternative world existed from which the family could have learned how to distance itself, how to discover different personal standards, and how to feel revulsion" (195).

Eva Zeller's mother also supports the Nazi regime, and even the skeptical grandmother is won over once the war begins; like Stern, Zeller herself is promoted within the BDM (Bund Deutscher Mädel [German Girls' Organization]) to *Jungmädelführerin.* But there the comparison stops. Zeller's matriarchal world view is intersected repeatedly (every vacation) by a contrasting paternal, anti-Nazi viewpoint. This supplies her with exactly the *Gegenwelt* (alternative world) that Stern complains she lacked. Although Zeller rejects her father's views for years because she rejects him personally, ultimately they have an effect on her. Partly because of the skepticism learned from her father, partly owing to an all-consuming, adolescent love affair, and partly because of Nazi offenses against her middle-class sensibilities and values, Eva avoids further involvement with the BDM and even escapes obligatory service in the *Reichsarbeitsdienst* (national work service). The emotional mother/daughter relationship in Zeller's works ("zwei Seelen, ein Gedanke" [two souls, one thought]) is nearly claustrophobic in its intensity. That the child is not smothered by mother-love is owing to the grandmother and to the puritan life-style and values of the villagers that prohibit the spoiling of children. It is the grandmother, not the mother, to whom Zeller turns for help in writing her autobiography. This help is both concrete in the form of the grandmother's *Vergissmeinnicht,* or diary, and spiritually as a "secret discussion partner" (*Solange* 147). Zeller confesses in a fictive conversation with the grandmother, "it would have been easy to make a super-ego [Über-Ich] out of you" (*Solange* 146). Even with so much female strength, it still takes all three women together, as Eva tells her classmates, "to barely manage [her] father" (*Solange* 222). Mothers and fathers remain inextricably linked with concepts of the fatherland throughout her life.

Zeller's confusion of her identity among maternal, paternal, and patriotic influences is representative of women's experience in general in the Nazi era, a topic addressed by all three authors. One should not be misled by the role of strong women in these texts; the paternal/patriarchal principle retains its currency: Stern's *Heesters* bow to tradition and leave all political matters to the men; Zeller's dominating grandmother admits grudging respect for her worldly former son-in-law (Eva's father) but herself succumbs to National Socialism; and even Christabel Bielenberg, who boldly requested an interrogation by the Gestapo in a desperate attempt to save Peter's life, is the moth purposefully circling the flame of her husband's life. She identifies Peter as her raison d'être: "[I saw] the figure of what I knew at that moment to be the only bit of Germany I had any interest in whatsoever" (220).

Patriarchy, which shares its etymological roots with both patriot and *patrie,* the French word for homeland, remained in both private and political realms firmly intact on a symbolic, public plane throughout the Nazi period. Various observers have, however, recorded subtle signs of its erosion, especially as the war progressed, such as Margaret Higonnet et al., who write in *Behind the Lines,* "Ironically, the Nazis' unparalleled intervention in reproduction and family life undermined the power of individual men within their families—the very power the government had vowed to preserve" (9). Similarly, Carola Stern told me, "I see our men, my grandfather, all of them, only as old and somewhat doddering; sitting in recliners. . . . My mother never took my uncle seriously. . . . Men are simply crazy, small [German: *lütt*], and silly—something along those lines." But significantly, Stern tacks onto the end of this summary the observation: "But there are also others" (33). Eva Zeller writes, for example, about one of "the others," namely her father, that he was an absolute king in his private castle, and not an especially benevolent one either: "Even my father . . . enjoyed his power and kept all those around him in their place. My father, who was always upset about the *Führer,* is in his own kingdom the absolute ruler, lord over wives, children, colleagues, who were all supposed to worship him" (*Nein* 224).[9]

Insistence on the use of the term *Vaterland* [fatherland] to refer to Germany, despite opposing "mother" usages such as "mother earth," "motherland," "mother lode," "mother tongue," and "mother wit" (in German: *Mutterboden, Muttererde, Mutterland, Muttersprache, Mutterwitz,* [*Wahrig,* 2612–2613]), already indicates the conflation of gender identification problems with issues of national identity. This interrelationship has been addressed by several scholars, representing different disciplinary approaches. Philippe Lacoue-Labarthe and Jean-Luc Nancy in their article on the Nazi myth, begin with an identity/racism linkage that evolves into an identity/gender linkage in the course of their argument. Their thesis begins: "It is because the German figure of totalitarianism is racism" (296). According to their reconstruction, Germans needed to base their identity in classical Greece, but that identification had already been appropriated: "German[y] . . . suffered an imitation *twice removed,* and saw itself obliged to imitate the imitation of antiquity that France did not cease to export for at least two centuries. Germany, in other words, was not only missing an identity but also lacked the ownership of its means of identification" (299). By consequence, in Lacoue-Labarthe's and Nancy's thesis, Germans, discovering that "Greece, in reality, had been double," chose to identify their cultural origins with "a buried Greece, nocturnal, somber (or too blindingly bright), the archaic, savage Greece of group rituals, of bloody sacrifices and collective intoxications, of the cult of the dead and of the Earth Mother" (301).

Maria-Antonietta Macciocchi adds to this analysis the gender factor. She relates "group rituals" to organized religion, commenting:

> In a political regime the question of the influential and active support of women is connected with the superstructure in its most dense form, namely religion. It is at the very moment when religion, the centuries-old scourge of women, is no longer adequate as an ideological shield for the power apparatus of the rising bourgeoisie . . . that fascism comes to the relief of the church guards. It is able to do this because of the submissiveness of women, whose instincts it can channel into a sort of new religious fervour which serves to support mass dictatorships and mass totalitarian regimes. (68)

On the "cult of the dead," Macciocchi cites Wilhelm Reich who "located the question of dictatorial domination in precisely the terms of a huge sexual repression which is tightly linked to death" (69). Macciocchi points out that the genius of both Italian fascism and German National Socialism was "to challenge women on their own ground: they make women both the reproducers of life and the guardians of death, without the two terms being contradictory" (70).

This interpretation is also supported by Nancy Huston, who comes to the conclusion that "men make war *because* women have children" (119). Toward the end of her essay Huston cites the "supreme irony" by which "many feminist authors now describe childbirth in such a way as explicitly to assimilate it to war" (134). Macciocchi pursues the psychosexual underpinnings of the fascist relation to women, especially in terms of the "virile puppet," Mussolini or Hitler (70). She recounts that on "The Day of Wedding Rings" in 1935, Italian women gave up their gold rings "to help the fatherland in its difficulty." For Macciocchi what followed was especially significant: "In exchange, the Duce distributed his own little iron rings, as if he had become *Husband* who was leading women to a second marriage, *a mystic marriage* under the sign of Death (war) and Birth (cradles)" (72).

All these elements are basic to understanding German women's (and girls') response to fascism: the mysticism and emotionalism identified by Lacoue-Labarthe and Nancy ("one of the essential ingredients in fascism is *emotion*, collective, mass emotion" 294), the linking of birth and death proposed by Huston ("The analogy between war and childbirth hinges on what might be called reciprocal metaphorization" 131), and the repression of sexuality discussed by Macciocchi ("The body of fascist discourse is rigorously chaste. . . . Its central aim is the death of sexuality" 75). If Mussolini symbolically married Italian women as both father and husband on "The Day of Wedding Rings," Hitler, the vigorous sounding, authoritatively acting, unmarried male appealed to masses of women without men in Germany; that is, he appealed to what Macciocchi terms "the necrophiliac femininity of the widows and mothers of men killed in the first world war" (68). When I asked Christabel Bielenberg if she thought a special relationship between Hitler and women had existed, she initially said "no" but then changed her mind:

> There were an awful lot of surplus women; that is an historical fact. Therefore if this fellow was attractive or the masculinity of his party was attractive, that could be. . . . I think that might be a phenomenon because in the front rows of his

> gatherings, I remember, there were always women sitting, sort of spinsterish figures, who were in . . . uniform. (Interview 37)

The supposed virile attraction of Hitler himself or the "masculinity of his party" were factors in the ideology of the BDM. Hitler's compelling blue eyes are legendary, and there are numerous accounts of the quasi-religious, "conversion" quality of individual decisions to embrace National Socialism. Some of the most convincing descriptions of these mystical, emotional "group rituals" are found in Melita Maschmann's *Fazit: Mein Weg in der Hitler-Jugend* (Net result; my path in the Hitler youth). As she writes, "We were dazzled [blinded] by the mystery that appeared to conceal itself with a magical force in the concept 'Greater Germany' " (174).

Like Maschmann and most German girls, both Eva Zeller and Carola Stern belonged to the BDM; in fact, both became group leaders. A number of other German writers have discussed the BDM experience, notably Christa Wolf, Ingeborg Drewitz, and Margarete Hannsmann. Martin Klaus summarizes the attraction of the BDM, especially to girls living in rural areas, like both Zeller and Stern: "The BDM-organization offers unity, a feeling of general belonging, that is created through common songs. . . . The new organization, which replaces the family, various loose friendships, and school contacts in the life of the girl, removes loneliness, creates security, and becomes a home" (17–18).

Both Zeller and Stern attempt to communicate their adolescent *Begeisterung* (enthusiasm) to the reader, although Stern believes ultimately that "nothing is as inexplicable as a former enthusiasm" (13). Nevertheless, Stern describes it in a fictive conversation with her goddaughter as "a children's birthday party. All the other children you know have been invited and are going, so you want to go, too, no matter what it will be like once you are there" (108). All the women who have described their experiences in the BDM talk about endless group rituals centered around sunrises, sunsets, and bonfires, and numerous activities performed en masse, including seemingly endless group singing.

One can regard these rituals as ersatz-religious ceremonies. Carola Stern says that her mother "was not a pious woman" and documents the erosion of traditional religion: "there was no more religious instruction in the school, and toward the end, we were supposed to celebrate a 'festival of lights' instead of Christmas" (196). National Socialism not only adeptly filled, through its exaggerated ritual, the vacuum created by a missing traditional religion, but also ensured there would be no foundation for spiritual opposition. Stern notes: "The Assmus family was too estranged from the church, to ever experience pangs of conscience about religion and world view" (196). Annemarie Tröger has noted the Nazi usurpation of religious (Christian) ideology vis-à-vis women: "Religions have built female victimization into a positive ideology of self-sacrifice as the highest virtue of womanhood, and fascism thrived on a secularized version of female sacrifice" (299). This religion-based masochism has its roots in the internalized female feelings of victimization inherent in patriarchy—a connection I discuss more fully later in this essay.

Zeller and Stern record their own enthusiastic participation in the BDM "group rituals" and "collective intoxications" (Lacoue-Labarthe/Nancy), but they also discuss their mothers' relations to National Socialism. Just as the appeal of the BDM was heightened for "fatherless" children like Zeller and Stern (Stern: "[I had] a need for recognition, and [suffered] low self-esteem" Interview 17), so, too, National Socialism was attractive to these two mothers-without-men—the former a divorcée, the latter a widow. A coincidence of their motherhood, both women were also forced by their husbands to undergo abortions—for Ella Assmus, three times in five years.[10] Both women attended local *NS Frauenschaft* (National Socialist women's group) meetings and were enthusiastic Nazis, but whereas Ella Assmus went on to a leadership role, Elisabeth Bertrand (Feldhaus) ultimately did not join the party. Despite this, she felt "absolute enthusiasm for the *Führer*" (*Solange* 227). With similar zeal Ella Assmus remains a believer until the very end, maintaining that "Hitler did not know about the things that were not good" (237) and that Goebbels would not lie, "Not at this hour! Not on the *Führer*'s birthday! No, no" (206).

The sexual chastity of Nazi ideology mentioned by Macciocchi is also apparent as a subtext in these works. Stern records her mother's reaction to news that Goebbels cheated on his wife Magda: "Frau Assmus and the aunts shook their heads disapprovingly; that was not good. But worse was to come" (197). After soldiers quartered in her house depart, Ella discovers Nazi fliers encouraging the conscripts to "multiply their valuable genes" without waiting for a wedding certificate. "She found that that went too far" (197). And finally she "pulled out her hair" when she read that there should be no distinction between wedded motherhood and motherhood out-of-wedlock: "Now I've had enough!" (197). The political agenda of distracting women from preoccupation with the life-and-death reality of wartime Germany becomes evident: "While every day thousands died, Eka argued with her schoolfriends whether one had to 'remain pure' up until marriage" (197). Zeller, on the other hand, connects the impossibility of Nazi "chastity ideology" with the emotions girls experience in puberty, a phase of life in which numerous women who have written on the Nazi era found themselves in the late 1930s and early 1940s.[11] Zeller said during our discussion, "At that age we were searching for our identity, we kept diaries, we fell in love for the first time. We were stewing in our own juices. I wanted to become 'I', and that was precisely what was forbidden" (37).

The development of an identity as an adolescent, not an easy task in any era or location, was complicated by the nature of Nazi ideology that did not encourage independent thinking, formation of individual opinions, or personal decision making. "When we had reached a point where we could have learned to think, and create an intellectual foundation," Melita Maschmann notes, "the period began in which thinking was considered a biologically negative activity of degenerate brains. We did not educate ourselves, we always just 'experienced'" (83). Annemarie Tröger argues that the same thwarting of identity development by Nazi ideology is still residually operative today in the memory-identity work of numerous writers.

Tröger makes two points important to a discussion of both past and present identity evolution. First, she notes that "war is often seen as a natural disaster, a catastrophe." As a result "there is no collective or personal responsibility for war; it just 'breaks out,' is not prepared for and not declared." By consequence one is allowed "to be against war . . . but at the same time to uphold nationalistic values" (298). Stern, Zeller, and Bielenberg are all—as are many writers—interested in this relationship of both exaggerated patriotism and nationalism to war.

Bielenberg identified her German friends as "patriots—not nationalists, but patriots" (Interview 7). According to dictionary definitions, patriotism and nationalism are both forms of national identity. A patriot is a "person who loves his [*sic*] country, zealously supporting and defending it and its interests," but a nationalist goes one step further to assert "the interests of a nation, viewed as *separate from* the interests of *other nations* or the *common interests* of all nations" (*American Dictionary* 1355, emphasis added). Echoing the thesis of Lacoue-Labarthe and Nancy above, Bielenberg speculates on the appeal of Hitler, especially to intelligent and educated citizens: "Would it have been that sense of national identity which he could conjure up with such mastery? That awareness of belonging somewhere, which in England just came naturally, but which I believed amongst Germans to be a rare, almost unique phenomenon?" (176). Zeller locates the turning point at which patriots, such as her grandmother, became nationalists at the beginning of the war. Because a patriot could not intentionally bring her country into danger, she became, of necessity, a nationalist. In language reminiscent of both Lacoue-Labarthe and Nancy and Macciocchi, Zeller summarizes this process thus: "The sanctification of Germany, the mythologizing of Germany had to be carried out in order to have the believers at one's disposal" (*Nein* 108). But the effects of such an ideology last a lifetime in the form of *Unheilbares* (the unhealable), as Carola Stern expresses it. "[Eka] can no longer find a natural relationship to the concepts patriotism and nationalism. A neurotic fear of renewed nationalism prevents her from recognition of any patriotic action or feeling whatsoever," Stern writes about herself after the war (255).

An immediate negative effect of nationalist sentiment was the belief that the ends justify the means; this feeling intensified once the war began, as people accepted "temporary" measures of all sorts in their lives. "Thus the strict regimentation of the ever-present government was perceived not as an imposition but as a necessity in order to secure *das grosse heilige Reich* (the great holy empire) against its internal and external enemies" (Zeller, *Nein* 108). When I queried Carola Stern about anti-Semitism and how far people would have gone with it, she replied that the answer she remembered hearing most was *wo gehobelt wird, fallen Späne* (24, literally: where there is planing, shavings fall; or, a comparable expression in English, 'you cannot make an omelet without breaking eggs.) She expanded: "They did not protest. Then there was: 'The *Führer* does not know about it; many things are happening that are not right, but the *Führer* does not know . . .

and we don't want to know either. After the war, everything will be better. This is just a time of transition'" (24).

Bielenberg addresses this same phenomenon of willful ignorance when she discusses people's frame of mind after the murder of Roehm. "Once everything distasteful had been neatly swept under the carpet, there was something almost touching about the anxious childlike pleasure with which so many tried to share in what they seemed to hope was a newly discovered respectability. Unpleasantness, of course there were unpleasantnesses; but such things if talked about at all, must be seen in production. There were after all so many more positive aspects of the regime to chat about" (27–8). While Bielenberg successfully captures the *tone* of what people were saying in this passage, Eva Zeller speculates on *why* people responded in this way in her second novel: "If I am honest, I admit: I too see the wounded people as being part of war. During my entire time in school they preached the war to us as a crusade that had to be waged against absolute evil. War: a heroic act of unique moral greatness, the glorified war, part of which was also the glorious sacrifice of the wounded" (*Nein* 68).

Annemarie Tröger's second point on the question of identity formation is closely related to the first: she explains how seeing the war as a "natural disaster" allows women—specifically the women she interviewed, but also women in general—to view themselves as victims. "The religious and popular symbol of the victim absolves the victim of responsibility and guilt. A victim of the war cannot be responsible for it" (299). As Tröger points out, women were indeed victims in the second half of the war, in the double sense of *victims* as both sufferers and those sacrificed.[12] But as Tröger also makes clear, postwar Germans have repeatedly substituted "war victimization" for "Nazi responsibility." In her own research, Tröger indicates that the argument "as a victim one cannot be held responsible for fascism" is one reason for why "interviewees brought up the war as soon as the uncomfortable issue of National Socialism was raised in the interview" (299). Suffering can act as a shield against recognition of personal responsibility, feelings of guilt, and the articulation of mea culpa.

The concept of victimization and the question of responsibility relate directly to episodes of *persönliches Versagen* (personal failure, shortcoming) in the lives and writings of Eva Zeller, Carola Stern, and, despite her claims to the contrary, of Christabel Bielenberg. At the heart is the question: Why did I write this book? The initial answers vary: to vindicate a friend, to set the record straight, to inform/warn the younger generation (Bielenberg: "I had a tremendous feeling of responsibility for having survived" Interview 3). But there are other, less clearly articulated reasons as well. None of these works would fall under the rubric of confessional literature, but they are nonetheless very much occupied with the *aute* aspect of autobiography, with the search for identity, culpable or not.

One is tempted to view Bielenberg separately because she was not German and was not raised in the Nazi era as were Zeller and Stern. I would argue, though, that her continued residence in Germany after 1935 offsets this initial difference. She herself details how impossible it was to avoid involvement: "it became increasingly difficult for us to escape the occasional compromise. By compromising we could learn how each small demand for our outward acquiescence could lead to the next, and with the gentle persistence of an incoming tide could lap at the walls of just that integrity we were so anxious to preserve" (26). Bielenberg indicts the German patrons in a pub for not wanting to get involved in an incident with three Jewish guests: "[what] stuck in my mind [was] . . . the hurried scrambling to depart, the jostle of *gutbürgerliche* backsides, the sudden void. It was not the agitation but the acquiescence that shocked me" (24–25). But only a few pages later, with no apparent sense of irony she describes her own and her husband's situation: "By consciously disassociating ourselves though from something we did not understand or approve of, we drifted into a way of life removed from the force of the mainstream and were forever being taken by surprise" (29).

Bielenberg's husband was, of course, involved peripherally in the plot to assassinate Hitler and as a result was arrested and incarcerated in Ravensbrück prison, which he miraculously survived. But her husband's resistance does not explain her own thoughts and actions. In our talk she said she did not participate in the numerous political discussions in which her husband was involved; she served coffee and listened. Her explanation for this was grounded in the distinction of being British: "I think it's not very British to talk much about things anyway and to go into deep, philosophical arguments, which Germans absolutely love" (17–18). Although she said in the interview, as quoted earlier, "I have no guilty conscience," (8) she recounts several incidents in the book that lead one to question the assertion; she also elaborates a lengthy self-defense in an imagined conversation with a Jewish family's housekeeper:

> I could have pleaded my cause, the cause of those who should know better. I could have told her that we were not yet thirty years of age and that our elders and supposedly betters . . . had not distinguished themselves by giving us a lead. I could have told her that since we were not Jews and there was no capricious higher authority to make up our minds for us, it was easy to bury one's head in the sand, but that we had tried often enough to fumble our way through the confusing fog of fact and fiction. I could have produced some exonerating evidence for her after all. (32)

Incidents of personal failure seem for Bielenberg to center around relations with Jews. The following passage, dealing with her reaction to the Nuremberg Laws is revealing:

> I could pinpoint no exact date when normal and natural association with Jewish friends became an act of defiance and then petered out, not because the friend was less close, but simply because such a relationship is an unnatural one, mutual embarrassment intervenes. . . . When was it that credulity turned to doubt, doubt to resignation, and to the unhappy, rather shamefaced admission that you were sorry, you could not help it, you happened to have been labelled an Aryan . . . and truth to tell you'd be mighty relieved to know that the good friend was safely off your conscience overseas? (30)

Key expressions in this passage are "mutual embarrassment," "shamefaced admission," "you could not help it," and "safely off your conscience," which reveal that she did have a conscience ("shamefaced admission") but perceived herself as a victim of the system too ("you could not help it") and that she even indulged mildly in a blame-the-victim mentality, whereby Jewish friends caused her discomfort ("mutual embarrassment") and unpleasant emotions/guilt ("off your conscience").

A later chapter is entitled somewhat oddly "A Jew Story," as if to universalize the Jewish experience—and perhaps also her own behavior in this situation. Asked to hide a Jewish couple, she seeks the advice of her neighbor, Carl Langbehn, who says, "You have your children, and while Peter is away you are my responsibility." Langbehn implies that there are other reasons, too, so she sends the Jews away. Bielenberg closes the anecdote with the image of a pot of forsythia twigs which she had neglected: "they had flowered long since, and the branches were covered with sickly green leaves" (115). The sickly leaves represent metaphorically the hunted Jewish couple, living in dark cellars, moving by night, but also possibly her own moral state. Before consulting the neighbor she had clearly considered the punishment for harboring Jews and what internment in a concentration camp would mean. In our interview, twenty-two years after writing this passage and forty-five years after the incident, her feelings about the experience and her role in it had become clearer: "I have an enormously guilty feeling about the Jews who came to my house, and I was told that I couldn't keep them. They were very, very nice people, and they finally were caught. When I heard from this friend that they had got caught, I most certainly loathed National Socialism more than ever in my life because I felt he [the friend] had involved me in murder" (24). Even in this account though, she characterizes herself as one of the victims; she is victimized by her friend who initially asked her to shelter the Jews. She does not make the decision to send the Jews away herself ("I was told . . ."); rather, the decision is dictated by another [male]—this from a woman who was brave enough to volunteer for a Gestapo interrogation when her own husband's life was at stake. She also views herself as a victim of National Socialism because it has obliged her to become an accomplice to murder. Annemarie Tröger writes of the women she interviewed, "That victims are responsible too, even for their own victimization, is never allowed to enter their minds" (299). Tröger remarks on the women's "deeply engraved identities as victims" and concludes that "the war . . . has not broken the vicious cycle." To a considerable extent, I think Tröger's comments are à propos in Bielenberg's case as well, although in her own defense, she argues, "I challenge anybody who has not lived under a dictatorship to understand what it is like, or how they would react themselves" (Interview 24).

Carola Stern argues in her book against precisely this mentality. In our interview she explained that "people of my generation always say 'We really could not do anything.' I say, 'Well, there were people who did do something'" (16). One of Stern's main reasons for including her husband's biography with her own was to demonstrate, year by year, that there were people who resisted the Nazis, who paid harsh penalties for that resistance, but who nonetheless persevered. Her own situation was, of course very different than her husband's because she belonged to the *Täter* (perpetrators). In our interview she gave one reason for writing her autobiography as "I did not want to die without having said that I participated in it" (2).

Stern records several instances of personal failure, such as hearing victims tortured by the Gestapo in the office below hers and not intervening or being asked to write a letter "to Berlin" on behalf of a friend's Jewish step-father and politely refusing on the grounds that it would not do any good anyway (195). In another instance, she curiously and eagerly surveys, in the company of schoolfriends, the damage after the *Kristallnacht;* later, as author, she poses the question, "Was there no bit of consternation mixed in with the curiosity at the scenes of the crime?" Her answer: "Eka does not dare answer" (121). She investigates her own excuses by compiling those of others. Noting, as Christa Wolf, Eva Zeller, and others have also noted, that basically everything was printed in the newspapers in the Nazi era—including information about the treatment of Jews—Stern asked friends and relatives their reflections on what they had read in the newspapers. A sampling of answers included: "It did not have anything to do with us, it concerned *the others,*" "We did not read it," "We thought the judgments were fair," and "We had accepted that one deals with enemies in an enemy-like fashion" (193). Stern's own alibis center on her tender age (she was six when the Nazis came to power), the isolation and ignorance of rural populations, and the lack of religious values in her family to offset the Nazi ideology, as mentioned earlier. Stern said in our discussion, "I don't hold it against myself that I was not in the resistance, because I never had the opportunity. I do hold it against myself that I failed as a human being. Since I had no alternative world at all, no other standard by which I could evaluate this system, it had to happen to me" (40). In her formulation of the problem here, she clearly identifies herself as a victim of a system which "*happened* to [her]." It is also evident that, although she admits to certain situations of personal failure, she neither regards her book as a confession nor herself as *die grosse Büsserin* (the great penitent): "It was clear to me that I had not been a criminal" (Interview 3).

A major concern in writing *In den Netzen der Erinnerung* was, according to Stern, developing "the right attitude toward [herself]" and "finding the right tone to speak about oneself" (3). Thus her task was not simply to tell the-truth-in-retrospect, rather to make it coincide with her contemporary self-perception.

But the lifting of layers of truth seems to be endless: in the interview she said she had omitted from the book that on 20 April 1944 she had joined the NSDAP because she was "too ashamed to write it" (3). In Stern's case, alibis and confessions seem to balance one another out.

Eva Zeller identifies herself much more clearly than Stern as a victim of patriarchy (her father), of politics (National Socialism), and of violence (the war). In the first volume she presents two *Stock- und Hiebfeste* (unassailable) alibis: the first is her youth (186), and the second, like the argument brought by Stern earlier, is that "we cannot confess to something we did not do, rather that they did something to us" (*Solange* 364). When she is forced to serve in the *Reichsarbeitsdienst,* she feels that she has been *ausgeliefert* (sacrificed up). Not until the second volume, does she record a situation in which she was an active rather than a passive agent. Traveling by train she is asked by two guards to accompany a female prisoner (an Eastern European worker) to the restroom. Once there the woman asks her to accept a folded-up piece of paper from her ("Du Frau, bitte" [You woman, please]), which she finally does. Forty years later she says:

> I should have touched her, her face, her shoulder, to indicate that I . . . I should have touched her. I didn't touch her. What one calls the prevailing relationships—these prevailing relationships are depressing, where could I have changed them? Maybe this one time, if I had patted her tear-stained face? When will I finally dare to know, what I already know? (*Nein* 233)

Her excuses were that she was afraid, she felt powerless, and she was pregnant. But at least she questions and thus grows beyond the sole perspective of herself as victim, by identifying and feeling pity for another victim.

If these women's autobiographies center on questions of identity and selfhood, it is because of the troubled and troubling nature of the selves they discover on the emotionally taxing journey backward in time. For several writers, the look backwards is accomplished by holding up a mirror, as if to deflect a direct gaze that would be too intense, too powerful, too threatening. Shari Benstock quotes Virginia Woolf at length about "the mirror stage" and notes "the shame of looking in the glass" (13). The next step after perceiving one's shame at looking at one's own face is to discover the reasons for that shame, a project dear to the hearts of many autobiographers of the Nazi era. Benstock says that the mirror stage gives rise to two insights: first, that the viewer is whole and complete, and second, that the image viewed is "that of an *other*" (14).

These two awarenesses have clear affinities with the autobiographical projects of Stern, Zeller, and Bielenberg. Their goal is to (re)make the self whole and complete by identifying and restoring all "others" to their rightful places. One means of "righting" those who were wronged is to *write* them. Barbara Saunders suggests that "in many peoples' lives there are certain propitious times for standing back and taking stock. . . . At these times the individual is more able to perceive patterns and connections in his [*sic*] life than at other times. Often it is clear that *episodes emerge partially through the process of writing itself,* although a defined shape to a life certainly exists prior to composition" (1, emphasis added). Bielenberg remarked on how her book ultimately assumed a life of its own: "I was just keeping the notes really. . . . I never expected more than very few notes and diaries for my children—this book sort of developed . . . I just got more and more involved" (Interview 5). Stern noted, even more explicitly, "Certain things only became clear to me during the writing [of the book]" (Interview 17).

The mirror's reflections of the "other" can be, in reality, another self. For Zeller, the gaze into the mirror was a nightmare of self-rejection. When she sees her face in the mirror as a child she finds it indescribably ugly "with colorless brows and lashes and pale eyes." When she looks into the mirror, her much-despised father, whom she physically resembles, gazes unrelentingly back (*Solange* 121). Bielenberg similarly sees an other self in the glass: "when I looked in the mirror a stranger looked back at me—a white-haired stranger with huge black-rimmed eyes and powdered lips" (171). Domna Stanton has maintained that "[an autobiography] can never inscribe the death of the speaking subject, the terminus of life" (10), but in this mirrored vision of herself as cadaver after a bombing raid, Bielenberg challenges that claim. This argument might well be extended to other autobiographies about the war in which death and life often seemed one (Bielenberg: "Living close to death I knew to be heightened living" 177).

If Zeller and Bielenberg, like Virginia Woolf before them, had literal encounters with mirrors, for Stern, the mirrors were her peers and the Nazi ideal of girlhood, both of which supplied traumatic reflections. She mirrors her own inadequacies: "Eka soon realizes that she can not do justice to her *Führer*'s ideal picture of a true German girl. . . . [She is] unathletic, messy, clumsy—unattractive, yes, that too" (109). She actively seeks ways as a child to alter this reflection. Bella Brodzki and Celeste Schenck write that, "beyond a woman's (always mediated) subjective relationship to her hand mirror is a range of ways in which she herself serves as mirror" (7). For Stern the solution is clear: "Eka does what she loves to do best, she performs and produces herself" (110). But maintaining a two-way mirror is strenuous, and she plays the clown for many years of her life in order "to entertain, to please, to be recognized, and to be loved. Thus she enjoys being an old woman much later. End of the nonsense/trickery" (110).

The act of writing can be both reflecting and self-reflective as discussed above, and it can also have "a global and essential therapeutic purpose" (Stanton 15). All the writers mentioned the pain and mental anguish of writing but also the satisfaction and comfort it brought (Stern: "It relieved me to write this book"; Bielenberg: "the book was for me a catharsis"). Relived pain and emotional stress would top a list of problems in writing autobiographically about the Nazi era. Several authors have also commented on their distress at making literary figures, or "characters," out of their friends and relatives (Zeller described this as "sacrificing them up"). Stern and Zeller were both concerned with *Rücksichtsnahme* (consideration) for people still alive. All three authors also address the problem of authenticity, the murky area that encompasses history, literature, and truth. Eva Zeller summarizes the difficulty thus: "Whoever attempts to write a piece of autobiography always sets him or herself up as omniscient. By avoiding the lies of invention, one falls victim to the lies of memory" (*Solange* 195).

Because all three of these writers not only strive to document but also transcend the personal and thus contribute to larger philosophical, historical, and political questions, they have created texts that are both authentic and valuable cultural artifacts. Given the difficulties of writing autobiography, including the unreliability of the memory, these authors have been remarkably successful at the art of distillation. James Olney's comment on Yeats's autobiography seems an appropriate evaluation of the autobiographies of Stern, Zeller, and Bielenberg as well: "we should be aware that very little in any of the volumes is intended to be taken as factual or incontrovertible. Yeats presents us instead with a truer truth than fact, a deeper reality than history" (263).

NOTES

1. Critical scholarship on Christa Wolf and on *Kindheitsmuster* has proliferated to a point where it might overwhelm any but the dedicated specialist. Thus a review of literature on *Kindheitsmuster* would claim the space of an entire essay in its own right. Wolf's work is not extensively treated here, in part because, as the introductory essay explains, this volume is intended to explore a wide variety of women's writings on the Nazi era including, in some cases, lesser-known authors. Additionally, *Kindheitsmuster* is already represented in this collection in Marie-Luise Gättens's unique juxtaposition of the work with Woolf's *Three Guineas* and Ruth Rehmann's *Der Mann auf der Kanzel* (The man in the pulpit).

2. Some recent works that have made important contributions to women's autobiography theory are: Estelle Jelinek, *Women's Autobiography* (1980), Domna Stanton, ed., *The Female Autograph* (1984), Sidonie Smith, *A Poetics of Women's Autobiography* (1987), Shari Benstock, ed., *The Private Self* (1988), Bella Brodzki and Celeste Schenck, eds., *Life/Lines* (1988), and Françoise Lionnet, *Autobiographical Voices* (1989).

3. Both Lejeune and Pike are quoted in Stanton, 11.

4. This is from our interview [unpublished], my translation. All further references cited in text.

5. This is from our interview [unpublished]. All further references cited in text.

6. Further references to Stern's novel cited in text. All are my translations.

7. As children, Stern and her schoolmates whimsically changed their names (and thus their identities) by spelling them backwards. She was known by the alias Akire Sumsa (*Netzen* 113).

8. For a more detailed discussion of Zeller's relationships to her father and her first husband, see my essay, "Patriarchy, Memory, and the Third Reich in the Autobiographical Novels of Eva Zeller," *Women in German Yearbook*, vol. 6 (1991): 47–62.

9. Further references to *Nein und Amen* cited in text. My translations. Compare Zeller's representation of her sexually aggressive, intellectual, fiercely patriarchal father with Barbara Bronnen's similar account of her fictionalized father, Arnolt Bronnen in Susan Figge's essay in this volume.

10. In our interview, Carola Stern elaborated on her mother's abortions and the family's reaction to her inclusion of it in the book: "[My aunt was upset] because I had written that my mother, her sister, had had an abortion. That is exactly how it was in the Nazi era: people were upset if a girl got pregnant, but they were

not upset if a Jew was taken away. This is that twisted, misanthropic *Kleinbürgerei* (petite bourgeoisie)" (25).

11. This group would include Melita Maschmann, Margarete Hannsmann, Christa Wolf, Carola Stern, Eva Zeller, Ingeborg Drewitz, and Wendelgard von Staden, among others.

12. Note also the corollary definition of victim as "a living creature sacrificed in religious rites" (*American Dictionary* 1355), which reiterates the religious-ritual/death-cult association argued by Macciocchi and others.

WORKS CITED

American College Dictionary. New York: Random House, 1966.

Benstock, Shari, ed. *The Private Self: Theory and Practice of Women's Autobiographical Writings.* Chapel Hill: University of North Carolina Press, 1988.

Bielenberg, Christabel. *The Past is Myself.* 1968. Reprint. London: Corgi, 1986.

———. Personal interview. Tullow, Ireland, 1 June 1988.

Brodzki, Bella, and Celeste Schenck, eds. *Life/Lines: Theorizing Women's Autobiography.* Ithaca: Cornell University Press, 1988.

Higonnet, Margaret, Jane Jenson, Sonya Michel, and Margaret Weitz, eds. *Behind the Lines: Gender and the Two World Wars.* New Haven: Yale University Press, 1987.

Huston, Nancy. "The Matrix of War: Mothers and Heroes." In *The Female Body in Western Culture,* ed. Susan Rubin Suleiman. Cambridge: Harvard University Press, 1986, 119–136.

Klaus, Martin. *Mädchen im Dritten Reich.* Cologne: Pahl-Ruggenstein, 1985.

Lacoue-Labarthe, Philippe, and Jean-Luc Nancy. "The Nazi Myth." Trans. Brian Holmes. *Critical Inquiry* 16 (Winter 1990): 291–312.

Macciocchi, Maria-Antonietta. "Female Sexuality in Fascist Ideology." Trans. and ed. Michèle Barrett, Judy Keiner, Karen Margolis, and Jennifer Stone. *Feminist Review* no. 1 (1979): 67–82.

Maschmann, Melita. *Fazit: Mein Weg in der Hitler-Jugend.* Munich: Deutscher Taschenbuch Verlag, 1979.

Olney, James. "Some Versions of Memory/Some Versions of *Bios:* The Ontology of Autobiography." In *Autobiography: Essays Theoretical and Critical,* ed. James Olney. Princeton: Princeton University Press, 1980. 236–267.

Saunders, Barbara. *Contemporary German Autobiography: Literary Approaches to the Problem of Identity.* London: University of London, Institute of Germanic Studies, 1985.

Smith, Sidonie. *A Poetics of Women's Autobiography: Marginality and the Fictions of Self-Representation.* Bloomington: Indiana University Press, 1987.

Stanton, Domna. "Autogynography: Is the Subject Different?" In *The Female Autograph,* ed. Domna Stanton. New York: New York Literary Forum, 1984.

Stern, Carola. *In den Netzen der Erinnerung: Lebensgeschichten Zweier Menschen.* Reinbek: Rowohlt, 1986.

———. Personal interview. Cologne, 11 June 1988.

Wahrig Deutsches Wörterbuch. Mosaik Verlag, 1980.

Wolf, Christa. *Kindheitsmuster.* Darmstadt: Luchterhand, 1979.

Zeller, Eva. *Nein und Amen.* Stuttgart: Deutsche Verlags-Anstalt, 1986.

———. *Solange ich denken kann.* Stuttgart: Deutsche Verlags-Anstalt, 1981.

———. Personal interview. Munich, 15 May 1986.

BARBARA MABEE

"I wash tears and sweat out of old moss": Remembrance of the Holocaust in the Poetry of Sarah Kirsch

With the unification of Germany on 3 October 1990, the quest for reflection on the history and historical responsibility that both Germanys share, has taken on new urgency. In his speech on the 53rd anniversary of *Reichskristallnacht* (Night of the crystal glass) and the second anniversary of the opening of the Berlin Wall on 9 November 1991, Eberhard Diepgen, the mayor of Berlin, captured united Germany's relationship to history with the poignant statement, "Remembering our history is our pain." As tens of thousands of Berliners rallied against racism and neo-Nazism in Berlin, carrying large banners with slogans such as "Solidarity Against Violence and Hate Against Foreigners," Germany's history loomed like a ghost over the rally. "Coming to terms with the past is a preoccupation and vital part of German political culture," the minister of technology for the German state of Brandenburg, formerly in the GDR (German Democratic Republic), declared at the rally (Lett 2E). United Germany is now challenged to embark on a joint coming to terms with the Nazi past (*Vergangenheitsbewältigung*).

The collapse of Marxist regimes in eastern and central Europe has intensified the interest in GDR (East German) writers like Sarah Kirsch, whose public defense of artistic freedom and dissident or disharmonious voices forced them to take up residence in the West, voluntarily or otherwise.[1] Kirsch, born in East Germany in 1935 and residing in West Germany since August 1977, has confronted in her poetic work human forgetfulness and false security. As early as 1965, in her first joint volume with her former husband Rainer Kirsch, *Gespräch mit dem Saurier* (Conversation with the Saurian), Kirsch ridicules self-satisfaction and self-aggrandizement in GDR society in the naively stylized image of a saurian from the north who eats the sun during the ice-age. In each of her poetry collections, Kirsch takes the reader on exploratory journeys through time and space, evoking mental associations with various forms of discrimination, fascist terror, oppressive power structures, and the most severe eradication of "otherness" in the systematically administered mass deaths of the Holocaust.[2] Kirsch's subjective confrontations with the past from the perspective of the present invite active participation in memory processes that lead to reflections on recent German history.

Kirsch left the GDR among the exodus of writers after the protest against the exile of the poet/singer Wolf Biermann in November 1976.[3] Her favorable view of "mein kleines wärmendes Land" (my small warming country) that she expressed in "Fahrt II" (Trip II) in 1967 in *Landaufenthalt* (A stay in the country), had become marred by the harassment and isolation she had suffered as an artist in support of Biermann's outspokenness at his Cologne concert in the Federal Republic of Germany (FRG). Kirsch stated in an interview with British Germanist Peter Graves on 10 July 1990 that the main reasons for her leaving the GDR was the repression that her eight-year-old son suffered after the Biermann affair and the deceitfulness and lies one had to teach a child in order to get ahead in the educational system (Graves, "Sarah Kirsch" 273). Biermann recently had generous praise for Kirsch's courage to "knit political motifs into her nature poetry" and for her outspokenness and honesty in contrast to some other GDR German poets (Biermann 44).

By 1977, Kirsch already had established herself as a formidable writer and had been awarded the East German Heinrich Heine Prize and the West German Petrarca Award. In the West, renowned awards quickly followed her lyric productivity: the Austrian Prize for European Literature in 1980, the West German Critics' Prize in 1982, the Friedrich Hölderlin Prize in 1984, and in 1988 the Art Prize in Schleswig-Holstein, her chosen state of residence in the FRG beginning in 1983 (prior to this she had lived in West Berlin and in Bothel, Lower Saxony). In the West German periodical *Der Spiegel,* the writer Rolf Schneider called Kirsch arguably "the most significant lyric poet writing in German today" (141). Elke Erb's 1989 GDR publication *Musik auf dem Wasser* (Music on the water), a volume of selected poetry by Sarah Kirsch from the East and the West and published before the Revolution, pays a generous tribute to Erb's close poet-friend and attests to a continued interest in Kirsch among her GDR readers after she moved to the West.

Critics and scholars have addressed Kirsch's intrinsically related and complex interests in travel and writing (Melin 199–204; Figge 167–184) and her characteristic topics of nature, love, and female self-assertion (Heukenkamp 354–367; Volkmann 95–134; Labroisse 145–195), emphasizing her seemingly effortless verse (Wolf 21), her public, spoken language (Erb 135), and the strong intensity of her "I-statements" that mix private and public concerns in free association spaces (Cosentino, "Sarah Kirschs Dichtung" 105, and Cosentino, *"Ein Spiegel"* 18). In his highly favorable and, for Kirsch's GDR reception, extremely influential review of the 1972 volume, *Zaubersprüche* (Conjurations), Adolf Endler (154) connected Kirsch's poetry with the genre of letters and diaries. Frequently critics have overemphasized the private voice in her writing and downplayed political and historical dimensions that are at the core of her interplay between subjective and objective realities. Peter Graves commented in his 1985 study, *Three Contemporary German Poets: Wolf Biermann, Sarah Kirsch, and Reiner Kunze* (17), that she speaks "with an altogether softer voice and, rarely touching upon public issues, deals above all with the sphere of personal and private relationships."

I intend to argue and show through close textual readings that much of Kirsch's multilayered "private poetry" displays a fundamental concern in working through German National Socialism and the history of domination over the "other," over nature and human consciousness, with the culmination of annihilation of "otherness" in recent German history. I focus on selected poetry, ranging from her first joint 1965 volume *Gespräch mit dem Saurier* to her last poetry volume *Schneewärme* (Snow warmth, 1989), and show how the Holocaust emerges as the actual locus for remembered and recorded human suffering and affects her choice of imagery and rupture of harmonious-idyllic settings. To scrutinize closely the crafted intricateness of the poetry and to draw attention to her gender, it is necessary to establish a background for the sociopolitical and cultural reality in her poetry. Furthermore, a short overview of the literary discussions and developments connected with post-1945 literature sets a context for an analysis of the Holocaust topos in her poetry.

How deeply Kirsch identifies with Jewish history manifests itself in her name change when she began to publish her poetry in the early 1960s. Born into a Protestant family as Ingrid Bernstein (one can assume a conversion from Judaism in previous generations), she took the penname Sarah as an antiracist statement and a means of showing solidarity with Jewish women in the Nazi era who had to assume the additional name Sara—mother of the Jews—in January 1939. Also, as she has stated in interviews (Serke 223), her father's ethnocentric thinking and her clergy-trained grandfather's intolerant religious attitude played a role in this decision. Kirsch's initial interest in a *personal* coming-to-terms with history and subjective mourning for the victims of the Holocaust must be viewed in the context of the state-directed, public antifascist reorganization in the GDR and a far-reaching campaign to expose Nazi ideology. Not surprisingly, Kirsch's poetry written in the GDR between 1965 and her move to the West in 1977 contains more explicit allusions to the Holocaust and Nazism than later volumes in northern Germany.

Anti-Semitism was viewed as "a problem of the bourgeoisie that would be automatically resolved through the overthrow of the capitalistic order" (Kwiet 180). In the historical narratives of the GDR, Europe between 1933 and 1945 was the site of an intense struggle between the "fascist dictatorship" and the "antifascist resistance" and instead of the word "Holocaust" terms such as "racial incitement," "anti-Semitism," and "persecution of the Jews" appear in the literature of the "first workers and peasants state on German soil."[4] Even in 1988, during the commemorations of the November 1938 pogrom against German Jews, GDR officials claimed—despite recent arrests of neo-Nazi "skinheads"—that they had eradicated anti-Semitism from their country (Fox 59).

The Eastern zone of Germany had adopted a state-regulated antifascist/democratic program between 1945 and 1949, which instilled a somewhat self-righteous belief in standing on the right side of history and led to an overemphasis on its collective innocence in dealing with fascism. Death camps and sites of Nazi torture were turned into hallowed grounds of warning (*Mahnmal*) for East German school children, foreign dignitaries, and tourists.

The term "victims of Nazism" was to include socialists and communists who had emigrated from Nazi Germany to become resistance fighters and became entitled to receive the same monthly pensions as Jewish victims. Until February 1990,[5] the GDR officially denied its responsibility for the crimes of Nazi Germany and refused to adopt the policies of the FRG regarding restitution for property and other losses suffered by individual Jews (Merritt 174). Literature from the early reorganization period avoided subjective mourning processes over atrocities committed in the twelve years of National Socialism. Returned exile writers wrote about heroic resistance fighters and exemplary workers engaged in the building of their new society (Hörnigk 79). In poetry, the theme of war and fascism was woven into political messages about the construction of their socialist state, as in Stephan Hermlin's traditionally rhymed Holocaust poem of 1947, "Die Asche von Birkenau" (The ashes of Birkenau). The aesthetic problem becomes manifest in the clash between mourning the victims of Birkenau, calling for participation in the German class struggle, and showing idealism:

Doch die sich entsinnen
sind da, sind viele, werden mehr.
Kein Mörder wird entrinnen,
kein Nebel fällt um ihn her.
Wo er den Menschen angreift,
da wird er gestellt.
Saat von eisernen Sonnen,
fliegt die Asche über die Welt.
Allen, Alten und Jungen,
wird die Asche zum Wurf gereicht,
schwer wie Erinnerungen
und wie Vergessen leicht.

Yet those who remember
are here, are many, will become more.
No murderer will get away,
no fog surrounds him.
Where it attacks people,
there they will be caught.
Seed from iron suns,
fly the ashes across the world.
All, old and young,

will be handed the ashes for the throw,
as difficult as remembering
and as easy as forgetting.[6]

The antifascist democratic program in the 1940s was accompanied by an antifascist renewal of humanistic German culture, and it established a premise that culture and politics must be closely linked and the classical tradition (*Erbepflege*) observed. Cultural policy was to support the progress of socialist society, and progress in turn would further the quality of cultural production (Stephan 75). The Socialist Union party (SED) assigned historians the task of enlightening their state of workers and peasants to the fact that Nazism was the creation of capitalist monopolists, Junkers (squires), and militarists and to prove that the GDR had no Nazi past, whereas potential dangers for creating a new fascism still existed in West Germany. Many writers in the early reconstruction period from the mid-1950s to the early 1960s were concerned with both getting the state constructed (*Aufbauperiode*) along the lines of their new social ethos and functioning in their literary productions by and large as a mouthpiece for the state if they wanted to be published in the GDR.

The negative effects of the categorical damnation of fascism in the GDR frequently have been viewed as corresponding to those of the "economic miracle" of the Adenauer era in the FRG. The general public in both German states by and large avoided and postponed private mourning, as indicated by the large body of literature from the 1970s and 1980s in both Germanys dealing with the personal working through the German past. In West German literature, the existential experience of "point zero" after the complete surrender in 1945 continued the apolitical and ahistorical literature along the lines of the "inner emigration" writers who had been silenced to a private treatment of universal themes by Hitler's cultural apparatus (Trommler 1–117; Daemmrich and Haenicke 350–404). In 1947, a group of West German writers became concerned with cleaning up the language of the Hitler period that had developed its own texts, language, and philosophy to legitimize its social reality. *Gruppe 47* (Group 47) under Heinrich Böll was founded with the intent of purging language of Nazi rhetoric, hysteria, and sentimentality. Immediately, these writers launched the reception of international modernism, German expressionism, and surrealism, which Hitler had aborted.

In the GDR, the reception of modernism began only in the

1960s as Kirsch was making her literary debut within the avant-garde movement of poetry called the "Lyric Wave." These young poets born between 1934 and 1935—Volker Braun, Bernd Jentzsch, Sarah Kirsch and Rainer Kirsch, Karl Mickel, Heinz Czechowski—began to draw attention to their poetry in Soviet-inspired public readings in 1962 and 1963. Even though they had a strong commitment to their state, they no longer wanted to give harmonious depictions of GDR reality but to uncover contradictions and problems in their society. They challenged the prescriptive aesthetics of socialist realism and Soviet-influenced antiformalism that had been part of the antifascist orientation of their state. To express their own relationship to art and history, they insisted on the right to assert their subjectivity in all aspects of their writing: "Historical consciousness is self-consciousness," a slogan coined by their spokesman Volker Braun, became a guiding principle for the group (Braun 139). In his essay, "Literature and Historical Consciousness," Volker Braun labels his view of reality "working history" and attributes it to Walter Benjamin's concept of working through history in the "time of the now"—*Jetztzeit* (Benjamin 265). In order to approach history authentically instead of through ideological slogans of progress and teleological history, this group of poets focused on a close interrelationship of past and present along the lines of Benjamin.

Walter Benjamin's understanding of remembrance in his "Theses on the Philosophy of History," formulated while contemplating the horrors of fascism just before he committed suicide in France in 1940, informs Kirsch's concept of remembrance and history. Kirsch wants to mediate moments of historic atrocities in the "now" between past and future. Benjamin's concept of history, which he saw captured in Paul Klee's painting of the mythic archetype "Angelus Novus," implies an abrupt merging of past and present in the moment of recognition of the "pile of debris" left by history. As stated in Benjamin's fifth and sixth theses of history: "The true picture of the past flits by. The past can be seized only as an image which flashes up at the instant when it can be recognized and is never seen again. . . . To articulate the past historically does not mean to recognize it 'the way it really was.' . . . It means to seize hold of a memory as it flashes up at a moment of danger. Historical materialism wishes to retain that image of the past which unexpectedly appears to man singled out by history at a moment of danger" (Benjamin 257). Benjamin's concept of remembrance (*Eingedenken*), developed in detail in his essays on the storyteller, Proust, Baudelaire, and in his "Theses on the Philosophy of History" represents a process of remembering that brings together past with present moments of oppression but does not universalize suffering. Instead, the rememberer "blasts open the continuum of history" (Benjamin 264) and retrieves the uniqueness of the experience.

The literary debate on appropriate aesthetic responses to the suffering of the Holocaust had been initiated in the 1950s by Theodor Adorno's often-quoted claim "to write poetry after Auschwitz would be barbaric" (Adorno, *Prismen* 31). Adorno believed that the aesthetic stylization principle and aesthetic enjoyment could not do justice to the victims; however, in 1965, he publicly refuted his earlier statement in connection with his reflections on the tension between the responsibility of art and the necessity of remembering the victims (Adorno, "Engagement," *Noten zur Literatur III* 125f.). Reinhard Baumgart, in his essay "Unmenschlichkeit beschreiben" (To Describe Inhumaneness), took up Adorno's earlier dictum when stating that Holocaust literature commits a grave injustice against the victims "by removing some of the horror" (Baumgart 12–36). Also, Michael Wyschogrod submits that the "attempt to transform the holocaust into art demeans the holocaust and must result in poor art" (Rosenfeld and Greenberg 3). George Steiner shares these negative views of Holocaust literature and carries them a step further when advocating silence: "The world of Auschwitz lies outside speech as it lies outside reason" (Steiner 54, 123).

Many critics assert the legitimacy of Holocaust literature and stress the importance of keeping the memory alive. Lawrence Langer's study, *The Holocaust and the Literary Imagination*, addresses the need for literary testimony that "the existence of Dachau and Auschwitz, . . . has altered not only our conception of reality, but its very nature. The challenge of the literary imagination is to find a way of making this fundamental truth accessible to the mind and emotions of the reader" (Langer XII). Rosenfeld sees Holocaust literature "as a testament of our times" (Rosenfeld and Greenberg 5). Elie Wiesel, a survivor of Auschwitz and author of many books that reflect on the Holocaust experience—and the 1986 recipient of the Nobel Peace Prize for his work as author, teacher, and witness—calls literature of the Holocaust a "contradiction in terms." Describing the conflict and pain he endures in writing testimonies "in order not to go mad," he states: "All I know is that Treblinka and Auschwitz cannot be told. And yet I have tried. God knows I have tried" (Rosenfeld and Greenberg 4, 205). In criticism of the literature of the Holocaust, key terms have been "Jewish" and "uniqueness," although these terms are not always used together. The fear of universalizing the Holocaust through imaginative rather than "authentic" treatment has been a focal point in literary discussions of the Holocaust. Ruth Angress, in her essay "Discussing Holocaust Literature," identifies problems with Alfred Rosenfeld's *A Double Dying. Reflections on the Holocaust.* Judging the book to be overall "informative and thoughtful," Angress criticizes its negative judgment of non-Jewish-oriented Holocaust literature. Problematic are Rosenfeld's criticism of Sylvia Plath's references to the Holocaust in her own poetic expressions of pain and his critique of William Styron's *Sophie's Choice* (Angress 192). The latter Rosenfeld charges with "misappropriating" the Holocaust. However, Rosenfeld's chapter, "Poetics of Expiration," receives praise from Angress for its succinct discussion of the relationship between linguistic experiments, silence, and negativity in the poetry of the Jewish poets Paul Celan and Nelly Sachs (191). Angress recommends taking the literature of the Holocaust out of its isolated place in literature and finding a more literary approach to this "quintessentially modern and deeply engaging body of work" (192).

Whereas survivors and Jewish writers have felt a great need to bear witness to the Holocaust through documentation of the horror in autobiographies, eye-witness reports, diaries, and novels, non-Jewish writers have focused more on imaginative/exegetical interpretation that would involve readers in reflection processes and a more affective relationship to the past. Kirsch, as a non-Jewish woman writer, born into a generation that experienced Nazi Germany only in early childhood, does not provide documentary testimonials to the victims of genocide. In her poetry she mediates memory processes that have the potential to increase her readers' sensibility toward the destruction of "otherness" and to bring committed atrocities into public consciousness. Readers are encouraged to probe their relationship to "otherness" and to recent German history. She challenges the readers to find intersections with their personal experiences. Kirsch herself has commented on her poetic principle in *Erklärung einiger Dinge* (Some things explained): "because I would like to write poems in which the readers have a space, where they can do something on their own. I do not want to restrict my readers completely. . . . There are only nudges, and everyone can move within the lines. . . . Somewhat of a small solidarity between the writer and the reader."[7]

Frequently Kirsch begins a poem with a concrete image drawn from nature (biology was her main area of academic study) in a bucolic setting, only to destroy its tranquility by turning to negative, paradoxical, oxymoronic stylistic devices that express inner affliction in the face of human atrocities. The tension she creates in this manner forces readers to come to terms with the dialectical shift and to rethink particularly dehumanizing events in the context of past, present, and future. For example, in "Reglos" (Motionless) from the 1984 volume *Katzenleben* (Catlives), Kirsch links a peaceful, snow-covered landscape in the present with buried memories of landscapes of death and war:

Der Tag kommt an aus den Wäldern
Unsichtbar es schneit in die Grenzen
Von gestern und heute . . .
Es ist nicht hell und wird nicht dunkel
Niemand geht auf den Feldern die Felder
Totenfelder wachsen hirtenlos stündlich . . .
Ich habe den Namen der Ortschaft vergessen . . .
Wir befinden uns kurz nach dem Frieden
Wir können uns nicht erinnern was
Alles geschah das ausgelöschte Bewusstsein
. . .

The day comes out of the forests
Invisible it snows into the borders
Between yesterday and today . . .
It is not light and does not get dark
Nobody walks in the fields the fields
Graveyards grow by the hour shepherdless . . .
I have forgotten the name of the town . . .
We are shortly after peace was made
We cannot remember what
All happened the blotted consciousness
. . .[8]

The deconstruction of idyllic landscapes and the poet's elliptic, disharmonious language, made up of interplay of light and dark, frequent use of paradox, oxymoron, irony, and blasphemy take on more significance in the context of post-Holocaust literature and its concern with language, silence, and appropriate mourning. For Kirsch, the literary treatment of the Holocaust requires a language that disrupts any false security and weaves opposites into one oxymoronic image, as she does in the title of her last volume of poetry, *Schneewärme* (Snow warmth).

In his essay, "Erziehung nach Auschwitz" (Education after Auschwitz), Theodor Adorno has shown how the destructive authority structures in German history and society are related to the barbarism of National Socialism. Adorno considers "autonomy, the strength for reflection, for self-determination, for non-participation as the only true strength against the principle of Auschwitz" (Adorno, "Erziehung nach Auschwitz" 678–679). Alexander Mitscherlich and Margarete Mitscherlich in their often cited 1960 study, *The Inability to Mourn: Principles of Collective Behavior* (tranlated from the original German edition, *Die Unfähigkeit zu trauern*) addressed the lack of personal confrontation with the past in West Germany. Drawing on Freudian psychoanalytic insights of the cathartic effect of memory, the Mitscherlichs focused on the need for a subjective interaction with avoidance of traumata and collective defense mechanisms. They saw the direction for authentic mourning in looking at the cultural "other" as a being with equal rights: "Mourning can occur only when one individual is capable of empathy with another. This other person enriche[s] . . . through his otherness, as man and woman can enrich each other by experiencing their difference" (Mitscherlich and Mitscherlich 27).

In her search for empathy with victims and for her own historically resonant authentic female poetic voice, Kirsch frequently historicizes the present of the lyrical or empirical "I" through dialogical strategies and historical allusions, as in her poem "Winter" from her first independent volume *Landaufenthalt* (A stay in the country, 22) in 1969. Here the "I" gazes from the interior of a room through its window and attempts to define her self as woman and poet in history. Implicitly the "double bind of the woman poet" is addressed, as Suzanne Juhasz and other female critics have frequently formulated theoretically since the 1970s (Juhasz 1–7). In registering personal and collective history, Kirsch's persona announces, "I am getting to know myself." By inserting an allusion to a newspaper clipping that mentions the Reichstag fire (on 28 February 1933), she establishes a link between the "I" and the beginnings of the Third Reich. This poem, with its chains of free association between subjective and historic matters and ambivalent images, was viciously attacked in the GDR in 1969 as "abstract empiricism" (Franz 1202–1203), the stylization of anecdotes, and flight into images. Kirsch's associative spaces and subjective memory processes were at that time considered to be in opposition to the officially sanctioned Soviet-inspired socialist realism from the 1930s and in sympathy with Western modernism. The "Kafka-Conference" in 1963 near Prague had brought the reception of literary modernism out into the open in the GDR.

Jost Hermand has described the heated disputes between the modernist tradition and the cultural heritage in the GDR in the 1960s and 1970s:

> In the opinion of the East, the West has sacrificed the "good old" for the "bad new." The GDR claims to have built on the "good old" while developing the "good new." By the "good old" they mean the literature of the rising revolutionary bourgeoisie, that is, the literature from 1750–1848. By the "bad new" they mean the literature of the declining bourgeoisie, that is western literature from 1848 to the present, from Baudelaire and Rimbaud to Benn and Beckett. (Hermand 87–88)

Western modernists were thought to be adhering to aimless avantgardism, and a new socialist literature, which is partisan and oriented to the people, could be achieved only by a synthesis of the "good old," meaning the classics, with the "good new," meaning critical and social realism (Hermand 88). Already in her early poetry of the 1960s, Kirsch adopted some techniques of Western modernism, such as simultaneity, alienation, montage, paradoxy, laconic-elliptic ruptures, an occasional break between signifier and signified. In various interviews, she has mentioned Raphael Alberti, Pablo Neruda, William Carlos Williams, Paul Celan, Georg Trakl, Ingeborg Bachmann, and Hans Magnus Enzensberger as modernists who affected her own work. Her early poetry in the 1960s shows Kirsch ahead of her time in its insistence on the emergence of the unconscious in dreams, fairy tales, and surreal disguises of the persona in the shape of animals, angels, witches, and natural elements. Frequently, Kirsch's reflections on the alienated artist or socially isolated individual lurk behind these disguises or masks.[9] Officially, there was a reluctance in the GDR to recognize the importance of Freud's psychoanalytical writing on such topics as the interpretations of dreams, the suppression of guilt, the function and healing powers of memory. Not until 1982 was a first selection of Freud's work published in the GDR under the title, *Trauer und Melancholie* (Mourning and melancholy).[10] Cultural officials feared that the emphasis on the subjective might lead to passive narcissism and away from affirmative expressions of commitment (*Parteilichkeit*) to Marxist-Leninist thought and socialist realism. In the public debates on lyric poetry in 1966, 1969, and 1972, questions about the role of subjectivity and its relation to writers' sociopolitical responsibilities as well as questions about the functions of literature stood in the foreground in public discussions in the GDR (Rosellini 152, Jäger 304–316).

Kirsch's poetry was directly involved in many literary discussions about artistic expressions of commitment necessary both to the GDR's political reality and to artistic freedom. Because traditionally art and literature in a socialist state are intended to fulfill a political function, the relationship between the individual and society played a much larger role than it did in the literature of the BRD. Kirsch's reception is a case in point regarding the shift in official policy toward art and commitment within the prescriptive mandates of socialist realism. The negative public criticism over the resignation and passivity of Kirsch's poem "Schwarze Bohnen" (Black beans) at the 6th Writers' Congress in 1969 was reversed in 1973, when the poem was praised for the "notwendige Vielfalt der Poesie" (the necessary plurality of poetry). This expansion of literary possibilities came after Erich Honecker's promising claim before the 4th Plenum in December 1971 that, if one starts from a secure position of socialism, there could be no taboos in art and literature (Honecker 427).

In her first collection *Gespräch mit dem Saurier* (22–23), a short Holocaust cycle attests to her attempt to include dream structures to express different facets of her personal experience of mourning the Holocaust victims. In "Mond vor meinem Fenster" (Moon outside of my window), the persona dreams of being able to dialogue with dead Holocaust victims in concrete GDR society. In the second stanza they disappear again in a memory journey to the many wasted minds which perished in the Holocaust (and implicitly also to the book burning on 10 May 1933, when libraries were "purged" of books by Jewish, humanist, Marxist, and foreign authors):

Sieh die Bücher,
die wir nicht lesen können,
weil die Erde
Gehirne frass, Phosphor gebar . . .
    Der Tod hinkt durch Gräben,
    lässt keinen am Leben.

Look at the books,
we cannot read,
because the earth
ate brains, bore phosphorus . . .
    Death limps through ditches
    leaves nobody alive.

In some of these early poems in *Gespräch mit dem Saurier* Kirsch interacts overtly with the poetry of the nature-magic school of poets in West Germany. Kirsch refers directly to Eich's early ahistorical "jay-poems" from the 1950s that explored human encounters with the mystery of nature. However, the presence of an historically beleaguered humankind is an essential element in Kirsch's landscapes—a commonality she shares with fellow-East Germans Peter Huchel and Johannes Bobrowski, both of whom Kirsch has recognized as mentors. Eich's peaceful nature images appear as alienated images in Kirsch's poetry. The deconstruction process of the beauty and mysteries in nature dispels harmony and draws attention to the threat of the eternal return of violence.

The poems that address the atrocities under Hitler's tyranny in "Gespräch mit dem Saurier" have an underlying tone of playful warning. They juxtapose remembering and forgetting and implicitly and explicitly reflect effects of inter-German antagonisms. Artistically some of the poems are simplistic in their rhyme schemes and "folksy" tone; for that reason the volume was neither taken seriously nor translated in the West. One must remember that the Soviet categories of art with their emphasis on the idea of literary "popularity," "solidarity with the people" (*Volksverbundenheit*) and the cultivation of folk art (Flores 53) influenced Kirsch's early writing. However, her poems with the serious subject matter of the German past anticipate her powerful and ambivalent imagery and the essence of her poetic landscapes.

Eichelhäher

Der Häher hat ein schattiges Haus,
der Häher kennt es nicht, er fliegt
am Tag und am Abend unterm Laub
und schreit in Erwartung des Henkers.

Der Henker wohnt in weissen Steinen
am Ufer des Sees; sein Boot
trägt ihn in dämmrige stille Buchten:
er liebt die Trauerweiden sehr.

Den schreienden Häher hört der Henker,
die Stimme geht viel zu weit;
(das Ohr ist gewöhnt an Taubengurren,
seine Kanarienhähne sind massvoll).

Da geht der Henker durch den Wald,
es blitzt auf seinem Rücken wie Gold,
die Sonne fällt ihm auf den Hut
und zeigt die Häherfeder.

The Jay

The jay has a house in the shadow,
the jay does not know it, it flies
night and day among the foliage
and shrieks in expectation of the executioner.

The executioner lives in white stones
on the shore of the lake; his boat
carries him into the dusk of silent coves:
he loves the weeping willows very much.

The executioner hears the screaming jay,
the voice carries much too far;
(the ear is accustomed to doves' cooing
his canaries are restrained).

Then the executioner goes through the forest,
his back flashes like gold,
the sun falls on his hat
and highlights the feather of the jay.[11]

The jay in this poem, seen against the foliage of the historic persecution of the Jews ("he has no house"), becomes the archetype of the wandering Jew. Throughout history he anticipated his status of outsider while he lives in the shade of the dominant culture: he "screams in expectation of the executioner." Kirsch establishes an antithetical relationship between the pariah existence of the homeless and the executioner's carefree life of indulgence in the "white stones" by the lake. He blissfully enjoys the peaceful evening atmosphere, the cooing of the domesticated doves and canaries, and the sight of the weeping willows. Associations can be drawn with the concentration camp official in Paul Celan's best-known Holocaust poem "Todesfuge" (Death Fuge). In Celan's poem, a German official spends his evenings writing sentimental letters to his Gretchen in Germany and his days driving Jews into death chambers (Celan 50–51).

In Kirsch's poem the feather of the jay signifies murder: to the bearer it is a symbol of his victory, but the poem also accuses him. Memory traces to the murderers in the Third Reich remain implicit. The lack of the executioner's memory is possibly an allusion to the denazification process in the GDR in contrast to the reinstatement of Nazis in political offices in the BRD. History follows him on his back in the form of a golden beam, displaying the booty on his hat, suggesting a biblical parallel to the sun (Ecclesiastes 3:11), which shines without judgment on both the just and the wicked. The executioner's successful game and glowing gold stir mental associations with fairy tale elements that taunt people with mysterious sacks of gold. One also might think of the appropriation of Jewish property under National Socialism. The feather becomes an encoded symbol of power and repeated violence; the executioner displays the feather as a symbol of his victory. If the symbol is decoded historically, the reader is drawn into memory processes of persecution, racism, and the extermination of innocent people.

In Kirsch's parody-filled title poem, "Der Saurier" (The Saurian, 30), the ambivalent image of the evil, powerful, and boastful sun-eating saurian from the north that dies out in the ice age suggests an allusion to Hitler's racist ideology with its worship of the blond Nordic race (Peukert 208). On another level, Kirsch's mocking of the saurian also can be related to a state of self-satisfaction or naive self-consciousness in the GDR that no longer questions contradiction, as Rainer Nägele has seen in this poem (Nägele 338–359). In another short poem she draws an analogy to Hitler's blind followers always ready to carry out orders from above—an attitude that she finds also among her fellow-citizens and in the general militaristic climate in the GDR as well. The poem is based upon a word play that juxtaposes the plant "Beifuss" (mugwort or artemisia) and the idiom "bei Fuss stehen" (to stand up straight).

Her short Holocaust cycle consists of three poems with female personae who acquire historical awareness and the ability to mourn: "Holunder" (Elderberry, 19), "Der Regen bin ich" (The rain am I, 20–21), and "Mond vor meinem Fenster" (Moon outside of my window, 22–23). If we examine the imagery closely in these three poems and compare it with Kirsch's later poetry, we find that many of her Holocaust-related images remain the same. She establishes an intertextuality with other writers also working through the Holocaust in this cycle, in particular with the modernist Paul Celan. Celan's poetry mourns the loss of his parents and lover and wrests language from the silence that befalls any attempt at poetic utterance. Celan's characteristically "disguised texts" (Lorenz 209–210), rich in imagery and self-reflecting with understated pain, appeal to Kirsch's poetic sensibility. Haunting images, such as whistle, hair, elderberry, stones, doves, moor, blood, and bones also can be found in the poetry of Nelly Sachs, Paul Celan, Ingeborg Bachmann, Peter Huchel, and Johannes Bobrowski, with whose works Kirsch continues to interact in future volumes.[12] In the case of Celan and Sachs: Kirsch later explicitly draws on titles from their works in her poetry after her move to the West. Kirsch's volumes from the FRG express references to the Holocaust more and more as highly subjective statements written about natural foliage and expressing apocalyptic imagery from a private landscape. The early cycle combines fantasy, present reality, dreams, historic and literary references in a highly subjective way, unknown up to that point in GDR literature. Both "Holunder" (19) and "Der Regen bin ich" (20–21) depict a learning and growth process of a female persona on several levels: a coming to terms with historical responsibility and "otherness," as well as human sexuality.

The hidden allusion to female sexuality and the female body relates to the "palimpsestic" quality of women's texts, the encoded female rebellion discernible beneath long established literary themes and forms, as developed in the seminal study by Sandra Gilbert and Susan Gubar, *The Madwoman in the Attic* (1979, 69–77, 80–83). The female component of Kirsch's imagery is conveyed in these poems in their focus on the female body and the female personae's associations with female fertility. After their initial phase of carefree childhood, they come to an understanding of historic-political guilt and violence in not only recent history but also history of patriarchy. In "The Rain Am I," the experience of the rain when crossing the moor can be read on one level as a departure-from-childhood motif. On another level the rain suggests a personified and mythological fairy tale–like being, that travels across the earth and uncovers experiences and things of significance. The "I" is a female person but is asexual at the same time. The feminine principle is portrayed here as being linked to the earth, biology, nature, and the body, but it is not to be confused with a biologically reduced concept of the feminine, which later in the 1970s was celebrated by one camp within the Western feminist movement. Biology does not represent reduction and confinement in these poems, but something pluralistic that attempts to establish in the writing process a link between "femininity" as expression of the body and the repressed regions of history and to break up old, stale beliefs through a critique of civilization.[13] Kirsch herself has frequently stated that she has no interest in Western style cultural feminism but only in political feminism—on an unorganized level—that works toward overcoming "otherness."

"Holunder" (Elderberry), traditionally an image in German folklore for honoring the dead, contains numerous literary allusions to images used by Paul Celan in his first volume *Mohn und Gedächtnis* (Poppy and memory). The whistle that the commander in Celan's "Death Fugue" used to "whistle his dogs up" and "to whistle his Jews out" becomes in Kirsch's poem the means by which "doves are called near" on a tranquil summer day:

Holunder

Staubiger Holunderbusch,
rundes Sommerhaus,

aus deinen Zweigen
klopf ich schäumendes Mark.

Dusty elderberry,
round summer house
out of your branches
I tap foaming marrow.

The multiple layers embedded in this first stanza suggests the enigmatic quality in Paul Celan's poems, in particular, his interweaving of eroticism and pain. If one also considers Johannes Bobrowski's poem "Holunderblüte" (Elderberry blossom) from 1961, in which he juxtaposes remembering and forgetting, the link to recent German history is immediately established in the first stanza. When connecting the title with the image of the dove and stone, death and destruction emerge as the prevailing atmospheric elements. As the doves "fall down like stones" and fan their feathers and scream, the light summer mood changes to witnessing acts of human violence. The birds take on the referential function of an ominous sign in the tradition of expressionist poetry. For poets such as Trakl or Heym birds were frequently messengers of death or bad tidings, fluctuating between negative and positive mood indicators. The stones signify nature's vessels for storing memories. Observing the violent acts and the uncanny atmosphere, the female persona turns to her mothers' usual activities in the kitchen that are carried out in total oblivion to the acts of violence outside:

Duftender Holunderbusch,
deinen Blütenteller
taucht die Mutter
morgen in Teig.

Morgen, morgens,

Die Kuchen
sind verbrannt,
die Tauben erschlagen,
und Stein ist nicht auf Stein.

Was brauch ich ein Pfeifchen
am Abend?

Fragrant elderberry bush,
your petals
the mother dips
tomorrow into dough.

Tomorrow, in the morning.

The cakes
are burnt,
the doves slaughtered,
and stone is not on stone.

Why should I want a whistle

in the evening?

In "Holunder," Kirsch delineates on several levels a girl's awareness of her mother's exclusive concerns with the fulfillment of the traditional role expectations of women as caretakers and nurturers. The mother's avoidance of guilt and pain become the center of the poetic memory journey to Nazi Germany—to the role and function that Nazi ideology assigned to women (Koonz 175–221; Stephenson 37–57). In Kirsch's association spaces, Hitler's well-documented address to the Nazi Socialist Women's Organization in 1934 comes to mind: "If we say the world of the man is the state, the world of the man is his commitment, his struggle on behalf of the community, we could then perhaps say that the world of the woman is a smaller world. For her world is her husband, her family, her children, and her home" (Mason 75). With Kirsch's chain of negative images, the inherited myth of women's innocence in the face of violence and oppression is dispelled. Kirsch's poetic destruction of this myth reflects the same intent and view of the second sex in the Third Reich that recently was conveyed by the historian Claudia Koonz in her *Mothers in the Fatherland: Women, the Family, and Nazi Politics.* The question at the end of the poem suggests that not only in haunting dreams at night can we remember the horrors of the camps but also in the midst of our everyday life we can encounter scenes that hold memories of violence. The time reference contained in the rhetorical question at the end of the poem, alludes on the one hand to the connection between whistle and evening as references to the continuity of control structures that potentially can destroy others—old sounds from the whistle have survived and continue to excercise their rule over others. The whistle as a phallic symbol in conjunction with "evening" takes up the erotic play of the opening lines and refers to the patriarchal moment of historic violence.

In "The Rain Am I," a girl's playful, naive roaming of the earth turns into a young woman's journey toward historical consciousness and self-awareness. Her walk at the outset turns into a nightmarish walk through the moors at concentration camp sites:

Der Regen bin ich

Der Regen bin ich
In grünseidenen Schuhn
gehe ich über die Erde.

Da tauchen die schuppigen Ähren
vom Grund der Felder auf;
das Gras setzt Knoten ein,
und die Kuh hinterm Haus
greift es mit sicherer Zunge.

Süsser singen die Vögel,
die Linden duften
ins geöffnete Fenster:
die Menschen besehen
das satt getrunkene Flüsschen.

Der Regen bin ich.
In dünnen Schuhn
gehe ich über das Moor.

Da wasche ich Tränen und Schweiss
aus altem Moos, ich höre
schmatzende Spaten und Schüsse,
die Schuhe färben sich rot.
Ich wasche und finde kein Ende.

Der Regen bin ich.
Ich gehe in verwaschenen Schuhen.

Eidechsen sehen mich an.
Frauenhaar duckt sich im Wind.

The Rain Am I

The rain am I,
in green silken shoes
I walk over the earth.

The scaly ears rise
from the soil of the fields;
the grass sprouts forth nodes,
and the cow behind the house
grasps it with a sure tongue.

More sweetly sing the birds,
the lime trees breathe
into the open window:
the people inspect
the brimming streamlet.

The rain am I.
In thin-soled shoes
I walk over the moor.

There I wash tears and sweat
out of old moss, I hear
smacking spades and shots,
my shoes turn red.
I wash and find no end.

The rain am I.
I walk in faded shoes.

Lizards look at me.
Maidenhair ducks in the wind.

In a naively stylized, peaceful nature scene, the persona's changing shoes become signs of a newly perceived reality—of a multiple growth process. The shoes' green color signifies unharmed nature as well as unencumbered childhood. With these shoes the girl becomes part of nature as she sets out on her journey to experience life. In the context of the poem, the shoes do not underscore reality, but rather emotional and atmospheric elements. While the persona as rain is wearing green shoes, nature is at its most luscious state. An abrupt break occurs with the distanced perspective from an open window. With the oscillating image of the "brimming streamlet," the mood and landscape change. As frequently in expressionistic and baroque poetry, the river points to a movement toward death. When relating the river to the red shoes, the reader recognizes behind the red shoes the blood that was shed by the victims. The moor now evokes memories of the most famous concentration camp song, the "Moorsoldatenlied" (song of the moor soldiers, *Börgermoor-Lied*), which was composed in 1933 at camp Börgermoor and has the refrain: "We are the moor soldiers / and go with our spades into the moor." Paul Celan also refers to the moorsoldiers and their enforced labor in the Nazi camps in his collection *Fadensonnen* (Threads of sun, 1968).

In Kirsch's poem the unfruitful landscape of the moor points to the guilt of collective forgetfulness about the atrocities in the camps. An analogy is set up between the rain's washing and the poetic memory process of the persona. The more the persona washes, that is, remembers the acts of terror, the more fruitful the moor can become again: "I wash and find no end."

The walk through the blood-stained landscape ends in an encounter with flora and fauna, with "maidenhair" that "ducks in the wind." Maidenhair is on one level a biological reference to the growth of a fern after years of "unfruitfulness." On another level, this multireferential image evokes allusions of Celan's Jewish female personae, for example, in his erotic memory poems with motifs from folk poetry about his mother and lover in *Mohn und Gedächtnis.* In "Espenbaum" (Aspentree) he mourns his mother's untimely, violent death in the images of the white of the leaves and of the hair: "Aspentree your leaves glance white into the dark. / My mother's hair was never white" (Celan 33). Also in Bachmann's poetry we encounter hair as the cipher for an expression of pain and the motif of departure from childhood (on a narrative level) to a new level of awareness. The reference to lizards at the end of Kirsch's poem alludes to the strange magic powers that were associated throughout history with Jews and were also connected with women and witches in the Middle Ages. By setting apart the two closing lines and connecting them in their referential function, Kirsch reminds the reader implicitly that Jews and women in male-dominated cultures were accused of witchcraft, magic and demonic powers (Trachtenberg 1–25).

With Kirsch's next volume, *Landaufenthalt* (A stay in the country) in 1967, she establishes herself in the East and West as an eminent writer. Most likely because of the Auschwitz trial in Frankfurt between 1962 and 1965, this volume contains two poems that are explicitly structured around the Holocaust, "Legende über Lilja" (Legend of Lilja, 29–31) and "Der Milchmann Schäuffele" (The Milkman Schäuffele, 44–45).

In "Legende über Lilja," the Auschwitz trial is directly woven into the structure of the poem through witness reports at the trial. Conflicting memory descriptions by survivors uncover small details and thus construct a mosaic of individual memories about the young Jewish woman from Poland. We participate in her final period of suffering in the camp and accompany her on her way to the gas chamber. Statements about Lilja's seven letters to her lover, passed among the inmates on the parade ground, can be only sketchy after the passing by of many years. Witnesses remember that a letter was exchanged for bread and that she was sent to the gas chamber because of a fellow-prisoner's betrayal. Her self-dignity stands out in people's memory:

> 5
> Lilja in der Schreibstube Lilja unterwegs Lilja im Bunker
> Schlag mit der Peitsche den Namen warum sagt sie nichts
>   wer weiss das
> warum schweigt sie im August wenn die Vögel
> singen im Rauch
>
> 6
> einer mit Uniform Totenkopf am Kragen Liebhaber
> alter Theaterstücke (sein Hund mit klassischem Namen)
>   erfand
> man sollte ihre Augen reden lassen

5
Lilja in the writing room Lilja walking Lilja in the bunker
lash with the whip the name why doesn't she say anything
   who knows
why is she silent in August when the birds
sing in the smoke

6
one in uniform death's-head on the collar lover
of old plays (his dog with classical name) determined
they should let her eyes speak[14]

The overt allusion to the classical education of the death camp official ("Meister"-"Master") in Paul Celan's "Death Fugue" indicates Kirsch's conscious expression of intersubjectivity with Jewish writers. Celan's "Meister" writes beautiful letters to his Margarethe in Germany (reference to Gothe's *Faust*) at night and whistles his dogs to chase Jews during the day, while Kirsch makes him into a lover of "old plays" and classical names. The witnesses remember Lilja's smile when meeting death—her last stroke over her hair to retain some form of human dignity before death approaches. When the testimony becomes too emotionally laden at this point, Kirsch has the judges break off the witness reports and state: "on record / obviously / legends were told this point / was to be struck from the indictment." With the judges' abrupt dismissal of the witnesses' reports, Kirsch indicts the entire West German post-1945 legal system and the well-documented reinstatement of former Nazis. The judges do not have the last word on Lilja in the poem because the last stanza (14) refers again to the letter that Lilja wrote: "in dem Brief soll gestanden haben wir / werden hier nicht rauskommen wir haben / zu viel gesehen" (in the letter was said to be written we / will not get out of here we have / seen too much). This all-pervasive fear of being killed because one had witnessed too many atrocities has frequently been documented in the literature by Holocaust survivors.

In "Der Milchmann Schäuffele," Kirsch interacts explicitly with Paul Celan's "Death Fugue" via a dialogue between a female persona and a Jewish milkman from Bohemia. The image of milk joins the two simultaneous dialogues. Celan's oxymoronic image of the "black milk," a cipher for Cyclon B used in the gas chambers and at the same time alluding to the evil that turned all values upside down, forms the antithesis to Kirsch's concrete "white milk." Schäuffele's name points to his second job as gravedigger (Schaufel = shovel) and forms also a connecting element to Celan's graves in the air and the haunting leitmotif/refrain of his "Death Fugue": "Schwarze Milch der Frühe wir trinken sie abends / wir trinken sie mittags und morgens wir trinken sie nachts / wir trinken und trinken" (Black milk of daybreak we drink it at sundown / we drink it at noon in the morning we drink it at night / we drink and we drink it"; Celan 50–53). In contrast, Schäuffele's milk in the rain is of a nourishing, pure quality; symbolically speaking, he pours his rich Jewish traditions and customs into vessels every morning only to be harassed later by the same people to whom he gave generously (pours generously into mugs into enamel pots and bulgy glasses).

Time does not manifest itself easily in this poem but we might assume that Schäuffele was driven out of his home in Bohemia and is now homeless except for his milk cart. Present, past, and future are woven around the caesura of the Holocaust. As the "I" becomes a witness to unspeakable cruelties, the time of the dialogue between the persona and Schäuffele could be read as the time before the Holocaust when persecution of the Jews and pogroms had begun. With the inverted phrase, "weil man muss Farbe bekennen" (because one must show one's colors), Kirsch alludes to Yiddish and the Holocaust and draws attention to Schäuffele's traditional Jewish attire, his "black coat" and "round glossy hat." Seen on the pre-Holocaust time level, Schäuffele's real burying of people before Hitler's tyranny is antithetically linked with Celan's "grave in the sky," amidst ascending smoke from the ovens. The halting syntax parallels the pauses and tensions that are created in their dialogue. Ultimately their dialogue leads to the brutalizing routine of the death camp that Celan depicts in the fugal structure of recurring abstract and concrete details of the Nazi official's playing with evil. Kirsch's time structure moves forward and backward as Schäuffele's concern about his future grows. Schäuffele becomes part of the poetic process itself and is asked—along with the reader—to ponder a reply to his question about the future of the "other" in society:

> . . . , das ist wichtig wo
> fahr ich hin auf deinem Papier, nach vorn die Zeit oder
>   zurück
> was wird dann aus mir?

Schäuffele
gäbs einen Grund dich gradaus fahrn zu lassen—da ist
keine Ausnahme für dich und das Pferd, Schäuffele fahr
vorsichtig dass
du die Milch nicht vergiesst
was ich tun kann
wär dir Familie zu geben eine gute Frau ein Enkelkind
ich bitt dich sagt er
allein
ist die Fahrt schon bös genug

. . . , this is important where
do I drive to on your paper, forward in time or backward
what will become of me?
Schäuffele
were there a reason to let you drive straight ahead—there is
no exception for you and the horse, Schäuffele drive
carefully so that
you don't spill the milk
what I could do
would be to give [to] you family a good wife a grandchild
I beg you he says
alone
the trip is already bad enough

From the pre-Holocaust vantage point of their dialogue, history has already provided the answer to Schäuffele's question. Shame and mourning linger on when the direct dialogue is broken off at the end between the persona and Schäuffele. A single line, set apart from the rest of the text, is given to Schäuffele's name. In contrast to the previous stanzas, which engaged the "I" directly in a conversation with Schäuffele, the conversational partner has been silenced forever (forebodingly expressed as future): "Schäuffele / wird man den Wagen zerschlagen das Zugtier blenden, bald / wird viel Milch verlaufen durch die / denen er reichlich im Regen gab" (Schäuffele's / wagon they will smash blind the cart horse, soon / much milk will spill because of those / to whom he gave generously in the rain). The reference to rain at the beginning and end can be read as a signifier for the continued washing away of guilt. The intended ambivalence of time elements in the poem also invites a post-Holocaust interpretation of the central time element of the dialogue with the murdered Jew returning to earth to find a witness. Wolfgang Wittkowski has rendered a convincing interpretation along these lines, posing questions as to anti-Semitism in the GDR, accountability of its citizens for Nazi crimes, and its future policies towards Jews and "others": If Schäuffele drives backward, he documents his fate as Jew under Hitlerfascism. However, if he drives forward, his fate means that something like this happens today, in each country, also *In diesem besseren Land* (In this better country), the title of a 1966 GDR poetry anthology by Endler and Mickel (Wittkowski 314).

In "Hirtenlied" (Sheperd's Song, *Landaufenthalt* 17), in the same volume with "Lilja" and "Schäuffele," Kirsch composes a poetological poem (reflecting on her poetics, craft, and self-understanding as poet), that explains her self-assigned role as a guardian of history in a country surrounded by "Draht" (wire) and the smell of "Brand" (fire):

Ich sitz über Deutschlands weissem Schnee
der Himmel ist aufgeschlitzt
Wintersamen
kommt auf mich wenn nicht Schlimmres
Haar wird zum Helm
die Flöte splittert am Mund
. . . .
Ich knote an Bäume mich lieg unter Steinen
streu Eis mir ins Hemd ich schneide
das Lid vom Aug da bleibe ich wach:
Meine tückische Herde
die sich vereinzelt die sich vermengt
meine dienstbare tückische Herde
wird Wolke sonst: winters noch
ist sie zerkracht

I sit above Germany's white snow
the sky is slit open
Winter seeds
come to me if nothing worse
hair becomes a helmet
the flute splinters in the mouth

. . . .
I tie myself to trees lie under stones
Sprinkle ice in my shirt I cut
the lid off my eye then I stay awake:
My insidious flock
which separates and mingles
my serviceable insidious flock
becomes a cloud otherwise: still in the winter
it burst

The poet's distancing perspective from "above white snow" underscores an ironic allusion to the pure conscience of both Germanys. When one examines the key words in the structure of the poem (hair, helmet, flute/whistle) and compares them with key words from the lyric poetry of Nelly Sachs, Paul Celan, Ilse Aichinger, and other post-Holocaust poets, the snow becomes aligned with death as is also the case in other snow poems in this volume, for example, "Der Schnee liegt schwarz in meiner Stadt" (The snow lies black in my city) and "Breughelbild" (Breughel picture). The "snow" in "Shepherd's Song" in conjunction with its key images and intertexuality aspects can be placed into the literary tradition of Holocaust or post-Holocaust writers. In the poetry of Celan, Sachs, Bobrowski, and Aichinger, snow designates the metaphorical context of death, ice, sleep, and silence and represents the cipher for guilt, forgetfulness, and petrification of Germans and Austrians. The slit sky, in conjunction with the oxymoron "Wintersamen" (Winter seed) and "Wolke" (cloud) at the end of the poem, signals the beginnings of chaos, a break with the cosmic order through the potential nuclear destruction of the entire earth.

As in her earlier Holocaust-cycle in *Gespräch mit dem Saurier*, Kirsch selects "hair" and "flute" as a gesture of solidarity with the suffering of the Jewish people. The splintering flute in the mouth symbolizes the inability to produce harmonious, full sounds after Auschwitz. It signals the poet's difficulty of working through the Holocaust aesthetically and the need to reflect the borders of her own poetic language. "Fire" and "wire" evoke the ovens of concentration camps, open fires into which small children were thrown, as well as the reality of the Berlin wall from 1961 until 1989. This reader is particularly reminded of Nelly Sachs's statement that her "metaphors are her wounds" and Ingeborg Bachmann's breaking away from the genre of poetry out of fear of aesthetization with the poignant question in her 1963 poem "Kleine Delikatessen" (Small delicacies"): "Shall I garnish you with a metaphor?"

Kirsch's poet-persona declares her dedication to remain awake at all cost and to cling to language—"I tie myself to trees lie under stones." The tree in Kirsch's poetry is frequently a cipher for language, paper, and handed-down traditions. The isolated images of "trees," "stones," "ice," and "eye" can all be found as motifs in the poetry of Jewish writers who have reflected on the problems of writing literature after Auschwitz. The logic of the imagery of the entire last stanza points to the poetological aspect of the poem and underscores Kirsch's close relationship between word and image. The poet's experiments with several different images lead to a personal charge to stay awake in order to be able to analyze social and historical processes, separating and mingling within cultural communities. The challenge will be to subdue "insidious" words until they become pliable and serviceable to mediate the horrors of the past, as well as those anticipated in the future, with linguistic power, strength of the imagination, and appropriate aesthetics.

In her next volume, *Zaubersprüche* (Conjurations, 1973) the poems are built on the construct of the witch, who evokes not so much associations with persecution but emancipatory female power and autonomy. Gerd Labroisse has praised this volume as groundbreaking for GDR poetry in its formulation of themes and its sketch of the possibility of female self-determination that breaks with traditional role expectations (Labroisse 151). In Kirsch's construct of the witch, Labroisse sees her creative exploration of possibilities for images that express autonomy. These poems are informed by a female "optic" that self-confidently explores and subversively confounds cultural male/female expectations, inherited myths, and petrified language patterns. By disrupting traditional notions of femininity, she creates new spaces for female interactions with cultural diversity.

In a section entitled "Lithographie" (Lithography), Kirsch takes the reader through fourteen travel experiences and imaginary dream-images. A self-confident "I" works through historical, mythical, sociopolitical, and personal material. In pursuit of historical traces, the "I" engages herself in human encounters in different cultural landscapes. The title poem of this section, "Lithographie," describes a visit to the Jewish cemetery in Prague. The visit, which turns into a reflection on the historic persecution, conveys again Kirsch's acute sensibility to the suffering in Jewish history and to the question of its aesthetic representation. The images of "paper," "stone," and "tree"—images that allude to the recording of Nazi atrocities as we find them in the literature of the Holocaust—invite confrontation with the "black marks" of history, captured ambiguously by the artist in the medium of lithography.[15]

Lithographie

Die Pforte war gebogen und wir kamen durch
Nachdem wir einen Mann mit weissen Haaren
Der noch nicht alt war, Geld bezahlten und er gab
Ein vogelstimmig Fräulein uns zur Seite

Die Alte flog voraus, nahm Weg durch Steine
Die uns wie Zähne eines Tiers erschienen
Wir wähnten einzugehn ins Maul des Wales
Der Jonas zu verschlingen einst geschickt war

Es waren Steine zum Gedächtnis alter Juden
Gewaltlos starben sie in dieser Stadt
Und sanken schichtweise in die Erde, weil der Platz
Gering war und von Häusern eingeschlossen

Nur grosse Bäume kamen auf an dieser Stelle
Sie standen blattlos in den dünnen Himmel
Doch schienen sie nicht schlecht im Saft zu sein.

Der eine wuchs dem Rabbi aus dem Kopf
Bis seine Wurzeln ihn verlassen mussten
Weil nichts mehr war, die Zweige zu ernähren

Das Vogelfräulein klappte mit dem Schnabel
Sie stopfte uns noch Jahre in die Ohren
Bevor sie aufflog im Geäst verschwand

Wir laufen Zickzack durch die schwarzen Male
Damit wir draussen gegenwärtig sind

Dies ist kein Ort, wir waren auf Papier
Vorher, auf Stein, gezeichnet und geätzt.

The gate was rounded and we got through
After we paid a man with white hair
Who was not yet very old, and he gave us
A bird-voiced woman guide

The old woman scurried ahead of us making her way
 through stones
That appeared to us like teeth of an animal
We thought we entered the mouth of the whale
That once was sent to swallow Jonah

They were stones commemorating old Jews
Without violence they died in this city
And sank in layers into the ground, because the space
Was limited being enclosed by houses

Only big trees grew in this place
They rose leafless into the thin sky
Yet they did not seem to be bad in their juices

One grew out of the Rabbi's head
Until its roots forced him to leave
Because nothing was there to nourish the branches

The bird-lady cloppered with her beak
She stuffed years into our ears
Before she flew up and disappeared into the branches

We run zig-zag through the black marks
So that outside we are again in the present
This is no place, we were on paper
Earlier, on stone, drawn and etched.

If one recalls that a lithograph is not only a graphic depiction but also a masterprint from which duplicates can be made, the poem gains multiple levels of meaning that focus on memory. As the title "lithography" suggests, the concrete image of the Jewish cemetery stands for many images—historical, artistic, literary, and biblical. The opening image of the bent gate immediately evokes death: the mythological gate to the afterlife but also the bent gate of Auschwitz and Buchenwald with the motto "Arbeit macht frei" (Work makes free) through which not many passed back out on the day of liberation by the Allies. The fact that the tourists are alive to get through—"we got through"—underscores the lingering reality of the death camps in this cemetery for those who remember. The young man with white hair, who organizes the tours of the old Jewish cemetery, could possibly be a former camp inmate. The bird-voiced sounding woman guide, hectically flying ahead and unaffectedly spitting out the historic facts of the site, forms a stark contrast to the peaceful gravesites.

The poet's imagination creates ambiguous imagery also in the second stanza: the tombstones appear "aggressive," like the teeth of an animal about to attack. The cemetery now has the effect of a whale's mouth, possibly suggesting that the visitors are outsiders, Jews who lived abroad or survived the camp experience and non-Jews like the poet, who feel uncomfortable and guilty. Just as Jonas's visit to the whale's stomach turned him/her into a prophet, the tourist's visit to the cemetery has the potential to make her/him a "storyteller." In other words, the poet can by means of poetic language take the reader to a place of memory that will create changes in perception or historical awareness.

In the third stanza the peaceful death of the Jews put to their final rest is antithetically linked with the violent, untimely mass deaths of the Jews in concentration camps, who died anonymously and have no individual grave markers. The fourth stanza, the center of the poem, significantly reinacts the violence of the atrocities in the poet's imagination. The juicy, growing trees form a contrast to the disruption of Jewish life and Jewish tradition during the Holocaust. The symbolic tree that grows out of the Rabbi's head suggests an analogy with the lineage of the twelve tribes of Israel. It becomes an image of death that creates memories of the systematic Nazi extermination of the Jews and their culture in Eastern and Western Europe. Racist Nazi ideology is evoked in the image of the branches that lead to the death of the lineage of Abraham, Isaac and Jacob, Sara, Rebecca, Rachel, and Lea. The six million murdered Jews and their broken family trees come into focus in the image of the branches. The uniqueness of this implemented ideology is underscored in the line, "Because nothing was there to nourish the branches." The antithesis of life and death in the image of the tree suggests influences of biblical images, of the Kabbala (Jewish theosophy) and the "word-mystical" images of the poet Nelly Sachs.

With the image of the *Vogelfräulein* (bird-lady) Kirsch points to the magical element associated with this old cemetery of Prague. The great magician, Rabbi Löw, is buried here, the alleged creator of the Golem of Prague and counselor to Rudolf von Habsburg, a ruler with an interest in alchemy. Löw's artificially created homunculus is the model for Kirsch's mysterious guide, who mechanically feeds the visitors dates and legends and who lacks the sensitivity to mourn.

In the last stanza, Kirsch switches from the (narrative) perfect tense to the (reflecting) present tense. The "we" at the end forms a contrast to the earlier "we," the visitors of the guided tour in the preceding stanzas. In the artistic/poetic memory process, the peacefully buried Jews undergo several transformations between the written word on their grave markers, the poet's printed word, and the reader's reception. The created space for the reader's reflection occurs explicitly in the last stanza, "Dies ist kein Ort" (This is no place). The images of paper, tree, and stone form a constellation of remembrance: Paper (tree as the basic material for paper and referent for the poetic creation) and stone can store history and names. They have the potential to establish connections between artist/writer/reader, concrete public burial sites, and sites of Jewish annihilation. Art can evoke the same memory processes as the real site in Prague. Art can bring the travel experience to its completion. The final artistic product, the poem "Lithography," is significantly structured into seven stanzas that end in a period, the only punctuation in the poem. The number seven, a symbolic number used frequently throughout Kirsch's poetry, underscores the aspect of "completion" of the holy number seven (creation). In the artist's monument to remembrance, processes come to completion. Poetry as mediation of history can have a cathartic effect.

After Kirsch's move to the West in 1977, history and remembrance take on a new urgency in her work. The association spaces become wider as her overt cultural-historical contexts fade. She radicalizes her concerns with subjective responsibility, suppression of human rights, Nazi ideology, power mechanisms, and global problems of human exploitation of nature. The titles of her volumes reflect the importance she places on natural settings: *Erdreich* (Earth kingdom, 1982), *Katzenleben*, (Catlives, 1984), *Landwege* (Country roads, 1985), *Irrstern* (Comet, 1986) *Schneewärme* (Snow warmth, 1989). As "wanderer, biologist, gardener, and shepherd" (Wolf 24), Kirsch enjoys roaming the earth in the role of chronicler and observer of humankind interacting with nature, as in "Ebene" (Plain) in *Scheewärme* (40): "Die grossen Bilder alltäglich . . . wie soll ich / Müde werden es zu benennen" (The big images ordinary . . . how should I get tired of naming it). She establishes "death games of the mind" that fluctuate between memory and forgetfulness and reveal the mechanisms that obstruct the productive and healing process of mourning and remembering (Mabee, "Im Totenspiel" 143–161). References to the Holocaust in the later poetry in the 1970s and 1980s, written in virtual isolation, appear more and more as hermeneutical statements and apocalyptic images from a private poetic cosmos—at times with intended allusions to works and images by Jewish poets Nelly Sachs and Paul Celan. Kirsch ends her poem "Erdrauch" (Earth smoke) in *Erdreich* (Earth kingdom, 1982) with the title of the first poetry volume by Sachs (1947), *In den Wohnungen des Todes* (In the dwellings of death). In this poem she addresses the problems of apathy and lack of sensibility in viewers of television and readers saturated by superficial mass media reports on death and violence.[16]

In "Selektion" (Selection, 58), also from *Erdreich* (Earth kingdom), the everyday experience of "rigidly separating" weeds in a woman's garden sets off a chain of associations with the selection process on a "parade ground" in a concentration camp.

Selektion

Welche Unordnung die Rosenblätter
Sind aus den Angeln gefallen der Wind
Blies sie ums Haus auf die Gemüsebeete.
Streng getrennt wachsen hier in den Gärten
Magen- und Augenpflanzen, der Schönheit
Bleibt ein einziges Beet
Während den ausgerichteten Reihen
Früher Kartoffeln Mohren Endivien Kohl
Ein Exerzierplatz eingeräumt wird.

What disorder the rose petals
Have fallen off the wind
Scattered them around the house onto the vegetable
beds.
Here in the gardens, separated rigidly grow
Plants for the stomach and the eye, for beauty
A single bed remains
While for the straightened rows
Formerly potatoes carrots endive cabbage
A parade ground is prepared.

In the allegorical image of the vegetable garden, the political sphere and the traditional, everyday life of women overlap. What is on one level an innocent activity of weeding, sorting out, and making room in the privacy of a backyard becomes on an historical level a demonstration of the core of Hitler's anti-Semitic ideology. The image of the "Gemüsebeete" (vegetable beds) loses its harmlessness when relating the title "selection" to "parade ground" and "disorder." Within this field of association, Kirsch evokes not only Darwin's theory of natural selection but the "administered" logic that informed the Nazi "selection" of Jews and others.[17] In the second stanza, the reader as observer of the scene follows the gardener (executioner) to the localized "Abfallhaufen" (compost heap), suggesting an analogy to the ovens and gas chambers, in which humans were exterminated as parasites.

Abrupt allusions to the Holocaust occur again and again in Kirsch's poetry collections after her move to the West. Frequently the last lines of a poem destroy a seemingly bucolic atmosphere (at times underscored by motifs from fairy tales), as in "Hinter der Mühle" (Behind the mill) (*Erdreich* 62–63), a poem that is built around a "memory walk" by mother and son to three "Zuckerhutberge" (sugarhut mountains) and their hidden scars of Germany's collective history: "on the inside of the arm, the many-digited number / and I know that the mourning which I felt / Was composed of anger and pain." The reader's task is to connect the artistic intricacies, allusions, and intertextual references (to Bobrowski's poem "Holunderblüte" and his novel *Levins Mühle* in this case), which were initially somewhat buried, with Kirsch's intended historic remembrance. In her last poetry collection to date, *Schneewärme* (Snow warmth), naming and evoking parts of nature as if to save them from human destruction (Wagner 75–81) is more dominant than remembering the Holocaust as an actual locus. Only one explicit reference to the Holocaust is given in "Kopfbild" (Image in the head, 50–51), where history unfolds in a vision that spans from the terrors of the Third Reich ("vergiss die / Herzklopfenden Mansarden das jüdische Fräulein"; forget the heart-pounding attics the Jewish woman) to the Kaiserreich and further back to the destruction of the Thirty Years War.

As chronicler and guardian of Germany's history, Kirsch continues to record the traces she encounters on her real and imaginary walks through the countryside. The title poem "Schneewärme" (Snow warmth, 41) shows fundamental similarities with her very early poem "Der Regen bin ich." Again a persona hears the moaning voices of history in nature.

> In der Dämmerung fand ich
> Tote Seelen die Schatten
> Erstarrter Seen und Flüsse
> Blank ohne Leben.
>
> Ein Fell war gewachsen.
> Das Eis zwischen den Krallen
> Rief Blut vor ich sah
> Wo ich herkam.
>
> At nightfall I found
> Dead souls the shadows
> Of solidified lakes and rivers
> Blank without life.
>
> Fur had grown.
> The ice between the claws
> Drew blood I saw
> From where I came.

Kirsch's apocalyptic and disfigured landscapes continue to evoke concepts that informed the Holocaust and signal visions of imminent death. The seemingly harmonious (nature) images of her surroundings at the Eider dike are never left intact but become tainted or relativized through paradox, irony or parody, as in her 1991 lyrical prose volume *Spreu* (Deadwood). Readers are brought face to face with their neglected relationship to the past and their "heart of stone" ("Steinherz," "Heart of Stone" is the telling title of a poem in the 1984 volume *Katzenleben* [*Catlives*], 59). The memory of the Holocaust as the eradication of "otherness" lurks beneath many of Kirsch's unsettling images of petrified, snow-covered, and iced-over landscapes. One may speculate that she will continue to write about "serious matters" (ernsthafte Dinge *Zaubersprüche* 43) in a playful-ironic style from the periphery of German culture amidst the rural tranquility of her sheep and donkey (*Spreu* 86).

NOTES

I want to thank my colleague Christopher Clason for his editorial comments.

1. Kirsch was one of the twelve original writers and artists who signed an open letter protesting Biermann's expulsion in November 1976. In the aftermath of the controversy, Kirsch was asked to give up her membership in the SED (Socialist Union party of German) and her seat on the executive board of the Writers' Union (Emmerich 249ff; Frisé).

2. The word *Holocaust* is used in this essay to denote the dehumanization, persecution, and systematic extermination of European Jewry, Sinti, and Roma ("gypsies"), Jehovah's Witnesses, political prisoners, homosexuals, the mentally and physically disabled, and the Slavs—Russians, Ukrainians, Serbians, Bulgarians, Slovaks, Croats, Byelorussians, and Poles—during the period from 1939 to 1945 in Germany. For a detailed study of the Holocaust in English, see Levin.

3. The better-known writers who left the GDR after 1976 and moved to the West before the collapse of the GDR include Kurt Bartsch, Jurek Becker, Thomas Brasch, Jürgen Fuchs, Karl-Heinz Jakobs, Bernd Jentzsch, Günter Kunert, Reiner Kunze, Erich Loest, Frank-Wolf Matthies, Klaus Poche, Hans Joachim Schädlich, Klaus Schlesinger, and Joachim Seypel.

4. See Robin Ostow, "'The Persecution of the Jews by the Fascists': GDR Textbook Examples of Terror and Resistance in Presocialist Europe," paper presented at the Fourteenth Annual German Studies Association Conference in Buffalo, New York, 4–7 October 1990.

5. In a letter, released on 8 February 1990, Prime Minister Hans Modrow said that "East Germany, abandoning four decades of denial, has recognized its people share responsibility for the Holocaust." In letters to Edgar Bronfman, president of the World Jewish Congress, and to the Israeli Foreign Ministry, Modrow pledged "material support" for the victims of Nazi persecution. Cf. "East Germany acknowledges responsibility for the Holocaust." AP and Free Press Staff. *Detroit Free Press*, 9 February 1990: 1 A.

6. My translation; it is a rather literal translation in order to show Hermlin's close interrelationship between remembering the ashes of the concentration camps and starting anew as an antifascist state.

7. Kirsch, *Erklärung einiger Dinge,* 13. My translation.

8. All translations of Sarah Kirsch's poems are my own unless otherwise indicated. Permission for citing my translated poetry was given by Sarah Kirsch. My translations are by and large literal and make no claim of doing justice to Kirsch's oscillating imagery, densely connotative language, and subtle distortions of syntax and grammar to enlarge the meaning of a poem. I should also like to thank Hugo Bekker for his collaboration on my translations. Cf. *Catlives* by Marina Roscher and Charles Fischman for translation of "Reglos" (27) and all other poems of Kirsch's *Katzenleben.*

9. For a more detailed discussion of Kirsch's representations of the isolated artist, see Cosentino's book, *"Ein Spiegel mit mir darin": Sarah Kirschs Lyrik,* 32–37.

10. Cf. Sigmund Freud, *Melancholie und Trauer,* eds. Franz Fühmann and Dietrich Simon (Berlin, 1982). Significantly, this text by Freud was edited by Fühmann, whose propagandistic style of his early poetry in the 1950s gave way to a determination to use elements of dreams and fantasies to express in more authentic terms the totality of his personal experience. For this he was widely criticized in the GDR by cultural officials and critics alike in the late 1950s and early 1960s (Cf. Tate 131–151).

11. My translation.

12. For a more detailed examination of Kirsch's intertextuality, see Mabee, *Die Poetik von Sarah Kirsch,* 50–77.

13. See Bovenschen's comment on the "feminine": "Is there a feminine aesthetic? Certainly there is, if one is talking about *aesthetic awareness* and *modes of sensory perception.* Certainly not, if one is talking about an unusual variant of artistic production or about a painstakingly constructed theory of art. Women's break with the formal, intrinsic laws of a given medium, the release of their imagination—these are unpredictable for an art with feminist intentions. There is, thank heavens, no premeditated strategy which can predict what happens when female sensuality is freed" (Bovenschen 49–50). For further discussion of 'femininity' as a cultural construct and socially constructed gender as Simone de Beauvoir defined it ("one is not born a woman one becomes one"), see Moi 122–124; Lennox 158.

14. I thank Wayne Kvam and Ohio University Press for their permission to use the translation of "The Milkman Schäuffele," and "Legend of Lilja." Cf. Wayne Kvam, *Conjurations,* 32–36, and 49–50.

15. My translation.

16. For a detailed discussion of "Erdrauch" and Kirsch's characteristic interlocking of time references and subjective/personal and collective/historical/political elements in her later poetry, see Mabee, "Im Totenspiel," 145–161.

17. See Zentner's study about modern anti-Semitic race theories. Zentner asserts that all modern anti-Semitic theories go back to the work of the French duke Gobineau (1816–1865), *Versuch über die Ungleichheit der Menschenrassen* (The Inequality of the Races, written between 1853 and 1855; 1898 translated into German). Hitler accepted Gobineau's book and Houston Chamberlain's *Die Grundlagen des neunzehnten Jahrhunderts* (The Foundations of the 19th Century)

in regard to their superiority of the "Arian-Germanic race" without any scientific examination of their validity.

WORK CITED

Adorno, Theodor W. "Engagement." *Noten zur Literatur III.* Frankfurt/M.: Suhrkamp, 1965.

———. "Erziehung nach Auschwitz." *Kulturkritik und Gesellschaft II. Stichworte.* Frankfurt/M.: Suhrkamp, 1977.

———. Prismen, *Kulturkritik und Gesellschaft.* Frankfurt/M.: Suhrkamp, 1955.

Angress, Ruth. "Discussing Holocaust Literature." In *Simon Wiesenthal Center Annual,* ed. Henry Friedländer and Sybil Milton. White Plains, N.Y.: Kraus International Publications, 1986. Vol. 2: 179–192.

Baumgart, Reinhard. "Unmenschlichkeit beschreiben." In *Literatur für Zeitgenossen,* ed. Reinhard Baumgart. Frankfurt/M.: Suhrkamp, 1966. 12–36.

Benjamin, Walter. "Theses on the Philosophy of History." In *Illuminations,* ed. Hannah Arendt. Frankfurt/M.: Suhrkamp, 1955. 255–267.

Biermann, Wolf. "Nur wer sich ändert, bleibt sich treu." *Die Zeit,* 24 August 1990: 44.

Bovenschen, Silvia. "Is There a Feminine Aesthetic?" Trans. Beth Weckmueller. In *Feminist Aesthetic,* ed. Gisela Ecker. Boston: Beacon, 1986. 23–50.

Braun, Volker. *Es genügt nicht die einfache Wahrheit.* Frankfurt/M: Suhrkamp. 1976.

Celan, Paul. *Paul Celan. Poems. A bilingual Edition.* Trans. Michael Hamburger. New York: Persea Books, 1980.

Cosentino, Christine. *"Ein Spiegel mit mir darin": Sarah Kirschs Lyrik.* Tübingen: Francke Verlag, 1990.

———. "Sarah Kirschs Dichtung in der DDR: Ein Rückblick." *Germanic Studies Review* 4, 1 (1981): 105–116.

Daemmrich, Horst, and Diether Haenicke. *The Challenge of German Literature.* Detroit: Wayne State University Press, 1971.

Emmerich, Wolfgang. *Kleine Literaturgeschichte der DDR.* Erweiterte Ausgabe. Frankfurt/M.: Luchterhand, 1989.

Endler, Adolf. "Sarah Kirsch und ihre Kritiker." *Sinn und Form* 27, 1 (1975): 142–170.

Erb, Elke, ed. "Nachwort." In *Sarah Kirsch. Musik auf dem Wasser.* Leipzig: Philipp Reclam jn., 1989.

Figge, Susan G. " 'Der Wunsch nach Welt': The Travel Motif in the Poetry of Sarah Kirsch." In *Studies in GDR Culture and Society 1,* ed. Margy Gerber et al. Washington: University Press of America, 1981. 167–182.

Flores, John. *Poetry in East Germany: Adjustments, Visions, Provocations, 1945–1970.* New Haven: Yale University Press, 1971.

Fox, Thomas. "A 'Jewish Question' in GDR Literature"? *German Life and Letters* 44, 1 (October 1990): 58–70.

Franz, Michael. "Zur Geschichte der DDR-Lyrik. 3. Teil: Wege zur poetischen Konkretheit." *Weimarer Beiträge* 15, 6 (1969): 1201–1203.

Frisé, Maria. "Zaubersprüche hinter dem Eiderdeich. Besuch bei Sarah Kirsch." *Frankfurter Allgemeine Zeitung*, 2 July 1984.

Gilbert, Sandra, and Susan Gubar. *The Madwoman in the Attic.* New Haven: Yale University Press, 1979.

Graves, Peter. "Sarah Kirsch: Some Comments and a Conversation." *German Life and Letters* 44, 3 (April 1991): 271–279.

———, ed. *Three Contemporary Poets: Wolf Biermann, Sarah Kirsch, Reiner Kunze.* Leicester: Leicester University Press, 1985.

Hermand, Jost. "The 'Good New' and the 'Bad New': Metamorphoses in the Modernism Debate in the GDR since 1956." *New German Critique* 5 (Fall 1974): 73–92.

Heukenkamp, Ursula. "Poetisches Subjekt und weibliche Perspektive. Zur Lyrik." In *Frauen Literatur Geschichte. Schreibende Frauen vom Mittelalter bis zur Gegenwart*, ed. Hiltrud Gnüg and Renate Möhrmann. Stuttgart: J. B. Metzler, 1985. 354–367.

Honecker, Erich. *Reden und Aufsätze.* Berlin: Dietz, 1975.

Hörnigk, Therese. "Das Thema Krieg und Faschismus in der Geschichte der DDR-Literatur." *Weimarer Beiträge* 24, 5 (1978): 73–105.

Jäger, Manfred. "Subjektivität als politische Kategorie. Zur Emanzipationsgeschichte der Lyrik in der DDR." In *Lyrik von allen Seiten*, ed. L. Jordan et al. Frankfurt/M.: Fischer, 1981. 304–316.

Juhasz. Suzanne. *Naked and Fiery Forms: Modern American Poetry by Women: A New Tradition.* New York: Harper & Row, 1976.

Kirsch, Sarah. *Drachensteigen.* Ebenhausen: Langewiesche-Brandt, 1979.

———. *Erdreich.* Stuttgart: Deutsche Verlags-Anstalt, 1982.

———. *Erklärung einiger Dinge.* Ebenhausen: Langewiesche-Brandt, 1978.

———. *Irrstern.* Stuttgart: Deutsche Verlags-Anstalt, 1986.

———. *Katzenleben.* Stuttgart: Deutsche Verlags-Anstalt, 1984. *Catlives: Sarah Kirschs 'Katzenleben.'* Eds. and Trans. Marina Roscher and Charles Fishman. Lubbock: Texas Tech University Press, 1991.

———. *La Pagerie.* Stuttgart: Deutsche Verlags-Anstalt, 1980.

———. *Landaufenthalt.* Berlin/Weimar: Aufbau, 1972; Ebenhausen: Langewiesche-Brandt, 1969/1977.

———. *Rückenwind.* Berlin/Weimar: Aufbau, 1976; Ebenhausen: Langewiesche-Brandt, 1977.

———. *Schneewärme.* Stuttgart: Deutsche Verlags-Anstalt, 1989.

———. *Spreu.* Göttingen: Speidl, 1991.

———. *Zaubersprüche.* Berlin/Weimar: Aufbau, 1972; Ebenhausen: Langewiesche-Brandt, 1973.

Kirsch, Sarah, and Rainer Kirsch. *Gespräch mit dem Saurier.* Berlin: Neues Leben, 1965.

Koonz, Claudia. *Mothers in the Fatherland: Women, the Family, and Nazi Politics 1919–1945.* New York: St. Martin's Press, 1987.

Kvam, Wayne, ed. and trans. *Conjurations. The Poems of Sarah Kirsch.* Athens: Ohio University Press, 1985.

Kwiet, Konrad. "Historians of the German Democratic Republic on Anti-Semitism and Persecution." *Leo Baeck Institute Yearbook*, 21 (1976): 170–181.

Labroisse, Gerd. "Frauenliteratur-Lyrik in der DDR." In *DDR-Lyrik im Kontext*, ed. Christine Cosentino, Wolfgang Ertl, and Gerd Labroisse. Amsterdam: Rodopi, 1988. 145–195.

Langer, Lawrence L. *The Holocaust and the Literary Imagination.* New Haven: Yale University Press, 1975.

Lennox, Sara. "Feminist Scholarship and Germanistik." *German Quarterly* 62, 2 (Spring 1989): 158–170.

Levin, Nora. *The Holocaust. The destruction of European Jewry 1933–1945.* New York: Schocken, 1973.

Lett, Mark. "Putting the pieces together hasn't been easy." *Detroit News* 28 November 1991, 1–2E.

Lorenz, Dagmar C. "Austrian Jewish Writers Since World War II." In *Simon Wiesenthal Center Annual*, ed. Henry Friedländer and Sybil Milton. White Plains, N.Y.: Kraus International Publications, 1986. Vol 3: 199–226.

Mabee, Barbara. *Die Poetik von Sarah Kirsch. Erinnerungsarbeit und Geschichtsbewusstsein.* Amsterdam/Atlanta: Rodopi, 1989.

———. "'Im Totenspiel ungewisser Bedeutung': Antirassistische Assoziationsräume in der Lyrik von Sarah Kirsch." In *Jahrbuch zur Literatur in der DDR 6*, ed. Paul Gerhard Klussmann and Heinrich Mohr. Bonn: Bouvier, 1988. 143–161.

Mason, Tim. *Women in Germany, 1925–1940: Family, Welfare & Work.* Part I and Part II. *History Workshop* 1 (Spring 1976): 74–113, 5–32.

Melin, Charlotte. "Landscape as Writing and Revelation in Sarah Kirsch's 'Death Valley.'" *Germanic Review* 62, 4 (Fall 1987): 199–204.

Merritt, Richard L. "Politics of Judaism in the GDR." In *Studies in GDR Culture and Society 9.* Selected Papers from the Fourteenth New Hampshire Symposium on the German Democratic Republic, ed. Margy Gerber et al. Lanham: University Press of America, 1989. 163–189.

Mitscherlich, Alexander, and Margarete Mitscherlich. *The Inability to Mourn: Principles of Collective Behavior.* Trans. Beverly R. Placzek. New York: Grove Press, 1975.

Moi, Toril. "Feminist, Female, Feminine." In *The Feminist Reader: Essays in Gender and the Politics of Literary Criticism*, ed. Catherine Belsey and Jane Moore. New York: Basil Blackwell, 1989. 117–132.

Nägele, Rainer. "Deutsche Demokratische Republik." In *Geschichte der politischen Lyrik in Deutschland*, ed. Walter Hinderer. Stuttgart: Reclam, 1978. 105–149.

Peukert, Detlev J. K. *Inside Nazi Germany: Conformity, Opposition, and Racism in Everyday Life.* Trans. Richard Devesen. New Haven: Yale University Press, 1987.

Rosellini, Jay. "Poetry and Criticism in the German Democratic Republic: The 1972 Discussion in the Context of Cultural Policy." *New German Critique* 9 (1978): 153–174.

Rosenfeld, Alvin H., and Irving Greenberg, ed. *Confronting the Holocaust: The Impact of Elie Wiesel.* Bloomington: Indiana University Press, 1978.

Rosenfeld, Alvin H. *A Double Dying. Reflections on the Holocaust.* Bloomington: Indiana University Press, 1980.

Schneider, Rolf. *Der Spiegel.* 20 July 1981, 141.

Serke, Jürgen. *Frauen schreiben.* Frankfurt/M.: Fischer, 1982.

Steiner, George. *Language and Silence.* New York: Atheneum, 1967.

Stephan, Alexander. "Johannes R. Becher and the Cultural Development of the GDR." Special Issue on the German Democratic Republic. *New German Critique* 2 (Spring 1974): 72–90.

Stephenson, Jill. *Women in Nazi Society.* New York: Harper & Row, 1975.

Tate, Dennis. "Subjective Authenticity in Franz Fühmann's Early Prose Writing." In *Studies in GDR Culture and Society 10.* Lanham: University Press of America, 1991. 135–151.

Trachtenberg, Joshua. *Jewish Magic and Superstition.* Cleveland: World Publishing Company, 1961.

Trommler, Frank. "Der zögernde Nachwuchs. Entwicklungsprobleme der Nachkriegsliteratur in Ost und West." In *Tendenzen der deutschen Literatur seit 1945,* ed. Thomas Koebner. Stuttgart: Kröner, 1971. 1–117.

Volckman, Silvia. *Zeit der Kirschen? Das Naturbild in der deutschen Gegenwartslyrik: Jürgen Becker, Sarah Kirsch, Wolf Biermann, Hans Magnus Enzensberger.* Königsstein/Ts: Athenäum, 1982. 95–134.

Wagner, Hans. *Sarah Kirsch.* Berlin: Colloquium, 1989.

Wiesel, Elie. "Why I Write." In *Confronting the Holocaust,* ed. Alvin Rosenfeld and Irving Greenberg. Bloomington: Indiana University Press, 1978.

Wittkowski, Wolfgang. "Sarah Kirsch: 'Der Milchmann Schäuffele.'" *German Quarterly* 54, 3 (1981): 311–317.

Wolf, Gerhard. "Ausschweifungen und Verwünschungen. Vorläufige Bemerkungen zu Motiven bei Sarah Kirsch." *Text und Kritik* 101 (January 1989): 13–28.

Zentner, Christian. *Adolph Hitlers 'Mein Kampf'. Eine kommentierte Auswahl.* München: List, 1974.

MARIA-REGINA KECHT

Resisting Silence: Brigitte Schwaiger and Elisabeth Reichart Attempt to Confront the Past

> What is past is not dead; it is not even past. We cut ourselves off from it: we preferred to be strangers.
>
> Christa Wolf,
> *Patterns of Childhood*

Austrian literature has acquired some notoriety for its political evasiveness, its escapism from social and historical reality, and its reluctance to function as a critical commentary on the country's state of affairs.[1] Among the many artistically accomplished and well-established postwar Austrian writers, few have felt compelled to either address the nation's role during the years of darkness or examine the social and psychological repercussions rippling through Austria after the fall of the Third Reich and the dissolution of the *Ostmark*. There are no Austrian counterparts to the West German Heinrich Böll, Günter Grass, Wolfgang Koeppen, Siegfried Lenz, Luise Rinser, and others who have been voices of conscience challenging their compatriots to face their Nazi past, assume responsibility for their acts, and learn how to grieve. Austrian literature has not shared the different stages of *Vergangenheitsbewältigung* (coming to terms with the past) that German literature has gone through since 1945.[2] If there are relatively few Austrian authors thematizing the experience of National Socialism or Austria's Nazi legacy, it is understandable that the number of women writers who have taken up the subject in some of their works is even smaller. Some of the women who have addressed the theme are Ilse Aichinger, Ingeborg Bachmann, Erika Mitterer, Marie-Thérèse Kerschbaumer, Elfriede Jelinek, Brigitte Schwaiger, Elisabeth Reichart, and Waltraud Anna Mitgutsch.[3]

It may seem curious that in the 1980s several young Austrian writers who were born only after the war have chosen the topic of the murky brown past for their critical investigation and literary representation.[4] This upsurge of interest in one of Austria's darkest historical periods—one that most Austrians have preferred to forget—cannot be sufficiently explained by the national and international controversies surrounding the country's presidential election in 1986. Surely, the polemics about Austria's role as a victim of or collaborator with Hitlerian aggression may have stirred the creative imagination of one or the other writer. But these young authors have reacted primarily against the decades of stifling silence shrouding the events of the Nazi past and rejected the unsatisfactory answers to their questions about Austria's participation in the building of the Third Reich.

Many psychologists have predicted correctly that the collective repression of the Nazi trauma would result in long-term damage to the children and grandchildren of those who experienced the rise and fall of National Socialism.[5] The Third Reich may be part of the past in the political and historical sense, but the Nazi ideology has had such a profound psychological impact on the German-speaking societies that its continued and pervasive influence can be counteracted only if it is finally addressed openly in families, schools, and the public.[6]

For some young writers, it may indeed be this ethical challenge that draws their critical attention to the Nazi legacy, but for others, it may be a very personal need that makes them articulate their confusion about their own attitude toward inherited Nazi beliefs and values. Common to most of them is the recognition that they cannot define their own identities without examining their own past and their own childhoods with parents who experienced Hitler's regime either as enthusiastic supporters, opportunistic collaborators, passive bystanders, or courageous opponents. They consider knowledge and understanding of the past crucial for an adequate assessment of the present, and therefore it becomes essential to study the complex layers of past experience—conscious and unconscious—that make up the intricate connections between generations.

Discovering the "truth" about the parents' ideological position then and now frequently leads to a painful scrutiny of one's own political and moral inheritance and to the revelation that its influence has been far more powerful than initially suspected. The important question, however, is whether these soul-searching efforts go beyond reproach and blame and so lead to admission of guilt, perhaps even to the acknowledgment that every individual bears personal responsibility for her or his acts. To put an end to the common strategies of negation, repression, and disavowal of the past, which always lead to a shifting of blame and guilt, a special kind of *Erinnerungsarbeit* (work of remembering) must be done before *Trauerarbeit* (work of mourning) can begin. Such a process of remembering would concern less the historical facts of National Socialism than its dominant patterns of behavior, moral values, emotions, and fantasies.[7] A formidable task indeed, but each individual effort deserves appreciation, and several young Austrian writers have made a significant contribution to this long-overdue *Erinnerungsarbeit.*

The two authors who belong to this group and are the focus of this essay—Brigitte Schwaiger and Elisabeth Reichart—illustrate two very different ways of tracing the forgotten past in the present, two different approaches to reaffirming the connections between generations, and two different strategies of confronting the question of individual responsibility. It has been suggested that women writers have a gender-based advantage in their sensitivity to the everyday symptoms of the Nazi legacy because women are painfully familiar with the "value-scheme" of patriarchal structures.[8] Therefore, my reading of Schwaiger's novel *Lange Abwesenheit* (Long absence, 1980) and Reichart's two texts *Februarschatten* (February shadows, 1984) and *Komm über den See* (Come across the lake, 1988) also addresses the question whether there is a specifically female mode of confronting the fascist past.

Brigitte Schwaiger's autobiographical novel can be seen as representative of the boom of "father obituaries" characterizing the German literary production of the late 1970s and early 1980s.[9] Like so many of her contemporaries, Schwaiger attempted only after her father's death to remove the psychological *Trümmer* (rubble) left in her mind and soul by her authoritarian, punitive father, a former officer in the *Wehrmacht.* As in so many other works belonging to this group, Schwaiger's *Lange Abwesenheit* focuses on the highly conflictual relationship between the female narrator and her father, especially on her sense of his having betrayed her and deprived her of affection and caring. What emerges is less a portrait of the father than one of the daughter: she wants to find the roots of her emotional life through reflecting on her father's behavior, especially his style of running the family. Regarding herself as the victim of a degrading and repressive upbringing, Schwaiger's narrator, mired in self-pity, is caught in *Wiederholungszwang* (compulsion to repeat). Like her father, who successfully avoided any confrontation with his own share of responsibility for the Nazi past and never overcame his feelings of betrayal by Hitler, the daughter is always ready to shift the blame for her anti-Semitism onto her father.

Schwaiger's book is typical of those fictional examinations of the past that do not venture beyond statements of personal aggression. First, the silence surrounding the Nazi past is broken only after the parent's death, when dialogue is safely impossible, and second, the mental world of the daughter is still neatly divided into good and evil, innocent and guilty. As a consequence, such righteous self-defense deflects any productive coping with the Nazi ideology and its impact.

Reichart's two works, *Februarschatten* and *Komm über den See,* are variations of this parent-child topos, but in these works, the mother-daughter relationships become vehicles to expand the theme of responsibility from the individual to society as a whole. The particular events involving the protagonists in Reichart's stories are representative of a broader set of events in Austrian history. *Februarschatten* and *Komm über den See* are thus examples of a recent and interesting literary trend that has rediscovered the importance of history and the necessity of understanding history when trying to understand an individual's development.[10]

The daughter-figures in both stories try to explore their mothers' wartime experience, the conditions of daily life and decisions then. Discovering that these mothers could not withstand pressure, and thus became complicitous, committed acts of betrayal, and finally withdrew into a silence of shame, the daughters question what the price of strong-mindedness and moral courage is today and how many people, indeed, show any ability to resist manipulation and social pressure.

In contrast to Schwaiger, who suggests that it is impossible to leave one's parents' patterns, Reichart's protagonists recognize that it is necessary to accept responsibility for their own behavior. For their own sake, the daughter-figures in *Februarschatten* and *Komm über den See* want to turn the "helplessness" of their mothers into strength and independence of spirit. It becomes clear that to avoid repeating the mistakes of the past—or being weighed down by the burden of the past—one has to make the past one's own through conscious introspection, turning memory into a living process. Only then can one gain control over one's life and stop being victimized by the past.

Giving expression to memory, suppressed emotions, and unconscious fears is the decisive first step toward an honest confrontation with the forces of the past. We still have to explore how much progress Schwaiger's and Reichart's characters make beyond this initial step.

I

Schwaiger's narrator in *Lange Abwesenheit* seems to have waited impatiently for her father's death in order to allow her memory to reconstruct what kind of man he was and what sorts of feelings he evoked in her. Her angry look back encompasses a bitter reminiscence both of her infantile adoration for the demigod doctor and teller of heroic war tales and of her life-long fear of the inaccessible, domineering parent. Her image of the father is split; on the one hand, the public ego of the friendly, conscientious, self-sacrificing physician, who enjoys his patients' respect and confidence, and on the other hand, the private ego of the angry, intolerant, and willful pater familias who takes satisfaction in humiliating his wife and daughters. This division corresponds to the daughter's twofold reaction to him: "I would like [others] to admire you as you deserve. I would like those who have known and respected you to hate you as you deserve."[11] The former Nazi officer has managed to preserve the qualities honored in Hitler's days: carrying out his duty no matter what and making sure that discipline and order are observed meticulously.

Realizing that it would be wrong to idealize this man further, the daughter, whose longing for affection he always met with stern reprimands and indifference, has come to terms with her father's power drive and its compensatory nature:

> If you had worn your captain's uniform from the war at home from the beginning, then perhaps a lot would have been clearer.

> A father, a real father, is someone who cannot be embraced, who cannot be interrupted when he is speaking, who must be answered even if he is asking the same thing for the fifth time and it appears as if he were asking for the fifth time in order to be sure that the daughters are always willing to answer; a father who may cut anybody off.[12]

The portrayed household is prototypical of a totalitarian regime where a tyrant can exert his power with impunity, where injustices and humiliation are not to be questioned, and peace at home "consists in some not saying how hungry they are so that the others can eat undisturbed."[13] It is not surprising that these hierarchies of strong over weak and male over female result in the daughter's developing a narrow emotional spectrum limited to admiration and disdain; she perpetuates fascination with figures of authority and contempt for submissive behavior.

For the daughter, writing a story about her dead father is a desperate attempt to free herself from his grip. She can finally express her wish to love without fear of instant rejection. And even though her reflections force her to realize how many objectionable values she has adopted from her father, she can now also prove her independence and creativity, which are beyond the father's interference. If the act of writing is seen as a chance for rebellion—a celebration of the tyrant's fall through cancer—it also results in a victory with a vengeance: the daughter, who always wanted to be one of her father's patients in order to be given care and attention, now feels that she has become a victim, a psychological cripple of her father's "sense of duty." In defiance, she refuses to make it her "filial duty" to show some pity and understanding for the dead man. Ironically, however, by exhibiting such emotional rigidity and coldness, she only confirms being her father's progeny. Her father's "black pedagogy" has worked.[14]

As long as her father is still alive, the daughter in *Lange Abwesenheit* tries to avoid her unconscious identification with him through another kind of revenge. Here too, the act of opposition turns into *Wiederholungszwang.* She searches for a father substitute in order to receive some male recognition and, simultaneously, to escape her father's powerful influence. Thus, she chooses a lover who is much older than she is, and who, like her father, enjoys instructing and guiding her, treating her like a little girl. Even in his mannerisms, gestures, and style of dress, there is a striking similarity between her father and her lover. But this "double," Birer, carries extra symbolic value: he is a Jew who survived the Holocaust through emigration.[15]

Birer offers the narrator contradictory possibilities of identification; to her he personifies both guilt and revenge. He typifies the victim of her father's blatant racism, and at the same time, he evokes in her deep-seated anti-Semitic feelings. Her guilt and shame derive from her adoption of the Nazi stereotype of Jews.

> Horny old Jew, I thought. And: maybe he is young in bed.
>
> His face came closer, our glasses clinked together when he kissed me. The kiss was good. Yes, I thought, he will be young. He will become my lover; with him I will assert myself against father. . . .
>
> I enter his bedroom, even though I am already tired of it. His bed is next to the wall. Here he wants to humiliate me.
>
> The old man. He is now taking a young body into his old bed. He tricked me. That's all he wants. He is a Jew. Jews are not to be trusted. Why did I not believe my father? Jews keep together and use us.[16]

Such anti-Semitic feelings, however, are constantly undercut by her perverse pride in having found a means to avenge herself on her father and humiliate him, which, of course, exacerbates her emotional conflict with Birer. "I will never have the courage to tell him why I really got involved with him,"[17] the narrator remarks. From this distorted perspective of desired *Rassenschande* (violation of racial purity), Birer is turned into the cunning and lascivious Jew who is eager to seduce a pretty gentile and thus stain the honor of the girl's family.

This kind of perception turns the narrator inexorably into a victim, thus allowing her two possibilities of self-definition: either she can establish an analogy between her victimization by her domineering father and that by her Jewish lover, or she can regard her supposed sacrifice as an act of piety and redemption, bringing her closer to a reconciliation with the race her father detests. The narrator favors the repeated victimization, which, it seems, foils any sincere confrontation with the fascist legacy. It does not occur to her that her internalization of paternal prejudices has placed her squarely on the side of the perpetrators. It hardly exculpates her to recognize the father's fascist mindset for what it is, imitate it, and then swiftly blame her upbringing for this legacy, or even try to deny the connection: "I do not want to be your daughter! . . . I want to save my neck, filthy Nazi pig!"[18]

Considering how conscious the narrator is of the anti-Semitism and authoritarianism that had made her father a fervent supporter of Hitler, it is surprising to see that the topics of World War II and the Holocaust remain practically untouched in her reflections. In the fragments of her childhood memories, associations, daydreams, and fantasies, the narrator constantly intertwines the two significant strands of her past: one connected to her father, the other to Birer. Both have profoundly influenced her mental and emotional life; nevertheless, she never explores the political dimension of either man's experiences and beliefs, even though politics is otherwise crucial to her cast of mind. Opportunities for questions were missed in the past, and these "sins of omission" are not made up for in the present. On the surface, there may be a great deal of eloquent anger and frustration, but beneath it, there is eerie silence from which no questions about life under National Socialism arise.

By joining the conspiracy of silence about the Nazi past, failing to ask the bigoted father what he saw, what he knew, and what he did, and by avoiding comparison of the father's and Birer's versions of history, the narrator in *Lange Abwesenheit* runs away from responsibility. She protects herself against admissions or confessions she does not want to hear and against horrors she cannot endure to learn about. On two occasions, she expresses guilt about Birer that she immediately suppresses by asking, "But what can I do about my thoughts, which are from my father?"[19] Such evasiveness prevents self-scrutiny and self-reproach, precludes *Trauerarbeit,* and creates the right conditions for self-pity and melancholy.[20]

Part of this defensive behavior is also the recurrent wish to kill her father and Birer. If the relationship with Birer allows the narrator to live out her incestuous desires (cf. Schwaiger 9, 41, 78, 89), thus experiencing a degree of intimacy that the father-daughter relationship was completely devoid of, it also reinforces feelings of hatred. Both men make her feel dependent, even trapped; experiences with them only augment her sense of inferiority and weakness, and her guilt. Just as the narrator, after she has broken off her relation with Birer, remarks, "And I would like to reach behind his face, pull the memories out of him; let me go free, let go", she tries to break out of her dead father's grip: "He has many voices, many arms and legs; he is invisible, but he can lie waiting to ambush me anytime and anywhere."[21] When she realizes, to her frustration, that not even the father's death can miraculously provide her with a new identity stripped of all the burdensome layers of the past, the narrator of *Lange Abwesenheit* should be able to perceive that unless she starts assuming responsibility for her thoughts and acts she will remain within the circle of her negative father-fixation. However, if she chooses not to face her responsibilities, then, as the epigraph to the novel suggests, the rebellion against the patriarch and his legacy will never develop into the revolution of *Erinnerungsarbeit* necessary for a better understanding of the past and the present: "The forehead of my father: a field of ice, on which a tiny figure is running. That's me running and running, but the head is revolving. So I am making no progress."[22]

II

The obstacles to individual responsibility and courage of spirit are more discerningly explored in Elisabeth Reichart's novel *Februarschatten* and her second work, the story *Komm über den See.* Her female protagonists seek ways of making progress despite pain. Reichart believes that an individual's behavior can best be understood in a specific social and historical context. Thus a narrow psychological focus—as in Schwaiger's *Lange Abwesenheit*—is shifted and the scope widened in Reichart's work.

The very titles of her books indicate how much Reichart cares about establishing links between the personal and the communal, the familial and the historical. The title *February Shadows* suggests two meanings: it refers both to the crimes that were committed on 2 February 1945 when the rural population of the area around the Austrian concentration camp Mauthausen brutally killed hundreds of fugitive Russian officers and the shadows that have been haunting Hilde, the story's main protagonist, ever since she betrayed the fugitive whom her brother Hannes was hiding during that February night, thus bringing about her brother's death. The shadows, a recurrent image throughout the novel, symbolize Hilde's guilt-ridden conscience.

The title "Come Across the Lake" also has dual connotations: the phrase itself is the final line of a poem by Sarah Kirsch—used as an epigraph in Reichart's story—which beckons one to cross the lake because the ice is showing cracks and might soon break up. This appeal becomes the leitmotif for the main character of the book, Ruth Berger, who must cross some treacherous territory of her psyche and make a painful journey into the past before she discovers her own identity. But the "lake" is also of historical relevance to Reichart's story, which is set in the lake region of the Austrian Salzkammergut, where, during the time of the *Anschluss* (annexation), some women and men organized themselves to resist National Socialism. To join the partisans in the mountains, one had to cross the lake, showing great courage and fearlessness, virtues that Ruth Berger is trying to emulate.

The strands of history and fiction, the layers of the present and the past, and the interdependence of the individual and the collective also pervade Reichart's depiction of the central human relationships in both her books. Women of different generations share not only their distressing common experience of weakness, subordination, and self-alienation but also their discovery of moral strength and inspiration through mutual support and trust.

In *Februarschatten,* Reichart's daughter-figure functions as a writer who seeks dialogue with her forlorn elderly mother in order to confront taboos, clarify past misunderstandings, and overcome alienation. The daughter strives stubbornly because she wants to repeat the success she had in establishing a candid relationship with her father before he died. In that relationship, personal and political questions could be raised and were answered. By writing her mother's life story, she intends to make up for her neglect, pay belated tribute to the mother, and prove to the mother that her life bears significance.

In contrast to Schwaiger, Reichart never lets the origin of the conflict between mother and daughter, the taboo of the Nazi past and its pathological consequences, disappear from her depiction of the parent-child relationship. The fictional motivation for this inclusion is rooted in the specific personality of the daughter that the author has chosen. She has created a young woman with a strong political consciousness and the courage to go against the grain who wants to satisfy her curiosity about the past in order to change the present. However, the daughter's intellectual and emotional independence intimidates and even hurts her weak and self-effacing mother.

Whereas the daughter attempts a reconciliation with her mother through her book project, the mother's resentment grows because she feels abused as an object of critical interest, as a mere case for an intellectual undertaking. After having glanced at a few pages of the manuscript, the mother's suspicions seem confirmed:

> This woman who is dealt with in broken off sentences. I am not this woman. She is a phantom of the daughter's imagination. . . . It is totally ridiculous that she is writing about me. How can she write about the mother whom she doesn't know? She can't know me. Because I haven't known her for the longest time.
>
> It is my life. Not her life. My life is no matter of concern for her. Of no concern. Why is she meddling in my life.[23]

Thus, the mother interprets gestures of sympathy and assistance as unwelcome intrusions into her personal recollections and secrets. Despite Hilde's seeing her daughter's persistent inquiry as provocation, the daughter refuses to give up because she is unwilling to accept that forgetting—as the mother has been preaching with her two most important words "forget it!"—is the only strategy of survival. She wants her mother to recognize the necessity of remembering but does not point her finger in angry accusation. Unlike the narrator in *Lange Abwesenheit,* she tries to become a confidante who can help her mother find a voice to allay the pain of silence.

Only gradually does Hilde reach the point where she is ready to break her life-long silence about her horrible childhood experience of the bloody manhunt and her complicity in Nazi terror. Her desire to share the burden and break out of her isolation finally overrides the powerful wish to forget. When her suffering turns her inner monologue into an interpersonal dialogue, she feels emotionally relieved, but she also feels malicious pleasure at the sight of her daughter's shock. Hilde passes on to her daughter the "february shadows," her painful knowledge, her guilt, and her frustrations, so that the balance of emotional power seems to have shifted, as several passages in the final chapter suggest:

> Hilde got into the driver's seat. The daughter didn't want her to drive. . . . The daughter stood indecisively. . . .
>
> Hilde drove slowly out of the village. Speeded up on the country road. . . .
>
> "Don't drive so fast. It is slippery."

> Hilde looked mockingly at the anxious daughter. Who still thought she knew everything better. Hilde stepped harder on the gas pedal. (FS 141)[24]

Hilde's sudden revelations have become burdensome knowledge for her daughter. Being informed may be more than the young woman can bear; it may be more than she was prepared to find out, and it may take her some time to recover her self-composure.

If readers of Reichart's *Februarschatten* are left to speculate how the daughter-figure will cope with her mother's overwhelming revelations and how they will affect her own way of thinking, acting, and living, it is in *Komm über den See* that we see how a supposedly protective silence may greatly harm the children of the war generation. Simultaneously, Reichart's second work also shows that exploring the past does not always automatically lead to an overcoming of and emancipation from it. Such searches may lead to an escapist immersion in the past that undercuts any successful contending with the present.

Ruth Berger certainly cannot be faulted with the amnesia from which most people around her suffer. On the contrary, she develops an obsessive interest in the Austrian resistance to National Socialism, writes her master's thesis on women in the underground, and is intent on spreading this knowledge in her history classes. Her intellectual fascination with forgotten heroes and heroines does not, however, spur Ruth's own process of remembering. Instead, her preoccupation with the courage and integrity of antifascist resistance becomes a substitute for a long overdue exploration of her personal past:

> A lack of my own personal past; from this arose later, much later my hunger—or maybe it arose right away and was articulated only later? It was not my mother alone but all Vienna had no memory. We children called ourselves "kids of the rubble," but we did not know where the rubble came from, . . . and no one explained, either, and only the rubble has been removed in the meantime.[25]

The obscurity veiling her childhood and her mother's role during the Third Reich has, strangely enough, never triggered Ruth's historical inquisitiveness despite her occasional awareness of that evasion: "Do I deny the darkness in which I stumble around as soon as I think of my mother, about whom I know so little, whom I can hardly remember?"[26]

Reichart suggestively illustrates that the blind spots in the personal history of her protagonist become the *Schmerzpunkte* (points of pain) of her life, resulting in confusion and alienation. Just as often as Ruth's dreams are filled with scenes of her childhood and images of her dead mother, she stubbornly refuses to undertake an odyssey through her own past to her self. If daughters define themselves through their mothers and cannot avoid resembling them, as much as they may resist, the daughter figure of *Komm über den See* has first to recognize who her mother was before she can discover her own identity.

Ruth's faint memory of her mother is inseparably connected with a traumatic incident that has haunted Ruth all her life, which perhaps explains her defensive repression of the past; as a small child, she witnessed her mother's arrest by the Gestapo. When the men were trying to grab Ruth, her mother told her to run away, which she did. What then seemed obedience later turned into a feeling of weakness and betrayal, burdening Ruth with guilt. Remembering how broken her mother was and then also that she died soon after release from prison, Ruth cannot help blaming herself. This "original sin" of disloyalty has later kept Ruth from developing friendships with other women for fear of further betrayal.

For forty years the daughter did not know that her guilt converges with her mother's; her mother denounced her best friend, a resistance fighter, to the Gestapo and simply could not recover from her guilt for the deed despite her strenuous efforts to suppress it. Nor did Ruth know that her mother then decided to have the four-year old daughter baptised and her name changed from *Brigitta* to *Ruth* because Brigitta's life had been the price for her denunciation. In effect, one could say, through a sacred ritual celebrating rebirth and absolution from original sin, Ruth's mother hoped to mark a new beginning, concerned more about her own salvation from torturing memories than about the psychological consequences of such a change of identity for her daughter.

Reichart's narrative, complex in its layers of recollections, associations, and dreams, does not clearly tell us why Ruth has been fleeing the truth about her mother. The reader's assumption that Ruth could not bear to have her illusions shattered—did *not want* to learn about her mother's weakness and self-loathing—is echoed in a remark by a friend of hers: "You are only afraid you'll have to recognize that your memories are merely wishful thinking! . . . Why keep alive the retouched images?"[27] And later, this fact is confirmed by Ruth herself: "For years I have acted blind—but in vain. We have developed extravagant fantasies out of our oversensitivity, our vulnerability, but in the end, we remain defenseless."[28] Ruth's sensitivity and vulnerability may have led her to make a taboo of her personal past under National Socialism and the mother's compliance with the evil, but her aunts who raised her certainly reinforced this taboo with their "law of obedience" enforcing silence.

As in her first novel, Reichart leads her protagonist out of the distressing predicament that has resulted from the repression of the past handed down from one generation to the next. In *Komm über den See,* Ruth finds a mother-substitute with whose help she can break out of her emotional isolation, overcome her fearfulness, and finally give her life a sense of direction. Through an encounter with Anna Zach, the former resistance fighter whom Ruth's mother betrayed, Ruth succeeds in putting the pieces of her memory puzzle together by sharing with Anna the pain of truth. Anna gives words to what Ruth has suspected for a long time but only now finds courage to confront and accept. Ruth finally crosses the lake.

It is of particular importance that Ruth would learn from Anna that her first, identity-forming name was Brigitta—the name she often heard herself scream in her nightmares without knowing whose name it was. For Ruth's mother, we can assume, changing the name from Brigitta to Ruth was to carry as much symbolic significance as the sacrament of baptism would. Through her choice of the name Ruth—after the biblical character Ruth who loyally followed her mother-in-law Naomi and earned respect and love for her faithfulness—the mother probably hoped to instill symbolically loyal friendship in her daughter that would redeem her own betrayal or, at least, make her forget it. For Ruth, the opportunity for an act of loyalty has arisen through her dialogue with Anna. Name and identity finally converge, and Ruth becomes more her own self.

Both of Reichart's works, *Komm über den See* and *Februarschatten,* make clear how much the women of different generations need each other's trust and support in order to come to terms with the Nazi past. As long as communication stays blocked and barriers remain between the past and the present, feelings of alienation and confusion prevail. Ruth and Hilde need encouragement and inspiration to recover from the paralysis that has developed out of their fear of repeatedly failing in their responsibility. Reichart vividly unfolds the inner worlds of her protagonists, which are full of self-reproach and shame, resentment and negativity. Far from trying to shift the burden of ethical decisions to others, these women suffer throughout their lives from the consequences of their first moral choice, which, they feel, was wrong.

The leitmotif of *Februarschatten* is *Schuld* (guilt), and significantly, its placement in the text frequently does not allow the reader to identify whose voice uttered it. In the context of the narrated events, such ambiguity suggests the guilt and shame that have been emotionally and morally corroding men and women ever since they decided to collaborate with the Nazi forces of evil.

Hilde's strong sense of guilt originates in her betrayal of her brother Hannes, but a sense of shame arises from her awareness of this weakness, from the recognition that she allowed herself to be seduced by the "warmth of Germany." She is conscious of her manic fear of being an outsider, which has always driven her to seek shelter under the shield of authority. Not surprisingly, her efforts to forget that horrible February night and the trauma of *Ohnmacht* (impotence) are nullified when Hilde loses her husband, whose strong personality and social status lent a new identity to her. At the side of her husband, Hilde could receive recognition and even respect; for such rewards her own self-effacement was not too great a sacrifice. After his death, Hilde has to give up her borrowed identity and immediately falls back into isolation, inferiority, and vulnerability, falls back into the past where the February shadows have been lurking. Suddenly, events in the present repeatedly evoke similar events in the past, erasing all the "good" years in between. To ease her fear and horror, Hilde tries to escape her predicament through alcohol, a temporary promise of oblivion:

> Wine will help me. The wine will find the words for me. The words for that night and that day. The words for the preceding nights and the days thereafter will come of their own accord.
>
> So it is true, what [the daughter] once told me. That everything one experiences, encounters, simply everything is stored in our brain. No erasable tape is available to us. Other

> than a forgetting which is limited in time. Yes. Forgetting was something I was able to do. That had been a good, usable erasable tape. (FS 116)[29]

Thrown back into her miserable past, into a childhood marked by poverty, abuse, humiliation, and loneliness, Hilde desperately tries to counteract the memory of her own wrongdoing with vivid recollections of her own victimization: how she was taught obedience and subordination by her father's rage and violence, how she was deprived of any emotional support and moral guidance in her family, and how she was told to forget the brutal killing of the Russian fugitives. Such attempts at explanation cannot, however, as Hilde recognizes in the end, excuse her act of betrayal.

The psychological and political dimensions of her own authoritarian upbringing escape Hilde's perception for the most part, but the reader can easily discern how the dynamics of her family would have prepared Hilde for her cooperation with the punitive system of National Socialism.[30] Furthermore, we become shockingly aware of the interdependence between the familial violation of Hilde's self and the institutionalized crime against innocent people in the Third Reich, the dehumanization of her *Lebenswelt* (environment) the savage extinction of human beings in concentration camps like Mauthausen.[31]

If Hilde in *Februarschatten* seeks to compensate for her negative self-image through identification with patriarchal authority, Ruth Berger in *Komm über den See* tries to forget her own weakness, her "voicelessness," through her skill in language. For nineteen years and with great ambition, Ruth pursues a career as an interpreter, always looking ahead and never back, when suddenly a psychosomatic ailment forces her to give up her work and take a close look at her life. Years later, when trying to find a job as a teacher, she still wonders, "Is the time not yet past in which you did not have your own language, in which you existed in the languages of the others, only in those of the others? But you were warned. . . . You did not want to hear the voice that was warning you. Eva's voice, 'You have a talent for all languages except your own.' Without the sentences of others you became speechless. But without language there is nothing."[32]

Finding her own language here means articulating her own views, expressing her own beliefs, thus refusing to let others speak for her and resisting manipulation. Language is identified with power; it becomes a means of intervention and change, whereas silence becomes the safe hideout for cowards and *Mitläufer* as well as the realm of forgetting. Ruth is acutely aware of her penchant for silence: "I do what comes easiest to me; I keep quiet, and as much as I sometimes feel this silence to be a fault, I live with it."[33] As long as Ruth hopes to find protection in silence and, as a result, shows herself guilty of passivity, accommodation, and opportunism because she is afraid of speaking out, of its risks and consequences, she incurs more and more "sins of omission"; she relives the traumatic childhood experience of her betraying her mother over and over again and makes a candid confrontation with her past an ever more daunting task.

Sensitive as Ruth is to her guilt, she has a great need for sublimation. So she admires the antifascist resistance fighters and praises their courage and great sense of responsibility. Once again she gives voice to others rather than dare to search for her own voice and show her own opposition to the manifold expressions of everyday fascism in her immediate surroundings. She fails to contradict her authoritarian colleague at the school where she is a replacement teacher when he tells her what kind of literature she ought to avoid, yields to the headmaster's pressure and patronizing control, and makes every effort to adjust to the social mores of the narrow-minded, gossipy provincial town where she is assigned to teach for a year.

The discrepancy between her inner beliefs and her outward behavior puts Ruth in permanent crisis. Therefore, it is indeed an accomplishment when she finally breaks her silence, musters her courage, and takes a stand against the headmaster—at the risk of losing her job—in an eloquent defense of Anna Zach. This first act of resistance against injustice and intimidation leads Ruth out of self-entrapment, allows her to discover her own voice, and find with the moral support of Anna the direction toward selfhood. Having overcome her cowardice, she is now prepared to cope with her past.

Reichart certainly endows her female protagonists with sensitive antennae that alert them to their problems. But their wish to overcome impotence and demonstrate courage–thus, transforming self-hatred into self-esteem—can hardly be realized unless they are given some encouragement from outside. Reichart's narratives illuminate the difficulty of developing an independent mind in a society that is bent on transmitting *Obrigkeitsdenken* (blind trust in authority) and *Untertanengeist* (submissiveness). As long as the institutions of family, school, church, and state aim at inculcating obedience, subordination, and accommodation as "virtues" for social advancement, status, and respect, it is very unlikely that individuals will learn to think for themselves, go against the grain, and make decisions for which they are willing to assume personal responsibility.

Growing up during the Third Reich and then living in a society that has, to a large extent, preserved the authoritarianism of the past, albeit in a less clearly threatening form, the protagonists of *Februarschatten* and *Komm über den See* face enormous obstacles in successfully coping with the Nazi legacy.

Hilde had to experience how her own neighbors dutifully followed the order to hunt down "Russian convicts, murderers, thieves, killers, enemies" (124), how they bestially attacked the emaciated bodies of these fugitives—"unarmed, helpless, frail" (126)—with hayforks, shovels, and other farm tools until they were dead "blood-smeared bundles" (134). Against her conscious wish, Hilde's memory has recorded this savagery carried out by ordinary Austrian citizens—an act that makes it impossible to shift responsibility for the atrocities of National Socialism to some higher authorities or special task forces. *Februarschatten* drives home to the reader "the banality of evil," as Hannah Arendt called it, the brutality of Hitlerian fascism acted out by common people who relished being needed for a great cause and meting out punishment.

The power of collective behavior, as Hilde encounters it, also manifests itself in the general agreement to forget the so-called "Rabbit Hunt of the Mill District" as soon as the Red Army arrives and the gates of Mauthausen are torn down. Her own desire to forget is buttressed by everyone else's immediate repression of the past, and the question of guilt and responsibility is shelved without hesitation.

> Why should I think about my childhood? I learned after all from the time I was little: the only way to survive is to forget. . . .
>
> Forget Hannes. Forget the cold February.
>
> At first because of the command of the adults. Forget what you have heard. What you have seen. Forget it! But soon it was no longer necessary to shout this command into her.

> Soon this command of all the other people became her own. Soon she would pass on this command to others. (FS 31)[34]

The chain of forgetting, as we know, is broken through the daughter. Just as the daughter succeeds in evoking her mother's recollections, a success that aids her in the delayed process of coming to terms with her repressed trauma, the story of *Februarschatten* may also very well succeed in compelling contemporary Austrian readers to confront their own complicity in the national process of forgetting, a fact that may shine some light into the shadows of the past.

To what degree these shadows still prevail in today's Austria is depicted in *Komm über den See* with circumspection. The daily life of Ruth Berger provides the reader with insight into the many manifestations of the Nazi legacy. We learn, among other things, that some teachers still have a list of banned writers (88); that respectable citizens annually celebrate the *Reichskristallnacht* in local inns and that the nationalized television refuses to broadcast reports critical of the practice (60f.); that some castles are still used as psychiatric clinics where patients disappear (148); that having a father who was a prominent Nazi helps in finding employment (96); that denunciation and the fear of it can still be part of surviving in one's career.

The facade of democracy, Reichart suggests, can barely hide the authoritarianism and discriminatory hierarchies, where the familiar dichotomy of Social Darwinism between the strong and the weak shapes one's thinking and appears in the common application of the dangerously simplistic categories of "good versus evil," "we versus they," and "men versus women." Various forms of censorship, surveillance, and punishment constitute the essential elements of a strong social pressure that requires adjustment, obedience, and silence. Clearly, such a society is not inclined to promote independence of mind and a sense of individual responsibility. It does not provide a foundation for resistance to manipulation of any kind because to resist means "first of all to survive emotionally. It require[s] the inner strength to cut oneself entirely loose from external systems of rewards and punishments and fashion a balance between conformity and opposition."[35]

Ruth Berger, who suffers from her own and others' daily opportunism and silent subordination, cannot rely on much support for her efforts to explore the past and counteract the perilous forces of the Nazi legacy. Even when she succeeds in her struggle for her emotional survival, she remains on the margin of society and experiences the isolation Anna Zach tells her about: "She would not have believed before that out of everything only the loneliness would be left, only the loneliness."[36]

III

It is impossible to predict whether the attempts of Reichart and Schwaiger to confront the past through their fiction can turn individual acts of *Erinnerungsarbeit* into collective efforts. Both writers break the silence about the past that has blocked communication between generations, but as we have seen, they take different approaches and reach different goals. The key to the difference in their accomplishments seems to lie in the authors' distinct perceptions of remembrance manifested in the structures of their works.

Schwaiger's *Lange Abwesenheit* is not a narrative of development; rather, it is circular, firmly linking the final chapter with the epigraph. The narrator of *Lange Abwesenheit,* caught in blind anger, frustration, and self-pity, moves in mental and emotional circles. She is interested only in finally ridding herself of her problems and holding her father responsible for his Nazi legacy of anti-Semitism, authoritarianism, and contempt for emotional expression (and any other form of "weakness"). It escapes the daughter's notice that, through her constant self-defense and denial of any responsibility, she is repeating the father's repression of any discomforting, unpleasant experience that could evoke guilt and shame.[37] The narrator of *Lange Abwesenheit* does not have the knowledge and strength to ask questions about either her father's Nazi past or Birer's Jewish experience; nor does she critically examine her own prejudices, so she fails to gain any insight that could guide her into the future.

Perhaps the lack of emotional distance from this autobiographical subject matter made it impossible for Schwaiger to break out of her entrapment in this vicious circle. If so, we should perhaps read *Lange Abwesenheit* as a fictional document confirming many psychoanalysts' gloomy observations that the young generation that does not feel guilty about the Nazi past has not begun to come to terms with it but, rather, has taken over its repression and disavowal.

If coming to terms with the past means traversing several cognitive stages—some of which are remembering, repeating, and working one's way through things—in order to overcome the unconscious and instinctual forces of self-protection (such as forgetting, denying, and projecting), then any literary account of such a process requires a composition depicting the protagonist's growth and transformation.

The structure of Elisabeth Reichart's books invites the reader not only to observe such a development but also to participate in the complex meanderings of the protagonists' memory. I think that most readers' response to Reichart's texts resembles Christa Wolf's experience described in her afterword to *Februarschatten:* "The book gripped my attention. The effort it cost me to read it seemed necessary, not gratuitous. The structure of the text which strives toward a disclosure, corresponds to the investigation, which the author undertook, and it corresponds also to the process of remembering. I had the feeling I was working along an excavation project, the results of which terrified me."[38]

Both *Februarschatten* and *Komm über den See* ask the reader to empathize with the protagonists' dilemma. They are caught between overwhelming desire to forget the dark past and the emotional urge to relieve themselves of the heavy burden by sharing it with someone else. In both works, the solution of the dilemma requires a painful and laborious "excavation," a mental and emotional digging more and more deeply until the source of the pain is revealed. It seems appropriate that Reichart decided to compose her texts like mystery stories, where all the textual elements, like individual pieces of a complicated puzzle, gradually come together to form a sudden revelation, shocking to the protagonist as well as to the reader. After all, secrets shrouded in decades of stifling silence are being explored and exposed.

It becomes clear in *Februarschatten* to what extent the divulging of a painful memory—the confession of a fault and the ensuing guilt—is still evaded even when reaching the stage of articulation. Hilde does not spell out her act of betrayal; in her revelations, there remains a gap that she leaves to the daughter (and the reader) to figure out: "Have I forgotten anything? She giggled. I hope I have forgotten something. So that at least there remains one secret." (FS 139)[39] In *Komm über den See,* the reader's identification with the "excavation project," as Christa Wolf so aptly describes it, is intensified through the insertion of narrative fragments preceding every chapter, spoken by the voice of an unidentified female resistance fighter. Only at the very end, when Ruth discovers her own true identity, does the reader discover that this voice belongs to Anna Zach. The two strands of *Erkenntnis* (insight)—Ruth's and the reader's—gradually converge.

The marked difference in depth or intensity of remembering that I have noted between Schwaiger's and Reichart's explorations of the past also applies, I suggest, to their feminism. Both writers see their female protagonists as having been socialized into obedience, subordination, and fear by the law of a patriarchal world. And both suggest that the microcosm of the authoritarian family reflects the larger social structure where power operates to intimidate and suppress all forms of opposition and deviation. Furthermore, Schwaiger and Reichart clearly believe that the fascist legacy is a manifestation of male domination as it still characterizes today's Austrian society.

But whereas Schwaiger depicts the victimization of the female narrator by her tyrannical father and patronizing lover without permitting her to recognize her own complicity, Reichart probes into the female contribution to the predominance of patriarchal values. Reichart's choice of female characters for her investigation of guilt and responsibility indicates that unlike many writers and historians, she does not share the idealization of women as mere victims of National Socialism or, for that matter, of male supremacy.[40] For Elisabeth Reichart, the world consists of many gray zones rather than stark blacks and whites.

Februarschatten and *Komm über den See* are literary exemplifications of Claudia Koonz's historical evidence that "German women varied in both support and opposition, as victims and perpetrators" and that "women, no less than men, destroyed ethical vision, debased humane traditions, and rendered decent people helpless. And other women, as victims and resisters, risked their lives to ensure Nazi defeat and preserve their own ideals."[41]

Reichart's mother-daughter stories are not so much calls to women for resistance against a male-dominated world as they are circumspect and passionate appeals to both women and men to develop courage and independence of mind in order to resist opportunism, hypocrisy, and submissiveness. Clearly, Reichart believes that women's role in nurturing these virtues already in children is particularly crucial; otherwise, democratic behavior, based on individual responsibility, cannot take root.[42] If women support each other in this endeavor, as the solidarity of Reichart's female characters ultimately suggests, social change for the better will come. Only from such a strong moral foundation can courage of one's convictions arise.

An honest confrontation with the past, as Reichart offers it to her readers, entails, to paraphrase Adorno, taking interest in one's personal self, strengthening one's confidence in selfhood.[43]

The reader has the choice of learning from this literature.

NOTES

1. The most influential studies on the issue are Claudio Magris, *Der habsburgische Mythos in der österreichischen Literatur* (Salzburg: Otto Müller, 1966) and Ulrich Greiner, *Der Tod des Nachsommers* (München: Hanser, 1979). Several scholars who contributed essays to the volume *Für und Wider eine österreichische Literatur,* ed. K. Bartsch et al. (Königstein: Athenäum, 1982) also support the thesis of "political doldrums" in Austrian literature. A sad acceptance of this claim as true characterizes most essays of the collection *Die Feder, ein Schwert?—Literatur und Politik in Österreich.* ed. Harald Seuter (Graz: Leykam, 1981), in which writers, journalists, historians, sociologists, and political scientists express their views on the relationship between literature and politics in Austria.

2. In her essay "Confronting the Fascist Past and Coming to Terms with It," *World Literature Today* 55, 4 (1981): 553–60, Ursula Mahlendorf outlines three stages in the development of German literature dealing with the topic of fascism. She notes a first wave of highly critical and artistically very good works written in exile, followed by an antifascist postwar literature around the Group 47. The third major confrontation with the fascist past started in the 1970s, carried out, for the most part, by the daughters and sons of the Nazi generation.

Mahlendorf's scheme cannot be transferred in its entirety to the Austrian literary scene. Only the third stage, the most recent reaction to National Socialism, can also be noted here. It should be stressed, however, that there are individual Austrian writers who fall into Mahlendorf's other categories, but they do not represent a wider literary phenomenon.

For another interesting historical survey of the treatment of fascism in postwar German literature, see Judith Ryan, *The Uncompleted Past* (Detroit: Wayne State University Press, 1983).

3. To provide the reader with some guide, it seems appropriate to list the authors and their works on the topic of fascism as a historical event or as a mentality characterizing daily life in postwar Austria:

Ilse Aichinger (born 1921), *Die grössere Hoffnung* (1948). In a highly poetic, almost surrealist fashion, the novel tells the story of a racially persecuted child.

Ingeborg Bachman (1926–1972), "Jugend in einer österreichischen Stadt" and "Unter Mödern und Irren" in the collection of stories *Das Dreissigste Jahr* (1961), *Der Fall Franza* (1966), and *Malina* (1971). In her novels, fascism primarily operates on the level of interpersonal relationships, whereas in her stories, the atmosphere of the war years and their effects on people's minds and souls is portrayed.

Erika Mitterer (born 1906), *Alle unsere Spiele* (1977). Her novel traces the stages of a woman's inner development from fanatical enthusiasm for the Nazis to gradual disillusionment and repentance.

Marie-Thérèse Kerschbaumer (born 1936), *Der weibliche Name des Widerstands* (1980). In this poetic document the author reconstructs the lives of seven Viennese women murdered under the Nazis because of their race or political convictions.

Elfriede Jelinek (born 1946), *Die Ausgesperrten* (1980) and the play *Burgtheater* (1983). The former work is a portrayal of violent youth gang members whose criminal behavior derives from the everyday fascism that marked their upbringing; the latter is a grotesque satire about the fascist traditions in Austrian culture.

Brigitte Schwaiger (born 1949), *Lange Abwesenheit* (1980).

Elisabeth Reichart (born 1953), *Februarschatten* (1984) and *Komm über den See* (1988).

Waltraud Anna Mitgutsch (born 1948), *Die Züchtigung* (1985). In this autobiographical novel, the author depicts a mother-daughter relationship whose pathological nature is conditioned by the traditions of authoritarian, fascist child rearing.

Two little-known Austrian women writers addressing the topic of fascism should perhaps also be mentioned here: Christine Haidegger (born 1942), who presents us the story of her childhood during the 1940s in *Zum Fenster hinaus* (1979), and Ingeborg Day (born 1940), who—after having moved to the United States in 1960—published her first novel *Ghost Waltz* (1980) in English before it appeared in German translation in 1983. Day presents reflections on her anti-Semitism, which she inherited in her childhood from her father, a former SS officer.

4. In addition to Jelinek, Schwaiger, Reichart, Mitgutsch, and Haidegger, the male writers Erich Hackl, Josef Haslinger, Reinhard Gruber, and Erwin Einzinger should be mentioned here. For more insight into the young generation's perspective on Austria's political past, see *Reden an Österreich. Schriftsteller ergreifen das Wort,* ed. Jochen Jung (Salzburg: Residenz, 1988).

5. See Alice Miller, *Du sollst nicht merken* (Frankfurt: Suhrkamp, 1980), Thea Bauriedl, *Die Wiederkehr des Verdrängten. Psychoanalyse, Politik und der Einzelne* (München: Piper, 1986), Horst Eberhard Richter, *Die Chance des Gewissens. Erinnerungen und Assoziationen* (Hamburg: Hoffmann und Campe, 1986), Margarete Mitscherlich, *Erinnerungsarbeit. Zur Psychoanalyse der Unfähigkeit zu trauern* (Frankfurt: Fisher, 1987), Nadine Hauer, "NS-Trauma und kein Ende," in *Das grosse Tabu. Österreichs Umgang mit seiner Vergangenheit,* ed. Anton Pelinka and E. Weinzierl (Wien: Edition S, 1987): 28–41.

6. This opinion has recently been confirmed again by Gabriele von Arnim, *Das grosse Schweigen. Von der Schwierigkeit, mit den Schatten der Vergangenheit zu leben* (München: Kindler, 1989).

7. In her recent study *Erinnerungsarbeit. Zur Psychologie der Unfähigkeit zu trauern,* Margarete Mitscherlich expresses great concern about the younger generation's failure to examine the Nazi past with anything other than the inherited

defense mechanisms. She writes, "Wenn aber Verleugnung, Verdrängung, Derealisierung der Vergangenheit an die Stelle der Durcharbeitung treten, ist ein Wiederholungszwang unvermeidbar, auch wenn er sich kaschieren lässt. Es wiederholt sich dabei nicht der Inhalt eines Systems, sondern die Struktur einer Gesellschaft. Nazisymbole und Nazivereinigungen kann man verbieten. "Nazistrukturen" (z.B. den autoritären Charakter) aus der Welt der Erziehung des Verhaltens, der Umgangs- und Denkweisen, der Politik zu vertreiben, ist nicht möglich ohne Trauerarbeit. Deswegen müssen wir heute erkennen, dass die junge Generation, die sich unschuldig fühlt, nicht die Bearbeitung unserer Vergangenheit angetreten, sondern deren Verleugnung und Verdrängung übernommen hat" (14).

8. See Mitscherlich, *Erinnerungsarbeit,* 34.

9. See Sandra Frieden, *Autobiography: Self Into Form. German-Language Autobiographical Writings of the 1970's* (Frankfurt: Peter Lang, 1983): 42–75; and Michael Schneider, "Väter und Söhne, posthum. Das beschädigte Verhältnis zweier Generationen," *Den Kopf verkehrt aufgesetzt* (Darmstadt: Luchterhand, 1981): 8–64.

10. Other recent Austrian novels thematizing fascism and illustrating this "rediscovery" of history are Andreas Okopenko, *Kindernazi* (Salzburg: Residenz, 1984), Franz Rieger, *Schattenschweigen oder Hartheim* (Graz: Styria, 1985), Peter Henisch, *Steins Paranoia* (Salzburg: Residenz, 1988), Gerald Szyszkowitz, *Puntigam oder die Kunst des Vergessens* (Wien: Zsolnay, 1988), Erich Hackl, *Abschied von Sidonie* (Zürich: Diogenes, 1989).

I would also like to point out that Elisabeth Reichart is a trained historian, who wrote her doctoral thesis on the Austrian resistance movement against the Nazis.

11. My translation of the original "Ich möchte, dass [andere] dich bewundern, wie du es verdienst. Ich möchte, dass die, die dich gekannt haben, dich hassen, wie du es verdienst." Brigitte Schwaiger, *Lange Abwesenheit* 10. All further translations are mine.

12. "Wenn du deine Hauptmannsuniform aus dem Krieg daheim getragen hättest von Anfang an, dann wäre vielleicht vieles deutlicher gewesen.

Ein Vater, ein richtiger Vater ist einer, den man nicht umarmen darf, den man nicht unterbrechen darf, wenn er spricht, dem man antworten muss, auch wenn er zum fünftenmal dasselbe fragt und es aussieht, als frage er zum fünftenmal, um sich zu vergewissern, ob die Töchter auch willig sind, stets zu antworten, ein Vater, der einem das Wort abschneiden darf." *Lange Abwesenheit* 19.

13. "[Der Friede], der darin besteht, dass die einen nicht sagen, wie hungrig sie sind, damit die anderen in Ruhe essen können." *Lange Abwesenheit* 20.

14. The term is taken from *Am Anfang war Erziehung* by Alice Miller, who has borrowed it from Katharina Rutschky's work *Schwarze Pädagogik* (Berlin: Ullstein, 1977). The main educational goal of "black pedagogy" is to suppress in the child any sign of *Eigensinn,* of selfhood and independence, which makes the child gradually internalize the will of the Other as his/her own.

15. In issue 35 of the periodical *Das Jüdische Echo* (October 1986), which deals exclusively with the question of fascism and anti-Semitism in Austria, Brigitte Schwaiger describes how her interest in the topic developed. About her encounter and friendship with Friedrich Torberg—fictionalized as Birer—she observes, "Dass Torberg Jude war, erschwerte unsere mit den Jahren sich festigende Freundschaft. Immer wieder misstraute ich ihm" (49).

16. "Geiler alter Jud, dachte ich. Und: Vielleicht ist er jung im Bett.

Sein Gesicht kam näher, unsere Brillen klirrten zusammen, als er mich küsste. Der Kuss war gut. Ja, dachte ich, er wird jung sein. Er wird mein Geliebter, mit ihm werde ich mich behaupten gegen Vater. . . .

Ich betrete sein Schlafzimmer, obwohl ich schon nicht mehr will. Ein Bett steht an der Wand. Hier will er mich demütigen.

Der alte Mann. Der holt sich jetzt einen jungen Körper in sein altes Bett. Er hat mich hinters Licht geführt. Er will nur das. Er ist Jude. Juden soll man nicht trauen. Warum habe ich meinem Vater nicht geglaubt? Juden halten zusammen und benützen uns." *Lange Abwesenheit* 28.

17. "Ich werde nie den Mut haben, ihm zu sagen, warum ich mich wirklich mit ihm eingelassen habe." *Lange Abwesenheit* 34.

18. "Ich will nicht deine Tochter sein! . . . Ich möchte meinen Kopf retten, Nazidrecksau!" *Lange Abwesenheit* 37.

19. "Aber was kann ich denn für die Gedanken, die von Vater sind?" *Lange Abwesenheit* 33. The second example can be found on p. 39.

20. On the difference between mourning and melancholy, Margarete Mitscherlich comments in *Erinnerungsarbeit. Zur Psychoanalyse der Unfähigkeit zu trauern:* "Im Unterschied zur Trauer geht die Melancholie mit einem Verlust des eigenen Selbstwerts einher, der auf die Ambivalenz in der Beziehung zum verlorenen Objekt zurückgeführt wird. . . . Der Melancholiker kreist um sein eigenes Elend, in ständiger Wiederholung äussert er alte Vorwürfe sich und anderen gegenüber, nichts Neues scheint in sein Denken und Fühlen, in seine Beziehungen zu Menschen mehr eindringen zu können" (70).

21. "Und möchte hinter sein Gesicht greifen, ihm die Erinnerungen herausreissen, gib mich frei, lass los." *Lange Abwesenheit* 57.

"Er hat viele Stimmen, viele Arme und Beine, ist unsichtbar und kann mir jederzeit und überall auflauern." *Lange Abwesenheit* 88.

22. "Die Stirne meines Vaters, ein Eisfeld, auf dem eine winzige Figur läuft. Das bin ich und laufe und laufe, aber der Kopf dreht sich. So komme ich nicht voran." Epigraph to *Lange Abwesenheit.*

23. Elisabeth Reichart, *February Shadows* 88. Henceforth the page references to the English edition of the novel (FS) are given in the text.

The original German passage in *Februarschatten* (Wien: Edition S, 1984) 120f., reads: "Diese Frau, von der in abgebrochenen Sätzen die Rede ist. Diese Frau bin nicht ich. Die ist ein Hirngespinst der Tochter. . . . Überhaupt ist es lächerlich, dass sie über mich schreibt. Wie kann sie über ihre Mutter schreiben, die sie nicht kennt. Sie kann mich nicht kennen. Denn ich kenne sie schon lange nicht mehr. Es ist mein Leben. Nicht ihr Leben. Mein Leben geht sie nichts an. Nichts. Warum mischt sie sich ein in mein Leben."

24. "Hilde setzte sich auf den Fahrersitz. Die Tochter wollte nicht, dass sie fuhr. . . . Hilde beachtete sie nicht. Die Tochter blieb unschlüssig stehen. . . .

Hilde fuhr langsam aus dem Dorf hinaus. Beschleunigte auf der Landstrasse. . . .

"Fahr' nicht so schnell. Es ist rutschig."

Hilde warf einen spöttischen Blick auf die ängstliche Tochter. Die noch immer alles besser wusste. Sie trat stärker auf das Gaspedal." *Februarschatten* 183.

25. My translation of the original passage "Die eigene Geschichtslosigkeit, aus der später, viel später der Hunger entstand—oder gleich entstand und sich erst später artikulierte? Nicht nur die Mutter, ganz Wien war ohne Gedächtnis. Wir Kinder nannten uns Trümmerkinder, aber woher die Trümmer kamen, wussten

wir nicht . . . und niemand erklärte, und nur die Trümmer sind inzwischen weggeräumt." *Komm über den See* (Frankfurt: Fischer, 1988) 174. All further translations from *Komm über den See* are mine.

26. "Verleugne ich die Dunkelheit, in der ich herumirre, sobald ich an meine Mutter denke, von der ich so wenig weiss, an die ich mich kaum erinnere." *Komm über den See* 40.

27. "Du hast doch nur Angst davor, erkennen zu müssen, dass deine Erinnerungen Wunschbilder sind! . . . Wozu die retuschierten Bilder am Leben erhalten?" *Komm über den See* 41.

28. "Jahrelang habe ich mich umsonst blind gestellt. Wir haben eine masslose Phantasie entwickelt aus unserer Überempfindlichkeit, unserer Verletzbarkeit, und bleiben doch Ausgelieferte." *Komm über den See* 187.

29. "Der Wein wird mir helfen. Er wird die Worte für mich finden. Die Worte für jene Nacht und jenen Tag. Die Worte für die Nächte und Tage vorher und nachher stellten sich schon ein.

So stimmt es, was [die Tochter] mir einmal erzählt hat. Daβ alles Erlebte. Erfahrene, einfach alles, in unserm Gehirn gespeichert wird. Kein Löschband stünde uns zur Verfügung. Ausser zeitbegrenztes Vergessen. Ja. Vergessen, das habe ich gekonnt. Das war ein gutes, brauchbares Löschband gewesen." *Februarschatten* 154f.

30. See Theodor Adorno's observations in his essay "Was bedeutet: Verarbeitung der Vergangenheit," *Eingriffe* (Frankfurt: Suhrkamp, 1963): "[Autoritätsgebundene Charaktere] identifizieren sich mit realer Macht schlechthin, vor jedem besonderen Inhalt. Im Grunde verfügen sie nur über ein schwaches Ich und bedürfen darum als Ersatz der Identifikation mit grossen Kollektiven und der Deckung durch diese" (133).

31. For a more detailed elaboration of this point, see Donna L. Hoffmeister's "Commentary" appended to *February Shadows* 147–62.

32. "Ist die Zeit, in der du ohne eigene Sprache warst, in der du in den Sprachen der anderen existiertest, nur in denen der anderen, noch nicht vorbei? Dabei bist du gewarnt worden. . . . Du wolltest die warnende Stimme nicht hören. Evas Stimme: 'Du bist für alle Sprachen begabt, ausser für deine eigene.' . . . Ohne die Sätze der anderen wurdest du sprachlos. Ohne Sprache aber ist nichts." *Komm über den See* 43.

33. "Ich tu, was mir am leichtesten fällt, ich schweige, und so sehr ich dieses Schweigen manchmal als Makel empfinde, ich lebe damit." *Komm über den See* 156.

34. "Wozu soll ich mich an meine Kindheit erinnern? Ich habe doch von klein auf gelernt: die einzige Möglichkeit zu überleben, ist zu vergessen. . . .

Hannes vergessen. Den kalten Februar vergessen.

Zuerst die Botschaft der Erwachsenen. Vergiss, was du gehört hast. Was du gesehen hast. Vergiss! Aber bald war es nicht mehr nötig, dieses Wort in sie hineinzuschreien. Bald war aller Wort ihr Wort. Bald würde sie selbst das Wort weitergeben wollen." *Februarschatten* 41f.

35. Claudia Koonz. *Mothers in the Fatherland. Women, the Family, and Nazi Politics* (New York: St. Martin's Press, 1987) 17.

36. "Das hätte sie früher nicht geglaubt, dass von allem nur die Einsamkeit bleibe, nur die Einsamkeit." *Komm über den See* 161.

37. In their influential study *Die Unfähigkeit zu trauern* (München: Piper,

1967), Alexander Mitscherlich and Margarete Mitscherlich note, "Wo psychologische Abwehrmechanismen wie etwa Verleugnung und Verdrängung bei der Lösung von Konflikten . . . eine übergrosse Rolle spielen, ist regelmässig zu beobachten, wie sich die Realitätswahrnehmung einschränkt und stereotype Vorurteile sich ausbreiten; in zirkulärer Verstärkung schützen dann die Vorurteile wiederum den ungestörten Ablauf des Verdrängungs—oder Verleugnungsvorganges" (24).

38. The American edition of *February Shadows* includes a reprint of Christa Wolf's "Afterword" (143–45) originally written for the East German edition of *Februarschatten* (Berlin: Aufbau Verlag, 1985). The quotation can be found on p. 143.

39. "Habe ich etwas vergessen? Sie kicherte. Hoffentlich habe ich etwas vergessen. Damit mir wenigstens ein Geheimnis geblieben ist." *Februarschatten* 181.

40. See Claudia Koonz's remark in *Mothers in the Fatherland:* "Historians have dismissed women as part of the timeless backdrop against which Nazi men made history, seeing men as active "subjects" and women as the passive 'other.'" (3)

In her essay "NS-Trauma und kein Ende," Nadine Hauer also comments on the conspicuous absence of women in research on the Nazi past: "Obwohl es fast ausschliesslich Frauen sind, die sich mit dem Thema NS-Zeit und psychische Folgen beschäftigen, sind Frauen auch heute im allgemeinen noch viel weniger bereit, über diese Zeit zu sprechen, und das gilt für die NS-Generation ebenso wie für deren "Kinder." . . . Frauen werden immer noch gerne—und sie selbst tun es auch—als Opfer angesehen. Opfer können nicht einmal "Mittäter" sein; vor allem Mütter gelten als jene, die sich für alle aufopfern." (37f.)

41. *Mothers in the Fatherland* 12, 17.

42. In my recent interview with Elisabeth Reichart (Vienna, 3 July 1989), she stated, "Es sollte auch aus meinen Büchern hervorgehen, dass die Zeit, in der die Töchter leben, nicht dazu angetan ist, Eigenverantwortung zu fördern, sozusagen ein demokratisches Grundverhalten. Und mit so einem Empfinden sind sie auch nicht aufgewachsen, da ist eher wieder die Ähnlichkeit mit den Müttern. Diese dargestellten Elternfiguren sind ja nicht gerade darauf vorbereitet, Eigenverantwortung und Selbstständigkeit gedeihen zu lassen. Das ist ein Samen, der bei den Kindern selbst nicht gefördert worden ist, und deshalb müssen sie selber dazu sehen, dass dieser Samen, wohl ein Grundbedürfnis, zum Wachsen gebracht wird."

43. "Was bedeutet: Aufarbeitung der Vergangenheit" 144.

WORKS CITED

Adorno, Theodor W. "Was bedeutet: Aufarbeitung der Vergangenheit." In *Eingriffe.* Frankfurt: Suhrkamp, 1963. 125–146.

Aichinger, Ilse. *Die grössere Hoffnung.* Frankfurt: Fischer, 1976.

Arnim, Gabriele von. *Das grosse Schweigen. Von der Schwierigkeit, mit den Schatten der Vergangenheit zu leben.* München: Kindler, 1989.

Bachmann, Ingeborg. *Erzählungen.* Vol. 2 of *Ingeborg Bachmann. Werke.* Ed. Christine Koschel et al. 4 vols. München: Piper, 1978.

———. *Todesarten.* Vol. 3 of *Ingeborg Bachmann. Werke.* Ed. Christine Koschel et al. 4 vols. München: Piper, 1978.

Bartsch, Karl, et al., eds. *Für und Wider eine österreichische Literatur.* Königstein: Anthenäum, 1982.

Bauriedl, Thea. *Die Wiederkehr des Verdrängten. Psychoanalyse, Politik und der Einzelne.* München: Piper, 1986.

Day, Ingeborg. *Geisterwalzer.* Trans. Ingeborg Day and Ulrich Fries. Salzburg: Residenz, 1983.

Frieden, Sandra. *Autobiography: Self into Form. German-Language Autobiographical Writings of the 1970's* Frankfurt: Peter Lang, 1983.

Greiner, Ulrich. *Der Tod des Nachsommers.* München: Hanser, 1979.

Hackl, Erich. *Abschied von Sidonie.* Zürich: Diogenes, 1989.

Haidegger, Christine. *Zum Fenster hinaus.* Reinbek bei Hamburg: Rowohlt, 1979.

Hauer, Nadine. "NS-Trauma und kein Ende." In *Das grosse Tabu. Österreichs Umgang mit seiner Vergangenheit,* ed. Anton Pelinka und E. Weinzierl. Wien: Edition S, 1987. 28–41.

Henisch, Peter. *Steins Paranoia.* Salzburg: Residenz, 1988.

Jelinek, Elfriede. *Die Ausgesperrten.* Reinbek bei Hamburg: Rowohlt, 1980.

———. *Burgtheater.* Köln: Prometh-Verlag, 1983.

Jung, Jochen, ed. *Reden an Österreich. Schriftsteller ergreifen das Wort.* Salzburg: Residenz, 1988.

Kerschbaumer, Marie-Thérèse. *Der weibliche Name des Widerstands.* Olten: Walter-Verlag, 1980.

Koonz, Claudia. *Mothers in the Fatherland. Women, the Family, and Nazi Politics.* New York: St. Martin's Press, 1987.

Magris, Claudio. *Der habsburgische Mythos in der österreichischen Literatur.* Salzburg: Otto Müller, 1966.

Mahlendorf, Ursula. "Confronting the Fascist Past and Coming to Terms with It." *World Literature Today* 55, 4 (1981): 553–560.

Miller, Alice. *Du sollst nicht merken.* Frankfurt: Suhrkamp, 1980.

Mitgutsch, Waltraud Anna. *Die Züchtigung.* Düsseldorf: Claassen, 1985.

Mitscherlich, Margarete. *Erinnerungsarbeit. Zur Psychoanalyse der Unfähigkeit zu trauern.* Frankfurt: Fischer, 1987.

Mitterer, Erika. *Alle unsere Spiele.* Frankfurt: Josef Knecht-Carolusdruckerei, 1977.

Okopenko, Andreas. *Kindernazi.* Salzburg: Residenz, 1984.

Reichart, Elisabeth. *Februarschatten.* Wien: Edition S, 1984.

———. *February Shadows.* Trans. Donna L. Hoffmeister. Riverside: Ariadne Press, 1989.

———. *Komm über den See.* Frankfurt: Fischer, 1988.

Richter, Horst Eberhard. *Die Chance des Gewissens. Erinnerungen und Assoziationen.* Hamburg: Hoffmann und Campe, 1986.

Rieger, Franz. *Schattenschweigen oder Hartheim.* Graz: Styria, 1985.

Ryan, Judith. *The Uncompleted Past.* Detroit: Wayne State University Press, 1983.

Schneider, Michael. "Väter und Söhne, posthum. Das beschädigte Verhältnis zweier Generationen." In *Den Kopf verkehrt aufgesetzt.* Darmstadt: Luchterhand, 1981. 8–64.

Schwaiger, Brigitte. *Lange Abwesenheit.* Reinbek bei Hamburg: Rowohlt, 1982.
———. "Mit Remarque." *Das Jüdische Echo* 35, 1 (1986): 47–49.
Seuter, Harald, ed. *Die Feder, ein Schwert?—Literatur und Politik in Österreich.* Graz: Leykam, 1981.
Szyszkowitz, Gerald. *Puntigam oder die Kunst des Vergessens* Wien: Zsolnay, 1988.

SUSAN G. FIGGE

Fathers, Daughters, and the Nazi Past: Father Literature and Its (Resisting) Readers

Since the mid 1970s the German literary project of *Vergangenheitsbewältigung* (overcoming the past) has included a series of narrative texts in which the postwar generation confronts its fathers as perpetrators of the Third Reich. By combining an account of the personal and public life of the father with an autobiographical narrative of the son or daughter, this literature constructs new understandings of the relationships between self, society, and history. In the father literature by women, daughters as subjects write their father's life and their own, portraying the father as icon for familial, cultural, and political authority. These texts make gender—as a social, cultural, and political category, as a basis for self-constitution, and as a determinant of lived experience—central to their representations of the Nazi past and its psycho-social legacy.

Fathers and daughters have been the focus of narratives by a disparate array of German and Austrian women writers, including Elisabeth Plessen, Ruth Rehmann, Barbara Bronnen, Monika Köhler, Brigitte Schwaiger, Jutta Schutting, Ingeborg Day, Herrad Schenck, and Marliese Fuhrmann.[1] Texts centered on fathers and sons have been written by Paul Kerstin, Christoph Meckel, Peter Härtling, Peter Henisch, and Peter Schneider, among others, all with previously established literary reputations.[2] New Left activist and theorist Bernward Vesper's autobiographical novel-essay *Die Reise* (The trip), treating his father, "Blood and Soil" poet Will

Vesper, was written before the author's suicide in 1971, published in 1977, reedited to include new material in 1983, and filmed in 1986.[3] In 1987 Niklas Frank's angry reckoning with his father Hans Frank, Hitler's governor-general in Poland, who was executed for war crimes in 1946, was serialized amidst considerable controversy in the German illustrated *Stern* under the title "Mein Vater, der Nazi Mörder" (My father, the Nazi murderer).[4] Although these treatments of fathers and sons have received serious attention in the popular and scholarly discussion of the father literature, the daughter narratives have often been marginalized and trivialized, their complex constructions of gender and fascism ignored.[5]

I want therefore to focus here on the uneven, controversial, and revealing reception of three father-centered texts by women writers, Ruth Rehmann, Barbara Bronnen, and Monika Köhler, in each of which a daughter is narrator and/or protagonist. By reception I mean the understandings and judgments of these texts that emerged in the media and in attempts by cultural commentators and literary critics to connect the father literature to literary trends and cultural politics in the Federal Republic of the late 1970s and early 1980s. I have looked at book reviews and feuilletonistic review essays in a cross-section of the mass circulation press, at transcriptions of radio interviews and commentaries, and at literary and cultural criticism.[6] And in 1987, the summer of the Kurt Waldheim controversy and the death of Rudolf Hess, I was able to discuss with the authors their own experience of the public response. In thinking about these dimensions of reception, I am particularly interested in how apparent expectations about gender and genre, about daughters and fathers and about the appropriate uses of fiction, documentary, biography, and autobiography have prompted many readers to resist attending to the relations constructed by these narratives between private and public, between patriarchy and politics, and between gender and German fascism.[7]

To understand the cultural and intellectual contexts of these resistances, it is helpful to look first at some early 1980s general assessments of the father literature. Here the daughter-centered texts encounter critical assumptions about a recurring theme in German literary history: the father-son conflict as paradigmatic for the struggles essential to self-definition and to social, political, and cultural change. In this interpretive tradition, by no means limited to the twentieth century, the literary overthrow, defeat or death of the father is understood to signify both the individual son's liberation from the bonds of particular authoritarian psychological and familial constraints and the potential creation of wider social and political freedoms.[8] Recent German literary preoccupation with fathers has been located by critics in that tradition, with the frequent subsequent exclusion of daughters' voices. The literary critic Wolfgang Frühwald sees contemporary father literature as a manifestation of the cultural dismantling of a Western father tradition. Passing over Elisabeth Plessen's 1976 novel, *Mitteilung an den Adel* (*Such Sad Tidings*), Frühwald considers Bernward Vesper's *Die Reise* (The trip, 1977) the seminal text in this current version of a recurring literary and cultural topos. For Frühwald this new and devastating destruction of the father as symbol of all repressive familial, cultural, and political authority leaves the sons' generation with no basis for personal, social, or literary identity. It is significant to Frühwald that Vesper committed suicide.[9] Clearly, however, the use of this literary paradigm of father and son conflict must either subsume or exclude consideration of fathers and daughters. Certainly it ignores the possible liberatory consequences for daughters attendant on what Frühwald describes as a break in "an immeasurably rich father tradition leading western thought back to antiquity."[10]

A related feature of Frühwald's analysis was anticipated by Michael Schneider in his 1981 essay "Fathers and Sons, Retrospectively: The Damaged Relationship between Two Generations." For Schneider contemporary father narratives are examples of a generational neurosis in which the children born just before or during the war, having rebelled actively and unsuccessfully in the late 1960s, revenge themselves again on the father who was psychologically unavailable to them in the postwar family. In this analysis the father literature embodies a failure of the sons' capacity to mourn either the father or the Nazi past, for which the father is held responsible.[11] Schneider's and Frühwald's attribution of narcissism and melancholy to the authors of the father literature, based on a Freudian model of mourning elaborated by psychoanalysts Alexander Mitscherlich and Margarete Mitscherlich in their widely read 1967 book *The Inability to Mourn,* largely excludes considerations of gender in its focus on fathers and sons and in its implicit mourning for the patriarchal family. Again, daughter-centered narratives do not fit easily into these interpretive paradigms.[12]

Recent feminist work on daughter and father texts moves beyond the oedipal model of psychological development or literary influence to suggest that while sons are traditionally expected to rebel culturally and textually against fathers, daughters are not. In literary representations of relations between father and daughter something other than the painful, if predictable, oedipal struggle in which one male replaces another may be at stake. According to critics Lynda Boose and Betty Flowers, the father-daughter bond serves as a "paradigm for women's relationship to male culture."[13] For authors and literary and social critics, "looking at fathers and daughters violates a protective taboo that has been transmitted by the disembodied voice of patriarchal culture."[14] And further, "when the threat of insurrection comes from the son, it fits the authorized structure of patriarchy. When it comes from the detached daughter, it engenders a vision of social inversion that must be quashed"[15] At the same time, Beth Kowaleski-Wallace and Patricia Yeager remind us that "when feminist writers construe the father as a metaphor for patriarchy, we lose sight of the complexities of paternity and the paternal function." The task then is not to reinstate the father's power through rebellion against his authority, nor is it to see the individual father only as a representative of patriarchy. It is perhaps rather "to reinvent the discourse of the father altogether, to move outside an oedipal dialectic that insists upon revealing the father as law, as the gaze, as bodiless, or as the symbolic, and to develop a new dialectic that refuses to describe the father function as if it were univocal and ahistorical."[16] As we look at the reception of the daughter-father texts, it is important to remember the multiple possibilities for change such narratives may suggest and the cultural traditions they may intersect and disrupt, as well as the likely responses to both processes.

In the recent German father literature it is, of course, not just a long tradition of symbolic rebellion against the father that is under revision. Also and importantly understandings of specific historical epochs are at stake. The father literature textually enacts both struggles with the power of the individual father and conflicts over the origin, meaning, and aftermath of the Third Reich. The daughter-centered narratives in particular construct the father as an icon of gendered power and as a deployer of that power in particular historical settings—the Nazi era and the postwar family. It is hardly surprising then that the fathers' stories told in daughters' voices might encounter ongoing cultural and political strategies for keeping silent about the Nazi past, even when appearing to speak. Wolfgang Frühwald's essay may serve as an example of such strategies, when he describes the father literature as embodying "the loosening from the traditionalism of form of a literature (or a life) which affirmed, concealed or powerlessly endured National Socialism, a loosening which mixes ideological components with the text, endangering the independence of literature by privatizing, historicizing and psychologizing."[17] For Frühwald and for many other critics and reviewers, narratives that appear to address particular existing fathers in relation to National Socialism, on the basis of what appears to be first hand experience, are disqualified from serious consideration as "literature" about the Nazi past.

In regard to traditions of such literature, it is useful to recall that the model for the canonical German novel of *Vergangenheitsbewältigung* was, until the mid 1970s, shaped by men. In the Federal Republic, Günter Grass, Heinrich Böll, Siegfried Lenz, and Peter Weiss were the canonized giants among the authors of the "uncompleted past."[18] Most novels of *Vergangenheitsbewältigung* represented sexual and gender politics in the family from the point of view of the male characters. However many autobiographical elements might be suspected—and indeed the authors' having lived through the Third Reich was a guarantee of the authenticity of the fiction—such novels were not understood to reveal the actual life of an individual father or of his child. By contrast, the father literature of the 1970s and 1980s, particularly from a daughter's perspective, moved away from such grotesque caricatures of petit bourgeois insecurity and vulnerability as Oscar Matzerath's father in Grass's *The Tin Drum* or from virtuous but mysterious presences such as Robert Fähmel in Böll's *Billiards at Half Past Nine.* Now historically existing fathers were appropriated, concealed, and revealed in ambiguous fictions that constructed connections between their failings as parents, their political gullibility or ethical culpability, and gendered power structures in the family and in German fascism.

In terms of critical categories evolving from more recent German literary trends, the contemporary father narratives are often labeled as depoliticized literature of the "new subjectivity," largely on the basis of their apparently unmediated autobiographical content. Critic Reinhard Baumgart, for example, reads these texts as examples of a 1960s and 1970s deprofessionalization of literature, of the belief that everyone, if they spoke of their own experience, could write. For Baumgart they represent a confusion of life and literature, replacing what Bernward Vesper had termed the aesthetics of domination of self and object with an aesthetics of self-revelation, vulnerability, and the ecstasy of powerlessness. This is a literature without imagination, serving "previously defined interests, whether green, feminist, narcissistic or pacifistic."[19] Clearly such characterizations undermine the project that much of the father literature undertakes: to construct genealogies of German fascism through the person of the father and to explore its cultural, social, and psychological aftermath in the person of the child. Gender and genre issues emerge again: particularly as women writers begin to explore the private sphere and the origins of their own subjectivity in the shadow of the Nazi past, their accounts, often construed either as narratives of personal experience or as fiction with focused feminist interests, are eliminated from consideration as serious contributions to the literary discussion of the legacy of National Socialism.

I want now to examine the reception of three texts that I take to be representative of the variety as well as of the commonality of daughter-centered father literature: Ruth Rehmann's *Der Mann auf der Kanzel. Fragen an einen Vater* (The man in the pulpit. Questions to a father, 1979); Barbara Bronnen's *Die Tochter* (The daughter, 1980); and Monika Köhler's *Die Früchte vom Machandelbaum* (The fruits of the juniper tree, 1980). The reception of these daughter narratives of the father especially reveals the changing but powerful cultural and literary traditions revolving around gender and genre and the German past.

Ruth Rehmann's 1979 memoir *Der Mann auf der Kanzel: Fragen an einen Vater* deals with the cultural, political, and theological origins of her Lutheran pastor father's failure to take a stand against National Socialism within his own congregation. Rehmann's father died in 1941, and she herself belongs to the generation just reaching adulthood at the beginning of the war. Not identified with the student movement and its political consequences, Rehmann had, at the time when the memoir appeared, a following as a popular novelist and short story writer, especially, but not exclusively among women. *Der Mann auf der Kanzel* enjoyed a very positive media reception and a considerable marketing success; it became a Bertelsmann Book Club selection in 1980.[20] Subsequently many correspondents shared their own memories with Rehmann, connecting them particularly to contemporary issues with complex moral and political dimensions.

Although some conservative Lutherans, including her own

pastor brother, questioned not only her theological acumen but also her daughterly piety, and criticism from the left focused on her lack of ideological rigor, most journalistic reviewers of *Der Mann auf der Kanzel* praised Rehmann especially for her affectionate, understanding, and even-handed treatment of her father, Reinhold Rehmann, pastor to a small Lutheran congregation in the Rhineland during the 1920s and 1930s.[21] The liberal theologian Helmut Gollwitzer called the book "a model for generational conflict, how it can be carried out without arrogance and fruitfully; a model for empathetic understanding, for being just without neglecting the revealing complaint and accusation."[22] In the *Frankfurter Allgemeine Zeitung* Walter Hink found Rehmann so convincing because in her writing "neither rage nor shame distorts the facts. The love of the daughter guarantees the believability of the father portrait."[23] For Hink the authenticity of Rehmann's memoir is assured by the absence of any strong emotion save love—a curious genre claim for a critic and one that may help explain the often negative reception of father texts written by angrier daughters.[24]

In part *Der Mann auf der Kanzel* invites this positive reception by the daughter's obvious affection for her father, her narrative posture as mediator between the generations, and her voice as apologist for her father to her son, a university student and the memoir's representative of the 1968 generation. His challenge, his questions, send the narrator on the literal and metaphorical journey that begins the book and the forays into her father's past and ultimately her own. She takes care to portray herself as without special authority, questioning her own ability to understand the past and commenting that she cannot even settle a quarrel among her children in "this family without a father, without an absolute command."[25] Part of the narrator's quest is also structured around her interviews with those she considers authorities: a former schoolteacher and family friend, a theologian. She includes results of her own research on Lutheran doctrine of church and state. In her loving and respectful portrayal of her father, in her employment of narrative strategies that authorize her in part through the authority of others, Rehmann behaves textually as a good daughter should.

Emphasizing the apparently dutiful daughterhood that constructs the affectionate portrait of her father in a self-effacing style, reviewers largely overlook the connections Rehmann makes between her father's uneasy accommodation to the Third Reich and the gendered power structure of his conservative Lutheran, antirepublican cultural world. In her description of his study, for example, the choice and arrangement of furniture, paintings and books represent a chain of fathers—God, head of state, pastor, and head of family—each symbolically validated by the other. Individuals, anchored by this chain, are relieved of responsibility to question beyond the available patriarchal paradigms of thought and belief appropriate to their tasks and station.[26] The narrative forges connections between the father's self-assured existence in a world of masculine authority and privilege and his failure to develop ethical and political insight about the events unfolding all around him. In this cultural text of fatherhood, Rehmann finds the patterns that explain both her father's political silence and the silencing of her mother and herself.

Thus her father can fail to see, although he interrupts the episode, that the church organist has tried to molest his teenage daughter. Thus, in 1933, as he administers last rites, he can fail to see that the dying Brown shirt member of his congregation has been shot in the back by his own comrades and not by the communist who will be accused of the murder. In his world of leftover Wilhelminian patriarchy, daughters are not sexual beings. Violence, sexual and otherwise, is the specialty of the proletariat, not of the bourgeois members of his own flock. In her reconstitution of her father's cultural and ethical imagination, Rehmann locates his personal and political blindness in his complex set of assumptions about gender and class, violence and sexuality, assumptions that are supported in turn by his own culturally validated "fatherly" authority.[27]

Rehmann recalls herself as the child who was allowed to stay in Reinhold's study, his *Vaterzimmer,* as long as she remained "as still as a mouse." As a teenager she did not dare to ask about her urgent and confusing sexual feelings. As an adult she avoided discussing sex and politics. Rehmann recalls her father's distress at a "bluestocking" female vicar who served briefly in the parish. He could not abide her outspoken opinions, especially because she was not "blessed with beauty and grace." "As far as the role of woman is concerned, he did feel that Paul's injunction that women should keep silent in the congregation was no longer in line with the times, but if the ladies were going to open their mouths, then something soft, praising, approving and encouraging should come out."[28] This most gentle, most pastoral authoritarianism, based on fundamental convictions about the hierarchy of the world, about respectability and order, saturated the daughter's childhood and adolescent experience.

Rehmann portrays her mother's posture as one of quiet self-sacrifice. To speak too much, like drinking when she was thirsty, was to let herself go. When the burden of her duties became too great, she took to her bed for a few days. When she was up and active again, everyone was relieved. "Mother is back. Now we can forget her."[29] Both the adult woman and the daughter growing up find their experiences passed over in silence. The gender constructs of her father's world affirm uncomplaining motherhood and exclude intellectual assertiveness and sexuality.

In this cultural paradigm of fatherhood Rehmann finds the origins of her pastor father's silence in the political sphere. For here too there is silence about those things that do not fit into the hierarchical patterns of patriarchy. Now it is her father himself who can find no voice to express his fears and disagreements. Rehmann wonders how, as a young army chaplain in the Great War, her father had dealt with the senseless dying, the final collapse, the flight of the Kaiser (that secular embodiment of divine fatherly authority). Her mother had said: "We didn't discuss it. . . . It hurt him too much."[30] Reinhold was appalled by the street politics of the Weimar Republic. Nor did he wish to be involved in church politics, keeping well out of the 1933 struggle with Hitler, which finally branded Niemöller and other members of the Confessing Church traitors to the fatherland. He did not approve of the Führer, but he did not want to be a traitor. It was his duty to serve as a loving father to his flock, not to mix in their politics.

Throughout *Der Mann auf der Kanzel* the theme of the father's silence, based on conservative patriarchal Wilhelminian notions of authority, of hierarchy, of propriety, crosses the boundaries between personal and political life. In a last conversation with her father the daughter finds that she cannot talk about love and sex, as she would like; he cannot say, although he secretly fears, that German officers might be sanctioning the slaughter of citizens of occupied countries; she does not hear as he tries to tell her of his fear of death. Rehmann locates the parameters of the father's cultural, intellectual, and emotional world within a culturally defined paradigm of fatherliness among the educated and conservative bourgeois that promised security, protection, and support in exchange for obedience, for silence, for loyalty. In her narrative it ultimately betrays both father and daughter.

Der Mann auf der Kanzel embodies a contradiction that readers can approach selectively; the book is thus palatable to an audience ranging from conservative clergy to contemporary liberal social commentators.[31] Retaining her posture as dutiful and loving daughter, the narrator mobilizes none of the conventions of the feminist novel of liberation, and she achieves a tone of nostalgia for the past of her childhood, even as she produces a stunning analysis of German patriarchal authoritarianism at its most attractive, deceptive, and dangerous. The memoir in no way overtly represents itself as a search for the narrator's identity or subjectivity in resistance to her father's authority. (Her son's questions, not her own, set the inquiry in motion.) Yet *Der Mann auf der Kanzel* is filled with the images of the institutional structures and psychosocial patterns that were able to accommodate National Socialism, beginning with the Wilhelminian pastor's family with its benevolent patriarch, its nostalgia through the Weimar Republic for the former era, and its assumptions about national, class, and racial superiority expressed in gendered terms. Rehmann sees herself as focusing on "the tiny emotional and intellectual decisions that are made daily on the basis of the ideologies which permeate every aspect of our lives."[32] At the same time, of course, the blindness (she repeatedly describes her father in terms of his inability to see) and speechlessness (her own and her father's) created by those ideologies may be read as adequate justification for failure to act. Embedded in the memoir's careful construction of the cultural ideologies that enabled so many good people to adjust to the Third Reich, is also a possible explanation and exculpation for both daughter and father.

Like *Der Mann auf der Kanzel,* Barbara Bronnen's novel *Die Tochter* (The daughter, 1980), is concerned with cultural and political ideologies, fascism and gender. The daughter of expressionist playwright and novelist, Arnolt Bronnen, Barbara Bronnen had already published a popular book on single parenthood and had produced with her husband a video series in which they discussed their own marriage. Her documentary television program on the life of her father had also been broadcast. This earlier work created some of the context for the reception of *Die Tochter,* Bronnen's first novel: she is perceived in part as the publicity-seeking daughter of a famous father and as a writer who would have done better to leave her father's life alone and exhaust her emancipatory impulses in straightforward women's fiction.

Die Tochter is a complex account of a daughter's attempt to reconstruct a famous author-father's psyche and politics, to understand her own childhood experiences of him, and to find a way out of a currently mired career and personal life. The novel begins with the present professional and emotional confusions of freelance writer Katharina Bebra—her problematic relationship to her mother and grandmother, her lover Walter, and her work. Divorced mother of a two-year-old son, barely recovered from her marriage to a brilliant and abusive husband, and unable to complete work on a promised book, Katharina temporarily abandons her extended maternal family and travels to the places and persons of her father's life. She seeks an explanation for her current perplexities with love and work in the psychic legacy of her long dead father, Alfret Bebra, self-proclaimed and publicly acknowledged poetic genius, consumer of women, and political chameleon with a Nazi and communist past.

While the first reviews were selectively positive about *Die Tochter,* a common critical mood was one of irritation at Bronnen's apparent transgressions against genre and gender. Unlike Ruth Rehmann, who conceals her narrator's quest for self-understanding behind the textual recreation of her father and his world, Bronnen shows her protagonist Katharina Bebra seeking her own autonomy as a writer and a woman in the face of an author/father, who believed in the power of his own poetic gifts and whose contempt for women's intellect and fear of their sexuality were titanic. "He bound her with a chain of illusory notions about what a woman should be: queen and whore and innocent girl and witch—and what she should not be—least of all an intellectual."[33] At the same time Katharina is seeking connectedness to her mother and grandmother, and the novel gives much greater narrative space to their lives and her own. The story of her search for her father and the memories of him that it evokes are framed by Katharina's accounts of her mother and grandmother. Apparently uncomfortable with this division of focus (if there is a father, he should take center stage), a variety of reviewers agree that Bronnen should have written either a biography of her father or a novel about female development and subjectivity, preferably the latter, because she obviously writes better about the everyday lives of women than about (male) issues of culture and politics.[34] For some critics there is an excessive and narcissistic focus on the lives of women. The issue is perhaps less that Barbara Bronnen constructs a portrait unmasking a great poet as a family tyrant and more that her search for him results in what is for her clearly the more important discovery: deeper understanding of her maternal family, commitment to her lover, and belief in herself.

In her mingling of Alfret Bebra's life story with Katharina's search for an authorial voice and an affirmation of her female identity, Bronnen has constructed a narrative about a daughter's imaginative exploration of the psychosexual ground common to her father's fascism and to his fear of and obsession with women. Academic Arnolt Bronnen scholarship, some of which is cited in the novel, has emphased Arnolt Bronnen's political and sexual excesses as weapons in his anarchic revolt against constraining and repressive cultural and social institutions. Barbara Bronnen has the fictional Katharina count the cost of such revolt in terms of the lives of his wives and children. While only the central third of the novel deals directly with the person and experiences of Alfret, the entire novel reflects the familial aftermath of his restless eroticism, which sought satisfaction in the fascist program of earth and soil, homeland and empire.[35] The father portrait in *Die Tochter* constructs the complex connections between the 1920s resistance to the New Woman and to newly ambiguous gender categories, the sense of loss of heroic masculinity, and a sexualized *Heimatliebe* (love of homeland)—all of which made this father, in the view of the novel, vulnerable to Nazi ideology.[36]

Related to the readings of *Die Tochter* as an unfortunate mixture of a father's biography with a daughter's emancipation story is a view of the book as either a failed biography or a faulty novel, satisfying neither set of genre conventions. Reviewers are particularly perturbed by Barbara Bronnen's apparent factual accuracy about her father's life conflated with the apparent extensive fictionalizing of her own. To what extent is the fictional Katharina the real Barbara?[37] Why is Arnolt Bronnen so thinly disguised in the person of Alfret? The use of names like Alfret Bebra for Arnolt Bronnen and Bancart Baal for Bertolt Brecht is seen as an inexplicable mystification of the father and a loss of authenticity that invalidates the narrative.[38] As one critic complained: "[Bronnen] allows authentic material to appear in the guise of fiction. In this way we get neither a documentation nor the report of the search for this father. Let alone a novel."[39]

In *Die Tochter*, Barbara Bronnen has joined elements of several genres—the *Frauenroman* (women's novel) which, as critic Sigrid

Weigel has shown, was by the late 1970s clearly established as a literary category; the autobiography, which had gained in popularity throughout the 1970s; and the biography.[40] The authenticity of Ruth Rehmann's memoir was guaranteed by her narrative posture of lovingly dutiful and self-deprecating daughterhood, by her use of external informants, and by her chronological and realistic representation. Most reviewers bemoan a lack of authenticity in Bronnen's father portrait, one seemingly originating from the fictionalized, hence potentially uncontrollable and unverifiable daughter's story with which the father's biography is mingled.

I would suggest, however, that by transparently disguising her famous father as the fictional Alfret Bebra, Bronnen represents Alfret/Arnolt's troubling psychosexual constitution not as a fictional invention but as an informing structure in the life and work of a recognizable historical individual. The substitution of the fictional Alfret for the historical Arnolt also suggests that the pattern is not unique to that individual. At the same time, by fictionalizing her own character and distancing herself through the use of the third person narrator, Bronnen avoids a reading that sees her dilemma as a personal problem for an individual daughter rather than as an ongoing cultural pattern. Although she uses her father's identity to show that a historically identifiable person was indeed hostage to the obsessions she describes, she disguises him and herself to achieve a validity that goes beyond one woman's story and beyond the prurient curiosity about the political and sexual pecadillos of a public persona. Bronnen is caught here in a tangle of issues of subjectivity and authenticity that revolve around gender and genre expectations. The claim to female subjectivity seems incompatible with the claim to general validity. At the same time, as Sigrid Weigel has pointed out, *Frauenliteratur* has come to mean a naive and direct confessional literature.[41] By writing fiction in the third person, Bronnen moves beyond this dilemma, claiming female subjectivity, wide validity, and historical authenticity together. The critical reception of *Die Tochter* reflects the novel's disruption and confusion of expected genre categories and conventions.

By embedding the quasi-documentary story of a father's life in the daughter's search for the self, by making Katharina's understanding of him and her ongoing relationship to him the necessary ground for her own further development, Barbara Bronnen as author tries to establish continuity rather than commit *Vater-*

mord (patricide), as Arnolt Bronnen had done in his 1922 play of that name. Nearly two-thirds of *Die Tochter* deals with Katharina's mother and grandmother and her relationship to them. The father quest leads her to deeper understanding of forces that have informed all their lives. Certainly the novel portrays a daughter's search for family connectedness, rather than the pattern of separation from and abandonment of family Arnolt/Alfret found essential to his creative genius.

In its focus on the novel as failed documentary or as faulty fiction, much of the reception of *Die Tochter* overlooks the novel's representation not only of links between sexual and political obsessions but also of the ways in which German fascism was shaped by and pandered to those psychological patterns. The novel constitutes these connections in its exploration of Katarina's own early experience of her father. She sees them persisting throughout her childhood in postwar Austria, where Alfret is honored as a communist and former resistance fighter, and she uncovers letters and diary accounts that trace the patterns of Alfret's sexual fears and political preoccupations back through several generations. The structure of Barbara Bronnen's novel explores the family as a site for understanding larger cultural patterns and claims the historical relevance of female experience. The critical position that women's fiction as the literature of female subjectivity, personal experience, and liberatory transformations cannot authentically join the discourses of literary *Vergangenheitsbewältigung* leaves Bronnen's portrayal of the psychosexual structures of one father's fascism unacknowledged.

The spectacularly contradictory reception of poet Monika Köhler's 1980 first novel *Die Früchte vom Machandelbaum* (The fruits of the juniper tree) is perhaps most instructive of all in matters of gender and genre. The radically divergent responses to Köhler's novel ranged among its designations as "the most important [book] in recent years," "horrifyingly kitschy" and "dishonest," and "the powerful model for the mourning work of an entire nation."[42] The substance and structure of *Die Früchte vom Machandelbaum* made it impossible to avoid issues of *Vergangenheitsaufarbeitung* (working through the past) and *Gegenwartsbewältigung* (coming to terms with the present) often sidestepped by the reviews of Rehmann's and Bronnen's texts. The Nazi past and the Federal Republic of the late 1970s converge in the first person narrative of the troubled and terrified protagonist. As readers we are unavoidably confronted with a fictional world in which the fruits of the Third Reich have only begun to ripen, horrifyingly, in contemporary German society. This was hardly a unique position on the German left during the turbulent period of witch hunts for suspected terrorists and sympathizers. All the same, the novel clearly raised questions for its largely liberal critics about permissible literary forms of *Vergangenheitsbewältigung,* and about appropriate gender and genre modes of literary mourning.

Die Früchte vom Machandelbaum portrays the search of an illegitimate daughter, Gudrun, for her unknown father, who was, Gudrun suspects, August Hirt, SS Obersturmbannführer and professor of anatomy at the University of Strasbourg. The historical August Hirt carried out experiments with poison gas on concentration camp inmates from Natzweiler and Auschwitz and had them selectively murdered for his collection of the skulls and skeletons of inferior races. Köhler introduces the figure of Hirt undisguised into the novel, inventing the connection to the fictional daughter Gudrun. Following clues from her psychotic and institutionalized mother, Gudrun begins personal detective work in the late 1970s that she believes reveals her father's identity and explains her mother's insanity. Gudrun's travels to uncover traces of the father's past bring her into contact with an oppressive German present, uncomfortably, in the novel, like the institutions and ideologies embodied in Hirt's life and crimes.

In his review for the popular German illustrated weekly *Stern,* editor Niklas Frank called the fictionalized use of the historical Hirt embarrassing and misleading. Köhler, according to Frank (and a number of other reviewers) would have done better to write a straightforward documentary about Hirt's medical experiments rather than invent a contemporary fictional context in which to resurrect them.[43] Like Christa Rotzoll in the *Frankfurter Allgemeine Zeitung,*[44] Frank claimed that Köhler had no authentic experience of Nazism or Nazi fathers around which to construct an imaginative narrative. Frank's attack on the mixing of fiction and documentary is based as well on his suspicion of Köhler's motives: "If one doesn't have a Nazi father, one has to seek one out. At least if one wants to participate in a German literature that for about the last four years has been settling accounts with the father generation."[45]

Indeed Monika Köhler shares in part the position of Barbara Bronnen: both are critically taken to task for embedding a real historical figure in a fictional context, Bronnen for exploiting a father who was, Köhler for usurping a father who was not, her own. Clearly by 1980 the father literature has been constituted as a genre accompanied by certain expectations. At stake once again is the question of authenticity, and the genre assumption that a fictional narrative cannot provide the testimony of first-hand experience or the accuracy of historical documentation that legitimate the project of *Vergangenheitsbewältigung* in the 1980s.[46] I would suggest however that Köhler's confounding of genres, her extensive use of documentary material on Nazi medical experiments, and her invention of a fictional daughter for a real Nazi criminal, represent a textual attempt to lay claim for a whole generation to the past of its elders. Aware that the fictional daughter Gudrun is not the daughter of the historical Hirt, Köhler makes her literally "illegitimate" in the novel, where she is the result of a fictional love affair between August Hirt and his children's nursemaid. On a different level Gudrun's illegitimacy represents Köhler's implicit awareness that she is not the "authentic" daughter of a Nazi father. In contrast to the other authors of father literature, Köhler is "illegitimate"—the one daughter not dealing, fictionally or not, with her own father. The daughter Gudrun in the novel even assumes a Jewish name, Sara, so that she can identify more fully with her father's victims—a textual doubling of Köhler's original invention and her further claiming of a heritage to which neither Gudrun nor Monika Köhler can claim a "legitimate" right. The novel implies that Nazi fathers belong to everyone.[47]

Gudrun's designation as illegitimate also suggests that the silence of the parents' generation has hidden from the children their true parentage and their legacy from the Third Reich, which, undealt with, will reemerge culturally, politically, and psychically. Gudrun is not searching for a father she knew, but rather for a father whose history has been carefully concealed from her and whose identity she can only suspect. Without familial or cultural resources to draw on in her quest for her father's identity and for her own historical inheritance, Gudrun is driven to construct the worst scenario—that her father was in fact a callous killer—an active participant in the Nazi crimes against humanity. Gudrun's mother's silence condemns her to finding a hidden Nazi parent and, because he has never been openly acknowledged, to seeing traces of him everywhere. For Gudrun, the past is resurrected in certain recent events in the Federal Republic: a reunion meeting of the Waffen-SS, the arrest and conviction of nuclear power plant protestors, and the treatment of accused terrorists. These and similar reappearances of Nazi institutions and reports of repressive political practices are juxtaposed throughout the novel with the documentary records of the concentration camp medical experiments. While critics often read this conflation of past and present as ahistorical manipulation and dogmatic left-wing political critique, within the structure of the novel Gudrun's obsession with parallels between past and present emerges as the result of the silence of the parents' generation and the confusions and fears that silence generated.[48]

The novel's fictional structure with its stream of consciousness narration creates the connections between past and present symbolically and associatively. Because as readers we are confined to the mind of Gudrun, these connections are inescapable. At one level the novel does indeed represent a simplistic characterization of the Federal Republic in the late 1970s as a fascist state. At another it represents the disturbed and disturbing psyche that is driven to create those characterizations in the face of familial and cultural silence and of a repressive political atmosphere.

A further narrative strategy in the novel that creates parallels between present and past as well as suggesting the uses of fiction is the introduction of the Grimm fairy tales as framing stories for realistic episodes. The title of the novel is an obvious reference to the Grimm tale "The Juniper Tree," in which an abusive second wife decapitates her stepson, cooks and feeds him to his father, giving his bones to her daughter to bury under the Juniper tree, where the boy's spirit returns as a bird and ultimately achieves his revenge. Gudrun, comfortably situated if unhappily married, is an illustrator of fairy tale literature. The Grimm tales that she interprets with her paintings, serve in multiple ways as representative cultural texts; they suggest first that fictions may create the imaginative associations and identifications unavailable to writers and readers of documentary. Partly through the language and images of the fairy tales Gudrun begins to understand and interpret her own situation. Second, the fairy tales, as essential German cultural baggage, appear to harbor, when Gudrun reads them in and through her life, patterns of violence and prejudice that are all too easily transmitted from one generation to the next. It is not that the tales themselves are insidious, but rather that they represent neutral traditions that may become tainted through exploitation or through the context in which they are told. Apparently harmless and trivial things, fairy tales or daily events, may signify wider cultural, social, and political patterns. And finally, through

Gudrun's interpretation of the Grimm tales in art and in life, the novel suggests that the perspective of the interpreter, whether of literary text or political context, may create either knowledge for survival or ignorance and death.[49]

In an episode that anticipates in some respects the novel's reception, Gudrun's husband has arranged an exhibition of her fairy tale paintings in the offices of a major bank. Because the art critic who speaks at the opening is unable to recognize the network of references in the paintings to the German past and present, he must invent a totally different explanation for these images, ascribing them to an obscure and long extinct religious cult. The critic treats Gudrun's painting as many of Köhler's reviewers would apparently prefer to treat her novel, transforming a complex of connections between a catastrophic past and a threatening present, connections created within an individual subjectivity and constituted out of one set of personal experiences, into a methodical documentary about matters relevant only to another time and place.[50]

That the individual subjectivity is female, and that it is increasingly frantic and terrified, compounds the genre confusions about Köhler's novel with issues of gender. A first-person narrative, the novel is mediated through the disintegrating consciousness of the fictional daughter Gudrun, who senses that she too is retreating into the insanity that has already confined her mother to an institution. Köhler introduces many themes—search for the self, issues of voicelessness, language, and silence, the effects of cultural misogyny, and gendered power structures within the family—that were clearly identified by 1980 with a textual teleology of women's emancipation. But the novel portrays only the impossibility of becoming a female subject in a world still governed by misogynist and repressive rules and institutions. Men are relentlessly identified with National Socialism or an array of present oppressions. Women are always their victims. Gudrun's mother is victim of not only her husband's past but also the male psychiatrists who now overmedicate her. Her left-wing journalist friend Barbara is harassed by male security police. Gudrun is herself caught in a shaky marriage to a scientist who designs computer programs for complex weapons systems and who, like her doctor, treats her growing anxiety about repressive political practices as a manifestation of emotional instability. Within the context of the novel Gudrun must choose between the insanity of her mother and the calculating reasonableness of her husband, between (male) instrumental reason and (female) irrationality. Even Gudrun's young son is implicated, as she sees him torturing a rabbit in their garden. Ruthlessly persistent in making connections between patriarchy and fascism, *Die Früchte vom Machandelbaum* borders on creating a simplistic dichotomy between blameless female victimhood and ruthless male brutality, foreclosing all hope for a better future and reinscribing men and women in an infinitely variable configuration of oppressor and oppressed.[51]

No reviewers take up these provocative and problematic aspects of the *Die Früchte vom Machandelbaum.* The critical silence on the constructions of gender and fascism in Köhler's novel in favor of a preoccupation with issues of authority and authenticity, documentary and fiction illustrates well some of the gender and genre dilemmas that potentially limit the daughter-authored father literature from influencing more fully the literary discourses of *Vergangenheitsbewältigung.*[52]

By the early 1980s the book market and book reviewers had clearly constituted "father literature" as a genre with a corresponding set of predictable conventions. The widely-used designations *Vaterbücher* (father books) or the even less elegant *Väterbücher* (fathers books) trivialized the genre by suggesting that these texts were not after all "literature."[53] In general critics tended to see them either as expressions of private animosities and resentments confined to individual families or as documents of postwar psychic deformations and disappointments over the failures of left-wing political activities. At the same time the grouping together of very disparate texts in reviews and feuilleton articles subsumed daughter narratives under a genre description based on the apparently nonfictional narratives of sons.[54] Such genre expectations came to include an authenticity grounded in the lived experience of a historically existing parent, a focus on the traditional literary topos of struggle between father and son as a locus for generational conflict and social rebellion, and an authority to speak publicly about private matters on the basis of an already established literary or professional reputation beyond the "limitations" of *Frauenliteratur.*

The examination of reader resistances to these texts is one way to locate their transgressions of the cultural limits placed on literature by women about the Nazi past, certainly and especially on books about fathers in the Federal Republic of the early 1980s.[55] While any treatment of the authoritarian patriarchal family as a reproducer of fascist ideologies and psyches might appear to introduce gender by implication into the discussion of the Nazi past, the narrating daughter's point of view, which often includes other female family members and foregrounds the struggle for legitimacy as narrator of the father and author of the self, focuses more directly on gendered power in the family and on the gender-specific constitution of subjectivity and experience.[56]

Constructing daughterhood as a narrative position in relation to National Socialism has led women authors of the father literature to cross boundaries between fiction, autobiography, and biography, between articulations of personal experience and analysis of documentary evidence, between conventions of the *Frauenroman* and of the canonized literature of the "uncompleted past." These texts of the 1970s and 1980s claim new territory for the continuing process of literary and cultural *Vergangenheitsbewältigung*. Daughter narratives in particular, if they reach a wider set of readers, may contribute crucial constructs of gender and genre to the changing dimensions of German historical memory.[57]

NOTES

An original version of this paper was presented at the session on Women's Writings About the Nazi Era, chaired by Elaine Martin and sponsored by the Coalition of Women in German, at the American Association of Teachers of German annual conference in Atlanta, November 1987. A grant from the Henry Luce Fund for Distinguished Scholarship at the College of Wooster supported summer research in 1987.

1. Elisabeth Plessen, *Mitteilung an den Adel. Roman* (Message to the nobility. novel) (Cologne: Benziger, 1976), trans. by Ruth Hein, *Such Sad Tidings* (New York: Viking, 1979); Ruth Rehmann, *Der Mann auf der Kanzel. Fragen an einen Vater* (The man in the pulpit. questions to a father) (Munich: Hanser, 1979); Barbara Bronnen, *Die Tochter. Roman* (The daughter. novel) (Munich: Piper, 1980); Monika Köhler, *Die Früchte vom Machandelbaum. Roman* (The fruits of the juniper tree. novel) (Munich: Winkler, 1980); Brigitte Schwaiger, *Lange Abwesenheit* (Long absence) (Vienna: Paul Zsolnay, 1980); Jutta Schutting, *Der Vater. Erzählung* (The father. story) (Salzburg: Residenz, 1980); Ingeborg Day, *Ghost Walz* (New York: Viking, 1980), published in German as *Geisterwalzer*, translated by Ingeborg Day and Ulrich Fries (Salzburg: Residenz, 1983); Marliese Fuhrmann, *Hexenringe. Dialog mit dem Vater* (Witch rings. dialogue with the father) (Frankfurt am Main: Fischer Taschenbuch Verlag, 1987), Herrad Schenck, *Die Unkündbarkeit der Ver-*

heissung. Roman (The irrevocableness of the promise) (Düsseldorf: Claasen, 1984). With the exception of Ingeborg Day's *Ghost Waltz,* originally published in English, and Elizabeth Plessen's *Mitteilung an den Adel,* none of these works had been translated into English as of December 1991, and the translations of titles are mine. The father literature has been largely a phenomenon of the Federal Republic and Austria. Interestingly there were no corresponding texts by women in the former GDR that I am aware of until the publication in 1989 of *Ungelegener Befund* (Inconvenient finding) by Helga Königsdorf. In Königsdorf's story the narrator is male.

2. Paul Kerstin, *Der alltägliche Tod meines Vaters. Erzählung* (The Ordinary Death of My Father. Story) (Cologne: Kiepenheuer und Witsch, 1978); Christoph Meckel, *Suchbild* (Image Sought) (Düsseldorf: Claassen, 1980); Peter Härtling, *Nachgetragene Liebe* (Love in Arrears) (Darmstadt: Luchterhand, 1980); Peter Henisch, *Die kleine Figur meines Vaters. Roman* (The Small Figure of my Father. Novel) (Salzburg: Residenz, 1987), trans. by Anne C. Ulmer, *Negatives of My Father* (Riverside: Ariadne, 1990), revised edition of *Die kleine Figur meines Vaters* (Frankfurt am Main: S. Fischer, 1975); Peter Schneider, *Vati* (Daddy) (Darmstadt: Luchterhand, 1987). None of these works, with the exception of Henisch's, had been translated into English as of December 1991, and the translations of titles are mine.

3. Bernward Vesper, *Die Reise. Romanessay* (The trip. novel-essay) (Reinbeck: Rowohlt, 1977).

4. Niklas Frank, "Mein Vater, der Nazi-Mörder" (My father, the Nazi murderer) *Stern* 22 (1987): 28–36; 23 (1987): 68–73, 245, 98–104; 24 (1987): 98–104; 25 (1987): 60–67; 26(1987): 72–80; 27 (1987): 62–67. Published as *Der Vater. eine Abrechnung* (The father. A reckoning) (Munich: C. Bertelsmann, 1987) (my translations). Trans. Arthur S. Wensinger, with Carole Clew-Hoey, *In the Shadow of the Reich* (New York: Alfred A. Knopf, 1991).

5. Reinhold Grimm points out that many treatments of the father literature have ignored daughter's narratives. At the same time he disposes of any possible feminist content or conclusions: "About a third of those who have published life stories of this sort up to now are women. Compared with the usual division of writers according to sex, a remarkable representation. But one should be on one's guard not to come to too comfortable or fashionable conclusions. One cannot in fact use this situation under discussion for feminist purposes." (Ungefähr ein Drittel derer, die bisher Lebensdarstellungen in diesem Sinne veröffentlicht haben, sind Frauen. Das ist, verglichen mit der üblichen Verteilung der Schreibenden auf die Geschlechter, ein bemerkenswert hoher Prozentsatz. Dennoch sollte man sich aber hüten, daraus allzu rasche, allzu bequeme und modische Schlüsse zu ziehen. Man kann die hier zur Debatte stehende Situation nämlich [nicht] . . . pauschal feministisch ausschlachten (my translation). "Elternspuren, Kindheitsmuster. Lebensdarstellungen in der jüngsten deutschsprachigen Prosa," in *Vom anderen und vom Selbst. Beiträge zu Fragen der Biographie und Autobiographie,* eds. Reinhold Grimm and Jost Hermand (Königstein/Ts.: Athenäum, 1982), 173.

6. Thanks here to the publishers, Piper and Hanser, and to the authors Barbara Bronnen and Monika Köhler, who kindly provided me with their entire clipping files of reviews; and to Dr. Fritz Arnold of Hanser Verlag, for helpful insights into matters of reception.

7. The concept of reader resistance here and the term "resisting reader" in the title of this paper come from Judith Fetterly, *The Resisting Reader: A Feminist Approach to American Fiction* (Bloomington: Indiana University Press, 1978).

8. For a useful, if methodologically dated constitution of this tradition, see Kurt T. Wais, *Das Vater-Sohn-Motiv in der Dichtung. Zweiter Teil: 1880–1930,* Stoff-und Motivgeschichte der deutschen Literatur, vol. 11, eds. Paul Merker and Gerhard Lüdtke (Berlin: Walter de Gruyter, 1930).

9. Wolfgang Frühwald, "Vaterland-Muttersprache. Zur literarischen Tradition moderner Väterliteratur," in *Communicatio fidei. Festschrift für Eugen Biser zum 65. Geburtstag,* eds. Horst Bürkle and Gerold Becker (Regensburg: Friedrich Pustet, 1983) 343–355.

10. "Einer das abendländische Denken bis tief in die Antike zurückführenden, unermeßlich reichen Vatertradition" Ibid., 344. This and all subsequent translations from Frühwald are mine.

11. Michael Schneider, "Fathers and Sons, Retrospectively: The Damaged Relationship between Two Generations, "*New German Critique* 31 (Winter 1984): 3–51. Orig. "Väter und Söhne posthum. Das beschädigte Verhältnis zweier Generationen," in *Den Kopf verkehrt aufgesetzt oder die melancholische Linke* (Darmstadt: Luchterhand, 1981): 8–64.

12. Cf. Frühwald, for whom Paul Kerstin's short story, "Der alltägliche Tod meines Vaters," is typical of the representations of the decomposing father image, "whereby in this decomposition the melancholy and narcissism of a significant part of the younger generation of writers are mirrored" (Wobei sich in dieser Dekomposition Melancholie und Narzissmus eines breträchtlichen Teiles der jüngeren Erzählergeneration spiegeln), 341. See also Alexander Mitscherlich and Margarete Mitscherlich, *The Inability to Mourn: Principles of Collective Behavior,* trans. Beverly R. Placzek (Ann Arbor: University of Michigan Press, 1978). Orig. *Die Unfähigkeit zu trauern. Grundlagen kollektiven Verhaltens* (Munich: Piper, 1967). My brief summaries in no way reflect the complexity or extent of the important analyses by Schneider or Frühwald. Both in fact refer to particular texts by daughters, but are unable to account for them satisfactorily except as anomalies. Schneider commends Ruth Rehmann for her even-handed treatment of her father, and Frühwald sets Jutta Schutting's *Der Vater* apart from his overall characterization of this literature. Both Schneider and Frühwald deploy interpretive models that betray what seem to me mourning for the loss of certain patriarchal traditions.

13. Lynda E. Boose and Betty S. Flowers, eds., *Daughters and Fathers* (Baltimore: Johns Hopkins University Press, 1989), 7.

14. Ibid., 6.

15. Lynda E. Boose, "The Father's House and the Daughter in It: The Structures of Western Culture's Daughter-Father Relationship," in Boose and Flowers, 34.

16. *Refiguring the Father: New Feminist Readings of Patriarchy,* eds. Patricia Yaeger and Beth Kowaleski-Wallace (Carbondale: University of Southern Illinois Press, 1989), x–xi.

17. "Die Ablösung vom Formtraditionalismus einer den Nationalsozialismus bestätigenden, ihn verschweigenden oder machtlos erduldenden Literatur (oder eines Lebens), [die] dem Text ideologische Komponenten beimischt, welche die Eigenständigkeit des Literarischen durch Privatisierung, Historisierung und Psychologisierung gefährdet." Frühwald 443.

18. Judith Ryan's study of postwar literary representations of the Third Reich, *The Uncompleted Past,* posits the missing Herakles in the Pergamene Altar as the potential but never realized individual hero who might have resisted but did not. She locates this gap in each of the works that she takes to comprise the

German canon of coming to terms with the past. Only Christa Wolf's *Kindheitsmuster (Patterns of Childhood)* fully joins the canon in this and in similar studies through 1980. Women filmmakers have come closer in the move from the margins to the center of this canon. *The Uncompleted Past. Postwar German Novels and the Third Reich* (Detroit: Wayne State University Press, 1983).

19. "Vordefinierte Interessen, ob grüne, feministische, narzisstische oder pazifistische." Reinhard Baumgart, "Das Leben—kein Traum? Vom Nutzen und Nachteil einer autobiographischen Literatur," in *Literatur aus dem Leben. Autobiographische Tendenzen in der deutschsprachigen Gegenwartsdichtung*, ed. Herbert Heckmann (Munich: Hanser, 1984), 21.

20. See Rehmann's own essay on the reception of her book, "Die Väter bitten um eine neue Sicht: Folgen einer Rezeption," *Süddeutsche Zeitung*, 11/12 April 1981: 130.

21. Ruth Rehmann, personal interview, 27 July 1987.

22. "Ein Muster für die Generationsauseinandersetzung, wie sie ohne Hochmut und fruchtbar geführt werden kann; ein Muster für einfühlsames Verstehen, für Gerechtwerden ohne Unterlassung der aufdeckenden Klage und Anklage" "Ein typisches Pastorenbild," *Deutsches Allgemeines Sonntagsblatt*, 16 September 1979: 12 [my translation]. Rehmann, who is now an active member of the Green party in Bavaria, described to me letters and conversations with friends, family, and acquaintances in which she felt these responses keenly. Personal interview, 27 July 1987.

23. "Weil hier weder Zorn noch Scham an den Fakten modeln . . . die Liebe der Tochter sichert hier die Glaubwürdigkeit des Vaterbildes." *Frankfurter Allgemeine Zeitung*, 1 September 1979 [my translation].

24. Brigitte Schwaiger, for example.

25. "In dieser Familie ohne Vater, ohne Machtwort." Rehmann 11. This and all subsequent translations are mine.

26. Ibid., 21–24.

27. See Marie-Luise Gättens's essay in this volume.

28. "Nicht gerade mit Schönheit und Anmut gesegnet ist." "Was die Rolle der Frau angeht, so hält er zwar das Paulus-Gebot 'die Frau schweige in der Gemeinde!' für nicht mehr ganz zeitgemäss, aber wenn die Damen schon den Mund auftun, dann sollte Sanftes herauskommen, Lobendes, Billigendes, Ermutigendes." Rehmann, 181.

29. "Die Mutter ist wieder da. Man kann sie vergessen." Ibid., 115.

30. "Wir haben nicht darüber gesprochen. . . . Es tat ihm zu weh." Ibid., 92.

31. Michael Schneider, for example, praises Rehmann's memoir, although he sees most of the father books as mourning the failure of the politics of the left and as expressions of political malaise, of narcissistic self-indulgence, and of rage against a generation now unable to defend itself. Cf. Schneider, "Väter und Söhne posthum."

32. Personal interview, 27 July 1987.

33. Bronnen, 125. Critic Elisabeth Endres begins her commentary on Bronnen with a nostalgic backward glance: "Last year there was a stroke of good luck: Ruth Rehmann, who made her father, The Man in the Pulpit, the object of a report which contained both piety and justice. Barbara Bronnen . . . , perhaps too captive to fashionable tendencies, has now also gone in search of her father, but with less literary luck." (Es gab voriges Jahr ein Glücksfall: Ruth Rehmann, die ihren Vater, den "Mann auf der Kanzel" zum Gegenstand eines Berichtes machte, in dem die

Gerechtigkeit wie die Pietät ihren Platz fanden. Barbara Bronnen . . . , die vielleicht allzusehr modischen Strömungen verhaftet nun auch auf Vatersuche auszog, hat literarisch weniger Glück.") "Kein Glück mit dem Vater," Review of *Die Tochter,* by Barbara Bronnen, *Frankfurter Allgemeine Zeitung,* 11 March 1980: 22 [my translation].

34. Cf. Eva Marie Lenz's commentary for the Südfunk: "in the ambitious segments of the novel, those dealing with Bronnen's biography and political and cultural developments, the conceptual and compositional incompetence of the author is clear" (In den ambitionierten Partien des Romans, die der Biografie Bronnens, der politischen und kulturellen Entwicklung gelten, tritt oft gedankliches und kompositorisches Unvermögen der Autorin zutage."] Review of *Die Tochter,* by Barbara Bronnen, "Lesezeichen," Süddeutscher Rundfunk, Stuttgart, 28 May 1980 [my translation]. And again Elizabeth Endres: "If only Barbara Bronnen had trusted in the tragedy of [the figures of the mother and grandmother] and only described them. And if only she had done without the father and above all without the wild happy end of a total reconciliation with the family and the world! It would have been an interesting book" ("Hätte sich doch Barbara Bronnen auf die Tragik derartiger Figuren [der Mutter und Grossmutter] verlassen, nur dies geschildert. Und hätte sie auf den Vater und vor allem auch auf das wilde *happy end* einer totalen Familien-und Weltversöhnung verzichtet! Es wäre ein interessantes Buch geworden). Endres 22 [my translation].

35. See Horst Denkler, "Blut, Vagina und Nationalflagge," in *Preis der Vernunft. Literatur und Kunst zwischen Aufklärung, Widerstand und Anpassung,* eds. Klaus Siebenhaar and Hermann Haarmann (Berlin: Medusa, 1982), 103–119.

36. For a treatment of these connections contemporary with Bronnen's novel, see Klaus Theweleit, *Männerphantasien,* vol. 1. *Frauen, Fluten, Körper, Geschichte* (Frankfurt am Main: Verlag Roter Stern, 1977).

37. Cf. Peter Elting's commentary for Deutsche Welle. Speaking of "certain difficulties of orientation" while reading," he asks: "Who is who here? What is 'fiction' and what is biographical? How far does the self presentation [of Barbara Bronnen] go?" (Wer ist hier wer? Was ist 'Roman,' was biographisch? Und wie weit reicht die Selbstdarstellung?) Review of *Die Tochter,* by Barbara Bronnen, "Bücherkiste," Deutsche Welle, Cologne, 6 June 1980; my translation.

38. Lenz, "Lesezeichen."

39. "Sie lässt das Authentische im Gewand der Fiktion auftreten. Dabei ist weder eine Dokumentation herausgekommen noch der Bericht über die Suche nach diesem Vater. Geschweige denn ein Roman." Jürgen Peters, "Aus dem Nest gefallen," *Frankfurter Rundschau,* 6 June 1980; my translation.

40. Sigrid Weigel, *Die Stimme der Medusa. Schreibweisen in der Gegenwartsliteratur von Frauen* (Dülmen-Hiddingsel: Tende, 1987), 19–23, and passim. Weigel also notes that women's first novels frequently draw on clearly autobiographical material, 154.

41. Ibid., 94–111. Associated with novels labeled *Frauenliteratur* (women's literature) in the 1970s is a female subject in the process of emancipation, becoming conscious and sure of herself, taking herself seriously, and forming judgments and norms for herself that are different from those of men. Weigel 98. That Bronnen's novel fits this pattern so well enabled readers to classify it as *Frauenliteratur* with the restricted scope and importance unfortunately attached to that term and to ignore the attempt to deal with the father's political as well as personal shadow.

42. "Das wichtigste [Buch] der letzte Jahren" Norbert Schachtsiek-Freitag, "Vom Genozid erzählen," *Frankfurter Rundschau,* 9 April 1981; "ein grauenvoll kitschiges Buch . . . ein unredliches Buch." Niklas Frank, "Vom Grauen zum Kitsch," *Stern,* no. 52 (1980): 103–104; "das erschütternde Modell für die Trauerarbeit einer Nation." Eva Haldiman, "Trauerarbeit für eine Nation," *Neue Zürcher Zeitung* 27 November 1980; these and all following translations are mine.

43. "And she mixes the real Hirt with the fictional experiences and thoughts of his fictional illegitimate daughter in a manner for which the word 'embarrassing' is in no way adequate" (Und sie mixt den realen Hirt mit den fiktiven Erlebnissen und Gedanken seiner fiktiven unehelichen Tochter in einer Weise, für die das Kennwort 'peinlich' bei weitem nicht ausreicht). Frank 103.

44. "Frau Köhler was born in 1941. Three-or four year-olds don't have a political conciousness or the experiences that they could use later to construct an image of this period" (Drei- oder Vierjährige haben noch kein politisches Bewusstsein, auch kaum Erfahrungen, die später für ein Zeitbild zu verwenden wären". Christa Rotzoll, "Von der SS zu Gudrun Ensslin," *Frankfurter Allgemeine Zeitung,* 27 November 1980; my translation.

45. "Hat man keinen Nazi zum Vater, muss man ihn sich suchen. Zumindest wenn man mitschreiben will an einer deutschen Literatur, die seit rund vier Jahren wieder mal mit der Vatergeneration abrechnet." Frank 103.

46. Cf. reviewer Armgard Seegers in *Die Zeit*: "Yet Köhler did not want to rely only on the emotions that a documentation of the murderous past of the Germans would call forth. So the novel also has to include pieces of a marriage in trouble." And further: "Monika Köhler could have shown us her important antifascist engagement with a documentation of the murdering SS- doctor Hirt. The fictional part of the book gives the whole work the appearance of a melodrama. The topic is wasted" (Doch auf die Betroffenheit allein, die eine Dokumentation der mörderischen Vergangenheit der Deutschen immer noch auslösen sollte, möchte sich Köhler nicht verlassen. So soll der Roman auch noch Bruchstücke einer Ehekrise liefern. . . . Monika Köhler hätte mit einer Dokumentation über den mordenden SS-Arzt Hirt ihr wichtiges antifaschistisches Engagement bekunden können. Der fiktive Teil des Buches gibt dem Ganzen aber den Anschein eines Rührstücks. Das Thema wird verschenkt. "Trauerarbeit? Rührstück?" Review of *Die Früchte vom Machandelbaum, Die Zeit,* 10 April 1981; my translation.

47. Norbert Schachtsiek-Freitag justifies Köhler's use of the historical Hirt as plausible because "Gudrun takes so seriously the theories of the critical social psychologists (like Alexander Mitscherlich) about the representative father figure which through its authority-fixated and conforming character helped establish fascism and is partly responsible for the Nazi crimes in the Third Reich, that she chooses a Nazi criminal for her father" (Gudrun nimmt die Ergebnisse der kritischen Sozialpsychologie [etwa eines Alexander Mitscherlich] über die repräsentative Vaterfigur, die durch ihren autoritätsfixierten, angepassten Charakter wesentlich zur Etablierung des Faschismus beigetragen und die Verbrechen des Dritten Reiches mitzuverantworten habe, so ernst, dass sie sich einen NS- Verbrecher zum Vater wählt); my translation. Schachtsiek-Freitag, "Vom Genozid erzählen."

48. Reinhold Grimm, for example, called Köhler's novel "probably the most monstrous . . . product of this kind" ("das vermutlich monströseste Produkt dieser

Art) and "her equation of father-world and fascism . . . not just false, but stupid" (Deren Gleichsetzung von Vaterwelt und Faschismus . . . nicht bloss falsch, sondern dumm). Grimm 173.

49. Cf. Helma Sanders-Brahms use of the Grimm tale "The Robber Bridegroom" in her film Deutschland, bleiche Mutter (*Germany, Pale Mother*).

50. Köhler 229–242.

51. A dichotomy that has been called into question for the Nazi period by feminist historians, notably Claudia Koonz. See her *Mothers in the Fatherland: Women, the Family and Nazi Politics* (New York: St. Martin's Press, 1986).

52. *Die Früchte vom Machandelbaum* had a short if controversial life. After the *Stern* review Kindler Verlag dropped all attempts to publicize the book. The *Stern* review of the novel led to a minor battle of reviewers in the winter of 1981, which centered around accusations, in print, that Frank had written so devastatingly about Köhler's book for reasons other than literary ones, including his own family background. *Die Früchte vom Machandelbaum* has, however, not been without successors in its focus on the borderline pathology of Gudrun and her mother. It prefigures, in that respect Niklas Frank's own autobiographical memoir of his Nazi father, Hans Frank, Hitler's governor general in Poland (see n. 4). Frank's memoir and other less sensational accounts such as Peter Sichrovsky's *Schuldig geboren. Kinder aus Nazifamilien* (Köln: Kiepenheuer and Witsch, 1987), trans. Jean Stainberg, *Born Guilty: Children of Nazi Families* (New York: Basic Books, 1989) diagnose the psychic wounds of a generation that grew up living with the knowledge (or silence) about its parents' atrocities. Surely Niklas Frank's startling representation of a son's emotional disturbance, his own duplication of the Nazi connection between sex, violence, and death, stands out in this legacy of pathology. Among the father books Monika Köhler's is ironically enough a clear forerunner.

53. I am grateful to the anonymous reader of this essay who called my attention to the trivialization inherent in the term "father books." I am aware that my own grouping together of these texts as "father literature" is likewise, if somewhat less, problematic.

54. In fact, the sons' narratives, while only exceptionally designated as fiction (although some subtitle themselves "Erzählung") are in fact highly crafted, complex works. See particularly works by Christoph Meckel, Paul Kerstin, Peter Härtling, and Peter Henisch, whose *Die kleine Figur meines Vaters,* was revised and republished as a novel (see n. 2).

55. The authorized women's texts of *Vergangenheitsbewältigung* are of course those by Christa Wolf, primarily *Nachdenken über Christa T (The Quest for Christa T.)* and *Kindheitsmuster (Patterns of Childhood)*, also Ingeborg Drewitz's novel *Gestern war heute. Hundert Jahre Gegenwart* (Yesterday was today. a hundred years of the present). Their connections to the father literature and its reception are worth pursuing. As recent controversies have shown, Wolf is also not immune to trivialization and attack in the press in the Federal Republic.

56. For an earlier attempt to define gender related narrative strategies in father literature by sons and daughters, see my essay "Father Books': Memoirs of the Children of Fascist Fathers," in *Revealing Lives,* eds. Susan Groag Bell and Marilyn Yalom (Albany: SUNY Press, 1990), 193–201.

57. Ruth Rehmann's memoir and Barbara Bronnen's novel have both been published in paperback by mainstream presses and continue in print. Other books narrated from a daughter's perspective have appeared since 1980. See n. 1.

WORKS CITED

Baumgart, Reinhard. "Das Leben—kein Traum? Vom Nutzen und Nachteil einer autobiographischen Literatur." In *Literature aus dem Leben. Autobiographische Tendenzen in der deutschsprachigen Gegenwartsdichtung*, ed. Herbert Heckmann. Munich: Hanser, 1984.

Boose, Lynda E. "The Father's House and the Daughter in It: The Structures of Western Culture's Daughter-Father Relationship." In *Daughters and Fathers*, ed. Boose and Flowers. 1974.

Boose, Lynda E., and Betty S. Flowers, eds. *Daughters and Fathers*. Baltimore: Johns Hopkins University Press, 1989.

Bronnen, Barbara. *Die Tochter. Roman.* 1980. Reprint. Munich. Knauer, 1985.

Day, Ingeborg. *Ghost Waltz*. New York: Viking, 1980; *Geisterwaltzer*, trans. Ingeborg Day and Ulrich Fries. Salzburg: Residenz, 1983.

Drewitz, Ingeborg. *Gestern war heute. Hundert Jahre Gegenwart.* Düsseldorf: Claassen, 1978.

Elting, Peter, Review of *Die Tochter*, by Barbara Bronnen. *Bücherkiste*. Deutsche Welle. Cologne. 6 June 1980.

Endres, Elisabeth. "Kein Glück mit dem Vater." Review of *Die Tochter*, by Barbara Bronnen. *Frankfurter Allgemeine Zeitung*, 11 March 1980: 22.

Fetterly, Judith. *The Resisting Reader. A Feminist Approach to American Fiction.* Bloomington: Indiana University Press. 1978.

Frank, Niklas. "Mein Vater, der Nazi-Mörder" (My father, the Nazi murderer). *Stern* 22 (1987): 28–36; 23 (1987): 68–73, 245, 98–104; 24 (1987): 98–104; 25 (1987): 60–67; 26 (1987): 72–80; 27 (1987): 62–67.

———. "Vom Grauen zum Kitsch." Review of *Die Früchte vom Machandelbaum*, by Monika Köhler. *Stern* 52 (1980): 103–104.

———. *Der Vater. eine Abrechnung.* Munich: C. Bertelsmann, 1987. Trans. Arthur S. Wensinger, with Carole Clew-Hoey. *In the Shadow of the Reich.* New York: Alfred A. Knopf, 1991.

Frühwald, Wolfgang. "Vaterland-Muttersprache. Zur literarischen Tradition moderner Väterliteratur." In *Communicatio fidei. Festschrift für Eugen Biser zum 65. Geburtstag*, ed. Horst Bürkle and Gerold Becker. Regensburg: Friedrich Pustet, 1983. 341–355.

Fuhrmann, Marliese. *Hexenringe. Dialog mit dem Vater.* Frankfurt am Main: Fischer Taschenbuch Verlag, 1987.

Gollwitzer, Helmut. "Ein typisches Pastorenbild." Review of *Der Mann auf der Kanzel*, by Ruth Rehmann. *Deutsches Allgemeines Sonntagsblatt* 16 September 1979: 12.

Grimm, Reinhold. "Elternspuren, Kindheitsmuster. Lebensdarstellungen in der jüngsten deutschsprachigen Prosa." In *Vom anderen und vom Selbst. Beiträge zu Fragen der Biographie und Autobiographie*, ed. Reinhold Grimm and Jost Hermand. Königstein/Ts.: Athenäum, 1982. 167–182.

Haldiman, Eva. "Trauerarbeit für eine Nation." Review of *Die Früchte vom Machandelbaum*, by Monika Köhler. *Neue Zürcher Zeitung*, 27 November 1980.

Härtling, Peter, *Nachgetragene Liebe*. Darmstadt: Luchterhand, 1980.

Henisch, Peter. *Die kleine Figur meines Vaters. Roman.* Salzburg Residenz, 1987. Rev. ed. of *Die kleine Figur meines Vaters*. Frankfurt am Main: S. Fischer,

1975. Trans. Anne C. Ulmer. *Negatives of My Father.* Riverside: Ariadne, 1990.

Hink, Walter. "Ein politischer Roman, weil er Privates ganz ernst nimmt." Review of *Der Mann auf der Kanzel,* by Ruth Rehmann. *Frankfurter Allgemeine Zeitung,* 1 September 1979.

Kerstin, Paul. *Der alltägliche Tod meines Vaters. Erzählung.* Cologne: Kiepenheuer und Witsch, 1978.

Königsdorf, Helga. *Ungelegener Befund. Erzählung.* Berlin: Aufbau Verlag, 1989.

Koonz, Claudia. *Mothers in the Fatherland. Women, the Family and Nazi Politics.* New York: St. Martin's Press, 1986.

Köhler, Monika. *Die Früchte vom Machandelbaum.* Munich: Kindler, 1980.

Lenz, Eva Marie. Review of *Die Tochter,* by Barbara Bronnen. *Lesezeichen.* Süddeutscher Rundfunk. Stuttgart. 28 May 1980.

Meckel, Christoph. *Suchbild.* Düsseldorf: Claassen, 1980.

Mitscherlich, Alexander, and Margarete Mitscherlich. *The Inability to Mourn: Principles of Collective Behavior.* Trans. by Beverly R. Placzek. Ann Arbor: University of Michigan Press, 1978. Orig. *Die Unfähigkeit zu trauern. Grundlagen kollektiven Verhaltens.* Munich: Piper, 1967.

Peters, Jürgen. "Aus dem Nest gefallen." Review of *Die Tochter,* by Barbara Bronnen. *Frankfurter Rundschau,* 6 June 1980.

Plessen, Elisabeth. *Mitteilung an den Adel. Roman.* Cologne: Benziger, 1976. Trans. Ruth Hein. *Such Sad Tidings.* New York: Viking. 1979.

Rehmann, Ruth. *Der Mann auf der Kanzel.* Munich: Hanser, 1979.

Rotzoll, Christa. "Von der SS zu Gudrun Ensslin." Review of *Die Früchte vom Machandelbaum,* by Monika Köhler. *Frankfurter Allgemeine Zeitung,* 27 November 1980.

Ryan, Judith. *The Uncompleted Past. Postwar German Novels and the Third Reich.* Detroit: Wayne State University Press, 1983.

Schachtsiek-Freitag, Norbert. "Vom Genozid erzählen" Review of *Die Früchte vom Machandelbaum,* by Monika Köhler. *Frankfurter Rundschau,* 9 April 1981.

Schenck, Herrad. *Die Unkündbarkeit der Verheissung. Roman.* Düsseldorf: Claassen, 1984.

Schneider, Michael, "Fathers and Sons, Retrospectively: The Damaged Relationship between Two Generations." *New German Critique* 31 (1984): 3–51. Orig. "Väter und Söhne posthum. Das beschädigte Verhältnis zweier Generationen." In *Den Kopf verkehrt aufgesetzt oder die melancholische Linke.* Darmstadt: Luchterhand, 1981. 8–64.

Schneider, Peter, *Vati Erzählung.* Darmstadt: Luchterhand, 1987.

Schutting, Jutta. *Der Vater. Erzählung.* Salzburg: Residenz, 1980.

Schwaiger, Brigitte. *Lange Abwesenheit.* Vienna: Paul Zsolnay, 1980.

Seegers, Armgard. "Trauerarbeit? Rührstück?" Review of *Die Früchte vom Machandelbaum,* by Monika Köhler. *Die Zeit,* 10 April 1981.

Sichrovsky, Peter. *Schuldig geboren. Kinder aus Nazifamilien.* Köln: Kiepenheuer and Witsch, 1987. Trans. Jean Stainberg. *Born Guilty: Children of Nazi Families.* New York: Basic Books, 1989.

Theweleit, Klaus. *Männerphantasien.* Vol. 1. *Frauen, Fluten, Körper, Geschichte.* Frankfurt am Main: Verlag Roter Stern, 1977.

Vesper, Bernward. *Die Reise. Romanessay.* Reinbeck: Rowohlt, 1977.

Wais, Kurt T. *Das Vater-Sohn Motiv in der Dichtung. Zweiter Teil: 1880–1930.*

Stoff-und Motivgeschichte der deutschen Literatur, vol. 11. Ed. Paul Merker and Gerhard Lüdtke. Berlin: Walter de Gruyter, 1930.

Weigel, Sigrid. *Die Stimme der Medusa. Schreibweisen in der Gegenwartsliteratur von Frauen.* Dülmen-Hiddingsel: Tende, 1987.

Wolf, Christa. *Kindheitsmuster.* Berlin: Aufbau, 1976. Trans. Ursule Molinaro and Hedwig Rappolt. *Patterns of Childhood.* New York: Farrar, Straus and Giroux, 1984.

———. *Nachdenken über Christa T.* Halle: Mitteldeutscher Verlag, 1968. Trans. Christopher Middleton. *The Quest for Christa T.* New York: Farrar, Straus and Giroux, 1979.

Yeager, Patricia, and Beth Kowaleski-Wallace, eds. *Refiguring the Father: New Feminist Readings of Patriarchy.* Carbondale: University of Southern Illinois Press, 1989.

CONTRIBUTORS

SUSAN FIGGE is an associate professor of German at The College of Wooster, where she has also directed the Women's Studies Program. She has published articles on the poet Sarah Kirsch and on German father literature and has worked extensively on German folk and fairy tale traditions, German women writers and feminist criticism, and the problems and challenges of interdisciplinary teaching and research. She is currently working on a monograph on the German father literature.

MARIE-LUISE GÄTTENS has studied in Hamburg, Bloomington, Indiana, and Austin, Texas, and holds a Ph.D. in comparative literature from the University of Texas. She is currently an assistant professor of German at Southern Methodist University in Dallas, where she teaches German and Women's Studies. She has recently finished a manuscript on the reconstruction of the National Socialist past by women.

DIANA ORENDI HINZE, a native of Frankfurt, Germany, is an associate professor of German at The Cleveland State University, Cleveland, Ohio. Her biography of Rahel Sanzara, an actress and writer of the 1920s appeared in Fischer TB in 1981. Besides feminist issues in German literature, she has done work on the legacy of the Holocaust. She has pursued the often asked question of the missing *Trauerarbeit* (mourning work) about the misdeeds of the past as this failure has expressed itself in German postwar literature. She is presently at work on an exploration of writings done by second generation survivors, young Jewish writers living in Germany today.

RITTA JO HORSLEY is an associate professor of German at the University of Massachusetts in Boston, where she teaches courses in language, literature, and women's studies. She has published articles on the European witch-hunts (with Richard A. Horsley), on Goethe's *Iphigenie,* and on twentieth-century authors (Ingeborg Bachmann, Irmgard Keun). She has reviewed twentieth-century, German-speaking women's literature and theory for a number of German and U.S. periodicals and is a regular contributor to the biographical calendar *Berühmte Frauen* (Luise F. Pusch, ed.). She is currently at work on a study of Irmgard Keun, Marieluise Fleisser, and Gabriele Tergit.

MARIA-REGINA KECHT is an assistant professor of German and Comparative Literature at the University of Connecticut, Storrs. She has published articles on contemporary Austrian literature and is the editor of *Pedagogy is Politics: Literary Theory and Critical Teaching.* Her current research focuses on the representation of female desire in the works of contemporary Austrian women writers.

BARBARA MABEE, an assistant professor of German at Oakland University in Rochester, Michigan, received her Ph.D. at Ohio State University in 1988. Her revised dissertation, *Die Poetik von Sarah Kirsch: Erinnerungsarbeit und Geschichtsbewusstsein,* was published by Rodopi Press in 1989. Other publications include articles on Sarah Kirsch, infanticide in eighteenth-century drama, images of femaleness in Musil's novella *Tonka,* the fantastic in GDR prose, and the witch as double in Morgner's *Amanda.* She is a regular book reviewer for the *GDR Bulletin* and *Holocaust and Genocide Studies* and has also published reviews on GDR poetry in *Germanic Review* and *German Studies Review.*

ELAINE MARTIN is an associate professor of German and Women Studies at the University of Alabama. A comparatist specializing in Franco-German literary relations and contemporary women writers, she has written on the female quest, Eva Zeller, and on Marie Cardinal and Sylvia Plath. She is currently writing a book about women's autobiographical reflections of the Third Reich and World War II.

OLGA ELAINE ROJER received her bachelors degree from Mount Holyoke College. After pursuing additional studies in Germany and Austria, she received her Ph.D. in German from the University of Maryland in 1985. Professor Rojer has written several articles on the subject of exile in Latin America and is the author of *Exile in Argentina 1933–1945. A Historical and literary Introduction.* She is currently an assistant professor of German at The American University in Washington, D.C.

INDEX